Aphra Behn

Five Plays

The Lucky Chance, The Rover Part I, The Widow Ranter, The False Count, Abdelazer

'Masterpieces are not single and solitary births; they are the outcome of many years of thinking in common, of thinking by the body of the people, so that the experience of the mass is behind the single voice . . . All women together ought to let flowers fall upon the tomb of Aphra Behn . . . for it was she who earned them the right to speak their minds.' Virginia Woolf

Dealing robustly with the main concerns of the age: politics and sex, Aphra Behn provides a vivid picture of her own times and society that stretches from the city alderman through the chimney-sweep to the Spanish courtesan and the Amerindian queen, embracing all ages and classes and a full range of human emotion from lust and greed to loyalty and courage.

Selected and introduced by Maureen Duffy.

APHRA BEHN

Aphra Behn was born in 1640 near Canterbury, Kent and began her career as a professional writer in 1670 when *The Forced Marriage* was performed by the Duke's Company at Lincoln's Inn Fields. Her other plays include: *The Amorous Prince* (1671); *The Dutch Lover* (1673); *Abdelazer* (1676); *The Rover* (1677); *The Debauchee* (1677); *The Counterfeit Bridegroom* (1677); *Sir Patient Fancy* (1678); *The Imaginary Invalid* (1678); *The Feigned Courtesans* (1679); *The Young King* (1679); *The Rover Part II* (1681); *The False Count* (1681); *The Roundheads* (1681); *The City Heiress* (1682); *Like Father, Like Son* (1682); *The Lucky Chance* (1686); *The Emperor of the Moon* (1687); *The Widow Ranter* (1690). She also wrote novels and poetry. Aphra Behn died in 1689.

APHRA BEHN

FIVE PLAYS

selected and introduced by Maureen Duffy

The Lucky Chance
The Rover Part I
The Widow Ranter
The False Count
Abdelazer

Methuen Drama

METHUEN WORLD DRAMATISTS

This collection first published in Great Britain in 1990
by Methuen Drama, Michelin House, 81 Fulham Road, London SW3 6RB
and distributed in the United States of America
by HEB Inc., 361 Hanover Street, Portsmouth, New Hampshire 03801
Reprinted 1991

The plays in this collection originally published in 1915.
Reprinted in six volumes in 1967 by Phaeton Press, New York.
Copyright © 1915, 1967, 1990.

This selection copyright © 1990 Maureen Duffy
Introduction copyright © 1990 Maureen Duffy
Chronology of Aphra Behn compiled by Simon Trussler.
The author of the Introduction has asserted her moral rights.

The painting on the front cover shows a detail from *The Family
of Jan Brueghel the Elder* by Peter Paul Rubens and appears by permission
of the Courtauld Institute Galleries, London (Princes Gate Collection).
The back cover shows a painting of Aphra Behn.

A CIP catalogue for this book is available from the British Library.

ISBN 0 413 17090 X

Printed and bound in Great Britain
by Cox & Wyman Ltd, Cardiff Road, Reading

Contents

Aphra Behn: a Brief Chronology

1640   Born at Harbledown, near Canterbury, Kent. Maiden name Johnson.

1663 c. Family in Surinam, but her father, who had been appointed Lieutenant-General, died on the voyage. Stayed on a local plantation.

1664   Returned to London in the spring. Presented an Indian costume to the King's Company.

1665 c. Marriage to Mr. Behn, probably a Dutch or German merchant, who died soon afterwards, perhaps during the Great Plague.

1666   Persuaded by Thomas Killigrew to serve as a spy in the Dutch Wars, but discovered little the government thought of value while in Antwerp, and remained unpaid for her services. Great Fire of London in her absence.

1667   Returned to London.

1668   Committed to prison for debt, despite petitions to Killigrew and the King. Date of release uncertain.

1670   Beginning of her career as a professional writer. December, her first play, the tragi-comic *The Forced Marriage*, performed by the Duke's Company at Lincoln's Inn Fields, with Betterton in the lead, achieving a run of six nights. Around this time, beginning of her long relationship with the dissolute lawyer John Hoyle.

1671   Her second tragi-comedy, *The Amorous Prince*, at Lincoln's Inn Fields in the spring.

1672   Possibly edited the collection of poetry, *The Covent-Garden Drollery*.

1673   Feb., failure of her comedy of intrigue *The Dutch Lover* at Dorset Garden.

1676   The passionate tragedy *Abdelazer* performed at Dorset Garden in July, followed there in September by a 'scandalous' comedy with brothel scenes, *The Town Fop*.

1677   March, *The Rover* produced at Dorset Garden. Two other plays attributed to her also seen at Dorset Garden, *The Debauchee* in February and *The Counterfeit Bridegroom* in September.

1678   January, *Sir Patient Fancy*, a comedy adapted from Molière's *The Imaginary Invalid*, at Dorset Garden. The Popish Plot 'revealed' by Titus Oates.

1679   Beginning of the exclusion crisis. The comedy *The Feigned Courtesans* seen in the spring, and the tragi-comedy *The Young King* in early autumn, both at Dorset Garden.

1680   Death of John Wilmot, Earl of Rochester, aged 33.

1681   April, *The Second Part of The Rover*; November, the farcical comedy *The False Count*; and December, the historical comedy *The Roundheads*: all at Dorset Garden.

1682   The anti-Whig political lampoon *The City Heiress* 'well-received' at Dorset Garden in the spring, but *Like Father, Like Son* which failed there, remained unprinted, and is now lost apart from prologue and epilogue. Increasing hostility from the Whigs leads to her arrest for the 'abusive' and 'scandalous' prologue she contributed in August to the anonymous *Romulus and Hersilia*: she was probably let off with a caution. Merging of the two theatre companies.

1683   Wrote three of her posthumously-published short novels, and the first part of *Love Letters between a Nobleman and His Sister*.

1684   Published her *Poems on Several Occasions*.

1685   Publication of her poetic *Miscellany*. Death of Charles II and accession of his brother James II.

1686   The prose work *La Montre; or, The Lover's Watch* published. Returned to the theatre in April with the comedy *The Lucky Chance* at Drury Lane.

1687   The *commedia*-style farce *The Emperor of the Moon*, one of her greatest successes, first seen at Drury Lane in March. Arrest and inconclusive trial of John Hoyle for sodomy.

1688   Published the short novels *The Fair Jilt*, *Agnes de Castro*, and *Oroonoko*, the latter based on her experiences in Surinam. The 'bloodless revolution' leads to the abdication of James II, and the protestant supremacy under William and Mary.

1689   16 April, died, and buried in Westminster Abbey. Posthumous production in November of her last play, the comedy *The Widow Ranter* at Drury Lane, a failure. The comedy *The Younger Brother* also first produced posthumously, at Drury Lane in February 1696.

Compiled by Simon Trussler

Introduction

Aphra Behn's first theatrical production was in September 1670, at *The Playhouse* in Lincoln's Inn Fields, the home of the Duke's Company, which had been managed by Sir William Davenant (said to be Shakespeare's bastard son) until his death in 1668 and had then passed to the actor manager Thomas Betterton. The play was *The Forced Marriage*, a romantic tragi-comedy which ran for a very successful six nights and gave Thomas Otway his only stage appearance in person as the old king. The prompter John Langbaine in his memoirs calls it 'a good play . . . that made its exit . . . to give room for a greater, *The Tempest*'. The prologue dealt boldly with the novelty of a woman daring to write for the stage, and the play was so successful that Behn's next piece was produced only six months later. She was launched upon a career as playwright that was to last the rest of her life, interspersed with writing fiction, poetry and translation, and which was to continue in posthumous productions for another ninety years, before an eclipse of nearly two centuries, until the twentieth-century revival of interest in her and her work.

The longest-lived of her plays, as it was the most popular in her lifetime, was *The Rover*, for which she took and completely transformed an old play, *Tommaso* by Thomas Killigrew who ran the rival King's Company at the Theatre Royal in Drury Lane. There is in the library at Columbia University what seems to be Aphra Behn's own copy of Killigrew's *Comedies and Tragedies*, published in 1664, with her signature as Mad Behn and marginal annotations. She mined this play for two of her own, both called *The Rover*, the second written as a sequel after the great success of the first at the request of the Duke of York, her patron, later to be crowned as James II.

Whereas Behn's male contemporaries derived their style and structure mainly from Ben Jonson, her spiritual begetter is Shakespeare, an allegiance she acknowledged in her preface to *The Dutch Lover*, and that's apparent in the texts themselves. The Rover, Wilmore, certainly owes something to Petrucchio in *The Taming of the Shrew*, but it's the women characters, in particular Hellena and the courtesan Angelica Bianca, whose individuality and

strength, derived from Shakespeare's own heroines, especially
Beatrice and Rosalind, set the play apart from the work of her male
colleagues, until the appearance of Congreve's Millament in *The
Way of the World*, eleven years after Behn's death.

Behn had already produced her only tragedy, *Abdelazer*, early
in 1677. Tragedy was in fashion, with Dryden and Otway, and
Behn's friend Edward Howard as its chief exponents. Once again
there's an Ur-text in a play called *Lust's Dominion* which may be by
Dekker, but *Abdelazer*'s true antecedents are *Othello* and *The
Duchess of Malfi*. It was revived after her death with new music by
Henry Purcell but he didn't, unfortunately, set her most famous
song which opens the play: 'Love in fantastick triumph sat'. The
part of Abdelazer was played by Thomas Betterton who is reputed
to have been magnificent as Othello, and Elizabeth Barry, Aphra
Behn's great friend who was to become one of the finest actresses of
her day, the friend of Nell Gwyn and lover of the Earl of Rochester
whose child she bore, appeared as the daughter of the lascivious
Queen of Spain.

If Restoration Comedy is seen by some contemporary directors
as so much theatrical wallpaper, which can be cut to any size and the
bits stuck together to make an evening of rollicking bawdy, the
tragedies of the period have suffered what is perhaps the even worse
fate of almost total neglect, apart from an occasional production of
Otway's *Venice Preserv'd*. The very full-bloodedness of Restoration
tragedies, closer to Webster and Marlowe than to either Shakespeare
or their French counterpart Racine, makes them sound alien to an
audience nourished on tragicomedy and understatement, a situation
akin to the difficulty of convincingly staging *opera seria*.
Nevertheless it seems important to include *Abdelazer*, Behn's only,
but highly successful, contribution to the genre in any representative
selection of her plays.

Several of her stage works are described on their title pages as
'A Farce'. *The False Count* belongs to a group of political writings
which were commissioned specifically by the two parties, Tory and
Whig, Court and Country, who were engaged in a bitter power
struggle for most of Behn's working life, a conflict which was only
finally resolved in 1688, a few months before her death, with the
flight of James II and the accession of William and Mary. Aphra
Behn came from an old royalist family, at least on her mother's side,
and she remained staunchly loyal to the Stuarts. It's a proof of her
success and popularity, if any is still needed, that the court should

have paid her for her services in writing what she described to a
friend as: 'Tory farce and doggerell'. *The False Count* however,
produced in 1682 when the battle was at its fiercest, goes beyond
mere political propaganda though she was perfectly capable of
writing this kind of simple theatrical pamphleteering as she showed
with *The Roundheads* or *The Good Old Cause* which followed a
couple of months after. So far, however, does *The False Count*
surpass its genre that it was given a new production in 1697 when
the Whigs were securely in the ascendant. Its true theme is money
and class but the play also embodies one of her favourite topics: the
sale of young women in marriage to old men, something she returns
to so often that the reader is forced to consider whether there wasn't
a personal experience informing this continued exploration of a
social issue. However so little is known about her own brief
marriage to the merchant Behn that this must be only speculation.

By the time *The Lucky Chance* was licensed for printing on
Shakespeare's birthday in 1686 Aphra Behn had only three years to
live. Ill and poor she was nevertheless writing furiously in every
medium. The theatres were in decline and it was hard to get new
plays staged. Her friend Tom Otway had died in great poverty
hiding out from his creditors in the London slum known as Alsatia,
and this gives her the core for the play in the plight of Gayman who
is finally rescued by his lover, the spirited Lady Fulbank who is
trapped in an unhappy marriage. The play ran into instant criticism
on the grounds of its immorality and Behn hurried it into print with
a preface in her own and the play's defence.

> All I ask is the privilege for my masculine part the poet in me
> (if any such you will allow me), to tread in those successful
> paths my predecessors have so long thrived in, to take those
> measures that both the ancient and modern writers have set
> me, and by which they have pleased the world so well. If I
> must not, because of my sex, have this freedom, but that you
> will usurp all to yourselves; I lay down my quill and you shall
> hear no more of me.

She couldn't of course afford to carry out such a threat but her next
work to be staged was an earlier play, written during the time of
Charles II and based on the commedia dell'arte characters, called
The Emperor of the Moon, which offended no one and was a great
success. The other play which seems to have been written about this
time but not produced until after her death, perhaps because she

thought it too controversial, was *The Widow Ranter*, 'a tragi-comedy' set in the colony of Virginia. As a young woman she had visited Surinam in 1663 and stayed for a few months waiting for a ship home. In 1688 she mined this experience for the novella *Oroonoko*, which Thomas Southerne was to make into a very successful play, and at much the same time must have used her 'American' material also for *The Widow Ranter*. It's as exotic as Dryden's *The Indian Queen* for which Aphra Behn claimed to have supplied some feathered costumes brought back from Surinam, and it was Dryden who was to supply the prologue and epilogue for the play which contain what sounds like his epitaph for her:

> She who so well could love's kind passion paint
> We piously believe, must be a saint.

The separate publication of the prologue and epilogue in folio form in 1689, before the play was even staged but after Dryden had been stripped of his laureateship by the new powers, reinforces this elegiac effect.

Not only did Aphra Behn produce more plays than any British playwright of her generation except Dryden, she also encompassed the whole range of available dramatic forms. Her fluent dialogue is less allusive than that of her contemporaries and therefore more accessible to a modern audience. The wit seems less striven for, and her characters' emotions, even when she is dealing with the theatrical stereotypes of the period, are much more fully explored. It's hard to think of another dramatist of her time, or indeed for the next two hundred years, who could have written, with such tenderness and subtlety, the opening scene of *The Rover* where the girls discuss their future lives and aspirations.

There is, however, nothing insipid about her work; that failing which her contemporaries identified in other women writers as 'tastes strongly of the sex is weak and poor'. Her plays are as rigorous and eventful as any by her male counterparts and she deals robustly with the main concerns of the age: politics and sex. It was her insistence on freedom and equality in both choice of theme and its treatment that gave her enemies and critics their weapons against her, both for her theatrical works and her fiction and poetry. There were times when she was forced to trim a little as in the timing of the production of *The Emperor of the Moon*, or in the play she dedicated to Nell Gwyn, *The Feigned Curtezans*, which adhered strictly to the classical unities of time, place and action and, without being in the least bland, gave no cause for offence – an important consideration, since the country was in the grip of hysteria over the so-called Popish Plot and at least one of Aphra Behn's friends, the dramatist Neville Payne, was in prison and in danger of his life. In the main, however, she was fearlessly outspoken and was herself imprisoned on one occasion for a prologue which cast aspersions on 'persons of quality', in other words the Duke of Monmouth in his rivalry with the Duke of York for the succession to the throne.

A knowledge of the political sub-text of Behn's work gives it, of course, an added stratum of meaning, yet even without this, her plays provide a vivid picture of her own times and society, that stretches from the city alderman through the chimney-sweep to the Spanish courtesan and the Amerindian queen, embracing all ages and classes and a full range of human emotion from lust and greed to loyalty and courage.

Maureen Duffy
August, 1990

THE LUCKY CHANCE; OR,
AN ALDERMAN'S BARGAIN.

To the Right Honourable *Laurence*, Lord *Hyde*, Earl of *Rochester*, one of his Majesty's most Honourable Privy Council, Lord High Treasurer of *England*, and Knight of the Noble Order of the Garter.

My Lord,

When I consider how Ancient and Honourable a Date Plays have born, how they have been the peculiar Care of the most Illustrious Persons of *Greece* and *Rome*, who strove as much to outdoe each other in Magnificence, (when by Turns they manag'd the great Business of the Stage, as if they had contended for the Victory of the Universe;) I say, my Lord, when I consider this, I with the greater Assurance most humbly address this Comedy to your Lordship, since by right of Antient Custom, the Patronage of Plays belong'd only to the great Men, and chiefest Magistrates. Cardinal *Richelieu*, that great and wise Statesman, said, That there was no surer Testimony to be given of the flourishing Greatness of a State, than publick Pleasures and Divertisements—for they are, says he—the Schools of Vertue, where Vice is always either punish't, or disdain'd. They are secret Instructions to the People, in things that 'tis impossible to insinuate into them any other Way. 'Tis Example that prevails above Reason or DIVINE PRECEPTS. (Philosophy not understood by the Multitude;) 'tis Example alone that inspires Morality, and best establishes Vertue, I have my self known a Man, whom neither Conscience nor Religion cou'd perswade to Loyalty, who with beholding in our Theatre a Modern Politician set forth in all his Colours, was converted, renounc'd his opinion, and quitted the Party.

The Abbot of *Aubignac* to show that Plays have been ever held most important to the very Political Part of Government, says, The Phylosophy of *Greece*, and the Majesty and Wisdom of the *Romans*, did equally concern their Great Men in making them Venerable, Noble, and Magnificent: Venerable, by their Consecration to their Gods: Noble, by being govern'd by their chiefest Men; and their Magnificency was from the publick Treasury, and the liberal Contributions of their Noble Men.

It being undeniable then, that Plays and publick Diversions were thought by the Greatest and Wisest of States, one of the most essential Parts of good Government, and in which so many great Persons were interested; suffer me to beg your Lordships Patronage for this little Endeavour, and believe it not below the Grandure of your Birth and State, the Illustrious Places you so justly hold in the Kingdom, nor your Illustrious Relation to the greatest Monarch of the World, to afford it the Glory of your Protection; since it is the Product of a Heart and Pen, that always faithfully serv'd that Royal Cause, to which your Lordship is by many Tyes so firmly fixt: It approaches you with that absolute Veneration, that all the World is oblig'd to pay you; and has no other Design than to express my sense of those excellent Vertues, that make your Lordship so truly admir'd and lov'd. Amongst which we find those two so rare in a Great Man and a Statesman, those of Gracious Speech and easie Access, and I believe none were ever sent from your Presence dissatisfied. You have an Art to please even when you deny; and something in your Look and Voice has an Air so greatly good, it recompences even for Disappointment, and we never leave your Lordship but with Blessings. It is no less our Admiration, to behold with what Serenity and perfect Conduct, that great Part of the Nations Business is carry'd on, by one single Person; who having to do with so vast Numbers of Men of all Qualitys, Interests, and Humours, nevertheless all are well satisfi'd, and none complain of Oppression, but all is done with Gentleness and Silence, as if (like the first Creator) you cou'd finish all by a Word. You have, my Lord, a Judgment so piercing and solid, a Wisdom so quick and clear, and a Fortitude so truly Noble, that those Fatigues of State, that wou'd even sink a Spirit of less Magnitude, is by yours accomplish't without Toil, or any Appearance of that harsh and crabbed Austerity, that is usually put on by the buisy Great. You, my Lord, support the Globe, as if you did not feel its Weight; nor so much as seem to bend beneath it : Your Zeal for the Glorious Monarch you love and serve, makes all things a Pleasure that advance his Interest, which is so absolutely your Care. You are, my Lord, by your generous Candor, your unbyast Justice, your Sweetness, Affability, and Condescending Goodness (those never-failing Marks of Greatness) above that Envy which reigns in Courts, and is aim'd at the most elevated Fortunes and Noblest Favourites of Princes : And when they consider your Lordship, with all the Abilitys and Wisdom of a great Counsellor, your unblemisht Vertue, your unshaken Loyalty, your constant Industry for the Publick Good, how all things under your Part of Sway have been refin'd and purg'd from those Grossnesses, Frauds, Briberys, and Grievances, beneath which so many of his Majestys Subjects groan'd, when we see Merit establish't and prefer'd, and Vice discourag'd; it imposes Silence upon Malice it self, and compells 'em to bless his Majesty's Choice of such a Pillar of the State, such a Patron of Vertue.

Long may your Lordship live to remain in this most Honourable Station, that his Majesty may be serv'd with an entire Fidelity, and the Nation be render'd perfectly Happy. Since from such Heads and Hearts, the Monarch reaps his Glory, and the Kingdom receives its Safety and Tranquility. This is the unfeign'd Prayer of

> My Lord,
> Your Lordships most Humble
> And most Obedient Servant
> A. Behn.

PREFACE.

THE little Obligation I have to some of the witty Sparks and Poets of the Town, has put me on a Vindication of this Comedy from those Censures that Malice, and ill Nature have thrown upon it, tho in vain : The Poets I heartily excuse, since there is a sort of Self-Interest in their Malice, which I shou'd rather call a witty Way they have in this Age, of Railing at every thing they find with pain successful, and never to shew good Nature and speak well of any thing; but when they are sure 'tis damn'd, then they afford it that worse Scandal, their Pity. And nothing makes them so thorough-stitcht an Enemy as a full Third Day, that's Crime enough to load it with all manner of Infamy; and when they can no other way prevail with the Town, they charge it with the old never failing Scandal— That 'tis not fit for the Ladys : As if (if it were as they falsly give it out) the Ladys were oblig'd to hear Indecencys only from their Pens and Plays and some of them have ventur'd to treat 'em as Coursely as 'twas possible, without the least Reproach from them; and in some of their most Celebrated Plays have entertained 'em with things, that if I should here strip from their Wit and Occasion that conducts 'em in and makes them proper, their fair Cheeks would perhaps wear a natural Colour at the reading them : yet are never taken Notice of, because a Man writ them, and they may hear that from them they blush at from a Woman But I make a Challenge to any Person of common Sense and Reason—that is not wilfully bent on ill Nature, and will in spight of Sense wrest a double *Entendre* from every thing, lying upon the Catch for a Jest or a Quibble, like a Rook for a Cully; but any unprejudic'd Person that knows not the Author, to read any of my Comedys and compare 'em with others of this Age, and if they find one Word that can offend the chastest Ear, I will submit to all their peevish Cavills; but Right or Wrong they must be Criminal because a Woman's; condemning them without having the Christian Charity, to examine whether it be guilty or not, with reading, comparing, or thinking; the Ladies taking up any Scandal on Trust from some conceited Sparks, who will in spight of Nature be Wits and *Beaus*; then scatter it for Authentick all over the Town and Court, poysoning of others Judgments with their false Notions, condemning it to worse than Death, Loss of Fame. And to fortifie their Detraction, charge me with all the Plays that have ever been offensive; though I wish with all their Faults I had been the Author of some of those they have honour'd me with.

For the farther Justification of this Play; it being a Comedy of Intrigue Dr. *Davenant* out of Respect to the Commands he had from Court, to take great Care that no Indecency should be in Plays, sent for it and nicely look't it over, putting out anything he but imagin'd the Criticks would play with. After that, Sir *Roger L'Estrange* read it and licens'd it, and found no such Faults as 'tis charg'd with : Then Mr. *Killigrew*, who more severe than any, from the strict Order he had, perus'd it with great

Circumspection; and lastly the Master Players, who you will I hope in some Measure esteem Judges of Decency and their own Interest, having been so many Years Prentice to the Trade of Judging.

I say, after all these Supervisors the Ladys may be convinc'd, they left nothing that could offend, and the Men of their unjust Reflections on so many Judges of Wit and Decencys. When it happens that I challenge any one, to point me out the least Expression of what some have made their Discourse, they cry, *That Mr.* Leigh *opens his Night Gown, when he comes into the Bride-chamber;* if he do, which is a Jest of his own making, and which I never saw, I hope he has his Cloaths on underneath? And if so, where is the Indecency? I have seen in that admirable Play of *Oedipus*, the Gown open'd wide, and the Man shown in his Drawers and Waist coat, and never thought it an Offence before. Another crys, *Why we know not what they mean, when the Man takes a Woman off the Stage, and another is thereby cuckolded;* is that any more than you see in the most Celebrated of your Plays? as the *City Politicks,* the *Lady Mayoress,* and the *Old Lawyers Wife,* who goes with a Man she never saw before, and comes out again the joyfull'st Woman alive, for having made her Husband a Cuckold with such Dexterity, and yet I see nothing unnatural nor obscene: 'tis proper for the Characters. So in that lucky Play of the *London Cuckolds,* not to recite Particulars. And in that good Comedy of *Sir Courtly Nice,* the *Taylor to the young Lady*—in the fam'd Sir *Fopling Dorimont* and *Bellinda,* see the very Words—in *Valentinian,* see the Scene between the *Court Bawds.* And *Valentinian* all loose and ruffd a Moment after the Rape, and all this you see without Scandal, and a thousand others The *Moor* of *Venice* in many places. The *Maids Tragedy*—see the Scene of undressing the Bride, and between the *King* and *Amintor,* and after between the *King* and *Evadne*— All these I Name as some of the best Plays I know; If I should repeat the Words exprest in these Scenes I mention, I might justly be charg'd with course ill Manners, and very little Modesty, and yet they so naturally fall into the places they are designed for, and so are proper for the Business, that there is not the least Fault to be found with them; though I say those things in any of mine wou'd damn the whole Peice, and alarm the Town. Had I a Day or two's time, as I have scarce so many Hours to write this in (the Play, being all printed off and the Press waiting,) I would sum up all your Beloved Plays, and all the Things in them that are past with such Silence by; because written by Men: such Masculine Strokes in me, must not be allow'd. I must conclude those Women (if there be any such) greater Critics in that sort of Conversation than my self, who find any of that sort in mine, or any thing that can justly be reproach't. But 'tis in vain by dint of Reason or Comparison to convince the obstinate Criticks, whose Business is to find Fault, if not by a loose and gross Imagination to create them, for they must either find the Jest, or make it; and those of this sort fall to my share, they find Faults of another kind for the Men Writers. And this one thing I will venture to say, though against my Nature, because it has a Vanity in it: That had the Plays I have writ come forth under any Mans Name, and never known to have been mine; I appeal to all unbyast Judges of Sense, if they had not said that Person had made as many good Comedies, as any one Man that has writ in our Age; but a Devil on't the Woman damns the Poet.

Ladies, for its further Justification to you, be pleas'd to know, that the first Copy of this Play was read by several Ladys of very great Quality, and unquestioned Fame, and received their most favourable Opinion, not one charging it with the Crime, that some have been pleas'd to find in the Acting. Other Ladys who saw it more than once, whose Quality and Vertue can sufficiently justifie any thing they design to favour, were pleas'd to say, they found an Entertainment in it very far from scandalous; and for the Generality of the Town, I found by my Receipts it was not thought so Criminal. However, that shall not be an Incouragement to me to trouble the Criticks with new Occasion of affronting me, for endeavouring at least to divert; and at this rate, both the few Poets that are left, and the Players who toil in vain will be weary of their Trade.

I cannot omit to tell you, that a Wit of the Town, a Friend of mine at *Wills* Coffee House, the first Night of the Play, cry'd it down as much as in him lay, who before had read it and assured me he never saw a prettier Comedy. So complaisant one pestilent Wit will be to another, and in the full Cry make his Noise too; but since 'tis to the witty Few I speak, I hope the better Judges will take no Offence, to whom I am oblig'd for better Judgments; and those I hope will be so kind to me, knowing my Conversation not at all addicted to the Indecencys alledged, that I would much less practice it in a Play, that must stand the Test of the censoring World. And I must want common Sense, and all the Degrees of good Manners, renouncing my Fame, all Modesty and Interest for a silly Sawcy fruitless Jest, to make Fools laugh, and Women blush, and wise Men asham'd; My self all the while, if I had been guilty of this Crime charg'd to me, remaining the only stupid, insensible. Is this likely, is this reasonable to be believ'd by any body, but the wilfully blind? All I ask, is the Priviledge for my Masculine Part the Poet in me, (if any such you will allow me) to tread in those successful Paths my Predecessors have so long thriv'd in, to take those Measures that both the Ancient and Modern Writers have set me, and by which they have pleas'd the World so well: If I must not, because of my Sex, have this Freedom, but that you will usurp all to your selves; I lay down my Quill, and you shall hear no more of me, no not so much as to make Comparisons, because I will be kinder to my Brothers of the Pen, than they have been to a defenceless Woman; for I am not content to write for a Third day only. I value Fame as much as if I had been born a *Hero*; and if you rob me of that, I can retire from the ungrateful World, and scorn its fickle Favours.

THE LUCKY CHANCE;

or, An Alderman's Bargain.

PROLOGUE,

Spoken by Mr. *Jevon*.

SINCE with old Plays you have so long been cloy'd,
As with a Mistress many years enjoy'd,
How briskly dear Variety you pursue;
Nay, though for worse ye change, ye will have New.
Widows take heed some of you in fresh Youth
Have been the unpitied Martyrs of this Youth.
When for a drunken Sot, that had kind hours,
And taking their own freedoms, left you yours;
'Twas your delib'rate choice your days to pass
With a damn'd, sober, self-admiring Ass,
Who thinks good usage for the Sex unfit,
And slights ye out of Sparkishness and Wit.
But you can fit him——Let a worse Fool come,
If he neglect, to officiate in his room.
Vain amorous Coxcombs every where are found,
Fops for all uses, but the Stage abound.
Though you shou'd change them oftener than your Fashions,
There still wou'd be enough for your Occasions:
But ours are not so easily supplied,
All that cou'd e'er quit cost, we have already tried.
Nay, dear sometimes have bought the Frippery stuff. ⎫
This, Widows, you—I mean the old and tough—— ⎬
Will never think, be they but Fool enough. ⎭

  Such will with any kind of Puppies play; ⎫
But we must better know for what we pay: ⎬
We must not purchase such dull Fools as they. ⎭

Shou'd we shew each her own partic'lar Dear,
What they admire at home, they wou'd loath here.
Thus, though the Mall, the Ring, the Pit is full,
And every Coffee-House still swarms with Fool;
Though still by Fools all other Callings live,
Nay our own Women by fresh Cullies thrive,
Though your Intrigues which no Lampoon can cure,
Promise a long Succession to ensure;
And all your Matches plenty do presage:
Dire is the Dearth and Famine on the Stage.
Our Store's quite wasted, and our Credit's small,
Not a Fool left to bless our selves withal.
We're forc't at last to rob, (which is great pity,
Though 'tis a never-failing Bank) the City.

   We show you one to day intirely new,
And of all Jests, none relish like the true.
Let that the value of our Play inhance,
Then it may prove indeed the Lucky Chance.

DRAMATIS PERSONÆ.

MEN.

Sir *Feeble Fainwou'd*, an old Alderman to be married to *Leticia*, } Mr. *Leigh*.

Sir *Cautious Fulbank*, an old Banker married to *Julia*, Mr. *Nokes*.

Mr. *Gayman*, a Spark of the Town, Lover of *Julia*, Mr. *Betterton*.

Mr. *Bellmour*, contracted to *Leticia*, disguis'd, and passes for Sir *Feeble's* Nephew, } Mr. *Kynaston*.

Mr. *Bearjest*, Nephew to Sir *Cautious*, a Fop, Mr. *Jevon*.

Capt. *Noisey*, his Companion, Mr. *Harris*.

Mr. *Bredwel*, Prentice to Sir *Cautious*, and Brother to *Leticia*, in love with *Diana*, } Mr. *Bowman*.

Rag, Footman to *Gayman*.

Ralph, Footman to Sir *Feeble*.

Dick, Footman to Sir *Cautious*.

Gingle, a Music Master.

A Post-man.

Two Porters.

A Servant.

WOMEN.

Lady *Fulbank*, in love with *Gayman*, honest and generous, } Mrs. *Barry*.

Leticia, contracted to *Bellmour*, married to Sir *Feeble*, young and virtuous, } Mrs. *Cook*.

Diana, Daughter to Sir *Feeble*, in love with *Bredwel*; virtuous, } Mrs. *Mountford*.

Pert, Lady *Fulbank's* Woman.

Gammer Grime, Landlady to *Gayman*, a Smith's Wife in *Alsatia*, } Mrs. *Powell*.

Susan, Servant to Sir *Feeble*.

Phillis, *Leticia's* Woman.

A Parson, Fidlers, Dancers and Singers.

The Scene, LONDON.

ACT I.

Scene I. *The Street, at break of Day.*

Enter Bellmour *disguis'd in a travelling Habit.*

Bel. Sure 'tis the day that gleams in yonder East,
The day that all but Lovers blest by Shade
Pay chearful Homage to:
Lovers! and those pursu'd like guilty me
By rigid Laws, which put no difference
'Twixt fairly killing in my own Defence,
And Murders bred by drunken Arguments,
Whores, or the mean Revenges of a Coward.
—This is *Leticia's* Father's House——   [*Looking about.*
And that the dear Balcony
That has so oft been conscious of our Loves;
From whence she has sent me down a thousand Sighs,
A thousand looks of Love, a thousand Vows.
O thou dear witness of those charming Hours,
How do I bless thee, how am I pleas'd to view thee
After a tedious Age of Six Months Banishment.

Enter Mr. Gingle *and several with Musick.*

Fid. But hark ye, Mr. *Gingle*, is it proper to play before
the Wedding?

Gin. Ever while you live, for many a time in playing after
the first night, the Bride's sleepy, the Bridegroom tir'd, and
both so out of humour, that perhaps they hate any thing that
puts 'em in mind they are married.   [*They play and sing.*

Enter Phillis *in the Balcony, throws 'em Money.*

RISE, Cloris, *charming Maid, arise!*
    And baffle breaking Day,
Shew the adoring World thy Eyes
    Are more surprizing gay;

The Gods of Love are smiling round,
And lead the Bridegroom on,
And Hymen *has the Altar crown'd.*
While all thy sighing Lovers are undone.

To see thee pass they throng the Plain;
The Groves with Flowers are strown,
And every young and envying Swain
Wishes the hour his own.
Rise then, and let the God of Day,
When thou dost to the Lover yield,
Behold more Treasure given away
Than he in his vast Circle e'er beheld.

Bel. Hah, *Phillis, Leticia's* Woman!

Ging. Fie, Mrs. *Phillis,* do you take us for Fiddlers that play for Hire? I came to compliment Mrs. *Leticia* on her Wedding-Morning because she is my Scholar.

Phil. She sends it only to drink her Health.

Ging. Come, Lads, let's to the Tavern then—

[*Ex. Musick.*

Bel. Hah! said he *Leticia?*
Sure, I shall turn to Marble at this News:
I harden, and cold Damps pass through my senseless Pores.
—Hah, who's here?

Enter Gayman *wrapt in his Cloke.*

Gay. 'Tis yet too early, but my Soul's impatient,
And I must see *Leticia.*   [*Goes to the door.*

Bel. Death and the Devil—the Bridegroom!
Stay, Sir, by Heaven, you pass not this way.

[*Goes to the door as he is knocking, pushes him away,*
and draws.

Gay. Hah! what art thou that durst forbid me Entrance?
—Stand off. [*They fight a little, and closing view each other.*

Bel. Gayman!

Gay. My dearest *Bellmour!*

Bel. Oh thou false Friend, thou treacherous base Deceiver!

Gay. Hah, this to me, dear *Harry?*

Bel. Whither is Honour, Truth and Friendship fled?

Gay. Why, there ne'er was such a Virtue,
'Tis all a Poet's Dream.

Bel. I thank you, Sir.

Gay. I'm sorry for't, or that ever I did any thing that could deserve it: put up your Sword—an honest man wou'd say how he's offended, before he rashly draws.

Bel. Are not you going to be married, Sir?

Gay. No, Sir, as long as any Man in *London* is so, that has but a handsom Wife, Sir.

Bel. Are you not in love, Sir?

Gay. Most damnably,—and wou'd fain lie with the dear jilting Gipsy.

Bel. Hah, who would you lie with, Sir?

Gay. You catechise me roundly—'tis not fair to name, but I am no Starter, *Harry;* just as you left me, you find me. I am for the faithless *Julia* still, the old Alderman's Wife.—'Twas high time the City should lose their Charter, when their Wives turn honest: But pray, Sir, answer me a Question or two.

Bel. Answer me first, what makes you here this Morning?

Gay. Faith, to do you service. Your damn'd little Jade of a Mistress has learned of her Neighbours the Art of Swearing and Lying in abundance, and is—

Bel. To be married!   [*Sighing.*

Gay. Even so, God save the Mark; and she'll be a fair one for many an Arrow besides her Husband's, though he an old *Finsbury* Hero this threescore Years.

Bel. Who mean you?

Gay. Why, thy Cuckold that shall be, if thou be'st wise.

Bel. Away;
Who is this Man? thou dalliest with me.

Gay. Why, an old Knight, and Alderman here o'th'
City, Sir *Feeble Fainwou'd*, a jolly old Fellow, whose
Activity is all got into his Tongue, a very excellent
Teazer; but neither Youth nor Beauty can grind his
Dudgeon to an Edge.

Bel. Fie, what Stuff's here!

Gay. Very excellent Stuff, if you have but the Grace
to improve it.

Bel. You banter me—but in plain *English*, tell me,
What made you here thus early,
Entring yon House with such Authority?

Gay. Why, your Mistress *Leticia*, your contracted Wife,
is this Morning to be married to old Sir *Feeble Fainwou'd*,
induc'd to't I suppose by the great Jointure he makes her,
and the improbability of your ever gaining your Pardon
for your high Duel—Do I speak *English* now, Sir?

Bel. Too well, would I had never heard thee.

Gay. Now I being the Confident in your Amours, the
Jack-go-between—the civil Pimp, or so—you left her in
charge with me at your Departure.

Bel. I did so.

Gay. I saw her every day; and every day she paid the
Tribute of a shower of Tears, to the dear Lord of all her
Vows, young *Bellmour*:
Till faith at last, for Reasons manifold,
I slackt my daily Visits.

Bel. And left her to Temptation—was that well done?

Gay. Now must I afflict you and my self with a long
tale of Causes why;
Or be charg'd with want of Friendship.

Bel. You will do well to clear that Point to me.

Gay. I see you're peevish, and you shall be humour'd.
—You know my *Julia* play'd me e'en such another Prank
as your false one is going to play you, and married old Sir
Cautious Fulbank here i'th' City; at which you know I
storm'd, and rav'd, and swore, as thou wo't now, and to

as little purpose. There was but one way left, and that was cuckolding him.

Bel. Well, that Design I left thee hot upon.

Gay. And hotly have pursu'd it : Swore, wept, vow'd, wrote, upbraided, prayed and railed ; then treated lavishly, and presented high—till, between you and I, *Harry*, I have presented the best part of Eight hundred a year into her Husband's hands, in Mortgage.

Bel. This is the Course you'd have me steer, I thank you.

Gay. No, no, Pox on't, all Women are not Jilts. Some are honest, and will give as well as take ; or else there would not be so many broke i'th' City. In fine, Sir, I have been in Tribulation, that is to say, Moneyless, for six tedious Weeks, without either Clothes, or Equipage to appear withal ; and so not only my own Love-affair lay neglected—but thine too—and I am forced to pretend to my Lady, that I am i'th' Country with a dying Uncle—from whom, if he were indeed dead, I expect two thousand a Year.

Bel. But what's all this to being here this Morning?

Gay. Thus have I lain conceal'd like a Winter-Fly, hoping for some blest Sunshine to warm me into life again, and make me hover my flagging Wings ; till the News of this Marriage (which fills the Town) made me crawl out this silent Hour, to upbraid the fickle Maid.

Bel. Didst thou?—pursue thy kind Design. Get me to see her ; and sure no Woman, even possest with a new Passion, Grown confident even to Prostitution,
But when she sees the Man to whom she's sworn so very
—very much, will find Remorse and Shame.

Gay. For your sake, though the day be broke upon us,
And I'm undone, if seen—I'll venture in—

[*Throws his Cloke over.*

Enter Sir Feeble Fainwou'd, *Sir* Cautious Fulbank, Bearjest *and* Noisey.   [*Pass over the Stage, and go in.*

Hah—see the Bridegroom !

And with him my destin'd Cuckold, old Sir *Cautious*
    Fulbank.
—Hah, what ail'st thou, Man?

  Bel. The Bridegroom!
Like *Gorgon's* Head he'as turned me into Stone.

  Gay. *Gorgon's* Head—a Cuckold's Head—'twas made
to graft upon.

  Bel. By Heaven, I'll seize her even at the Altar,
And bear her thence in Triumph.

  Gay. Ay, and be borne to *Newgate* in Triumph, and be
hanged in Triumph—'twill be cold Comfort, celebrating
your Nuptials in the Press-Yard, and be wak'd next
Morning, like Mr. *Barnardine* in the Play—Will you
please to rise and be hanged a little, Sir?

  Bel. What wouldst thou have me do?

  Gay. As many an honest Man has done before thee—
Cuckold him—cuckold him.

  Bel. What—and let him marry her! She that's mine
by sacred Vows already! By Heaven, it would be flat
Adultery in her!

  Gay. She'll learn the trick, and practise it the better
with thee.

  Bel. Oh Heavens! *Leticia* marry him! and lie with
    him!—
Here will I stand and see this shameful Woman,
See if she dares pass by me to this Wickedness.

  Gay. Hark ye, *Harry*—in earnest have a care of
betraying your self; and do not venture sweet Life for a
fickle Woman, who perhaps hates you.

  Bel. You counsel well—but yet to see her married!
How every thought of that shocks all my Resolution!—
But hang it, I'll be resolute and saucy,
Despise a Woman who can use me ill,
And think my self above her.

  Gay. Why, now thou art thy self—a Man again.
But see, they're coming forth, now stand your ground.

Enter Sir Feeble, *Sir* Cautious, Bearjest, Noisey, Leticia
sad, Diana, Phillis.   [*Pass over the Stage.*

Bel. 'Tis she; support me, *Charles,* or I shall sink to
Earth,
—Methought in passing by she cast a scornful glance at me;
Such charming Pride I've seen upon her Eyes,
When our Love-Quarrels arm'd 'em with Disdain—
—I'll after 'em, if I live she shall not 'scape me.

[*Offers to go,* Gay. *holds him.*

Gay. Hold, remember you're proscribed,
And die if you are taken.

Bel. I've done, and I will live, but he shall ne'er enjoy
her.
—Who's yonder, *Ralph,* my trusty Confident?

Enter Ralph.

Now though I perish I must speak to him.
—Friend, what Wedding's this?

Ral. One that was never made in Heaven, Sir;
'Tis Alderman *Fainwou'd,* and Mrs. *Leticia Bredwel.*

Bel. Bredwel—I have heard of her,—she was Mistress—

Ral. To fine Mr. *Bellmour,* Sir,—ay, there was a
Gentlemen
—But rest his Soul—he's hang'd, Sir.   [*Weeps.*

Bel. How! hang'd?

Ral. Hang'd, Sir, hang'd—at the *Hague* in *Holland.*

Gay. I heard some such News, but did not credit it.

Bel. For what, said they, was he hang'd?

Ral. Why, e'en for High Treason, Sir, he killed one
of their Kings.

Gay. Holland's a Commonwealth, and is not rul'd by
Kings.

Ral. Not by one, Sir, but by a great many; this was
a Cheesemonger—they fell out over a Bottle of Brandy,
went to Snicker Snee; Mr. *Bellmour* cut his Throat, and
was hang'd for't, that's all, Sir.

Bel. And did the young Lady believe this?

Ral. Yes, and took on most heavily—the Doctors gave her over—and there was the Devil to do to get her to consent to this Marriage—but her Fortune was small, and the hope of a Ladyship, and a Gold Chain at the Spittal Sermon, did the Business—and so your Servant, Sir.   [*Ex.* Ralph.

Bel. So, here's a hopeful Account of my sweet self now.

Enter Post-man with Letters.

Post. Pray, Sir, which is Sir *Feeble Fainwou'd's?*

Bel. What wou'd you with him, Friend?

Post. I have a Letter here from the *Hague* for him.

Bel. From the *Hague!* Now have I a curiosity to see it—I am his Servant—give it me—[*Gives it him, and Exit.*
—Perhaps here may be the second part of my Tragedy, I'm full of Mischief, *Charles*—and have a mind to see this Fellow's Secrets. For from this hour I'll be his evil Genius, haunt him at Bed and Board; he shall not sleep nor eat; disturb him at his Prayers, in his Embraces; and teaze him into Madness.

Help me, Invention, Malice, Love, and Wit:

[*Opening the Letter.*

Ye Gods, and little Fiends, instruct my Mischief.

[*Reads.*

Dear Brother,

ACCORDING to your desire I have sent for my Son from St. Omer's, *whom I have sent to wait on you in* England; *he is a very good Accountant, and fit for Business, and much pleas'd he shall see that Uncle to whom he's so obliged, and which is so gratefully acknowledged by— Dear Brother, your affectionate Brother,*

Francis Fainwou'd.

—Hum—hark ye, *Charles*, do you know who I am now?

Gay. Why, I hope a very honest Friend of mine, *Harry Bellmour.*

Bel. No, Sir, you are mistaken in your Man.

Gay. It may be so.

Bel. I am, d'ye see, *Charles*, this very individual, numerical young Mr.—*what ye call'um Fainwou'd*, just come from *St. Omers* into *England*—to my Uncle the Alderman. I am, *Charles*, this very Man.

Gay. I know you are, and will swear't upon occasion.

Bel. This lucky Thought has almost calm'd my mind. And if I don't fit you, my dear Uncle, May I never lie with my Aunt.

Gay. Ah, Rogue—but prithee what care have you taken about your Pardon? 'twere good you should secure that.

Bel. There's the Devil, *Charles*,—had I but that— but I have had a very góod Friend at work, a thousand Guyneys, that seldom fails; but yet in vain, I being the first Transgressor since the Act against Duelling. But I impatient to see this dear delight of my Soul, and hearing from none of you this six weeks, came from *Brussels* in this disguise—for the *Hague* I have not seen, though hang'd there—but come—let's away, and compleat me a right *St. Omer's* Spark, that I may present my self as soon as they come from Church.   [*Exeunt.*

SCENE II. *Sir* Cautious Fulbank's *House.*

Enter Lady Fulbank, Pert *and* Bredwel. Bredwel *gives her a Letter.*

Lady Fulbank *reads.*

DID my Julia *know how I languish in this cruel Separation, she would afford me her pity, and write oftner. If only the Expectation of two thousand a year kept me from you, ah!* Julia, *how easily would I abandon that Trifle for your more valued sight; but that I know a Fortune will render me more agreeable to the charming* Julia, *I should quit all my Interest here, to throw my self at her Feet, to make her sensible how I am intirely her Adorer.*

Charles Gayman.

—Faith, *Charles*, you lie—you are as welcome to me now,
Now when I doubt thy Fortune is declining,
As if the Universe were thine.

Pert. That, Madam, is a noble Gratitude. For if his
Fortune be declining, 'tis sacrificed to his Passion for your
Ladyship.

—'Tis all laid out on Love.

L. Ful. I prize my Honour more than Life,
Yet I had rather have given him all he wish'd of me,
Than be guilty of his Undoing.

Pert. And I think the Sin were less.

L. Ful. I must confess, such Jewels, Rings and Presents
as he made me, must needs decay his Fortune.

Bred. Ay, Madam, his very Coach at last was turned
into a Jewel for your Ladyship. Then, Madam, what
Expences his Despair have run him on—
As Drinking and Gaming, to divert the Thought of your
marrying my old Master.

L. Ful. And put in Wenching too.—

Bred. No, assure your self, Madam—

L. Ful. Of that I would be better satisfied—and you
too must assist me, as e'er you hope I should be kind to
you in gaining you *Diana*.   [*To* Bredwel.

Bred. Madam, I'll die to serve you.

Pert. Nor will I be behind in my Duty.

L. Ful. Oh, how fatal are forc'd Marriages!
How many Ruins one such Match pulls on!
Had I but kept my Sacred Vows to *Gayman*,
How happy had I been—how prosperous he!
Whilst now I languish in a loath'd embrace,
Pine out my Life with Age—Consumptions, Coughs.
—But dost thou fear that *Gayman* is declining?

Bred. You are my Lady, and the best of Mistresses—
Therefore I would not grieve you, for I know
You love this best—but most unhappy Man.

L. Ful. You shall not grieve me—prithee on.

Bred. My Master sent me yesterday to Mr. *Crap,* his Scrivener, to send to one Mr. *Wasteall,* to tell him his first Mortgage was out, which is two hundred pounds a Year—and who has since ingaged five or six hundred more to my Master; but if this first be not redeem'd, he'll take the Forfeit on't, as he says a wise Man ought.

L. Ful. That is to say, a Knave, according to his Notion of a wise Man.

Bred. Mr. *Crap,* being busy with a borrowing Lord, sent me to Mr. *Wasteall,* whose Lodging is in a nasty Place called *Alsatia,* at a Black-Smith's.

L. Ful. But what's all this to *Gayman?*

Bred. Madam, this *Wasteall* was Mr. *Gayman.*

L. Ful. Gayman! Saw'st thou *Gayman?*

Bred. Madam, Mr. *Gayman,* yesterday.

L. Ful. When came he to Town?

Bred. Madam, he has not been out of it.

L. Ful. Not at his Uncle's in *Northamptonshire?*

Bred. Your Ladyship was wont to credit me.

L. Ful. Forgive me—you went to a Black-Smith's—

Bred. Yes, Madam; and at the door encountred the beastly thing he calls a Landlady; who lookt as if she had been of her own Husband's making, compos'd of moulded Smith's Dust. I ask'd for Mr. *Wasteall,* and she began to open—and did so rail at him, that what with her *Billinsgate,* and her Husband's hammers, I was both deaf and dumb— at last the hammers ceas'd, and she grew weary, and call'd down Mr. *Wasteall;* but he not answering—I was sent up a Ladder rather than a pair of Stairs; at last I scal'd the top, and enter'd the inchanted Castle; there did I find him, spite of the noise below, drowning his Cares in Sleep.

L. Ful. Whom foundst thou? *Gayman?*

Bred. He, Madam, whom I waked—and seeing me, Heavens, what Confusion seiz'd him! which nothing but my own Surprize could equal. Asham'd—he wou'd have turn'd away;

But when he saw, by my dejected Eyes, I knew him,
He sigh'd, and blusht, and heard me tell my Business:
Then beg'd I wou'd be secret; for he vow'd his whole
Repose and Life depended on my silence. Nor had I told
it now,
But that your Ladyship may find some speedy means to
draw him from this desperate Condition.

L. Ful. Heavens, is't possible?

Bred. He's driven to the last degree of Poverty—
Had you but seen his Lodgings, Madam!

L. Ful. What were they?

Bred. 'Tis a pretty convenient Tub, Madam. He may
lie a long in't, there's just room for an old join'd Stool
besides the Bed, which one cannot call a Cabin, about the
largeness of a Pantry Bin, or a Usurer's Trunk; there had
been Dornex Curtains to't in the days of Yore; but they
were now annihilated, and nothing left to save his Eyes
from the Light, but my Landlady's Blue Apron, ty'd by
the strings before the Window, in which stood a broken
six-penny Looking-Glass, that shew'd as many Faces as
the Scene in *Henry* the Eighth, which could but just stand
upright, and then the Comb-Case fill'd it.

L. Ful. What a leud Description hast thou made of his
Chamber?

Bred. Then for his Equipage, 'tis banisht to one small
Monsieur, who (saucy with his Master's Poverty) is rather
a Companion than a Footman.

L. Ful. But what said he to the Forfeiture of his Land?

Bred. He sigh'd and cry'd, Why, farewel dirty Acres;
It shall not trouble me, since 'twas all but for Love!

L. Ful. How much redeems it?

Bred. Madam, five hundred Pounds.

L. Ful. Enough—you shall in some disguise convey this
Money to him, as from an unknown hand: I wou'd not
have him think it comes from me, for all the World:
That Nicety and Virtue I've profest, I am resolved to keep.

Pert. If I were your Ladyship, I wou'd make use of Sir *Cautious*'s Cash: pay him in his own Coin.

Bred. Your Ladyship wou'd make no Scruple of it, if you knew how this poor Gentleman has been us'd by my unmerciful Master.

L. Ful. I have a Key already to his Counting-House; it being lost, he had another made, and this I found and kept.

Bred. Madam, this is an excellent time for't, my Master being gone to give my Sister *Leticia* at Church.

L. Ful. 'Tis so, I'll go and commit the Theft, whilst you prepare to carry it, and then we'll to dinner with your Sister the Bride.   [*Exeunt.*

SCENE III.   *The House of Sir* Feeble.

Enter Sir Feeble, Leticia, *Sir* Cautious, Bearjest, Diana, Noisey.   *Sir* Feeble *sings and salutes 'em.*

Sir Feeb. Welcome, *Joan Sanderson*, welcome, welcome.
                              [*Kisses the Bride.*
Ods bobs, and so thou art, Sweet-heart.   [*So to the rest.*

Bear. Methinks my Lady Bride is very melancholy.

Sir Cau. Ay, ay, Women that are discreet, are always thus upon their Wedding-day.

Sir Feeb. Always by day-light, Sir *Cautious.*

> *But when bright* Phœbus *does retire,*
> *To* Thetis' *Bed to quench his fire,*
> *And do the thing we need not name,*
> *We Mortals by his influence do the same.*
> *Then then the blushing Maid lays by*
> *Her simpering, and her Modesty;*
> *And round the Lover clasps and twines*
> *Like Ivy, or the circling Vines.*

Sir Feeb. Here, *Ralph*, the Bottle, Rogue, of Sack, ye Rascal; hadst thou been a Butler worth hanging, thou wou'dst have met us at the door with it.—Ods bods, Sweet-heart, thy health.

Bear. Away with it, to the Bride's *Haunce in Kelder*.

Sir *Feeb*. Gots so, go to, Rogue, go to, that shall be, Knave, that shall be the morrow morning; he—ods bobs, we'll do't, Sweet heart; here's to't.   [*Drinks again*.

Let. I die but to imagine it, wou'd I were dead indeed.

Sir *Feeb*. Hah—hum—how's this? Tears upon the Wedding day? Why, why—you Baggage, you, ye little Ting, Fools-face—away, you Rogue, you're naughty, you're naughty. [*Patting and playing, and following her*. Look—look—look now,—buss it—buss it—buss it—and Friends; did'ums, did'ums beat its none silly Baby—away, you little Hussey, away, and pledge me—
          [*She drinks a little*.

Sir *Cau*. A wise discreet Lady, I'll warrant her; my Lady would prodigally have took it off all.

Sir *Feeb*. Dear's its nown dear Fubs; buss again, buss again, away, away—ods bobs, I long for Night—look, look, Sir *Cautious*, what an Eye's there!

Sir *Cau*. Ay, so there is, Brother, and a modest Eye too.

Sir *Feeb*. Adad, I love her more and more, *Ralph*—call old *Susan* hither—come, Mr. *Bearjest*, put the Glass about. Ods bobs, when I was a young Fellow, I wou'd not let the young Wenches look pale and wan—but would rouse 'em, and touse 'em, and blowze 'em, till I put a colour in their Cheeks, like an Apple *John*, affacks—Nay, I can make a shift still, and Pupsey shall not be jealous.

Enter Susan, *Sir* Feeble *whispers her, she goes out*.

Let. Indeed, not I; Sir. I shall be all Obedience.

Sir *Cau*. A most judicious Lady; would my *Julia* had a little of her Modesty; but my Lady's a Wit.

Enter Susan *with a Box*.

Sir *Feeb*. Look here, my little Puskin, here's fine Playthings for its nown little Coxcomb—go—get you gone—get you gone, and off with this St. *Martin's* Trumpery, these Play-house Glass Baubles, this Necklace, and these

Pendants, and all this false Ware; ods bobs, I'll have no Counterfeit Geer about thee, not I. See—these are right as the Blushes on thy Cheeks, and these as true as my Heart, my Girl. Go, put 'em on, and be fine. [*Gives 'em her.*

Let. Believe me, Sir, I shall not merit this kindness.

Sir Feeb. Go to—More of your Love, and less of your Ceremony—give the old Fool a hearty buss, and pay him that way—he, ye little wanton Tit, I'll steal up—and catch ye and love ye—adod, I will—get ye gone—get ye gone.

Let. Heavens, what a nauseous thing is an old Man turn'd Lover!   [*Ex.* Leticia *and* Diana.

Sir Cau. How, steal up, Sir *Feeble*—I hope not so; I hold it most indecent before the lawful hour.

Sir Feeb. Lawful hour! Why, I hope all hours are lawful with a Man's own Wife.

Sir Cau. But wise Men have respect to Times and Seasons.

Sir Feeb. Wise young Men, Sir *Cautious;* but wise old Men must nick their Inclinations; for it is not as 'twas wont to be, for it is not as 'twas wont to be—

[*Singing and Dancing.*

Enter Ralph.

Ral. Sir, here's a young Gentleman without wou'd speak with you.

Sir Feeb. Hum—I hope it is not that same *Bellmour* come to forbid the Banes—if it be, he comes too late—therefore bring me first my long Sword, and then the Gentleman.   [*Exit Ralph.*

Bea. Pray, Sir, use mine, it is a travell'd Blade I can assure you, Sir.

Sir Feeb. I thank you, Sir.

Enter Ralph *and* Bellmour *disguis'd, gives him a Letter, he reads.*

How—my Nephew!

Francis Fainwou'd!   [*Embraces him.*

Bel. I am glad he has told me my Christian name.

Sir *Feeb.* Sir *Cautious*, know my Nephew—'tis a young *St. Omers* Scholar—but none of the Witnesses.

Sir *Cau.* Marry, Sir, and the wiser he; for they got nothing by't.

Bea. Sir, I love and honour you, because you are a Traveller.

Sir *Feeb.* A very proper young Fellow, and as like old *Frank Fainwou'd* as the Devil to the Collier; but, *Francis*, you are come into a very leud Town, *Francis*, for Whoring, and Plotting, and Roaring, and Drinking; but you must go to Church, *Francis*, and avoid ill Company, or you may make damnable Havock in my Cash, *Francis*,—what, you can keep Merchants Books?

Bel. That's been my study, Sir.

Sir *Feeb.* And you will not be proud, but will be commanded by me, *Francis*?

Bel. I desire not to be favour'd as a Kinsman, Sir, but as your humblest Servant.

Sir *Feeb.* Why, thou'rt an honest Fellow, *Francis*,—and thou'rt heartily welcome—and I'll make thee fortunate. But come, Sir *Cautious*, let you and I take a turn i'th' Garden, and get a right understanding between your Nephew Mr. *Bearjest*, and my Daughter *Dye*.

Sir *Cau.* Prudently thought on, Sir, I'll wait on you.—

[*Ex. Sir* Feeble, *and Sir* Cautious.

Bea. You are a Traveller, I understand.

Bel. I have seen a little part of the World, Sir.

Bea. So have I, Sir, I thank my Stars, and have performed most of my Travels on Foot, Sir.

Bel. You did not travel far then, I presume, Sir?

Bea. No, Sir, it was for my diversion indeed; but I assure you, I travell'd into *Ireland* a-foot, Sir.

Bel. Sure, Sir, you go by shipping into *Ireland*?

Bea. That's all one, Sir, I was still a-foot, ever walking on the Deck.

Bel. Was that your farthest Travel, Sir?

Bea. Farthest—why, that's the End of the World—and sure a Man can go no farther.

Bel. Sure, there can be nothing worth a Man's Curiosity?

Bea. No, Sir, I'll assure you, there are the Wonders of the World, Sir: I'll hint you this one. There is a Harbour which since the Creation was never capable of receiving a Lighter, yet by another Miracle the King of *France* was to ride there with a vast Fleet of Ships, and to land a hundred thousand Men.

Bel. This is a swinging Wonder—but are there store of Mad-men there, Sir?

Bea. That's another Rarity to see a Man run out of his Wits.

Noi. Marry, Sir, the wiser they I say.

Bea. Pray, Sir, what store of Miracles have you at St. *Omers*?

Bel. None, Sir, since that of the wonderful *Salamanca* Doctor, who was both here and there at the same Instant of time.

Bea. How, Sir? why, that's impossible.

Bel. That was the Wonder, Sir, because 'twas impossible.

Noi. But 'twas a greater, Sir, that 'twas believed.

Enter L. Fulb. *and* Pert, *Sir* Cau. *and Sir* Feeb.

Sir *Feeb.* Enough, enough, Sir *Cautious*, we apprehend one another. Mr. *Bearjest*, your Uncle here and I have struck the Bargain, the Wench is yours with three thousand Pound present, and something more after Death, which your Uncle likes well.

Bea. Does he so, Sir? I'm beholding to him; then 'tis not a Pin matter whether I like or not, Sir.

Sir *Feeb.* How, Sir, not like my Daughter *Dye?*

Bea. Oh, Lord, Sir,—die or live, 'tis all one for that, Sir—I'll stand to the Bargain my Uncle makes.

Pert. Will you so, Sir? you'll have very good luck if you do.   [*Aside.*

Bea. Prithee hold thy Peace, my Lady's Woman.

L. *Ful.* Sir, I beg your pardon for not waiting on you to Church—I knew you wou'd be private.

Enter Let. *fine in Jewels.*

Sir *Feeb.* You honour us too highly now, Madam.

           [Presents his Wife, who salutes her.

L. *Ful.* Give you Joy, my dear *Leticia!* I find, Sir, you were resolved for Youth, Wit and Beauty.

Sir *Feeb.* Ay, ay, Madam, to the Comfort of many a hoping Coxcomb: but *Lette,*—Rogue *Lette*—thou wo't not make me free o'th' City a second time, wo't thou entice the Rogues with the Twire and the wanton Leer —the amorous Simper that cries, come, kiss me—then the pretty round Lips are pouted out—he, Rogue, how I long to be at 'em!—well, she shall never go to Church more, that she shall not.

L. *Ful.* How, Sir, not to Church, the chiefest Recreation of a City Lady?

Sir *Feeb.* That's all one, Madam, that tricking and dressing, and prinking and patching, is not your Devotion to Heaven, but to the young Knaves that are lick'd and comb'd and are minding you more than the Parson—ods bobs, there are more Cuckolds destin'd in the Church, than are made out of it.

Sir *Cau.* Hah, ha, ha, he tickles ye, i'faith, Ladies.

           [To his Lady.

Bel. Not one chance look this way—and yet
I can forgive her lovely Eyes,
Because they look not pleas'd with all this Ceremony;
And yet methinks some sympathy in Love
Might this way glance their Beams—I cannot hold—
—Sir, is this fair Lady my Aunt?

Sir *Feeb.* Oh, *Francis!* Come hither, *Francis.*
Lette, here's a young Rogue has a mind to kiss thee.

           [Puts them together, she starts back.

—Nay, start not, he's my own Flesh and Blood,
My Nephew—Baby—look, look how the young
Rogues stare at one another; like will to like, I see that.

Let. There's something in his Face so like my *Bellmour*,
it calls my Blushes up, and leaves my Heart defenceless.

Enter Ralph.

Ralph. Sir, Dinner's on the Table.

Sir *Feeb.* Come, come—let's in then—Gentlemen and
   Ladies,
And share to day my Pleasures and Delight,
But—
Adds bobs, they must be all mine own at Night.   [*Exeunt.*

ACT II.

SCENE I. Gayman's *Lodging.*

Enter Gayman *in a Night-Cap, and an old Campaign Coat*
tied about him, very melancholy.

Gay. Curse on my Birth! Curse on my faithless Fortune!
Curse on my Stars, and curst be all—but Love!
That dear, that charming Sin, though t'have pull'd
Innumerable Mischiefs on my head,
I have not, nor I cannot find Repentance for.
Nor let me die despis'd, upbraided, poor:
Let Fortune, Friends and all abandon me—
But let me hold thee, thou soft smiling God,
Close to my heart while Life continues there.
Till the last pantings of my vital Blood,
Nay, the last spark of Life and Fire be Love's!

Enter Rag.

—How now, *Rag*, what's a Clock?

Rag. My Belly can inform you better than my Tongue.

Gay. Why, you gormandizing Vermin you, what have
you done with the Three pence I gave you a fortnight ago.

Rag. Alas, Sir, that's all gone long since.

Gay. You gutling Rascal, you are enough to breed a Famine in a Land. I have known some industrious Footmen, that have not only gotten their own Livings, but a pretty Livelihood for their Masters too.

Rag. Ay, till they came to the Gallows, Sir.

Gay. Very well, Sirrah, they died in an honourable Calling—but hark ye, *Rag*,—I have business, very earnest business abroad this Evening; now were you a Rascal of Docity, you wou'd invent a way to get home my last Suit that was laid in Lavender—with the Appurtenances thereunto belonging, as Perriwig, Cravat, and so forth.

Rag. Faith, Master, I must deal in the black Art then, for no human means will do't—and now I talk of the black Art, Master, try your Power once more with my Landlady.

Gay. Oh! name her not, the thought on't turns my Stomach—a sight of her is a Vomit; but he's a bold Hero that dares venture on her for a kiss, and all beyond that sure is Hell it self—yet there's my last, last Refuge —and I must to this Wedding—I know not what,—but something whispers me,—this Night I shall be happy—and without *Julia* 'tis impossible!

Rag. *Julia*, who's that? my Lady *Fulbank*, Sir?

Gay. Peace, Sirrah—and call—a—no—Pox on't, come back—and yet—yes—call my fulsome Landlady.

[*Exit* Rag.

Sir *Cautious* knows me not by Name or Person.
And I will to this Wedding, I'm sure of seeing *Julia* there.
And what may come of that—but here's old Nasty coming.
I smell her up—hah, my dear Landlady.

Enter Rag *and* Landlady.

Quite out of breath—a Chair there for my Landlady.

Rag. Here's ne'er a one, Sir.

Land. More of your Money and less of your Civility, good Mr. *Wasteall*.

Gay. Dear Landlady—

Land. Dear me no Dears, Sir, but let me have my Money—Eight Weeks Rent last Friday ; besides Taverns, Ale-houses, Chandlers, Landresses' Scores, and ready Money out of my Purse; you know it, Sir.

Gay. Ay, but your Husband don't ; speak softly.

Land. My Husband ! what, do you think to fright me with my Husband ?—I'd have you to know I'm an honest Woman, and care not this—for my Husband. Is this all the thanks I have for my kindness, for patching, borrowing and shifting for you ; 'twas but last Week I pawn'd my best Petticoat, as I hope to wear it again, it cost me six and twenty shillings besides Making; then this Morning my new *Norwich* Mantua followed, and two postle Spoons, I had the whole dozen when you came first ; but they dropt, and dropt, till I had only *Judas* left for my Husband.

Gay. Hear me, good Landlady.

Land. Then I've past my word at the *George Tavern*, for forty Shillings for you, ten Shillings at my Neighbour *Squabs* for Ale, besides seven Shillings to Mother *Suds* for Washing; and do you fob me off with my Husband ?

Gay. Here, *Rag*, run and fetch her a Pint of Sack— there's no other way of quenching the Fire in her flabber Chops. [*Exit* Rag.
—But, my dear Landlady, have a little Patience.

Land. Patience ! I scorn your Words, Sir—is this a place to trust in ? tell me of Patience, that us'd to have my money before hand ; come, come, pay me quickly— or old *Gregory Grimes* house shall be too hot to hold you.

Gay. Is't come to this, can I not be heard ?

Land. No, Sir, you had good Clothes when you came first, but they dwindled daily, till they dwindled to this old Campaign—with tan'd coloured Lining—once red —but now all Colours of the Rain-bow, a Cloke to sculk in a Nights, and a pair of piss-burn'd shammy Breeches. Nay, your very Badge of Manhood's gone too.

Gay. How, Landlady ! nay then, i'faith, no wonder if you rail so.

Land. Your Silver Sword I mean—transmogrified to this two-handed Basket Hilt—this old Sir *Guy* of *Warwick* —which will sell for nothing but old Iron. In fine, I'll have my money, Sir, or i'faith, *Alsatia* shall not shelter you.

Enter Rag.

Gay. Well, Landlady—if we must part—let's drink at parting ; here, Landlady, here's to the Fool—that shall love you better than I have done.   [*Sighing, drinks.*

Land. Rot your Wine—dy'e think to pacify me with Wine, Sir?
     [*She refusing to drink, he holds open her Jaws,* Rag
          throws a Glass of Wine into her Mouth.
—What, will you force me?—no—give me another Glass, I scorn to be so uncivil to be forced, my service to you, Sir—this shan't do, Sir.
                    [*She drinks, he, embracing her, sings.*

> *Ah,* Cloris, *'tis in vain you scold,*
> *Whilst your Eyes kindle such a Fire.*
> *Your Railing cannot make me cold,*
> *So fast as they a Warmth inspire.*

Land. Well, Sir, you have no reason to complain of my Eyes nor my Tongue neither, if rightly understood.
                                        [*Weeps.*

Gay. I know you are the best of Landladies,
As such I drink your Health—   [*Drinks.*
But to upbraid a Man in Tribulation—fie—'tis not done like a Woman of Honour, a Man that loves you too.
                                        [*She drinks.*

Land. I am a little hasty sometimes, but you know my good Nature.

Gay. I do, and therefore trust my little wants with you. I shall be rich again—and then, my dearest Landlady—

Land. Wou'd this Wine might ne'er go through me, if I wou'd not go, as they say, through Fire and Water— by Night or by Day for you.   [*She drinks.*

Gay. And as this is Wine I do believe thee. [*He drinks.*

Land. Well—you have no money in your Pocket now, I'll warrant you—here—here's ten Shillings for you old *Greg'ry* knows not of.

[*Opens a great greasy purse.*

Gay. I cannot in Conscience take it, good Faith, I cannot—besides, the next Quarrel you'll hit me in the Teeth with it.

Land. Nay, pray no more of that; forget it, forget it. I own I was to blame—here, Sir, you shall take it.

Gay. Ay,—but what shou'd I do with Money in these damn'd Breeches?—No, put it up—I can't appear abroad thus—no, I'll stay at home, and lose my business.

Land. Why, is there no way to redeem one of your Suits?

Gay. None—none—I'll e'en lay me down and die.

Land. Die—marry, Heavens forbid—I would not for the World—let me see—hum—what does it lie for?

Gay. Alas! dear Landlady, a Sum—a Sum.

Land. Well, say no more, I'll lay about me.

Gay. By this kiss but you shall not—*Assafœtida*, by this Light.

Land. Shall not? that's a good one, i'faith: shall you rule, or I?

Gay. But shou'd your Husband know it?—

Land. Husband—marry come up, Husbands know Wives secrets? No, sure, the World's not so bad yet—where do your things lie? and for what?

Gay. Five Pounds equips me—*Rag* can conduct you—but I say you shall not go, I've sworn.

Land. Meddle with your matters—let me see, the Caudle Cup that *Molly's* Grandmother left her, will pawn for about that sum—I'll sneak it out—well, Sir, you shall have your things presently—trouble not your head, but expect me.

[*Ex.* Landlady *and* Rag.

Gay. Was ever man put to such beastly shifts? 'Sdeath, how she stunk—my senses are must luxuriously regal'd—there's my perpetual Musick too—

[Knocking of Hammers on a Anvil.

The ringing of Bells is an Ass to't.

Enter Rag.

Rag. Sir, there's one in a Coach below wou'd speak to you.

Gay. With me, and in a Coach! who can it be?

Rag. The Devil, I think, for he has a strange Countenance.

Gay. The Devil! shew your self a Rascal of Parts, Sirrah, and wait on him up with Ceremony.

Rag. Who, the Devil, Sir?

Gay. Ay, the Devil, Sir, if you mean to thrive.

[Exit Rag.

Who can this be—but see he comes to inform me—withdraw.

Enter Bredwel drest like a Devil.

Bred. I come to bring you this—   [*Gives him a Letter.*

Gayman reads.

RECEIVE what Love and Fortune present you with, be grateful and be silent, or 'twill vanish like a dream, and leave you more wretched that it found You.

Adieu.

—hah—   [*Gives him a bag of Money.*

Bred. Nay, view it, Sir, 'tis all substantial Gold.

Gay. Now dare not I ask one civil question for fear it vanish all—   [*Aside.*

But I may ask, how 'tis I ought to pay for this great Bounty.

Bred. Sir, all the Pay is Secrecy—

Gay. And is this all that is required, Sir?

Bred. No, you're invited to the Shades below.

Gay. Hum, Shades below !—I am not prepared for such a Journey, Sir.

Bred. If you have Courage, Youth or Love, you'll follow me :
When Night's black Curtain's drawn around the World,
And mortal Eyes are safely lockt in sleep,

[In feign'd Heroick Tone.

And no bold Spy dares view when Gods caress,
Then I'll conduct thee to the Banks of Bliss.
—Durst thou not trust me ?

Gay. Yes, sure, on such substantial security.

[Hugs the Bag.

Bred. Just when the Day is vanish'd into Night,
And only twinkling Stars inform the World,
Near to the Corner of the silent Wall,
In Fields of *Lincoln's-Inn*, thy Spirit shall meet thee.
—Farewell.   *[Goes out.*

Gay. Hum—I am awake sure, and this is Gold I grasp.
I could not see this Devil's cloven Foot ;
Nor am I such a Coxcomb to believe,
But he was as substantial as his Gold.
Spirits, Ghosts, Hobgoblins, Furies, Fiends and Devils,
I've often heard old Wives fright Fools and Children with,
Which, once arriv'd to common Sense, they laugh at.
—No, I am for things possible and Natural :
Some Female Devil, old and damn'd to Ugliness,
And past all Hopes of Courtship and Address,
Full of another Devil called Desire,
Has seen this Face—this Shape—this Youth,
And thinks it's worth her Hire. It must be so :
I must moil on in the damn'd dirty Road,
And sure such Pay will make the Journey easy :

And for the Price of the dull drudging Night,
All Day I'll purchase new and fresh Delight.   *[Exit.*

SCENE II. *Sir* Feeble's *House*.

Enter Leticia, *pursu'd by* Phillis.

Phil. Why, Madam, do you leave the Garden,
For this retreat to Melancholy?

Let. Because it suits my Fortune and my Humour;
And even thy Presence wou'd afflict me now.

Phil. Madam, I was sent after you; my Lady *Fulbank*
has challeng'd Sir *Feeble* at Bowls, and stakes a Ring of
fifty Pound against his new Chariot.

Let. Tell him I wish him Luck in every thing,
But in his Love to me—
Go tell him I am viewing of the Garden.   [*Ex.* Phillis.

Enter Bellmour *at a distance behind her*.

—Blest be this kind Retreat, this 'lone Occasion,
That lends a short Cessation to my Torments,
And gives me leave to vent my Sighs and Tears. [*Weeps.*

Bel. And doubly blest be all the Powers of Love,
That give me this dear Opportunity.

Let. Where were you, all ye pitying Gods of Love?
That once seem'd pleas'd at *Bellmour's* Flame and mine,
And smiling join'd our Hearts, our sacred Vows,
And spread your Wings, and held your Torches high.

Bel. Oh—   [*She starts, and pauses.*

Let. Where were you now? When this unequal Marriage
Gave me from all my Joys, gave me from *Bellmour*;
Your Wings were flag'd, your Torches bent to Earth,
And all your little Bonnets veil'd your Eyes;
You saw not, or were deaf and pitiless.

Bel. Oh my *Leticia!*

Let. Hah, 'tis there again; that very voice was *Bellmour's*:
Where art thou, Oh thou lovely charming Shade?
For sure thou canst not take a Shape to fright me.
—What art thou?—speak!
                    [*Not looking behind her yet for fear.*

Bel. Thy constant true Adorer,
Who all this fatal Day has haunted thee
To ease his tortur'd Soul.   [*Approaching nearer.*

Let. My Heart is well acquainted with that Voice,
But Oh, my Eyes dare not encounter thee.
                    [*Speaking with signs of fear.*

Bel. Is it because thou'st broken all thy Vows?
—Take to thee Courage, and behold thy Slaughters.

Let. Yes, though the Sight wou'd blast me, I wou'd
    view it.   [*Turns.*
—'Tis he—'tis very *Bellmour!* or so like—
I cannot doubt but thou deserv'st this Welcome.
                              [*Embraces him.*

Bel. Oh my *Leticia!*

Let. I'm sure I grasp not Air; thou art no Fantom:
Thy Arms return not empty to my Bosom,
But meet a solid Treasure.

Bel. A Treasure thou so easily threw'st away;
A Riddle simple Love ne'er understood.

Let. Alas, I heard, my *Bellmour*, thou wert dead.

Bel. And was it thus you mourn'd my Funeral?

Let. I will not justify my hated Crime:
But Oh! remember I was poor and helpless,
And much reduc'd, and much impos'd upon.
                              [*Bellmour weeps.*

Bel. And Want compell'd thee to this wretched Marriage—did it?

Let. 'Tis not a Marriage, since my *Bellmour* lives;
The Consummation were Adultery.
I was thy Wife before, wo't thou deny me?

Bel. No, by those Powers that heard our mutual Vows,
Those Vows that tie us faster than dull Priests.

Let. But oh my *Bellmour*, thy sad Circumstances
Permit thee not to make a publick Claim:
Thou art proscribed, and diest if thou art seen.

Bel. Alas!

Let. Yet I wou'd wander with thee o'er the World,
And share thy humblest Fortune with thy Love.

Bel. Is't possible, *Leticia*, thou wou'dst fly
To foreign Shores with me?

Let. Can *Bellmour* doubt the Soul he knows so well?

Bel. Perhaps in time the King may find my Innocence,
and may extend his Mercy:
Mean time I'll make provision for our Flight.

Let. But how 'twixt this and that can I defend
My self from the loath'd Arms of an impatient Dotard,
That I may come a spotless Maid to thee?

Bel. Thy native Modesty and my Industry
Shall well enough secure us.
Feign your nice Virgin-Cautions all the day;
Then trust at night to my Conduct to preserve thee.
—And wilt thou yet be mine? Oh, swear a-new,
Give me again thy Faith, thy Vows, thy Soul;
For mine's so sick with this Day's fatal Business,
It needs a Cordial of that mighty strength;
Swear—swear, so as if thou break'st—
Thou mayst be—any thing—but damn'd, *Leticia*.

Let. Thus then, and hear me, Heaven!   [*Kneels.*
Bel. And thus—I'll listen to thee.   [*Kneels.*

Enter Sir Feeble, *L.* Fulbank, *Sir* Cautious.

Sir *Feeb.* *Lette*, *Lette*, *Lette*, where are you, little Rogue,
Lette?
—Hah—hum—what's here—
        [*Bel. snatches her to his Bosom, as if she fainted.*
Bel. Oh Heavens, she's gone, she's gone!

Sir *Feeb.* Gone—whither is she gone?—it seems she
had the Wit to take good Company with her—
        [*The Women go to her, take her up.*
Bel. She's gone to Heaven, Sir, for ought I know.

Sir *Cau.* She was resolv'd to go in a young Fellow's
Arms, I see.

Sir *Feeb*. Go to, *Francis*—go to.

L. Ful. Stand back, Sir, she recovers.

Bel. Alas, I found her dead upon the Floor,
—Shou'd I have left her so—if I had known your mind—

Sir *Feeb*. Was it so—was it so?—Got so, by no means,
Francis.—

Let. Pardon him, Sir, for surely I had died,
Bur for his timely coming.

Sir *Feeb*. Alas, poor Pupsey—was it sick—look here—
here's a fine thing to make it well again. Come, buss, and
it shall have it—oh, how I long for Night.
Ralph, are the Fidlers ready?

Ral. They are tuning in the Hall, Sir.

Sir *Feeb*. That's well, they know my mind. I hate that
same twang, twang, twang, fum, fum, fum, tweedle,
tweedle, tweedle, then scrue go the Pins, till a man's Teeth
are on an edge; then snap, says a small Gut, and there we
are at a loss again. I long to be in bed with a—hey tredodle,
tredodle, tredodle,—with a hay tredool, tredodle, tredo—
                    [*Dancing and playing on his Stick like a Flute.*

Sir *Cau*. A prudent Man would reserve himself—
Good-facks, I danc'd so on my Wedding-day, that when
I came to Bed, to my Shame be it spoken, I fell fast asleep,
and slept till morning.

L. Ful. Where was your Wisdom then, Sir *Cautious?*
But I know what a wise Woman ought to have done.

Sir *Feeb*. Odsbobs, that's Wormwood, that's Wormwood—I shall have my young Hussey set a-gog too; she'll
hear there are better things in the World than she has at
home, and then odsbobs, and then they'll ha't, adod, they
will, Sir *Cautious*. Ever while you live, keep a Wife
ignorant, unless a Man be as brisk as his Neighbours.

Sir *Cau*. A wise Man will keep 'em from baudy
Christnings then, and Gossipings.

Sir *Feeb*. Christnings and Gossipings! why, they are the
very Schools that debauch our Wives, as Dancing-Schools
do our Daughters.

    Sir *Cau.* Ay, when the overjoy'd good Man invites 'em all against that time Twelve-month: Oh, he's a dear Man, cries one—I must marry, cries another, here's a Man indeed—my Husband—God help him—

    Sir *Feeb.* Then he falls to telling of her Grievance, till (half maudlin) she weeps again : Just my Condition, cries a third : so the Frolick goes round, and we poor Cuckolds are anatomiz'd, and turn'd the right side outwards; adsbobs, we are, Sir *Cautious.*

    Sir *Cau.* Ay, ay, this Grievance ought to be redrest, Sir *Feeble;* the grave and sober part o'th' Nation are hereby ridicul'd,—

Ay, and cuckolded too for ought I know.

    L. Ful. Wise Men knowing this, should not expose their Infirmities, by marrying us young Wenches; who, without Instruction, find how we are impos'd upon.

Enter Fiddles playing, Mr. Bearjest and Diana dancing;
Bredwel, Noisey, &c.

    L. Ful. So, Cousin, I see you have found the way to Mrs. *Dy's* Heart.

    Bea. Who, I, my dear Lady Aunt? I never knew but one way to a Woman's Heart, and that road I have not yet travelled; for my Uncle, who is a wise Man, says Matrimony is a sort of a—kind of a—as it were, d'ye see, of a Voyage, which every Man of Fortune is bound to make one time or other : and Madam—I am, as it were —a bold Adventurer.

    Dia. And are you sure, Sir, you will venture on me?

    Bea. Sure!—I thank you for that—as if I could not believe my Uncle; For in this case a young Heir has no more to do, but to come and see, settle, marry, and use you scurvily.

    Dia. How, Sir, scurvily?

    Bea. Very scurvily, that is to say, be always fashionably drunk, despise the Tyranny of your Bed, and reign

absolutely—keep a Seraglio of Women, and let my Bastard
Issue inherit; be seen once a Quarter, or so, with you in
the Park for Countenance, where we loll two several ways
in the gilt Coach like *Janus*, or a Spread-Eagle.

Dia. And do you expect I shou'd be honest the while?

Bea. Heaven forbid, not I, I have not met with that
Wonder in all my Travels.

L. Ful. How, Sir, not an honest Woman?

Bea. Except my Lady Aunt—Nay, as I am a Gentleman and the first of my Family—you shall pardon me,
here—cuff me, cuff me soundly.   [*Kneels to her.*

Enter Gayman *richly drest.*

Gay. This Love's a damn'd bewitching thing—Now
though I should lose my Assignation with my Devil, I
cannot hold from seeing *Julia* to night: hah—there, and
with a Fop at her Feet.—Oh Vanity of Woman!
          [*Softly pulls her.*

L. Ful. Oh, Sir, you're welcome from *Northamptonshire.*

Gay. Hum—surely she knows the Cheat.   [*Aside.*

L. Ful. You are so gay, you save me, Sir, the labour of
asking if your Uncle be alive.

Gay. Pray Heaven she have not found my Circum-
          stances!   [*Aside.*
But if she have, Confidence must assist me—
—And, Madam, you're too gay for me to inquire
Whether you are that *Julia* which I left you?

L. Ful. Oh, doubtless, Sir—

Gay. But why the Devil do I ask—Yes, you are still
the same; one of those hoiting Ladies, that love nothing
like Fool and Fiddle; Crouds of Fops; had rather be
publickly, though dully, flatter'd, than privately ador'd:
you love to pass for the Wit of the Company, by talking
all and loud.

L. Ful. Rail on, till you have made me think my Virtue
at so low Ebb, it should submit to you.

Gay. What—I'm not discreet enough;
I'll babble all in my next high Debauch,
Boast of your Favours, and describe your Charms
To every wishing Fool.

L. Ful. Or make most filthy Verses of me—
Under the name of *Cloris*—you *Philander*,
Who in leud Rhimes confess the dear Appointment;
What Hour, and where, how silent was the Night,
How full of Love your Eyes, and wishing mine.
Faith, no; if you can afford me a Lease of your Love,
Till the old Gentleman my Husband depart this wicked
     World,
I'm for the Bargain.

Sir Cau. Hum—what's here, a young Spark at my
Wife?   [*Goes about 'em.*

Gay. Unreasonable *Julia*, is that all,
My Love, my Sufferings, and my Vows must hope?
Set me an Age—say when you will be kind,
And I will languish out in starving Wish:
But thus to gape for Legacies of Love,
Till Youth be past Enjoyment,
The Devil I will as soon—farewel.   [*Offers to go.*

L. Ful. Stay, I conjure you stay.

Gay. And lose my Assignation with my Devil.
                                   [*Aside.*

Sir Cau. 'Tis so, ay, ay, 'tis so—and wise Men will
perceive it; 'tis here—here in my forehead, it more than
buds; it sprouts, it flourishes.

Sir Feeb. So, that young Gentleman has nettled him,
stung him to the quick: I hope he'll chain her up—the
Gad-Bee's in his Quonundrum—in Charity I'll relieve
him—Come, my Lady *Fulbank*, the Night grows old
upon our hands; to dancing, to jiggiting—Come, shall I
lead your Ladyship?

L. Ful. No, Sir, you see I am better provided—
                              [*Takes* Gayman's *hand.*

Sir *Cau.* Ay, no doubt on't, a Pox on him for a young handsome Dog.   [*They dance all.*

Sir *Feeb.* Very well, very well, now the Posset; and then—ods bobs, and then—

Dia. And then we'll have t'other Dance.

Sir *Feeb.* Away, Girls, away, and steal the Bride to Bed; they have a deal to do upon their Wedding-nights; and what with the tedious Ceremonies of dressing and undressing, the smutty Lectures of the Women, by way of Instruction, and the little Stratagems of the young Wenches —odds bobs, a Man's cozen'd of half his Night: Come, Gentlemen, one Bottle, and then—we'll toss the Stocking.

[*Exeunt all but L.* Ful. Bred. *who are talking, and* Gayman.

L. Ful. But dost thou think he'll come?

Bred. I do believe so, Madam—

L. Ful. Be sure you contrive it so, he may not know whither, or to whom he comes.

Bred. I warrant you, Madam, for our Parts.

[*Exit* Bredwel, *stealing out* Gayman.

L. Ful. How now, what, departing?

Gay. You are going to the Bride-Chamber.

L. Ful. No matter, you shall stay—

Gay. I hate to have you in a Croud.

L. Ful. Can you deny me—will you not give me one lone hour i'th' Garden?

Gay. Where we shall only tantalize each other with dull kissing, and part with the same Appetite we met— No, Madam; besides, I have business—

L. Ful. Some Assignation—is it so indeed?

Gay. Away, you cannot think me such a Traitor; 'tis more important business—

L. Ful. Oh, 'tis too late for business—let to morrow serve.

Gay. By no means—the Gentleman is to go out of Town.

L. Ful. Rise the earlier then—

Gay. —But, Madam, the Gentleman lies dangerously
—sick—and should he die—

L. Ful. 'Tis not a dying Uncle, I hope, Sir?

Gay. Hum—

L. Ful. The Gentleman a dying, and to go out of
Town to morrow?

Gay. Ay—a—he goes—in a Litter—'tis his Fancy,
Madam—Change of Air may recover him.

L. Ful. So may your change of Mistress do me, Sir—
farewel.   [*Goes out.*

Gay. Stay, *Julia*—Devil, be damn'd—for you shall
tempt no more, I'll love and be undone—but she is gone—
And if I stay, the most that I shall gain
Is but a reconciling Look, or Kiss.
No, my kind Goblin—

> *I'll keep my Word with thee, as the least Evil;*
> *A tantalizing Woman's worse than Devil.*   [*Exit.*

ACT III.

Scene I. *Sir* Feeble's *House.*

The Second Song before the Entry.

A SONG made by Mr. *Cheek.*

NO more, Lucinda, *ah! expose no more*
   To the admiring World those conquering Charms :
In vain all day unhappy Men adore,
   What the kind Night gives to my longing Arms.
Their vain Attempts can ne'er successful prove,
Whilst I so well maintain the Fort of Love.

Yet to the World with so bewitching Arts,
   Your dazling Beauty you around display,
And triumph in the Spoils of broken Hearts,
   That sink beneath your feet, and croud your Way.
Ah! suffer now your Cruelty to cease,
And to a fruitless War prefer a Peace.

Enter Ralph *with Light,* Sir *Feeble, and* Bellmour
sad.

Sir *Feeb.* So, so, they're gone—Come, *Francis,* you
shall have the Honour of undressing me for the Encounter ;
but 'twill be a sweet one, *Francis.*

Bel. Hell take him, how he teazes me !

[*Undressing all the while.*

Sir *Feeb.* But is the young Rogue laid, *Francis*—is she
stoln to Bed ? What Tricks the young Baggages have
to whet a man's Appetite ?

Bel. Ay, Sir—Pox on him—he will raise my Anger
up to Madness, and I shall kill him to prevent his going
to Bed to her. [*Aside.*

Sir *Feeb.* A pise of those Bandstrings—the more haste
the less speed.

Bel. Be it so in all things, I beseech thee, *Venus.*

Sir *Feeb.* Thy aid a little, *Francis*—oh, oh—thou choak-
est me, 'sbobs, what dost mean ? [*Pinches him by the Throat.*

Bel. You had so hamper'd 'em, Sir—the Devil's very
mischievous in me. [*Aside.*

Sir *Feeb.* Come, come, quick, good *Francis,* adod, I'm
as yare as a Hawk at the young Wanton—nimbly, good
Francis, untruss, untruss.

Bel. Cramps seize ye—what shall I do? the near
Approach distracts me. [*Aside.*

Sir *Feeb.* So, so, my Breeches, good *Francis.* But well,
Francis, how dost think I got the young Jade my Wife ?

Bel. With five hundred pounds a year Jointure, Sir.

Sir *Feeb.* No, that wou'd not do, the Baggage was
damnably in love with a young Fellow they call *Bellmour,*
a handsome young Rascal he was, they say, that's truth
on't ; and a pretty Estate : but happening to kill a Man
he was forced to fly.

Bel. That was great pity, Sir.

Sir *Feeb.* Pity ! hang him, Rogue, 'sbobs, and all the
young Fellows in the Town deserve it ; we can never

keep our Wives and Daughters honest for rampant young
Dogs; and an old Fellow cannot put in amongst 'em,
under being undone, with Presenting, and the Devil and
all. But what dost think I did? being damnably in love
—I feign'd a Letter as from the *Hague*, wherein was a
Relation of this same *Bellmour's* being hang'd.

Bel. Is't possible, Sir, you cou'd devise such News?

Sir *Feeb.* Possible, Man! I did it, I did it; she swooned
at the News, shut her self up a whole Month in her
Chamber; but I presented high: she sigh'd and wept,
and swore she'd never marry: still I presented; she hated,
loathed, spit upon me; still, adod, I presented, till I presented my self effectually in Church to her; for she at
last wisely considered her Vows were cancell'd, since
Bellmour was hang'd.

Bel. Faith, Sir, this was very cruel, to take away his
Fame, and then his Mistress.

Sir *Feeb.* Cruel! thou'rt an Ass, we are but even with
the brisk Rogues, for they take away our Fame, cuckold
us, and take away our Wives: so, so, my Cap, *Francis*.

Bel. And do you think this Marriage lawful, Sir?

Sir *Feeb.* Lawful! it shall be when I've had Livery
and Seisin of her Body—and that shall be presently Rogue,
—quick—besides, this *Bellmour* dares as well be hang'd
as come into *England*.

Bel. If he gets his Pardon, Sir—

Sir *Feeb.* Pardon! no, no, I have took care for that,
for I have, you must know, got his Pardon already.

Bel. How, Sir! got his Pardon, that's some amends for
robbing him of his Wife.

Sir *Feeb.* Hold, honest *Francis:* What, dost think 'twas
in kindness to him! No, you Fool, I got his Pardon my
self, that no body else should have it, so that if he gets
any body to speak to his Majesty for it, his Majesty cries
he has granted it; but for want of my appearance, he's
defunct, trust up, hang'd, *Francis*.

Bel. This is the most excellent Revenge I ever heard of.

Sir *Feeb.* Ay, I learnt it of a great Politician of our Times.

Bel. But have you got his Pardon?——

Sir *Feeb.* I've done't, I've done't; Pox on him, it cost me five hundred pounds though: Here 'tis, my Solicitor brought it me this Evening.　　　　　　[*Gives it him.*

Bel. This was a lucky hit—and if it scape me, let me be hang'd by a Trick indeed.　　　　　　　　[*Aside.*

Sir *Feeb.* So, put it into my Cabinet,—safe, *Francis*, safe.

Bel. Safe, I'll warrant you, Sir.

Sir *Feeb.* My Gown, quick, quick,—t'other Sleeve, Man—so now my Night-cap; well, I'll in, throw open my Gown to fright away the Women, and jump into her Arms.　　　　　　　　　　　　[*Exit Sir* Feeble.

Bel. He's gone, quickly, oh Love inspire me!

Enter a Footman.

Foot. Sir, my Master, Sir *Cautious Fulbank*, left his Watch on the little Parlor-Table to night, and bid me call for't.

Bel. Hah—the Bridegroom has it, Sir, who is just gone to Bed, it shall be sent him in the Morning.

Foot. 'Tis very well, Sir—your Servant—

　　　　　　　　　　　　　　　　[*Exit* Footman.

Bel. Let me see—here is the Watch, I took it up to keep for him—but his sending has inspir'd me with a sudden Stratagem, that will do better than Force, to secure the poor trembling *Leticia*—who, I am sure, is dying with her Fears.　　　　　　　[*Exit* Bellmour.

SCENE II. *Changes to the Bed-chamber;* Leticia *in an undressing by the Women at the Table.*

Enter to them Sir Feeble Fainwou'd.

Sir *Feeb.* What's here? what's here? the prating Women still. Ods bobs, what, not in Bed yet? for shame of Love, *Leticia.*

Let. For shame of Modesty, Sir; you wou'd not have me go to Bed before all this Company.

Sir *Feeb.* What, the Women! why, they must see you laid, 'tis the fashion.

Let. What, with a Man? I wou'd not for the World. Oh, *Bellmour*, where art thou with all thy promised aid?

[*Aside.*

Dia. Nay, Madam, we shou'd see you laid indeed.

Let. First in my Grave, *Diana.*

Sir *Feeb.* Ods bobs, here's a Compact amongst the Women—High Treason against the Bridegroom—therefore, Ladies, withdraw, or, adod, I'll lock you all in.

[*Throws open his Gown, they run all away, he locks the Door.*

So, so, now we're alone, *Leticia*—off with this foolish Modesty, and Night Gown, and slide into my Arms.

[*She runs from him.*

H'e', my little Puskin—what, fly me, my coy *Daphne,*

[*He pursues her. Knocking.*

Hah—who's that knocks—who's there?—

Bel. [*Within.*] 'Tis I, Sir, 'tis I, open the door presently.

Sir *Feeb.* Why, what's the matter, is the House o-fire?

Bel. [*Within.*] Worse, Sir, worse—

[*He opens the door,* Bellmour *enters with the Watch in his hand.*

Let. 'Tis *Bellmour*'s Voice!

Bel. Oh, Sir, do you know this Watch?

Sir *Feeb.* This Watch!

Bel. Ay, Sir, this Watch?

Sir *Feeb.* This Watch!—why, prithee, why dost tell me of a Watch? 'tis Sir *Cautious Fulbank*'s Watch; what then, what a Pox dost trouble me with Watches?

[*Offers to put him out, he returns.*

Bel. 'Tis indeed his Watch, Sir, and by this Token he has sent for you, to come immediately to his House, Sir.

Sir *Feeb.* What a Devil, art mad, *Francis?* or is his

Worship mad, or does he think me mad?—go, prithee tell him I'll come to him to morrow. [*Goes to put him out.*

Bel. To morrow, Sir! why all our Throats may be cut before to morrow.

Sir *Feeb.* What sayst thou, Throat cut?

Bel. Why, the City's up in Arms, Sir, and all the Aldermen are met at *Guild-Hall;* some damnable Plot, Sir.

Sir *Feeb.* Hah—Plot—the Aldermen met at *Guild-Hall!*—hum—why, let 'em meet, I'll not lose this Night to save the Nation.

Let. Wou'd you to bed, Sir, when the weighty Affairs of State require your Presence?

Sir *Feeb.* —Hum—met at *Guild-Hall;*—my Clothes, my Gown again, *Francis*, I'll out—out! what, upon my Wedding-night? No—I'll in.

[*Putting on his Gown pausing, pulls it off again.*

Let. For shame, Sir, shall the Reverend Council of the City debate without you?

Sir *Feeb.* Ay, that's true, that's true; come truss again, *Francis*, truss again—yet now I think on't, *Francis*, prithee run thee to the Hall, and tell 'em 'tis my Wedding-night, d'ye see, *Francis;* and let some body give my Voice for—

Bel. What, Sir?

Sir *Feeb.* Adod, I cannot tell; up in Arms, say you! why, let 'em fight Dog, fight Bear; mun, I'll to Bed—go—

Let. And shall his Majesty's Service and his Safety lie unregarded for a slight Woman, Sir?

Sir *Feeb.* Hum, his Majesty!—come, haste, *Francis*, I'll away, and call *Ralph*, and the Footmen, and bid 'em arm; each Man shoulder his Musket, and advance his Pike —and bring my Artillery Implements quick—and let's away: Pupsey—b'u'y, Pupsey, I'll bring it a fine thing yet before Morning, it may be—let's away: I shall grow fond, and forget the business of the Nation—Come, follow me, *Francis.*—   [*Exit Sir* Feeble, Bellmour *runs to* Leticia.

Bel. Now, my *Leticia*, if thou e'er didst Love,
If ever thou design'st to make me blest—
Without delay fly this adulterous Bed.

Sir *Feeb.* Why, *Francis*, where are you, Knave?

[*Sir* Feeb. *within.*

Bel. I must be gone, lest he suspect us—I'll lose him,
and return to thee immediately—get thy self ready.—

Let. I will not fail, my Love.   [*Exit* Bellmour.

> *Old Man forgive me—thou the Aggressor art,*
> *Who rudely forc'd the Hand without the Heart.*
> *She cannot from the Paths of Honour rove,*
> *Whose Guide's Religion, and whose End is Love.* [Exit.

SCENE III. *Changes to a Wash-house, or Out-House.*

Enter with a Dark-lanthorn Bredwel *disguis'd like a Devil,*
leading Gayman.

Bred. Stay here till I give notice of your coming.

[*Exit* Bredwel, *leaves his Dark-Lanthorn,*

Gay. Kind Light, a little of your aid—now must I be
peeping, though my Curiosity should lose me all—hah—
Zouns, what here—a Hovel or a Hog-sty? hum, see the
Wickedness of Man, that I should find no time to swear
in, but just when I'm in the Devil's Clutches.

Enter Pert, *as an old Woman, with a Staff.*

Old W. Good Even to you, fair Sir.

Gay. Ha—defend me; if this be she, I must rival the
Devil, that's certain.

Old W. Come, young Gentleman, dare not you venture?

Gay. He must be as hot as *Vesuvius* that does—I shall
never earn my Morning's Present.

Old W. What, do you fear a longing Woman, Sir?

Gay. The Devil I do—this is a damn'd Preparation
to Love.

Old W. Why stand you gazing, Sir? A Woman's

Passion is like the Tide, it stays for no man when the hour is come——

Gay. I'm sorry I have took it at its Turning; I'm sure mine's ebbing out as fast.

Old W. Will you not speak, Sir—will you not on?

Gay. I wou'd fain ask—a civil Question or two first.

Old W. You know too much Curiosity lost Paradise.

Gay. Why, there's it now.

Old W. Fortune and Love invite you, if you dare follow me.

Gay. This is the first thing in Petticoats that ever dar'd me in vain. Were I but sure she were but human now—for sundry Considerations she might down—but I will on—— [*She goes, he follows; both go out.*

SCENE IV. *A Chamber in the Apartments of L.* Fulbank.

Enter Old Woman *follow'd by* Gayman *in the dark.*

[*Soft Musick plays, she leaves him.*

Gay. —Hah, Musick—and Excellent!

SONG.

OH! *Love, that stronger art than Wine,*
Pleasing Delusion, Witchery divine,
Want to be priz'd above all Wealth,
Disease that has more Joys than Health;
Though we blaspheme thee in our Pain,
And of thy Tyranny complain,
We all are better'd by thy Reign.

What Reason never can bestow,
We to this useful Passion owe.
Love wakes the dull from sluggish Ease,
And learns a Clown the Art to please:
Humbles the Vain, kindles the Cold,
Makes Misers free, and Cowards bold.
'Tis he reforms the Sot from Drink,
And teaches airy Fops to think.

When full brute Appetite is fed,
And choak'd the Glutton lies, and dead;
Thou new Spirits dost dispense,
And fine'st the gross Delights of Sense.
Virtue's unconquerable Aid,
That against Nature can persuade;
And makes a roving Mind retire
Within the Bounds of just Desire.
Chearer of Age, Youth's kind Unrest,
And half the Heaven of the blest.

Gay. Ah, *Julia, Julia!* if this soft Preparation
Were but to bring me to thy dear Embraces;
What different Motions wou'd surround my Soul,
From what perplex it now.

   Enter Nymphs and Shepherds, and dance.

  [*Then two dance alone. All go out but* Pert *and a*
   Shepherd.

—If these be Devils, they are obliging ones:
I did not care if I ventur'd on that last Female Fiend.

     Man sings.

Cease your Wonder, cease your Guess,
Whence arrives your happiness.
Cease your Wonder, cease your Pain,
Human Fancy is in vain.

Chorus. *'Tis enough, you once shall find,*
Fortune may to Worth be kind; [gives him Gold.
And Love can leave off being blind.

     Pert sings.

You, before you enter here
On this sacred Ring must swear, [Puts it on his
By the Figure which is round,   Finger, holds
Your Passion constant and profound; his Hand.
By the Adamantine Stone,
To be fixt to one alone:

> *By the Lustre, which is true,*
> *Ne'er to break your sacred Vow.*
> *Lastly, by the Gold that's try'd,*
> *For Love all Dangers to abide.*

They all dance about him, while those same two sing.

Man. *Once about him let us move,*
   To confirm him true to Love.   [bis.

Pert. *Twice with mystick turning Feet,*
   Make him silent and discreet.   [bis.

Man. *Thrice about him let us tread,*
   To keep him ever young in Bed.   [bis.

    Gives him another part.

Man. *Forget Aminta's proud Disdain;*
   Haste here, and sigh no more in vain,
   The Joy of Love without the Pain.

Pert. *That God repents his former Slights,*
   And Fortune thus your Faith requites.

Both. *Forget Aminta's proud Disdain;*
   Then taste, and sigh no more in vain,
   The Joy of Love without the Pain,
   The Joy of Love without the Pain.

[*Exeunt* all Dancers. Looks on himself, and feels
     about him.

Gay. What the Devil can all this mean? If there be
a Woman in the Case—sure I have not liv'd so bad a
Life, to gain the dull Reputation of so modest a Coxcomb,
but that a Female might down with me, without all this
Ceremony. Is it care of her Honour?—that cannot be—
this Age affords none so nice: Nor Fiend nor Goddess can
she be, for these I saw were Mortal. No—'tis a Woman
—I am positive. Not young nor handsom, for then Vanity
had made her glory to have been seen. No—since 'tis
resolved, a Woman—she must be old and ugly, and will

not balk my Fancy with her sight, but baits me more with
this essential Beauty.

> *Well——be she young or old, Woman or Devil,*
> *She pays, and I'll endeavour to be civil.*   [*Exit.*

SCENE V. *In the same House. The flat Scene of the Hall.*

After a Knocking, enter Bredwel *in his masking Habit, with
his Vizard in the one Hand, and a Light in t'other, in haste.*

Bred. Hah, knocking so late at our Gate——

[*Opens the door.*

Enter Sir Feeble *drest, and arm'd Cap-a-pee, with a broad
Waste-Belt stuck round with Pistols, a Helmet, Scarf,
Buff-coat and half Pike.*

Sir Feeb. How now, how now, what's the matter here?

Bred. Matter, what, is my Lady's innocent Intrigue
found out?——Heavens, Sir, what makes you here in this
warlike Equipage?

Sir Feeb. What makes you in this showing Equipage, Sir?

Bred. I have been dancing among some of my Friends.

Sir Feeb. And I thought to have been fighting with
some of my Friends. Where's Sir *Cautious*, where's Sir
Cautious?

Bred. Sir *Cautious*——Sir, in Bed.

Sir Feeb. Call him, call him——quickly, good *Edward*.

Bred. Sure my Lady's Frolick is betray'd, and he
comes to make Mischief. However, I'll go and secure
Mr. *Gayman.*   [*Exit* Bredwel.

Enter Sir Cautious *and* Dick *his Boy with Light.*

Dick. Pray, Sir, go to Bed, here's no Thieves; all's
still and well.

Sir Cau. This last Night's misfortune of mine, *Dick*,
has kept me waking, and methought all night, I heard a
kind of a silent Noise. I am still afraid of Thieves; mercy
upon me, to lose five hundred Guineas at one clap, *Dick.*

—Hah—bless me! what's yonder? Blow the great Horn,
Dick—Thieves—Murder, Murder!

Sir *Feeb*. Why, what a Pox, are you mad? 'Tis I, 'tis
I, man.

Sir *Cau*. I, who am I? Speak—declare—pronounce.

Sir *Feeb*. Your Friend, old *Feeble Fainwou'd*.

Sir *Cau*. How, Sir *Feeble*! At this late hour, and on
his Wedding-Night—why, what's the matter, Sir—is it
Peace or War with you?

Sir *Feeb*. A Mistake, a Mistake, proceed to the business,
good Brother, for time you know is precious.

Sir *Cau*. Some strange Catastrophe has happened between
him and his Wife to Night, and makes him disturb me
thus—   [*Aside.*
—Come, sit, good Brother, and to the business as you say—
> [*They sit one at one end of the Table, the other at the
> other; Dick sets down the Light and goes out—both
> sit gaping and staring, and expecting when either
> should speak.*

Sir *Feeb*. As soon as you please, Sir. Lord, how wildly
he stares! He's much disturb'd in's mind—Well, Sir, let
us be brief—

Sir *Cau*. As brief as you please, Sir—Well, Brother—
                                                    [*Pausing still.*

Sir *Feeb*. So, Sir.

Sir *Cau*. How strangely he stares and gapes—some deep
concern.

Sir *Feeb*. Hum—hum—

Sir *Cau*. I listen to you, advance—

Sir *Feeb*. Sir?

Sir *Cau*. A very distracted Countenance—pray Heaven
he be not mad, and a young Wife is able to make an old
Fellow mad, that's the Truth on't.   [*Aside.*

Sir *Feeb*. Sure 'tis something of his Lady—he's so loth
to bring it out—I am sorry you are thus disturb'd, Sir.

Sir *Cau*. No disturbance to serve a Friend—

Sir *Feeb.* I think I am your Friend indeed, Sir *Cautious*, or I wou'd not have been here upon my Wedding-Night.

Sir *Cau.* His Wedding-Night—there lies his Grief, poor Heart! Perhaps she has cuckolded him already— [*Aside.* —Well, come, Brother—many such things are done—

Sir *Feeb.* Done—hum—come, out with it; Brother— what troubles you to Night?

Sir *Cau.* Troubles me—why, knows he I am robb'd? [*Aside.*

Sir *Feeb.* I may perhaps restore you to the Rest you've lost.

Sir *Cau.* The Rest; why, have I lost more since? Why, know you then who did it?—Oh, how I'd be reveng'd upon the Rascal!

Sir *Feeb.* 'Tis—Jealousy, the old Worm that bites— [*Aside.*

Who is it you suspect?

Sir *Cau.* Alas, I know not whom to suspect, I wou'd I did; but if you cou'd discover him—I wou'd so swinge him—

Sir *Feeb.* I know him—what, do you take me for a Pimp, Sir? I know him—there's your Watch again, Sir; I'm your Friend, but no Pimp, Sir— [*Rises in Rage.*

Sir *Cau.* My Watch; I thank you, Sir—but why Pimp, Sir?

Sir *Feeb.* Oh, a very thriving Calling, Sir,—and I have a young Wife to practise with. I know your Rogues.

Sir *Cau.* A young Wife!—'tis so, his Gentlewoman has been at Hot-Cockles without her Husband, and he's Horn-mad upon't. I suspected her being so close in with his Nephew—in a Fit with a Pox—[*Aside.*] Come, come, Sir *Feeble*, 'tis many an honest Man's Fortune.

Sir *Feeb.* I grant it, Sir—but to the business, Sir, I came for.

Sir *Cau.* With all my Soul—

[*They sit gaping, and expecting when either should speak. Enter* Bredwel *and* Gayman *at the door.* Bredwel *sees them, and puts* Gayman *back again.*

Bred. Hah—Sir *Feeble*, and Sir *Cautious* there—what shall I do? For this way we must pass, and to carry him back wou'd discover my Lady to him, betray all, and spoil the Jest—retire, Sir, your Life depends upon your being unseen. [*Go out.*

Sir *Feeb.* Well, Sir, do you not know that I am married, Sir? and this my Wedding Night?

Sir *Cau.* Very good, Sir.

Sir *Feeb.* And that I long to be in bed?

Sir *Cau.* Very well, Sir.

Sir *Feeb.* Very good, Sir, and very well, Sir—why then what the Devil do I make here, Sir? [*Rises in a rage.*

Sir *Cau.* Patience, Brother—and forward.

Sir *Feeb.* Forward! lend me your hand, good Brother; let's feel your Pulse; how has this Night gone with you?

Sir *Cau.* Ha, ha, ha—this is the oddest Quonudrum—sure he's mad—and yet now I think on't, I have not slept to night, nor shall I ever sleep again, till I have found the Villain that robb'd me. [*Weeps.*

Sir *Feeb.* So, now he weeps—far gone—this Laughing and Weeping is a very bad sign! [*Aside.*] Come, let me lead you to your Bed.

Sir *Cau.* Mad, stark mad—no, now I'm up 'tis no matter—pray ease your troubled Mind—I am your Friend —out with it—what, was it acted? or but designed?

Sir *Feeb.* How, Sir?

Sir *Cau.* Be not asham'd, I'm under the same Premunire I doubt, little better than a—but let that pass.

Sir *Feeb.* Have you any Proof?

Sir *Cau.* Proof of what, good Sir?

Sir *Feeb.* Of what! why, that you're a Cuckold; Sir, a Cuckold, if you'll ha't.

Sir *Cau.* Cuckold! Sir, do ye know what ye say?

Sir *Feeb.* What I say?

Sir *Cau.* Ay, what you say, can you make this out?

Sir *Feeb.* I make it out!

Sir Cau. Ay, Sir—if you say it, and cannot make it out, you're a—

Sir Feeb. What am I, Sir? What am I?

Sir Cau. A Cuckold as well as my self, Sir; and I'll sue you for *Scandalum Magnatum*; I shall recover swinging Damages with a City-Jury.

Sir Feeb. I know of no such thing, Sir.

Sir Cau. No, Sir?

Sir Feeb. No, Sir.

Sir Cau. Then what wou'd you be at, Sir?

Sir Feeb. I be at, Sir! what wou'd you be at, Sir?

Sir Cau. Ha, ha, ha—why this is the strangest thing—to see an old Fellow, a Magistrate of the City, the first Night he's married, forsake his Bride and Bed, and come arm'd Cap-a-pee, like *Gargantua*, to disturb another old Fellow, and banter him with a Tale of a Tub; and all to be-cuckold him here—in plain *English*, what's your Business?

Sir Feeb. Why, what the Devil's your Business, and you go to that?

Sir Cau. My Business, with whom?

Sir Feeb. With me, Sir, with me; what a Pox do you think I do here?

Sir Cau. 'Tis that I wou'd be glad to know, Sir.

Enter Dick.

Sir Feeb. Here, *Dick*, remember I've brought back your Master's Watch; next time he sends for me o'er Night, I'll come to him in the Morning.

Sir Cau. Ha, ha, ha, I send for you! Go home and sleep, Sir—Ad, and ye keep your Wife waking to so little purpose, you'll go near to be haunted with a Vision of Horns.   [*Exit* Dick.

Sir Feeb. Roguery, Knavery, to keep me from my Wife—Look ye, this was the Message I receiv'd.
          [*Tells him seemingly.*

Enter Bredwel *to the Door in a white Sheet like a Ghost,
speaking to* Gayman *who stands within.*

Bred. Now, Sir, we are two to two, for this way you
must pass or be taken in the Lady's Lodgings—I'll first
adventure out to make you pass the safer, and that he
may not, if possible, see Sir *Cautious*, whom I shall fright
into a Trance, I am sure.

And Sir *Feeble*, the Devil's in't if he know him.   [*Aside.*
   Gay. A brave kind Fellow this.

   Enter Bredwel *stalking on as a Ghost by them.*

   Sir *Cau.* Oh—undone,—undone; help, help;—I'm
dead, I'm dead.   [*Falls down on his Face; Sir* Feeble
                                  stares,—and stands still.
   Bred. As I could wish.   [*Aside, turns.*
Come on, thou ghastly thing, and follow me.

   Enter Gayman *like a Ghost, with a Torch.*

   Sir *Cau.* Oh Lord, oh Lord!
   Gay. Hah!—old Sir *Feeble Fainwou'd*—why, where
the Devil am I?—'Tis he:—and be it where it will, I'll
fright the old Dotard for cozening my Friend of his Mis-
tress.   [*Stalks on.*
   Sir *Feeb.* Oh, guard me,—guard me—all ye Pow'rs!
                                          [*Trembling.*
   Gay. Thou call'st in vain, fond Wretch—for I am
Bellmour,

        *Whom first thou robb'st of Fame and Life,
        And then what dearer was,—his Wife.*

                  [*Goes out, shaking his Torch at him.*
   Sir *Cau.* Oh Lord—oh Lord!

   Enter L. Fulbank *in an undress, and* Pert *undrest.*

   L. Ful. Heavens, what noise is this?—So he's got safe
out I see—hah, what thing art thou?
                                  [*Sees Sir* Feeble *arm'd.*

Sir Feeb. Stay, Madam, stay—'tis I, a poor trembling Mortal.

L. Ful. Sir *Feeble Fainwou'd!*—rise,—are you both mad?

Sir Cau. No, no,—Madam, we have seen the Devil.

Sir Feeb. Ay, and he was as tall as the Monument.

Sir Cau. With Eyes like a Beacon—and a Mouth,—Heaven bless us, like *London* Bridge at a full Tide.

Sir Feeb. Ay, and roar'd as loud.

L. Ful. Idle Fancies, what makes you from your Bed? and you, Sir, from your Bride?

Enter Dick *with Sack.*

Sir Feeb. Oh! that's the business of another day, a mistake only, Madam.

L. Ful. Away, I'm ashamed to see wise Men so weak; the Fantoms of the Night, or your own Shadows, the Whimseys of the Brain for want of Rest, or perhaps *Bredwel,* your Man—who being wiser than his Master, play'd you this Trick to fright you both to Bed.

Sir Feeb. Hum—adod, and that may be, for the young Knave when he let me in to Night, was drest up for some Waggery—

Sir Cau. Ha, ha, ha, 'twas even so, sure enough, Brother—

Sir Feeb. Ads bobs, but they frighted me at first basely—but I'll home to Pupsey, there may be Roguery, as well as here—Madam, I ask your Pardon, I see we're all mistaken.

L. Ful. Ay, Sir *Feeble,* go home to your Wife.

[*Ex. severally.*

SCENE VI. *The Street.*

Enter Bellmour *at the door, knocks, and enter to him from the House,* Phillis.

Phil. Oh, are you come, Sir? I'll call my Lady down.

Bel. Oh, haste, the Minutes fly—leave all behind.
And bring *Leticia* only to my Arms.   [*A noise of People.*

—Hah, what noise is that? 'Tis coming this way,
I tremble with my fears—hah, Death and the Devil,
'Tis he—

Enter Sir Feeble *and his Men arm'd, goes to the door, knocks.*

Ay, 'tis he, and I'm undone—what shall I do to kill
him now? besides, the Sin wou'd put me past all Hopes
of pardoning.

    Sir *Feeb.* A damn'd Rogue to deceive me thus.—

    Bel. Hah—see, by Heaven *Leticia,* Oh, we are ruin'd!

    Sir *Feeb.* Hum—what's here, two Women?—

                                [*Stands a little off.*

Enter Leticia *and* Phillis *softly, undrest, with a Box.*

    Let. Where are you, my best Wishes? Lord of my
Vows—and Charmer of my Soul? Where are you?

    Bel. Oh, Heavens!—   [*Draws his Sword half-way.*

    Sir *Feeb.* Hum, who's here? My Gentlewoman—she's
monstrous kind of the sudden. But whom is't meant to?

                                        [*Aside.*

    Let. Give me your hand, my Love, my Life, my All
—Alas! where are you?

    Sir *Feeb.* Hum—no, no, this is not to me—I am jilted,
cozen'd, cuckolded, and so forth.—

            [*Groping, she takes hold of Sir* Feeb.

    Let. Oh, are you here? indeed you frighted me with your
Silence—here, take these Jewels, and let us haste away.

    Sir *Feeb.* Hum—are you thereabouts, Mistress? was I
sent away with a Sham-Plot for this!—She cannot mean
it to me.   [*Aside.*

    Let. Will you not speak?—will you not answer me?
—do you repent already?—before Enjoyment are you
cold and false?

    Sir *Feeb.* Hum, before Enjoyment—that must be me.
Before Injoyment—Ay, ay, 'tis I—I see a little Prolonging
a Woman's Joy, sets an Edge upon her Appetite.

                                      [*Merrily.*

Let. What means my Dear? shall we not haste away?

Sir *Feeb.* Haste away! there 'tis again—No—'tis not me she means: what, at your Tricks and Intrigues already?—Yes, yes, I am destin'd a Cuckold—

Let. Say, am I not your Wife? can you deny me?

Sir *Feeb.* Wife! adod, 'tis I she means—'tis I she means—   [*Merrily.*

Let. Oh *Bellmour, Bellmour.*

[*Sir* Feeb. *starts back from her hands.*

Sir *Feeb.* Hum—what's that—*Bellmour!*

Let. Hah! Sir *Feeble!*—he would not, Sir, have us'd me thus unkindly.

Sir *Feeb.* Oh—I'm glad 'tis no worse—*Bellmour*, quoth a! I thought the Ghost was come again.

Phil. Why did you not speak, Sir, all this while?— my Lady weeps with your Unkindness.

Sir *Feeb.* I did but hold my peace, to hear how prettily she prattled Love: But, fags, you are naught to think of a young Fellow—ads bobs, you are now.

Let. I only say—he wou'd not have been so unkind to me.

Sir *Feeb.* But what makes ye out at this Hour, and with these Jewels?

Phil. Alas, Sir, we thought the City was in Arms, and packt up our things to secure 'em, if there had been a necessity for Flight. For had they come to plundering once, they wou'd have begun with the rich Aldermen's Wives, you know, Sir.

Sir *Feeb.* Ads bobs, and so they would—but there was no Arms, nor Mutiny—where's *Francis?*

Bel. Here, Sir.

Sir *Feeb.* Here, Sir—why, what a story you made of a Meeting in the Hall, and—Arms, and—a—the Devil of any thing was stirring, but a couple of old Fools, that sat gaping and waiting for one another's business—

Bel. Such a Message was brought me, Sir.

Sir Feeb. Brought! thou'rt an Ass, *Francis*—but no more—come, come, let's to bed—

Let. To Bed, Sir! what, by Day-light?—for that's hasting on—I wou'd not for the World—the Night wou'd hide my Blushes—but the Day—wou'd let me see my self in your Embraces.

Sir Feeb. Embraces, in a Fiddlestick; why, are we not married?

Let. 'Tis true, Sir, and Time will make me more familiar with you, but yet my Virgin Modesty forbids it. I'll to *Diana's* Chamber, the Night will come again.

Sir Feeb. For once you shall prevail; and this damn'd Jant has pretty well mortified me:—a Pox of your Mutiny, *Francis.*—Come, I'll conduct thee to *Diana*, and lock thee in, that I may have thee safe, Rogue.—

We'll give young Wenches leave to whine and blush,
And fly those Blessings which—ads bobs, they wish.

[*Exeunt.*

ACT IV.

SCENE I. *Sir* Feeble's *House.*

Enter Lady Fulbank, Gayman *fine, gently pulling her back*
by the hand; and Ralph *meets 'em.*

L. Ful. How now, *Ralph*—Let your Lady know I am come to wait on her.   [*Exit* Ralph.

Gay. Oh, why this needless Visit—
Your Husband's safe, at least till Evening safe.
Why will you not go back,
And give me one soft hour, though to torment me?

L. Ful. You are at leisure now, I thank you, Sir.
Last Night when I with all Love's Rhetorick pleaded,
And Heaven knows what last Night might have produced,
You were engag'd! False Man, I do believe it,
And I am satisfied you love me not. [*Walks away in scorn.*

Gay. Not love you!
Why do I waste my Youth in vain pursuit,

Neglecting Interest, and despising Power?
Unheeding and despising other Beauties.
Why at your feet are all my Fortunes laid,
And why does all my Fate depend on you?

    L. Ful. I'll not consider why you play the Fool,
Present me Rings and Bracelets; why pursue me;
Why watch whole Nights before my senseless Door,
And take such Pains to shew your self a Coxcomb.

    Gay. Oh! why all this?
By all the Powers above, by this dear Hand,
And by this Ring, which on this Hand I place,
On which I've sworn Fidelity to Love;
I never had a Wish or soft Desire
To any other Woman,
Since *Julia* sway'd the Empire of my Soul.

    L. Ful. Hah, my own Ring I gave him last night. [*Aside.*
—Your Jewel, Sir, is rich:
Why do you part with things of so much value,
So easily, and so frequently?

    Gay. To strengthen the weak Arguments of Love.

    L. Ful. And leave your self undone?

    Gay. Impossible, if I am blest with *Julia.*

    L. Ful. Love's a thin Diet, nor will keep out Cold.
You cannot satisfy your Dunning Taylor,
To cry—I am in Love!
Though possible you may your Seamstress.

    Gay. Does ought about me speak such Poverty?

    L. Ful. I am sorry that it does not, since to maintain
This Gallantry, 'tis said you use base means,
Below a Gentleman.

    Gay. Who dares but to imagine it's a Rascal,
A Slave, below a beating—what means my *Julia?*

    L. Ful. No more dissembling, I know your Land is gone
—I know each Circumstance of all your Wants;
Therefore—as e'er you hope that I should love you ever—
Tell me—where 'twas you got this Jewel, Sir.

Gay. Hah—I hope 'tis no stol'n Goods;   [*Aside.*
Why on the sudden all this nice examining?

L. Ful. You trifle with me, and I'll plead no more.

Gay. Stay—why—I bought it, Madam—

L. Ful. Where had you Money, Sir? You see I am
No Stranger to your Poverty.

Gay. This is strange—perhaps it is a secret.

L. Ful. So is my Love, which shall be kept from you.
                             [*Offers to go.*

Gay. Stay, *Julia*—your Will shall be obey'd, [*Sighing.*
Though I had rather die than be obedient,
Because I know you'll hate me when 'tis told.

L. Ful. By all my Vows, let it be what it will,
It ne'er shall alter me from loving you.

Gay. I have—of late—been tempted—
With Presents, Jewels, and large Sums of Gold.

L. Ful. Tempted! by whom?

Gay. The Devil, for ought I know.

L. Ful. Defend me, Heaven! the Devil?
I hope you have not made a Contract with him.

Gay. No, though in the Shape of Woman it appear'd.

L. Ful. Where met you with it?

Gay. By Magick Art I was conducted—I know not how,
To an inchanted Palace in the Clouds,
Where I was so attended—
Young dancing, singing Fiends innumerable.

L. Ful. Imagination all!

Gay. But for the amorous Devil, the old *Proserpine.*—

L. Ful. Ay, she—what said she?—

Gay. Not a word: Heaven be prais'd, she was a silent
Devil—but she was laid in a Pavilion, all form'd of gilded
Clouds, which hung by Geometry, whither I was con-
veyed, after much Ceremony, and laid in Bed with her;
where with much ado, and trembling with my Fears—
I forc'd my Arms about her.

L. Ful. And sure that undeceiv'd him.   [*Aside.*

Gay. But such a Carcase 'twas—deliver me—so rivell'd, lean and rough—a Canvas Bag of wooden Ladles were a better Bed-fellow.

L. Ful. Now though I know that nothing is more distant than I from such a Monster—yet this angers me. Death! cou'd you love me and submit to this?

Gay. 'Twas that first drew me in—
The tempting Hope of Means to conquer you,
Wou'd put me upon any dangerous Enterprize:
Were I the Lord of all the Universe,
I am so lost in Love,
For one dear Night to clasp you in my Arms,
I'd lavish all that World—then die with Joy.

L. Ful. 'Slife, after all to seem deform'd, old, ugly—
                                 [*Walking in a fret.*

Gay. I knew you would be angry when you heard it.
                     [*He pursues her in a submissive posture.*

Enter Sir Cautious, Bearjest, Noisey *and* Bredwel.

Sir *Cau.* How, what's here?—my Lady with the Spark that courted her last Night?—hum—with her again so soon?—Well, this Impudence and Importunity undoes more City-Wives than all their unmerciful Finery.

Gay. But, Madam—

L. Ful. Oh, here's my Husband—you'd best tell him your Story—what makes him here so soon?—   [*Angry.*

Sir *Cau.* Me his Story! I hope he will not tell me he 'as a mind to cuckold me.

Gay. A Devil on him, what shall I say to him?

L. Ful. What, so excellent at Intrigues, and so dull at an Excuse?   [*Aside.*

Gay. Yes, Madam, I shall tell him—

Enter Bellmour.

L. Ful. —Is my Lady at leisure for a Visit, Sir?

Bel. Always to receive your Ladyship. [*She goes out.*

Sir *Cau.* With me, Sir, wou'd you speak?

Gay. With you, Sir, if your name be *Fulbank*.

Sir Cau. Plain *Fulbank!* methinks you might have had a Sirreverence under your Girdle, Sir; I am honoured with another Title, Sir—— [*Goes talking to the rest.*

Gay. With many, Sir, that very well become you——

[*Pulls him a little aside.*

I've something to deliver to your Ear.

Sir Cau. So, I'll be hang'd if he do not tell me, I'm a Cuckold now: I see it in his Eyes. My Ear, Sir! I'd have you to know I scorn any man's secrets, Sir;—for ought I know you may whisper Treason to me, Sir. Pox on him, how handsom he is, I hate the sight of the young Stallion.

[*Aside.*

Gay. I wou'd not be so uncivil, Sir, before all this Company.

Sir Cau. Uncivil! Ay, ay, 'tis so, he cannot be content to cuckold, but he must tell me so too.

Gay. But since you will have it, Sir—you are—a Rascal —a most notorious Villain, Sir, d'ye hear——

Sir Cau. Yes, yes, I do hear—and am glad 'tis no worse. [*Laughing.*

Gay. Griping as Hell—and as insatiable—worse than a Brokering Jew, not all the Twelve Tribes harbour such a damn'd Extortioner.

Sir Cau. Pray, under favour, Sir, who are you?

[*Pulling off his Hat.*

Gay. One whom thou hast undone——

Sir Cau. Hum—I'm glad of that however.[*Aside smiling.*

Gay. Racking me up to a starving Want and Misery, Then took advantages to ruin me.

Sir Cau. So, and he'd revenge it on my Wife——

[*Aside smiling.*

Gay. Do not you know one *Wasteall*, Sir?

Enter Ralph *with* Wine, *sets it on a Table.*

Sir Cau. *Wasteall*—ha, ha, ha,—if you are any Friend

to that poor Fellow—you may return and tell him, Sir—
d'ye hear—that the Mortgage of two hundred pound a
Year is this day out, and I'll not bait him an hour, Sir—ha,
ha, ha,—what, do you think to hector civil Magistrates?

Gay. Very well, Sir, and is this your Conscience?

Sir *Cau.* Conscience! what do you tell me of Conscience? Why, what a noise is here—as if the undoing a
young Heir were such a Wonder; ods so I've undone a
hundred without half this ado.

Gay. I do believe thee—and am come to tell you—I'll be
none of that Number—for this Minute I'll go and redeem
it—and free myself from the Hell of your Indentures.

Sir *Cau.* How, redeem it! sure the Devil must help
him then.—Stay, Sir—stay—Lord, Sir, what need you
put your self to that trouble? your Land is in safe hands,
Sir; come, come, sit down—and let us take a Glass of
Wine together, Sir—

Bel. Sir, my service to you.   [*Drinks to him.*

Gay. Your Servant, Sir. Wou'd I cou'd come to speak
to *Bellmour*, which I dare not do in publick, lest I betray
him. I long to be resolv'd where 'twas Sir *Feeble* was last
night—if it were he—by which I might find out my
invisible Mistress.

Noi. Noble Mr. *Wasteall*— [*Salutes him, so does* Bearjest.

Bel. Will you please to sit, Sir?

Gay. I have a little business, Sir—but anon I'll wait
on you—your Servant, Gentlemen—I'll to *Crap* the
Scrivener's.   [*Goes out.*

Sir *Cau.* Do you know this *Wasteall*, Sir?— [*To* Noisey.

Noi. Know him, Sir! ay, too well—

Bea. The World's well amended with him, Captain,
since I lost my Money to him and you at the *George* in
White-Fryers.

Noi. Ay, poor Fellow—he's sometimes up, and sometimes down, as the Dice favour him—

Bea. Faith, and that's pity; but how came he so fine

o'th' sudden? 'Twas but last week he borrowed eighteen
pence of me on his Waste-Belt to pay his Dinner in an
Ordinary.

Bel. Were you so cruel, Sir, to take it?

Noi. We are not all one Man's Children; faith, Sir,
we are here to Day, and gone to Morrow——

Sir *Cau.* I say 'twas done like a wise Man, Sir; but
under favour, Gentlemen, this *Wasteall* is a Rascal——

Noi. A very Rascal, Sir, and a most dangerous Fellow
——he cullies in your Prentices and Cashiers to play——
which ruins so many o'th' young Fry i'th' City——

Sir *Cau.* Hum——does he so——d'ye hear that, *Edward?*

Noi. Then he keeps a private Press, and prints your
Amsterdam and *Leyden* Libels.

Sir *Cau.* Ay, and makes 'em too, I'll warrant him; a
dangerous Fellow——

Noi. Sometimes he begs for a lame Soldier with a
wooden Leg.

Bea. Sometimes as a blind Man, sells Switches in
New-Market Road.

Noi. At other times he runs the Country like a Gipsey
——tells Fortunes and robs Hedges, when he's out of Linen.

Sir *Cau.* Tells Fortunes too!——nay, I thought he dealt
with the Devil——Well, Gentlemen, you are all wide o'
this Matter——for to tell you the Truth——he deals with
the Devil, Gentlemen——otherwise he could never have
redeem'd his Land.   [*Aside.*

Bel. How, Sir, the Devil!

Sir *Cau.* I say the Devil; Heaven bless every wise Man
from the Devil.

Bea. The Devil, sha! there's no such Animal in
Nature; I rather think he pads.

Noi. Oh, Sir, he has not Courage for that——but he's
an admirable Fellow at your Lock.

Sir *Cau.* Lock! My Study-Lock was pickt——I begin
to suspect him——

Bea. I saw him once open a Lock with the Bone of a Breast of Mutton, and break an Iron Bar asunder with the Eye of a Needle.

Sir *Cau.* Prodigious!—well, I say the Devil still.

Enter Sir Feeble.

Sir *Feeb.* Who's this talks of the Devil?—a Pox of the Devil,
I say, this last night's Devil has so haunted me—

Sir *Cau.* Why, have you seen it since, Brother?

Sir *Feeb.* In Imagination, Sir.

Bel. How, Sir, a Devil?

Sir *Feeb.* Ay, or a Ghost.

Bel. Where, good Sir?

Bea. Ay, where? I'd travel a hundred Mile to see a Ghost—

Bel. Sure, Sir, 'twas Fancy.

Sir *Feeb.* If 'twere a Fancy, 'twas a strong one; and Ghosts and Fancy are all one if they can deceive. I tell you—if ever I thought in my Life—I thought I saw a Ghost—Ay, and a damnable impudent Ghost too; he said he was a—a Fellow here—they call *Bellmour.*

Bel. How, Sir!

Bea. Well, I wou'd give the world to see the Devil, provided he were a civil affable Devil, such an one as *Wasteall's* Acquaintance is—

Sir *Cau.* He can show him too soon, it may be. I'm sure as civil as he is, he helps him to steal my Gold, I doubt—and to be sure—Gentlemen, you say he's a Gamester—I desire when he comes anon, that you wou'd propose to sport a Dye, or so—and we'll fall to play for a Teaster, or the like—and if he sets any money, I shall go near to know my own Gold, by some remarkable Pieces amongst it; and if he have it, I'll hang him, and then all his six hundred a Year will be my own, which I have in Mortgage.

Bea. Let the Captain and I alone to top upon him—mean time, Sir, I have brought my Musick, to entertain my Mistress with a Song.

Sir *Feeb.* Take your own methods, Sir—they are at leisure—while we go drink their Healths within. Adod, I long for night, we are not half in kelter, this damn'd Ghost will not out of my Head yet.

[Exeunt all but Bellmour.

Bel. Hah—a Ghost! what can he mean? A Ghost, and *Bellmour's!*
—Sure my good Angel, or my Genius,
In pity of my Love, and of *Leticia*—
But see *Leticia* comes, but still attended—

Enter Leticia, *Lady* Fulbank, Diana.

—Remember—oh, remember to be true?
[Aside to her, passing by goes out.

L. *Ful.* I was sick to know with what Christian Patience you bore the Martyrdom of this Night.

Let. As those condemn'd bear the last Hour of Life.
A short Reprieve I had—and by a kind Mistake,
Diana only was my Bedfellow—   *[Weeps.*

Dia. And I wish for your Repose you ne'er had seen my Father.   *[Weeps.*

Let. And so do I, I fear he has undone me—

Dia. And me, in breaking of his word with *Bredwel*—

L. *Ful.* —So—as *Trincolo* says, wou'd you were both hang'd for me, for putting me in mind of my Husband. For I have e'en no better luck than either of you—
—Let our two Fates warn your approaching one:
I love young *Bredwel* and must plead for him.

Dia. I know his Virtue justifies my Choice:
But Pride and Modesty forbids I shou'd unlov'd pursue him.

Let. Wrong not my Brother so, who dies for you—

Dia. Cou'd he so easily see me given away,
Without a Sigh at parting?

For all the day a Calm was in his Eyes,
And unconcern'd he look'd and talk'd to me;
In dancing never prest my willing Hand,
Nor with a scornful Glance reproach'd my Falshood.

    Let. Believe me, that Dissembling was his Master-piece.
    Dia. Why should he fear, did not my Father promise him?
    Let. Ay, that was in his wooing time to me:
But now 'tis all forgotten—   [*Musick at the door.*

      After which enter Bearjest *and* Bredwel.

    L. *Ful.* How now, Cousin! Is this high piece of Gallantry from you?
    Bea. Ay, Madam, I have not travel'd for nothing—
    L. *Ful.* I find my Cousin is resolv'd to conquer, he assails with all his Artillery of Charms; we'll leave him to his success, Madam.— [*Ex.* Leticia *and* L. Fulbank.
    Bea. Oh Lord, Madam, you oblige me—look, *Ned*, you had a mind to have a full view of my Mistress, Sir, and —here she is.   [*He stands gazing.*
Go, salute her—look how he stands now; what a sneaking thing is a Fellow who has never travel'd and seen the World!—Madam—this is a very honest Friend of mine, for all he looks so simply.
    Dia. Come, he speaks for you, Sir.
    Bea. He, Madam! though he be but a Banker's Prentice, Madam, he's as pretty a Fellow of his Inches as any i'th' City—he has made love in Dancing-Schools, and to Ladies of Quality in the middle Gallery, and shall joke ye—and repartee with any Fore-man within the Walls—prithee to her—and commend me, I'll give thee a new Point Crevat.
    Dia. He looks as if he cou'd not speak to me.
    Bea. Not speak to you! yes, Gad, Madam, and do any thing to you too.
    Dia. Are you his Advocate, Sir?   [*In scorn.*

Bea. For want of a better—

      [Stands behind him, pushing him on.

Bred. An Advocate for Love I am,

And bring you such a Message from a Heart—

Bea. Meaning mine, dear Madam.

Bred. That when you hear it, you will pity it.

Bea. Or the Devil's in her—

Dia. Sir, I have many Reasons to believe,

It is my Fortune you pursue, not Person.

Bea. There is something in that, I must confess.

            [Behind him.

But say what you will, *Ned.*

Bred. May all the Mischiefs of despairing Love

Fall on me if it be.

Bea. That's well enough—

Bred. No, were you born an humble Village-Maid,

That fed a Flock upon the neighbouring Plain ;

With all that shining Vertue in your Soul,

By Heaven, I wou'd adore you—love you—wed you—

Though the gay World were lost by such a Nuptial.

        [Bear. looks on him.

—This—I wou'd do, were I my Friend the Squire.

          [Recollecting.

Bea. Ay, if you were me—you might do what you pleas'd ; but I'm of another mind.

Dia. Shou'd I consent, my Father is a Man whom Interest sways, not Honour ; and whatsoever Promises he'as made you, he means to break 'em all, and I am destin'd to another.

Bea. How, another—his Name, his Name, Madam— here's *Ned* and I fear ne'er a single Man i'th' Nation, What is he—what is he?—

Dia. A Fop, a Fool, a beaten Ass—a Blockhead.

Bea. What a damn'd Shame's this, that Women shou'd be sacrificed to Fools, and Fops must run away with Heiresses—whilst we Men of Wit and Parts dress and

dance, and cock and travel for nothing but to be tame
Keepers.

Dia. But I, by Heaven, will never be that Victim:
But where my Soul is vow'd, 'tis fix'd for ever.

Bred. Are you resolv'd, are you confirm'd in this?
Oh my *Diana*, speak it o'er again.

[Runs to her, and embraces her.
Bless me, and make me happier than a Monarch.

Bea. Hold, hold, dear *Ned*—that's my part, I take it.

Bred. Your Pardon, Sir, I had forgot my self.
—But time is short—what's to be done in this?

Bea. Done! I'll enter the House with Fire and Sword,
d'ye see, not that I care this—but I'll not be fob'd off—
what, do they take me for a Fool—an Ass?

Bred. Madam, dare you run the risk of your Father's
Displeasure, and run away with the Man you love?

Dia. With all my Soul—

Bea. That's hearty—and we'll do it—*Ned* and I here—
and I love an Amour with an Adventure in't like *Amadis
de Gaul*—Harkye, *Ned*, get a Coach and six ready to night
when 'tis dark, at the back Gate—

Bred. And I'll get a Parson ready in my Lodging, to
which I have a Key through the Garden, by which we
may pass unseen.

Bea. Good—Mun, here's Company—

Enter Gayman *with his Hat and Money in't, Sir* Cautious
in a rage, Sir Feeble, *Lady* Fulbank, Leticia, *Captain*
Noisey, Bellmour.

Sir *Cau.* A hundred Pound lost already! Oh Coxcomb,
old Coxcomb, and a wise Coxcomb—to turn Prodigal at
my Years, why, I was bewitcht!

Sir *Feeb.* Shaw, 'twas a Frolick, Sir, I have lost a hundred
Pound as well as you. My Lady has lost, and your Lady
has lost, and the rest—what, old Cows will kick sometimes, what's a hundred Pound?

Sir Cau. A hundred Pound! why, 'tis a sum, Sir—a sum—why, what the Devil did I do with a Box and Dice!

L. Ful. Why, you made a shift to lose, Sir? And where's the harm of that? We have lost, and he has won; anon it may be your Fortune.

Sir Cau. Ay, but he could never do it fairly, that's certain. Three hundred Pound! why, how came you to win so unmercifully, Sir?

Gay. Oh, the Devil will not lose a Gamester of me, you see, Sir.

Sir Cau. The Devil!—mark that, Gentlemen—

Bea. The Rogue has damn'd luck sure, he has got a Fly—

Sir Cau. And can you have the Conscience to carry away all our Money, Sir?

Gay. Most assuredly, unless you have the courage to retrieve it. I'll set it at a Throw, or any way: what say you, Gentlemen?

Sir Feeb. Ods bobs, you young Fellows are too hard for us every way, and I'm engag'd at an old Game with a new Gamester here, who will require all an old Man's stock.

L. Ful. Come, Cousin, will you venture a Guinea? Come, Mr. *Bredwel.*

Gay. Well, if no body dare venture on me, I'll send away my Cash—   [*They all go to play at the Table, but*
                    Sir Cau. *Sir* Feeb. *and* Gay.

Sir Cau. Hum—must it all go?—a rare sum, if a Man were but sure the Devil wou'd but stand Neuter now— [*Aside.*]—Sir, I wish I had any thing but ready Money to stake: three hundred Pound—a fine Sum!

Gay. You have Moveables, Sir, Goods—Commodities—

Sir Cau. That's all one, Sir; that's Money's worth, Sir: but if I had any thing that were worth nothing—

Gay. You wou'd venture it,—I thank you, Sir,—I wou'd your Lady were worth nothing—

Sir Cau. Why, so, Sir?

Gay. Then I wou'd set all this against that Nothing.

Sir Cau. What, set it against my Wife?

Gay. Wife, Sir! ay, your Wife—

Sir Cau. Hum, my Wife against three hundred Pounds!
What, all my Wife, Sir?

Gay. All your Wife! Why, Sir, some part of her wou'd
serve my turn.

Sir Cau. Hum—my Wife—why, if I shou'd lose, he
cou'd not have the Impudence to take her.   [*Aside.*

Gay. Well, I find you are not for the Bargain, and so
I put up—

Sir Cau. Hold, Sir—why so hasty—my Wife? no—
put up your Money, Sir—what, lose my Wife for three
hundred Pounds!—

Gay. Lose her, Sir!—why, she shall be never the worse
for my wearing, Sir—the old covetous Rogue is considering
on't, I think—What say you to a Night? I'll set it to a
Night—there's none need know it, Sir.

Sir Cau. Hum—a Night!—three hundred Pounds for
a Night! why, what a lavish Whore-master's this! We
take Money to marry our Wives, but very seldom part
with 'em, and by the Bargain get Money—For a Night,
say you?—Gad, if I shou'd take the Rogue at his word,
'twou'd be a pure Jest.   [*Aside.*

Sir Feeb. You are not mad, Brother.

Sir Cau. No, but I'm wise—and that's as good; let me
consider.—

Sir Feeb. What, whether you shall be a Cuckold or not?

Sir Cau. Or lose three hundred Pounds—consider that.
A Cuckold!—why, 'tis a word—an empty sound—'tis
Breath—'tis Air—'tis nothing:—but three hundred
Pounds—Lord, what will not three hundred Pounds do?
You may chance to be a Cuckold for nothing, Sir—

Sir Feeb. It may be so—but she shall do't discretly then.

Sir Cau. Under favour, you're an Ass, Brother; this is
the discreetest way of doing it, I take it.

Sir Feeb. But wou'd a wise man expose his Wife?

Sir *Cau.* Why, *Cato* was a wiser Man than I, and he lent his Wife to a young Fellow they call'd *Hortensius*, as Story says; and can a wise Man have a better Precedent than *Cato?*

Sir *Feeb.* I say, *Cato* was an Ass, Sir, for obliging any young Rogue of 'em all.

Sir *Cau.* But I am of *Cato's* mind. Well, a single Night you say.

Gay. A single Night—to have—to hold—possess—and so forth, at discretion.

Sir *Cau.* A Night—I shall have her safe and sound i'th' Morning.

Sir *Feeb.* Safe, no doubt on't—but how sound.—

Gay. And for Non-performance, you shall pay me three hundred Pounds, I'll forfeit as much if I tell—

Sir *Cau.* Tell?—why, make your three hundred pounds six hundred, and let it be put into the *Gazet*, if you will, Man.—But it's a Bargain?

Gay. Done—Sir *Feeble* shall be witness—and there stands my Hat.

> [*Puts down his Hat of Money, and each of 'em take a Box and Dice, and kneel on the Stage, the rest come about 'em.*

Sir *Cau.* He that comes first to One and thirty wins—
> [*They throw and count.*

L. Ful. What are you playing for?

Sir *Feeb.* Nothing, nothing—but a Trial of Skill between an old Man and a Young—and your Ladyship is to be Judge.

L. Ful. I shall be partial, Sir.

Sir *Cau.* Six and five's Eleven—
> [*Throws, and pulls the Hat towards him.*

Gay. Cater Tray—Pox of the Dice—

Sir *Cau.* Two fives—one and twenty—
> [*Sets up, pulls the Hat nearer.*

Gay. Now, Luck—Doublets of sixes—nineteen.

 Sir *Cau.* Five and four—thirty—

        [*Draws the Hat to him.*

 Sir *Feeb.* Now if he wins it, I'll swear he has a Fly indeed—'tis impossible without Doublets of sixes—

 Gay. Now Fortune smile—and for the future frown.

           [*Throws.*

 Sir *Cau.* —Hum—two sixes—

      [*Rises and looks dolefully round.*

 L. *Ful.* How now? what's the matter you look so like an Ass, what have you lost?

 Sir *Cau.* A Bauble—a Bauble—'tis not for what I've lost—but because I have not won—

 Sir *Feeb.* You look very simple, Sir—what think you of *Cato* now?

 Sir *Cau.* A wise Man may have his failings—

 L. *Ful.* What has my Husband lost?—

 Sir *Cau.* Only a small parcel of Ware that lay dead upon my hands, Sweet-heart.

 Gay. But I shall improve 'em, Madam, I'll warrant you.

 L. *Ful.* Well, since 'tis no worse, bring in your fine Dancer, Cousin, you say you brought to entertain your Mistress with.   [*Bearjest goes out.*

 Gay. Sir, you'll·take care to see me paid to Night?

 Sir *Cau.* Well, Sir—but my Lady, you must know, Sir, has the common frailties of her Sex, and will refuse what she even longs for, if persuaded to't by me.

 Gay. 'Tis not in my Bargain to sollicit her, Sir, you are to procure her—or three hundred pounds, Sir; chuse you whether.

 Sir *Cau.* Procure her! with all my soul, Sir; alas, you mistake my honest meaning, I scorn to be so unjust as not to see you a-bed together; and then agree as well as you can, I have done my part—In order to this, Sir— get but your self conveyed in a Chest to my house, with a Direction upon't for me; and for the rest—

 Gay. I understand you.

Sir Feeb. Ralph, get supper ready.

Enter Bea. *with Dancers; all go out but Sir* Cautious.

Sir Cau. Well, I must break my Mind, if possible, to
my Lady—but if she shou'd be refractory now—and make
me pay Three hundred Pounds—why, sure she won't
have so little Grace—Three hundred Pounds sav'd, is
three hundred pounds got—by our account—Cou'd All—

> *Who of this City-Privilege are free,*
> *Hope to be paid for Cuckoldom like me;*
> *Th' unthriving Merchant, whom gray Hair adorns,*
> *Before all Ventures wou'd ensure his Horns;*
> *For thus, while he but lets spare Rooms to hire,*
> *His Wife's crack'd Credit keeps his own entire.* [*Exit.*

ACT V.

SCENE I. *Sir* Cautious *his House.*

Enter Bellmour *alone, sad.*

Bel. The Night is come, oh my *Leticia!*
The longing Bridegroom hastens to his Bed;
Whilst she with all the languishment of Love,
And sad Despair, casts her fair Eyes on me,
Which silently implore, I would deliver her.
But how! ay, there's the Question—hah—   [*Pausing.*
I'll get my self hid in her Bed-chamber—
And something I will do—may serve us yet—
If all my Arts should fail—I'll have recourse
                                    [*Draws a dagger.*
To this—and bear *Leticia* off by force.
—But see she comes—

Enter Lady Fulbank, *Sir* Cautious, *Sir* Feeble, Leticia,
     Bearjest, Noisey, Gayman. *Exit* Bellmour.

Sir Feeb. Lights there, *Ralph.*
And my Lady's Coach there— [*Bearjest goes to* Gayman.

Bea. Well, Sir, remember you have promised to grant
me my diabolical Request, in shewing me the Devil—

Gay. I will not fail you, Sir.

L. Ful. Madam, your Servant; I hope you'll see no
more Ghosts, Sir *Feeble.*

Sir *Feeb.* No more of that, I beseech you, Madam:
Prithee, Sir *Cautious,* take away your Wife—Madam,
your Servant—   [*All go out after the Light.*
—Come, *Lette, Lette;* hasten, Rogue, hasten to thy
Chamber; away, here be the young Wenches coming—
                [*Puts her out, he goes out.*

Enter Diana, *puts on her Hood and Scarf.*

Dia. So—they are gone to Bed; and now for *Bredwel*
—the Coach waits, and I'll take this opportunity.

> *Father, farewell—if you dislike my course,*
> *Blame the old rigid Customs of your Force.* [*Goes out.*

Scene II. *A Bed-chamber.*

Enter Sir Feeble, Leticia, *and* Phillis.

Let. Ah, *Phillis!* I am fainting with my Fears,
Hast thou no comfort for me? [*He undresses to his Gown.*

Sir *Feeb.* Why, what art doing there—fiddle fadling—
adod, you young Wenches are so loth to come to—but
when your hands in, you have no mercy upon us poor
Husbands.

Let. Why do you talk so, Sir?

Sir *Feeb.* Was it anger'd at the Fool's Prattle? tum
a-me, tum a-me, I'll undress it, effags, I will—Roguy.

Let. You are so wanton, Sir, you make me blush—
I will not go to bed, unless you'll promise me—

Sir *Feeb.* No bargaining, my little Hussey—what, you'll
tie my hands behind me, will you? [*She goes to the Table.*

Let. —What shall I do?—assist me, gentle Maid,
Thy Eyes methinks put on a little hope.

Phil. Take Courage, Madam—you guess right—be confident.

Sir *Feeb.* No whispering, Gentlewoman—and putting Tricks into her head; that shall not cheat me of another Night—Look on that silly little round Chitty-face— look on those smiling roguish loving Eyes there—look— look how they laugh, twire, and tempt—he, Rogue—I'll buss 'em there, and here, and every where—ods bods— away, this is fooling and spoiling of a Man's Stomach, with a bit here, and a bit there—to Bed—to Bed—

[*As she is at the Toilet, he looks over her shoulder, and sees her Face in the Glass.*

Let. Go you first, Sir, I will but stay to say my Prayers, which are that Heaven wou'd deliver me.   [*Aside.*

Sir *Feeb.* Say thy Prayers!—What, art thou mad! Prayers upon thy Wedding-night! a short Thanksgiving or so—but Prayers quoth a—'Sbobs, you'll have time enough for that, I doubt—

Le. I am asham'd to undress before you, Sir; go to Bed—

Sir *Feeb.* What, was it asham'd to shew its little white Foots, and its little round Bubbies—well, I'll go, I'll go —I cannot think on't, no I cannot—

[*Going towards the Bed,* Bellmour *comes forth from between the Curtains, his Coat off, his Shirt bloody, a Dagger in his hand, and his Disguise off.*

Bel. Stand—

Sir *Feeb.* Ah—

Let. and *Phil.* [*squeak*]—Oh, Heavens!—why, is it *Bellmour?*   [*Aside to* Phil.

Bel. Go not to Bed, I guard this sacred Place,
And the Adulterer dies that enters here.

Sir *Feeb.* Oh—why do I shake?—sure I'm a Man, what art thou?

Bel. I am the wrong'd, the lost and murder'd *Bellmour.*

Sir *Feeb.* O Lord! it is the same I saw last night—Oh! —hold thy dread Vengeance—pity me, and hear me—

Oh! a Parson—a Parson—what shall I do—Oh! where shall I hide my self?

Bel. I'th' utmost Borders of the Earth I'll find thee—
Seas shall not hide thee, nor vast Mountains guard thee:
Even in the depth of Hell I'll find thee out,
And lash thy filthy and adulterous Soul.

Sir *Feeb.* Oh! I am dead, I'm dead; will no Repentence save me? 'twas that young Eye that tempted me to sin; Oh!—

Bel. See, fair Seducer, what thou'st made me do;
Look on this bleeding Wound, it reach'd my Heart,
To pluck my dear tormenting Image thence,
When News arriv'd that thou hadst broke thy Vow.

Sir *Feeb.* Oh Lord! oh! I'm glad he's dead though.

Let. Oh, hide that fatal Wound, my tender Heart faints with a Sight so horrid!   [*Seems to Weep.*

Sir *Feeb.* So, she'll clear her self, and leave me in the Devil's Clutches.

Bel. You've both offended Heaven, and must repent or die.

Sir *Feeb.* Ah,—I do confess I was an old Fool,—bewitcht with Beauty, besotted with Love, and do repent most heartily.

Bel. No, you had rather yet go on in Sin:
Thou wou'dst live on, and be a baffled Cuckold.

Sir *Feeb.* Oh, not for the World, Sir! I am convinc'd and mortifi'd.

Bel. Maintain her fine, undo thy Peace to please her, and still be Cuckol'd on,—believe her,—trust her, and be Cuckol'd still.

Sir *Feeb.* I see my Folly—and my Age's Dotage—and find the Devil was in me—yet spare my Age—ah! spare me to repent.

Bel. If thou repent'st, renounce her, fly her sight;—
Shun her bewitching Charms, as thou wou'dst Hell,
Those dark eternal Mansions of the dead—
Whither I must descend.

Sir *Feeb.* Oh—wou'd he were gone!—

Bel. Fly—be gone—depart, vanish for ever from her to some more safe and innocent Apartment.

Sir *Feeb.* Oh, that's very hard!—

[*He goes back trembling,* Bellmour *follows in with his Dagger up; both go out.*

Let. Blest be this kind Release, and yet methinks it grieves me to consider how the poor old Man is frighted.

[Bellmour *re-enters, puts on his Coat.*

Bel. —He's gone, and lock'd himself into his Chamber— And now, my dear *Leticia,* let us fly—

> Despair till now did my wild Heart invade,
> But pitying Love has the rough Storm allay'd.
>
> [*Exeunt.*

SCENE III. *Sir* Cautious *his Garden.*

Enter two Porters and Rag, *bearing* Gayman *in a Chest; set it down, he comes forth with a Dark-lanthorn.*

Gay. Set down the Chest behind yon hedge of Roses —and then put on those Shapes I have appointed you— and be sure you well-favour'dly bang both *Bearjest* and *Noisey,* since they have a mind to see the Devil.

Rag. Oh, Sir, leave 'em to us for that; and if we do not play the Devil with 'em, we deserve they shou'd beat us. But, Sir, we are in Sir *Cautious* his Garden, will he not sue us for a Trespass?

Gay. I'll bear you out; be ready at my Call. [*Exeunt.* —Let me see—I have got no ready stuff to banter with —but no matter, any Gibberish will serve the Fools— 'tis now about the hour of Ten—but Twelve is my appointed lucky Minute, when all the Blessings that my Soul could wish, shall be resign'd to me.

Enter Bredwel.

—Hah! who's there? *Bredwel?*

Bred. Oh, are you come, Sir—and can you be so kind to a poor Youth, to favour his Designs, and bless his Days?

Gay. Yes, I am ready here with all my Devils, both to secure you your Mistress, and to cudgel your Captain and Squire, for abusing me behind my Back so basely.

Bred. 'Twas most unmanly, Sir, and they deserve it— I wonder that they come not.

Gay. How durst you trust her with him?

Bred. Because 'tis dangerous to steal a City-Heiress, and let the Theft be his—so the dear Maid be mine— Hark—sure they come—

Enter Bearjest, *runs against* Bredwel.

—Who's there? Mr. *Bearjest?*

Bea. Who's that? *Ned?* Well, I have brought my Mistress, hast thou got a Parson ready, and a License?

Bred. Ay, ay, but where's the Lady?

Bea. In the Coach, with the Captain at the Gate. I came before, to see if the Coast be clear.

Bred. Ay, Sir; but what shall we do? here's Mr. *Gayman* come on purpose to shew you the Devil, as you desir'd.

Bea. Sho! a Pox of the Devil, Man—I can't attend to speak with him now.

Gay. How, Sir! D'ye think my Devil of so little Quality, to suffer an Affront unrevenged?

Bea. Sir, I cry his Devilship's Pardon: I did not know his Quality. I protest, Sir, I love and honour him, but I am now just going to be married, Sir; and when that Ceremony's past, I'm ready to go to the Devil as soon as you please.

Gay. I have told him your Desire of seeing him, and shou'd you baffle him?

Bea. Who, I, Sir! Pray, let his Worship know, I shall be proud of the Honour of his Acquaintance; but, Sir, my Mistress and the Parson wait in *Ned's* Chamber.

Gay. If all the World wait, Sir, the Prince of Hell will stay for no Man.

Bred. Oh, Sir, rather than the Prince of the Infernals shall be affronted, I'll conduct the Lady up, and entertain her till you come, Sir.

Bea. Nay, I have a great mind to kiss his—Paw, Sir; but I cou'd wish you'd shew him me by day-light, Sir.

Gay. The Prince of Darkness does abhor the Light. But, Sir, I will for once allow your Friend the Captain to keep you company.

Enter Noisey *and* Diana.

Bea. I'm much oblig'd to you, Sir; oh, Captain— [*Talks to him.*

Bred. Haste, Dear; the Parson waits,
To finish what the Powers design'd above.

Dia. Sure nothing is so bold as Maids in Love!

[*They go out.*

Noi. Psho! he conjure—he can flie as soon.

Gay. Gentlemen, you must be sure to confine your selves to this Circle, and have a care you neither swear, nor pray.

Bea. Pray, Sir! I dare say neither of us were ever that way gifted.

A horrid Noise.

Gay. *Cease your Horror, cease your Haste.*
And calmly as I saw you last,
Appear! Appear!
By thy Pearls and Diamond Rocks,
By thy heavy Money-Box,
By thy shining Petticoat,
That hid thy cloven Feet from Note;
By the Veil that hid thy Face,
Which else had frighten'd humane Race: [Soft
Appear, that I thy Love may see, Musick
Appear, kind Fiends, appear to me. ceases.

A Pox of these Rascals, why come they not?

Four enter from the four corners of the Stage, to Musick that
plays; they dance, and in the Dance, dance round
'em, and kick, pinch, and beat 'em.

Bea. Oh, enough, enough! Good Sir, lay 'em, and
I'll pay the Musick—

Gay. I wonder at it—these Spirits are in their Nature
kind, and peaceable—but you have basely injur'd some
body—confess, and they will be satisfied—

Bea. Oh, good Sir, take your *Cerberuses* off—I do confess,
the Captain here, and I have violated your Fame.

Noi. Abus'd you,—and traduc'd you,—and thus we
beg your pardon—

Gay. Abus'd me! 'Tis more than I know, Gentlemen.

Bea. But it seems your Friend the Devil does.

Gay. By this time *Bredwel's* married.
—Great *Pantamogan*, hold, for I am satisfied, [*Ex. Devils.*
And thus undo my Charm—

                    [*Takes away the Circle, they run out.*
So, the Fools are going, and now to *Julia's* Arms. [*Going.*

SCENE IV.   *Lady* Fulbank's *Anti-chamber.*

She discover'd undrest at her Glass; Sir Cautious *undrest.*

L. Ful. But why to Night? indeed you're wondrous
kind methinks.

Sir Cau. Why, I don't know—a Wedding is a sort of
an Alarm to Love; it calls up every Man's courage.

L. Ful. Ay, but will it come when 'tis call'd?

Sir Cau. I doubt you'll find it to my Grief—   [*Aside.*
—But I think 'tis all one to thee, thou car'st not for my
Complement; no, thou'dst rather have a young Fellow.

L. Ful. I am not us'd to flatter much; if forty Years
were taken from your Age, 'twou'd render you something
more agreeable to my Bed, I must confess.

Sir Cau. Ay, ay, no doubt on't.

L. Ful. Yet you may take my word without an Oath,
Were you as old as Time, and I were young and gay
As *April* Flowers, which all are fond to gather;
My Beauties all should wither in the Shade,
E'er I'd be worn in a dishonest Bosom.

Sir *Cau.* Ay, but you're wondrous free methinks, sometimes, which gives shreud suspicions.

L. Ful. What, because I cannot simper, look demure,
and justify my Honour, when none questions it?
—Cry fie, and out upon the naughty Women,
Because they please themselves—and so wou'd I.

Sir *Cau.* How, wou'd, what cuckold me?

L. Ful. Yes, if it pleas'd me better than Vertue, Sir.
But I'll not change my Freedom and my Humour,
To purchase the dull Fame of being honest.

Sir *Cau.* Ay, but the World, the World—

L. Ful. I value not the Censures of the Croud.

Sir *Cau.* But I am old.

L. Ful. That's your fault, Sir, not mine.

Sir *Cau.* But being so, if I shou'd be good-natur'd, and
give thee leave to love discreetly—

L. Ful. I'd do't without your leave, Sir.

Sir *Cau.* Do't—what, cuckold me?

L. Ful. No, love discreetly, Sir, love as I ought, love
honestly.

Sir *Cau.* What, in love with any body, but your own
Husband?

L. Ful. Yes.

Sir *Cau.* Yes, quoth a—is that your loving as you ought?

L. Ful. We cannot help our Inclinations, Sir,
No more than Time, or Light from coming on—
But I can keep my Virtue, Sir, intire.

Sir *Cau.* What, I'll warrant, this is your first Love,
Gayman?

L. Ful. I'll not deny that Truth, though even to you.

Sir *Cau.* Why, in consideration of my Age, and your

Youth, I'd bear a Conscience—provided you do things wisely.

L. Ful. Do what thing, Sir?

Sir *Cau.* You know what I mean—

L. Ful. Hah—I hope you wou'd not be a Cuckold, Sir.

Sir *Cau.* Why—truly in a civil way—or so.

L. Ful. There is but one way, Sir, to make me hate you; And that wou'd be tame suffering.

Sir *Cau.* Nay, and she be thereabouts, there's no dis-covering.

L. Ful. But leave this fond discourse, and, if you must, Let us to Bed.

Sir *Cau.* Ay, ay, I did but try your Virtue, mun—dost think I was in earnest?

Enter Servant.

Serv. Sir, here's a Chest directed to your Worship.

Sir *Cau.* Hum, 'tis *Wasteall*—now does my heart fail me—A Chest say you—to me—so late;—I'll warrant it comes from Sir *Nicholas Smuggle*—some prohibited Goods that he has stoln the Custom of, and cheated his Majesty —Well, he's an honest Man, bring it in— [*Exit Servant.*

L. Ful. What, into my Apartment, Sir, a nasty Chest!

Sir *Cau.* By all means—for if the Searchers come, they'll never be so uncivil to ransack thy Lodgings; and we are bound in Christian Charity to do for one another—Some rich Commodities, I am sure—and some fine Knick-knack will fall to thy share, I'll warrant thee—Pox on him for a young Rogue, how punctual he is!   [*Aside.*

Enter with the Chest.

—Go, my Dear, go to Bed—I'll send Sir *Nicholas* a Receit for the Chest, and be with thee presently— [*Ex. severally.*

[*Gayman peeps out of the Chest, and looks round him wondring.*

Gay. Hah, where am I? By Heaven, my last Night's Vision—'Tis that inchanted Room, and yonder's the

Alcove! Sure 'twas indeed some Witch, who knowing of
my Infidelity—has by Inchantment brought me hither—
'tis so—I am betray'd—   [*Pauses.*

Hah! or was it *Julia*, that last night gave me that lone
Opportunity?—but hark, I hear some coming—

                                   [*Shuts himself in.*

Enter Sir Cautious.

Sir Cau. [*Lifting up the Chest-lid.*] So, you are come,
I see—   [*Goes, and locks the door.*

Gay. Hah—he here! nay then, I was deceiv'd, and it
was *Julia* that last night gave me the dear Assignation.

                                              [*Aside.*

[*Sir* Cautious *peeps into the Bed-chamber.*

L. Ful. [*Within.*] Come, Sir *Cautious*, I shall fall asleep,
and then you'll waken me.

Sir Cau. Ay, my Dear, I'm coming—she's in Bed—
I'll go put out the Candle, and then—

Gay. Ay, I'll warrant you for my part—

Sir Cau. Ay, but you may over-act your part, and spoil
all—But, Sir, I hope you'll use a Christian Conscience in
this business.

Gay. Oh, doubt not, Sir, but I shall do you Reason.

Sir Cau. Ay, Sir, but—

Gay. Good Sir, no more Cautions; you, unlike a fair
Gamester, will rook me out of half my Night—I am
impatient—

Sir Cau. Good Lord, are you so hasty? if I please, you
shan't go at all.

Gay. With all my soul, Sir; pay me three hundred
Pound, Sir—

Sir Cau. Lord, Sir, you mistake my candid meaning still.
I am content to be a Cuckold, Sir—but I wou'd have
things done decently, d'ye mind me?

Gay. As decently as a Cuckold can be made, Sir.
—But no more disputes, I pray, Sir.

Sir *Cau.* I'm gone—I'm gone—but harkye, Sir, you'll rise before day?   [*Going out, returns.*

Gay. Yet again—

Sir *Cau.* I vanish, Sir—but harkye—you'll not speak a word, but let her think 'tis I?

Gay. Be gone, I say, Sir—   [*He runs out.*
I am convinc'd last night I was with *Julia.*
Oh Sot, insensible and dull!

Enter softly Sir Cautious.

Sir *Cau.* So, the Candle's out—give me your hand.
                    [*Leads him softly in.*

SCENE V. *Changes to a Bed-chamber.*

Lady Fulbank *suppos'd in Bed. Enter Sir* Cautious *and*
Gayman *by dark.*

Sir *Cau.* Where are you, my Dear? [*Leads him to the bed.*
L. Ful. Where shou'd I be—in Bed; what, are you by dark?

Sir *Cau.* Ay, the Candle went out by Chance.
          [Gayman *signs to him to be gone; he makes grimaces
          as loath to go, and Exit.*

SCENE VI. *Draws over, and represents another Room
in the same House.*

Enter Parson, Diana, *and* Pert *drest in* Diana's *Clothes.*

Dia. I'll swear, Mrs. *Pert,* you look very prettily in my Clothes; and since you, Sir, have convinc'd me that this innocent Deceit is not unlawful, I am glad to be the Instrument of advancing Mrs. *Pert* to a Husband, she already has so just a Claim to.

Par. Since she has so firm a Contract, I pronounce it a lawful Marriage—but hark, they are coming sure—

Dia. Pull your Hoods down, and keep your Face from the Light.   [*Diana runs out.*

Enter Bearjest *and* Noisey *disorder'd.*

Bea. Madam, I beg your Pardon—I met with a most devilish Adventure ;—your Pardon too, Mr. Doctor, for making you wait.—But the business is this, Sir—I have a great mind to lie with this young Gentlewoman to Night, but she swears if I do, the Parson of the Parish shall know it.

Par. If I do, Sir, I shall keep Counsel.

Bea. And that's civil, Sir—Come, lead the way,
  With such a Guide, the Devil's in't if we can go astray.
                                                    [*Exeunt.*

Scene VII. *Changes to the Anti-chamber.*

Enter Sir Cautious.

Sir *Cau.* Now cannot I sleep, but am as restless as a Merchant in stormy Weather, that has ventur'd all his Wealth in one Bottom.—Woman is a leaky Vessel.—if she should like the young Rogue now, and they should come to a right understanding—why, then I am a—Wittal—that's all, and shall be put in Print at *Snow-hill*, with my Effigies o'th' top, like the sign of Cuckolds Haven.—Hum —they're damnable silent—pray Heaven he have not murdered her, and robbed her—hum—hark, what's that?— a noise !—he has broke his Covenant with me, and shall forfeit the Money—How loud they are ? Ay, ay, the Plot's discovered, what shall I do ?—Why, the Devil is not in her sure, to be refractory now, and peevish ; if she be, I must pay my Money yet—and that would be a damn'd thing. —sure they're coming out—I'll retire and hearken how 'tis with them.   [*Retires.*

Enter Lady Fulbank *undrest,* Gayman, *half undrest upon his Knees, following her, holding her Gown.*

L. Ful. Oh ! You unkind—what have you made me do? Unhand me, false Deceiver—let me loose—

Sir *Cau.* Made her do ?—so, so—'tis done—I'm glad of that—   [*Aside peeping.*

Gay. Can you be angry, *Julia?*
Because I only seiz'd my Right of Love.

L. Ful. And must my Honour be the Price of it?
Could nothing but my Fame reward your Passion?
—What, make me a base Prostitute, a foul Adulteress?
Oh—be gone, be gone—dear Robber of my Quiet.
[Weeping.

Sir *Cau.* Oh, fearful!—

Gay. Oh! Calm your rage, and hear me; if you are so,
You are an innocent Adulteress.
It was the feeble Husband you enjoy'd
In cold imagination, and no more;
Shily you turn'd away—faintly resign'd.

Sir *Cau.* Hum, did she so?—

Gay. Till my Excess of Love betray'd the Cheat.

Sir *Cau.* Ay, ay, that was my Fear.

L. Ful. Away, be gone—I'll never see you more—

Gay. You may as well forbid the Sun to shine.
Not see you more!—Heavens! I before ador'd you,
But now I rave! And with my impatient Love,
A thousand mad and wild Desires are burning!
I have discover'd now new Worlds of Charms,
And can no longer tamely love and suffer.

Sir *Cau.* So—I have brought an old House upon my Head,
Intail'd Cuckoldom upon my self.

L. Ful. I'll hear no more—Sir *Cautious,*—where's my
          Husband?
Why have you left my Honour thus unguarded?

Sir *Cau.* Ay, ay, she's well enough pleas'd, I fear,
for all.

Gay. Base as he is, 'twas he expos'd this Treasure;
Like silly *Indians* barter'd thee for Trifles.

Sir *Cau.* O treacherous Villain!—

L. Ful. Hah—my Husband do this?

Gay. He, by Love, he was the kind Procurer,
Contriv'd the means, and brought me to thy Bed.

L. Ful. My Husband! My wise Husband!
What fondness in my Conduct had he seen,
To take so shameful and so base Revenge?

Gay. None—'twas filthy Avarice seduc'd him to't.

L. Ful. If he cou'd be so barbarous to expose me,
Cou'd you who lov'd me—be so cruel too?

Gay. What—to possess thee when the Bliss was offer'd?
Possess thee too without a Crime to thee?
Charge not my Soul with so remiss a flame,
So dull a sense of Virtue to refuse it.

L. Ful. I am convinc'd the fault was all my Husband's—
And here I vow—by all things just and sacred,
To separate for ever from his Bed.   [*Kneels.*

Sir Cau. Oh, I am not able to indure it—
Hold—oh, hold, my Dear—   [*He kneels as she rises.*

L. Ful. Stand off—I do abhor thee—

Sir Cau. With all my Soul—but do not make rash Vows.
They break my very Heart—regard my Reputation.

L. Ful. Which you have had such care of, Sir, already—
Rise, 'tis in vain you kneel.

Sir Cau. No—I'll never rise again—Alas! Madam, I
was merely drawn in; I only thought to sport a Dye or
so: I had only an innocent design to have discover'd
whether this Gentleman had stoln my Gold, that so I
might have hang'd him—

Gay. A very innocent Design indeed!

Sir Cau. Ay, Sir, that's all, as I'm an honest man.—

L. Ful. I've sworn, nor are the Stars more fix'd than I.

Enter Servant.

Serv. How! my Lady and his Worship up?
—Madam, a Gentleman and a Lady below in a Coach
knockt me up, and say they must speak with your Ladyship.

L. Ful. This is strange!—bring them up—
                    [*Exit Servant.*
Who can it be, at this odd time of neither Night nor Day?

Enter Leticia, Bellmour, *and* Phillis.

Let. Madam, your Virtue, Charity and Friendship to
me, has made me trespass on you for my Life's security,
and beg you will protect me, and my Husband—

          [*Points at* Bellmour.

Sir *Cau.* So, here's another sad Catastrophe!

L. Ful. Hah—does *Bellmour* live? is't possible?
Believe me, Sir, you ever had my Wishes;
And shall not fail of my Protection now.

Bel. I humbly thank your Ladyship.

Gay. I'm glad thou hast her, *Harry*; but doubt thou
durst not own her; nay dar'st not own thy self.

Bel. Yes, Friend, I have my Pardon—
But hark, I think we are pursu'd already—
But now I fear no force. [*A noise of some body coming in.*

L. Ful. However, step into my Bed-chamber.

       [*Exeunt* Leticia, Gayman *and* Phillis.

Enter Sir Feeble *in an Antick manner.*

Sir *Feeb.* Hell shall not hold thee—nor vast Mountains
cover thee, but I will find thee out—and lash thy filthy
and Adulterous Carcase.

     [*Coming up in a menacing manner to Sir* Cau.

Sir *Cau.* How—lash my filthy Carcase?—I defy thee,
Satan—

Sir *Feeb.* 'Twas thus he said.

Sir *Cau.* Let who's will say it, he lies in's Throat.

Sir *Feeb.* How, the Ghostly—hush—have a care—for
'twas the Ghost of *Bellmour*—Oh! hide that bleeding
Wound, it chills my Soul!— [*Runs to the Lady* Fulbank.

L. Ful. What bleeding Wound?—Heavens, are you
frantick, Sir?

Sir *Feeb.* No—but for want of rest, I shall e'er Morning.

              [*Weeps.*

—She's gone—she's gone—she's gone— [*He weeps.*

Sir *Cau.* Ay, ay, she's gone, she's gone indeed.

            [*Sir Cau. weeps.*

Sir *Feeb*. But let her go, so I may never see that dreadful Vision—harkye, Sir—a word in your Ear—have a care of marrying a young Wife.

Sir *Cau*. Ay, but I have married one already. [*Weeping*.

Sir *Feeb*. Hast thou? Divorce her—flie her, quick—depart—be gone, she'll cuckold thee—and still she'll cuckold thee.

Sir *Cau*. Ay, Brother, but whose fault was that?—Why, are not you married?

Sir *Feeb*. Mum—no words on't, unless you'll have the Ghost about your Ears; part with your Wife, I say, or else the Devil will part ye.

L. *Ful*. Pray go to Bed, Sir.

Sir *Feeb*. Yes, for I shall sleep now, I shall lie alone;
[*Weeps*.
Ah, Fool, old dull besotted Fool—to think she'd love me—'twas by base means I gain'd her—cozen'd an honest Gentleman of Fame and Life—

L. *Ful*. You did so, Sir, but 'tis not past Redress—you may make that honest Gentleman amends.

Sir *Feeb*. Oh, wou'd I could, so I gave half my Estate—

L. *Ful*. That Penitence atones with him and Heaven. —Come forth, *Leticia*, and your injur'd Ghost.

Enter Leticia, Bellmour, *and* Phillis.

Sir *Feeb*. Hah, Ghost—another Sight would make me mad indeed.

Bel. Behold me, Sir, I have no Terror now.

Sir *Feeb*. Hah—who's that, *Francis!*—my Nephew *Francis?*

Bel. *Bellmour*, or *Francis*, chuse you which you like, and I am either.

Sir *Feeb*. Hah, *Bellmour!* and no Ghost?

Bel. *Bellmour*—and not your Nephew, Sir.

Sir *Feeb*. But art alive? Ods bobs, I'm glad on't, Sirrah; —But are you real, *Bellmour?*

Bel. As sure as I'm no Ghost.

Gay. We all can witness for him, Sir.

Sir *Feeb.* Where be the Minstrels, we'll have a Dance—adod, we will—Ah—art thou there, thou cozening little Chits-face?—a Vengeance on thee—thou madest me an old doting loving Coxcomb—but I forgive thee—and give thee all thy Jewels, and you your Pardon, Sir, so you'll give me mine; for I find you young Knaves will be too hard for us.

Bel. You are so generous, Sir, that 'tis almost with grief I receive the Blessing of *Leticia*.

Sir *Feeb.* No, no, thou deservest her; she would have made an old fond Blockhead of me, and one way or other you wou'd have had her—ods bobs, you wou'd—

Enter Bearjest, Diana, Pert, Bredwel, *and* Noisey.

Bea. Justice, Sir, Justice—I have been cheated—abused—assassinated and ravisht!

Sir *Cau.* How, my Nephew ravisht!—

Pert. No, Sir, I am his Wife.

Sir *Cau.* Hum—my Heir marry a Chamber-maid!

Bea. Sir, you must know I stole away Mrs. *Dy*, and brought her to *Ned's* Chamber here—to marry her.

Sir *Feeb.* My Daughter *Dy* stoln—

Bea. But I being to go to the Devil a little, Sir, whip—what does he, but marries her himself, Sir; and fob'd me off here with my Lady's cast Petticoat—

Noi. Sir, she's a Gentlewoman, and my Sister, Sir.

Pert. Madam, 'twas a pious Fraud, if it were one; for I was contracted to him before—see, here it is—

[*Gives it 'em.*

All. A plain Case, a plain Case.

Sir *Feeb.* Harkye, Sir, have you had the Impudence to marry my Daughter, Sir?

[*To* Bredwel, *who with* Diana *kneels.*

Bred. Yes, Sir, and humbly ask your Pardon, and your Blessing—

Sir *Feeb.* You will ha't, whether I will or not—rise, you are still too hard for us: Come, Sir, forgive your Nephew—

Sir *Cau.* Well, Sir, I will—but all this while you little think the Tribulation I am in, my Lady has forsworn my Bed.

Sir *Feeb.* Indeed, Sir, the wiser she.

Sir *Cau.* For only performing my Promise to this Gentleman.

Sir *Feeb.* Ay, you showed her the Difference, Sir; you're a wise man. Come, dry your Eyes—and rest your self contented, we are a couple of old Coxcombs; d'ye hear, Sir, Coxcombs.

Sir *Cau.* I grant it, Sir; and if I die, Sir, I bequeath my Lady to you—with my whole Estate—my Nephew has too much already for a Fool.   [*To* Gayman.

Gay. I thank you, Sir—do you consent, my *Julia?*

L. *Ful.* No, Sir—you do not like me—a canvas Bag of wooden Ladles were a better Bed-fellow.

Gay. Cruel Tormenter! Oh, I could kill myself with shame and anger!

L. *Ful.* Come hither, *Bredwel*—witness for my Honour —that I had no design upon his Person, but that of trying his Constancy.

Bred. Believe me, Sir, 'tis true—I feigned a danger near—just as you got to bed—and I was the kind Devil, Sir, that brought the Gold to you.

Bea. And you were one of the Devils that beat me, and the Captain here, Sir?

Gay. No truly, Sir, those were some I hired—to beat you for abusing me to day.

Noi. To make you 'mends, Sir, I bring you the certain News of the death of Sir *Thomas Gayman*, your Uncle, who has left you Two thousand pounds a year—

Gay. I thank you, Sir—I heard the news before.

Sir *Cau.* How's this; Mr. *Gayman*, my Lady's first

Lover? I find, Sir *Feeble*, we were a couple of old Fools indeed, to think at our Age to cozen two lusty young Fellows of their Mistresses; 'tis no wonder that both the Men and the Women have been too hard for us; we are not fit Matches for either, that's the truth on't.

> *The Warrior needs must to his Rival yield,*
> *Who comes with blunted Weapons to the Field.*

EPILOGUE,

Written by a Person of Quality, Spoken by Mr. *Betterton*.

LONG have we turn'd the point of our just Rage
On the half Wits, and Criticks of the Age.
Oft has the soft, insipid Sonneteer
In Nice *and* Flutter, *seen his Fop-face here.*
Well was the ignorant lampooning Pack
Of shatterhead Rhymers whip'd on Craffey's *back;*
But such a trouble Weed is Poetaster,
The lower 'tis cut down, it grows the faster.
Though Satir then had such a plenteous crop,
An After Math of Coxcombs is come up;
Who not content false Poetry to renew,
By sottish Censures wou'd condemn the true.
Let writing like a Gentleman—fine appear,
But must you needs judge too en Cavalier?
These whiffling Criticks, 'tis our Auth'ress fears,
And humbly begs a Trial by her Peers:
Or let a Pole of Fools her fate pronounce,
There's no great harm in a good quiet Dunce.
But shield her, Heaven! from the left-handed blow
Of airy Blockheads who pretend to know.
On downright Dulness let her rather split,
Than be Fop-mangled under colour of Wit.

Hear me, ye Scribling Beaus,—
Why will you in sheer Rhyme, without one stroke
Of Poetry, Ladies just Disdain provoke,
And address Songs to whom you never spoke?
In doleful Hymns for dying Felons fit,
Why do you tax their Eyes, and blame their Wit?
Unjustly of the Innocent you complain,
'Tis Bulkers give, and Tubs must cure your pain.
Why in Lampoons will you your selves revile?
'Tis true, none else will think it worth their while:
But thus you're hid! oh, 'tis a politick Fetch;
So some have hang'd themselves to ease Jack Ketch.
Justly your Friends and Mistresses you blame,
For being so they well deserve the shame,
'Tis the worst scandal to have borne that name.
* At Poetry of late, and such whose Skill
Excels your own, you dart a feeble Quill;
Well may you rail at what you ape so ill.
With virtuous Women, and all Men of Worth,
You're in a state of mortal War by Birth.
Nature in all her Atom-Fights ne'er knew
Two things so opposite as Them and You.
On such your Muse her utmost fury spends,
They're slander'd worse than any but your Friends.
More years may teach you better; the mean while,
If you can't mend your Morals, mend your Style.

* See the late Satir on Poetry.

THE ROVER; OR,
THE BANISH'D CAVALIERS.
PART I.

THE ROVER;
or, the Banish'd Cavaliers.

PART I.

PROLOGUE,

Written by a Person of Quality.

WITS, like Physicians, never can agree,
When of a different Society;
And Rabel's Drops were never more cry'd down
By all the Learned Doctors of the Town,
Than a new Play, whose Author is unknown:
Nor can those Doctors with more Malice sue
(And powerful Purses) the dissenting Few,
Than those with an insulting Pride do rail
At all who are not of their own Cabal.

If a Young Poet hit your Humour right,
You judge him then out of Revenge and Spite;
So amongst Men there are ridiculous Elves,
Who Monkeys hate for being too like themselves:
So that the Reason of the Grand Debate,
Why Wit so oft is damn'd, when good Plays take,
Is, that you censure as you love or hate.
Thus, like a learned Conclave, Poets sit
Catholick Judges both of Sense and Wit,
And damn or save, as they themselves think fit.
Yet those who to others Faults are so severe,
Are not so perfect, but themselves may err.
Some write correct indeed, but then the whole
(Bating their own dull Stuff i'th' Play) is stole:

As Bees do suck from Flowers their Honey-dew,
So they rob others, striving to please you.

Some write their Characters genteel and fine,
But then they do so toil for every Line,
That what to you does easy seem, and plain,
Is the hard issue of their labouring Brain.
And some th' Effects of all their Pains we see,
Is but to mimick good Extempore.
Others by long Converse about the Town,
Have Wit enough to write a leud Lampoon,
But their chief Skill lies in a Baudy Song.
In short, the only Wit that's now in Fashion
Is but the Gleanings of good Conversation.
As for the Author of this coming Play,
I ask'd him what he thought fit I should say,
In thanks for your good Company to day:
He call'd me Fool, and said it was well known,
You came not here for our sakes, but your own.
New Plays are stuff'd with Wits, and with Debauches,
That croud and sweat like Cits in May-day Coaches.

DRAMATIS PERSONÆ.

MEN.

Don *Antonio*, the Vice-Roy's Son,	Mr. *Jevorne.*
Don *Pedro*, a Noble *Spaniard*, his Friend,	Mr. *Medburne.*
Belvile, an *English* Colonel in love with *Florinda*,	Mr. *Betterton.*
Willmore, the *ROVER*,	Mr. *Smith.*
Frederick, an *English* Gentleman, and Friend to *Belvile* and *Blunt*,	Mr. *Crosbie.*
Blunt, an *English* Country Gentleman,	Mr. *Underhill.*
Stephano, Servant to Don *Pedro*,	Mr. *Richards.*
Philippo, *Lucetta's* Gallant,	Mr. *Percival.*
Sancho, Pimp to *Lucetta*,	Mr. *John Lee.*
Bisky and *Sebastian*, two Bravoes to *Angelica*.	
Diego, Page to Don *Antonio*.	
Page to *Hellena*.	
Boy, Page to *Belvile*.	
Blunt's Man.	
Officers and Soldiers.	

WOMEN.

Florinda, Sister to Don *Pedro*,	Mrs. *Betterton.*
Hellena, a gay young Woman design'd for a Nun, and Sister to *Florinda*,	Mrs. *Barrey.*
Valeria, a Kinswoman to *Florinda*,	Mrs. *Hughes.*
Angelica Bianca, a famous Curtezan,	Mrs. *Gwin.*
Moretta, her Woman,	Mrs. *Leigh.*
Callis, Governess to *Florinda* and *Hellena*,	Mrs. *Norris.*
Lucetta, a jilting Wench,	Mrs. *Gillow.*

Servants, other Masqueraders, Men and Women.

SCENE *Naples*, in Carnival-time.

ACT I.

Scene I. *A chamber.*

Enter Florinda *and* Hellena.

Flor. What an impertinent thing is a young Girl bred in a Nunnery! How full of Questions! Prithee no more, *Hellena;* I have told thee more than thou understand'st already.

Hell. The more's my Grief; I wou'd fain know as much as you, which makes me so inquisitive; nor is't enough to know you're a Lover, unless you tell me too, who 'tis you sigh for.

Flor. When you are a Lover, I'll think you fit for a Secret of that nature.

Hell. 'Tis true, I was never a Lover yet—but I begin to have a shreud Guess, what 'tis to be so, and fancy it very pretty to sigh, and sing, and blush and wish, and dream and wish, and long and wish to see the Man; and when I do, look pale and tremble; just as you did when my Brother brought home the fine *English* Colonel to see you—what do you call him? Don *Belvile.*

Flor. Fie, *Hellena.*

Hell. That Blush betrays you—I am sure 'tis so—or is it Don *Antonio* the Vice-Roy's Son?—or perhaps the rich old Don *Vincentio*, whom my father designs for your Husband?—Why do you blush again?

Flor. With Indignation; and how near soever my Father thinks I am to marrying that hated Object, I shall let him see I understand better what's due to my Beauty, Birth and Fortune, and more to my Soul, than to obey those unjust Commands.

Hell. Now hang me, if I don't love thee for that dear Disobedience. I love Mischief strangely, as most of our

Sex do, who are come to love nothing else—But tell me, dear *Florinda*, don't you love that fine *Anglese?*—for I vow next to loving him my self, 'twill please me most that you do so, for he is so gay and so handsom.

Flor. *Hellena*, a Maid design'd for a Nun ought not to be so curious in a Discourse of Love.

Hell. And dost thou think that ever I'll be a Nun? Or at least till I'm so old, I'm fit for nothing else. Faith no, Sister; and that which makes me long to know whether you love *Belvile*, is because I hope he has some mad Companion or other, that will spoil my Devotion; nay I'm resolv'd to provide my self this Carnival, if there be e'er a handsom Fellow of my Humour above Ground, tho I ask first.

Flor. Prithee be not so wild.

Hell. Now you have provided your self with a Man, you take no Care for poor me—Prithee tell me, what dost thou see about me that is unfit for Love—have not I a world of Youth? a Humour gay? a Beauty passable? a Vigour desirable? well shap'd? clean limb'd? sweet breath'd? and Sense enough to know how all these ought to be employ'd to the best Advantage: yes, I do and will. Therefore lay aside your Hopes of my Fortune, by my being a Devotee, and tell me how you came acquainted with this *Belvile;* for I perceive you knew him before he came to *Naples*.

Flor. Yes, I knew him at the Siege of *Pampelona*, he was then a Colonel of *French* Horse, who when the Town was ransack'd, nobly treated my Brother and my self, preserving us from all Insolencies; and I must own, (besides great Obligations) I have I know not what, that pleads kindly for him about my Heart, and will suffer no other to enter—But see my Brother.

Enter Don Pedro, Stephano, *with a Masquing Habit, and* Callis.

Pedro. Good morrow, Sister. Pray, when saw you your Lover Don *Vincentio?*

Flor. I know not, Sir—*Callis*, when was he here? for I consider it so little, I know not when it was.

Pedro. I have a Command from my Father here to tell you, you ought not to despise him, a Man of so vast a Fortune, and such a Passion for you—*Stephano*, my things—

[*Puts on his Masquing Habit.*

Flor. A Passion for me! 'tis more than e'er I saw, or had a desire should be known—I hate *Vincentio*, and I would not have a Man so dear to me as my Brother follow the ill Customs of our Country, and make a Slave of his Sister—And Sir, my Father's Will, I'm sure, you may divert.

Pedro. I know not how dear I am to you, but I wish only to be rank'd in your Esteem, equal with the *English* Colonel *Belvile*—Why do you frown and blush? Is there any Guilt belongs to the Name of that Cavalier?

Flor. I'll not deny I value *Belvile*: when I was expos'd to such Dangers as the licens'd Lust of common Soldiers threatned, when Rage and Conquest flew thro the City— then *Belvile*, this Criminal for my sake, threw himself into all Dangers to save my Honour, and will you not allow him my Esteem?

Pedro. Yes, pay him what you will in Honour—but you must consider Don *Vincentio's* Fortune, and the Jointure he'll make you.

Flor. Let him consider my Youth, Beauty and Fortune; which ought not to be thrown away on his Age and Jointure.

Pedro. 'Tis true, he's not so young and fine a Gentleman as that *Belvile*—but what Jewels will that Cavalier present you with? those of his Eyes and Heart?

Hell. And are not those better than any Don *Vincentio* has brought from the *Indies*?

Pedro. Why how now! Has your Nunnery-breeding taught you to understand the Value of Hearts and Eyes?

Hell. Better than to believe *Vincentio* deserves Value

from any woman—He may perhaps encrease her Bags, but not her Family.

Pedro. This is fine—Go up to your Devotion, you are not design'd for the Conversation of Lovers.

Hell. Nor Saints yet a while I hope.   [*Aside.* Is't not enough you make a Nun of me, but you must cast my Sister away too, exposing her to a worse confinement than a religious Life?

Pedro. The Girl's mad—Is it a Confinement to be carry'd into the Country, to an antient Villa belonging to the Family of the *Vincentio's* these five hundred Years, and have no other Prospect than that pleasing one of seeing all her own that meets her Eyes—a fine Air, large Fields and Gardens, where she may walk and gather Flowers?

Hell. When? By Moon-Light? For I'm sure she dares not encounter with the heat of the Sun ; that were a Task only for Don *Vincentio* and his *Indian* Breeding, who loves it in the Dog-days—And if these be her daily Divertisements, what are those of the Night? to lie in a wide Moth-eaten Bed-Chamber with Furniture in Fashion in the Reign of King *Sancho* the First ; the Bed that which his Forefathers liv'd and dy'd in.

Pedro. Very well.

Hell. This Apartment (new furbisht and fitted out for the young Wife) he (out of Freedom) makes his Dressing-room ; and being a frugal and a jealous Coxcomb, instead of a Valet to uncase his feeble Carcase, he desires you to do that Office—Signs of Favour, I'll assure you, and such as you must not hope for, unless your Woman be out of the way.

Pedro. Have you done yet?

Hell. That Honour being past, the Giant stretches it self, yawns and sighs a Belch or two as loud as a Musket, throws himself into Bed, and expects you in his foul Sheets, and e'er you can get your self undrest, calls you with a Snore or two— And are not these fine Blessings to a young Lady?

Pedro. Have you done yet?

Hell. And this man you must kiss, nay, you must kiss none but him too—and nuzle thro his Beard to find his Lips—and this you must submit to for threescore Years, and all for a Jointure.

Pedro. For all your Character of Don *Vincentio*, she is as like to marry him as she was before.

Hell. Marry Don *Vincentio!* hang me, such a Wedlock would be worse than Adultery with another Man: I had rather see her in the *Hostel de Dieu*, to waste her Youth there in Vows, and be a Handmaid to Lazers and Cripples, than to lose it in such a Marriage.

Pedro. You have consider'd, Sister, that *Belvile* has no Fortune to bring you to, is banisht his Country, despis'd at home, and pity'd abroad.

Hell. What then? the Vice-Roy's Son is better than that Old Sir Fisty. Don *Vincentio!* Don *Indian!* he thinks he's trading to *Gambo* still, and wou'd barter himself (that Bell and Bawble) for your Youth and Fortune.

Pedro. *Callis*, take her hence, and lock her up all this Carnival, and at Lent she shall begin her everlasting Penance in a Monastery.

Hell. I care not, I had rather be a Nun, than be oblig'd to marry as you wou'd have me, if I were design'd for't.

Pedro. Do not fear the Blessing of that Choice—you shall be a Nun.

Hell. Shall I so? you may chance to be mistaken in my way of Devotion—A Nun! yes I am like to make a fine Nun! I have an excellent Humour for a Grate: No, I'll have a Saint of my own to pray to shortly, if I like any that dares venture on me.   [*Aside.*

Pedro. *Callis*, make it your Business to watch this wild Cat. As for you, *Florinda*, I've only try'd you all this while, and urg'd my Father's Will; but mine is, that you would love *Antonio*, he is brave and young, and all that can compleat the Happiness of a gallant Maid—This Absence of my Father will give us opportunity to free you from *Vincentio*, by marrying here, which you must do to morrow.

Flor. To morrow !

Pedro. To morrow, or 'twill be too late—'tis not my Friendship to *Antonio*, which makes me urge this, but Love to thee, and Hatred to *Vincentio*—therefore resolve upon't to morrow.

Flor. Sir, I shall strive to do, as shall become your Sister.

. *Pedro.* I'll both believe and trust you—Adieu.

[*Ex.* Ped. *and* Steph.

Hell. As become his Sister !—That is, to be as resolved your way, as he is his—   [Hell. *goes to* Callis.

Flor. I ne'er till now perceiv'd my Ruin near,
I've no Defence against *Antonio*'s Love,
For he has all the Advantages of Nature,
The moving Arguments of Youth and Fortune.

Hell. But hark you, *Callis*, you will not be so cruel to lock me up indeed : will you ?

Call. I must obey the Commands I hate—besides, do you consider what a Life you are going to lead ?

Hell. Yes, *Callis*, that of a Nun : and till then I'll be indebted a World of Prayers to you, if you let me now see, what I never did, the Divertisements of a Carnival.

Call. What, go in Masquerade ? 'twill be a fine farewell to the World I take it—pray what wou'd you do there ?

Hell. That which all the World does, as I am told, be as mad as the rest, and take all innocent Freedom— Sister, you'll go too, will you not ? come prithee be not sad—We'll out-wit twenty Brothers, if you'll be ruled by me—Come put off this dull Humour with your Clothes, and assume one as gay, and as fantastick as the Dress my Cousin *Valeria* and I have provided, and let's ramble.

Flor. *Callis*, will you give us leave to go ?

Call. I have a youthful Itch of going my self. [*Aside.*
—Madam, if I thought your Brother might not know it,
and I might wait on you, for by my troth I'll not trust
young Girls alone.

Flor. Thou see'st my Brother's gone already, and thou
shalt attend and watch us.

Enter Stephano.

Steph. Madam, the Habits are come, and your Cousin
Valeria is drest, and stays for you.

Flor. 'Tis well—I'll write a Note, and if I chance to
see *Belvile*, and want an opportunity to speak to him, that
shall let him know what I've resolv'd in favour of him.

Hell. Come, let's in and dress us.   [*Exeunt.*

Scene II.   *A Long Street.*

Enter Belvile, *melancholy,* Blunt *and* Frederick.

Fred. Why, what the Devil ails the Colonel, in a time
when all the World is gay, to look like mere Lent thus?
Hadst thou been long enough in *Naples* to have been in love,
I should have sworn some such Judgment had befall'n thee.

Belv. No, I have made no new Amours since I came
to *Naples*.

Fred. You have left none behind you in *Paris*.

Belv. Neither.

Fred. I can't divine the Cause then; unless the old
Cause, the want of Mony.

Blunt. And another old Cause, the want of a Wench—
Wou'd not that revive you?

Belv. You're mistaken, *Ned.*

Blunt Nay, 'Sheartlikins, then thou art past Cure.

Fred. I have found it out; thou hast renew'd thy
Acquaintance with the Lady that cost thee so many Sighs
at the Siege of *Pampelona*—pox on't, what d'ye call her
—her Brother's a noble *Spaniard*—Nephew to the dead
General—*Florinda*—ay, *Florinda*—And will nothing

serve thy turn but that damn'd virtuous Woman, whom on my Consicience thou lov'st in spite too, because thou seest little or no possibility of gaining her?

Belv. Thou art mistaken, I have Interest enough in that lovely Virgin's Heart, to make me proud and vain, were it not abated by the Severity of a Brother, who perceiving my Happiness——

Fred. Has civilly forbid thee the House?

Belv. 'Tis so, to make way for a powerful Rival, the Vice-Roy's Son, who has the advantage of me, in being a Man of Fortune, a *Spaniard*, and her Brother's Friend; which gives him liberty to make his Court, whilst I have recourse only to Letters, and distant Looks from her Window, which are as soft and kind as those which Heav'n sends down on Penitents.

Blunt. Hey day! 'Sheartlikins, Simile! by this Light the Man is quite spoil'd——*Frederick*, what the Devil are we made of, that we cannot be thus concern'd for a Wench?——'Sheartlikins, our *Cupids* are like the Cooks of the Camp, they can roast or boil a Woman, but they have none of the fine Tricks to set 'em off, no Hogoes to make the Sauce pleasant, and the Stomach sharp.

Fred. I dare swear I have had a hundred as young, kind and handsom as this *Florinda;* and Dogs eat me, if they were not as troublesom to me i'th' Morning as they were welcome o'er night.

Blunt. And yet, I warrant, he wou'd not touch another Woman, if he might have her for nothing.

Belv. That's thy Joy, a cheap Whore.

Blunt. Why, 'dsheartlikins, I love a frank Soul——When did you ever hear of an honest Woman that took a Man's Mony? I warrant 'em good ones——But, Gentlemen, you may be free, you have been kept so poor with Parliaments and Protectors, that the little Stock you have is not worth preserving——but I thank my Stars, I have more Grace than to forfeit my Estate by Cavaliering.

Belv. Methinks only following the Court should be sufficient to entitle 'em to that.

Blunt. 'Sheartlikins, they know I follow it to do it no good, unless they pick a hole in my Coat for lending you Mony now and then; which is a greater Crime to my Conscience, Gentlemen, than to the Common-wealth.

Enter Willmore.

Will. Ha! dear *Belvile!* noble Colonel!

Belv. *Willmore!* welcome ashore, my dear Rover!— what happy Wind blew us this good Fortune?

Will. Let me salute you my dear *Fred*, and then command me—How is't honest Lad?

Fred. Faith, Sir, the old Complement, infinitely the better to see my dear mad *Willmore* again—Prithee why camest thou ashore? and where's the Prince?

Will. He's well, and reigns still Lord of the watery Element—I must aboard again within a Day or two, and my Business ashore was only to enjoy my self a little this Carnival.

Belv. Pray know our new Friend, Sir, he's but bashful, a raw Traveller, but honest, stout, and one of us.

[*Embraces* Blunt.

Will. That you esteem him, gives him an Interest here.

Blunt. Your Servant, Sir.

Will. But well— Faith I'm glad to meet you again in a warm Climate, where the kind Sun has its god-like Power still over the Wine and Woman.—Love and Mirth are my Business in *Naples;* and if I mistake not the Place, here's an excellent Market for Chapmen of my Humour.

Belv. See here be those kind Merchants of Love you look for.

Enter several Men in masquing Habits, some playing on Musick, others dancing after ; Women drest like Curtezans, with Papers pinn'd to their Breasts, and Baskets of Flowers in their Hands.

Blunt. 'Sheartlikins, what have we here!

Fred. Now the Game begins.

Will. Fine pretty Creatures! may a stranger have leave
to look and love?—What's here—*Roses for every Month!*

[*Reads the Paper.*

Blunt. Roses for every Month! what means that?

Belv. They are, or wou'd have you think they're
Curtezans, who here in *Naples* are to be hir'd by the Month.

Will. Kind and obliging to inform us—Pray where
do these Roses grow? I would fain plant some of 'em
in a Bed of mine.

Wom. Beware such Roses, Sir.

Will. A Pox of fear: I'll be bak'd with thee between
a pair of Sheets, and that's thy proper Still, so I might but
strow such Roses over me and under me—Fair one, wou'd
you wou'd give me leave to gather at your Bush this idle
Month, I wou'd go near to make some Body smell of it all
the Year after.

Belv. And thou hast need of such a Remedy, for thou
stinkest of Tar and Rope-ends, like a Dock or Pesthouse.

[*The Woman puts her self into the Hands of a Man, and*
Exit.

Will. Nay, nay, you shall not leave me so.

Belv. By all means use no Violence here.

Will. Death! just as I was going to be damnably in
love, to have her led off! I could pluck that Rose out of
his Hand, and even kiss the Bed, the Bush it grew in.

Fred. No Friend to Love like a long Voyage at Sea.

Blunt. Except a Nunnery, *Fred.*

Will. Death! but will they not be kind, quickly be
kind? Thou know'st I'm no tame Sigher, but a rampant
Lion of the Forest.

*Two Men drest all over with Horns of several sorts, making
    Grimaces at one another, with Papers pinn'd on their Backs,
    advance from the farther end of the Scene.*

Belv. Oh the fantastical Rogues, how they are dress'd! 'tis a Satir against the whole Sex.

Will. Is this a Fruit that grows in this warm Country?

Belv. Yes: 'Tis pretty to see these *Italian* start, swell, and stab at the Word *Cuckold*, and yet stumble at Horns on every Threshold.

Will. See what's on their Back—*Flowers for every Night.*   [*Reads.*
—Ah Rogue! And more sweet than Roses of ev'ry Month! This is a Gardiner of *Adam's* own breeding.

                              [*They dance.*

Belv. What think you of those grave People?—is a Wake in *Essex* half so mad or extravagant?

Will. I like their sober grave way, 'tis a kind of legal authoriz'd Fornication, where the Men are not chid for't, nor the Women despis'd, as amongst our dull *English*; even the Monsieurs want that part of good Manners.

Belv. But here in *Italy* a Monsieur is the humblest best-bred Gentleman——Duels are so baffled by Bravo's that an age shews not one, but between a *Frenchman* and a Hang-man, who is as much too hard for him on the Piazza, as they are for a *Dutchman* on the new Bridge—— But see another Crew.

Enter Florinda, Hellena, *and* Valeria, *drest like Gipsies;* Callis *and* Stephano, Lucetta, Philippo *and* Sancho *in Masquerade.*

Hell. Sister, there's your *Englishman*, and with him a handsom proper Fellow——I'll to him, and instead of telling him his Fortune, try my own.

Will. Gipsies, on my Life—Sure these will prattle if a Man cross their Hands. [*Goes to* Hellena] — Dear pretty (and I hope) young Devil, will you tell an amorous Stranger what Luck he's like to have?

Hell. Have a care how you venture with me, Sir, lest I pick your Pocket, which will more vex your *English* Humour, than an *Italian* Fortune will please you.

Will. How the Devil cam'st thou to know my Country and Humour?

Hell. The first I guess by a certain forward Impudence, which does not displease me at this time; and the Loss of your Money will vex you, because I hope you have but very little to lose.

Will. Egad Child, thou'rt i'th' right; it is so little, I dare not offer it thee for a Kindness—But cannot you divine what other things of more value I have about me, that I would more willingly part with?

Hell. Indeed no, that's the Business of a Witch, and I am but a Gipsy yet—Yet, without looking in your Hand, I have a parlous Guess, 'tis some foolish Heart you mean, an inconstant *English* Heart, as little worth stealing as your Purse.

Will. Nay, then thou dost deal with the Devil, that's certain—Thou hast guess'd as right as if thou hadst been one of that Number it has languisht for—I find you'll be better acquainted with it; nor can you take it in a better time, for I am come from Sea, Child; and *Venus* not being propitious to me in her own Element, I have a world of Love in store—Wou'd you would be good-natur'd, and take some on't off my Hands.

Hell. Why—I could be inclin'd that way—but for a foolish Vow I am going to make—to die a Maid.

Will. Then thou art damn'd without Redemption; and as I am a good Christian, I ought in charity to divert so wicked a Design—therefore prithee, dear Creature, let me know quickly when and where I shall begin to set a helping hand to so good a Work.

Hell. If you should prevail with my tender Heart (as I begin to fear you will, for you have horrible loving Eyes) there will be difficulty in't that you'll hardly undergo for my sake.

Will. Faith, Child, I have been bred in Dangers, and wear a Sword that has been employ'd in a worse Cause,

than for a handsom kind Woman—Name the Danger—
let it be any thing but a long Siege, and I'll undertake it.

Hell. Can you storm?

Will. Oh, most furiously.

Hell. What think you of a Nunnery-wall? for he that
wins me, must gain that first.

Will. A Nun! Oh how I love thee for't! there's no
Sinner like a young Saint—Nay, now there's no denying
me: the old Law had no Curse (to a Woman) like dying
a Maid; witness *Jephtha's* Daughter.

Hell. A very good Text this, if well handled; and I
perceive, Father Captain, you would impose no severe
Penance on her who was inclin'd to console her self before
she took Orders.

Will. If she be young and handsom.

Hell. Ay, there's it—but if she be not—

Will. By this Hand, Child, I have an implicit Faith,
and dare venture on thee with all Faults—besides, 'tis
more meritorious to leave the World when thou hast tasted
and prov'd the Pleasure on't; then 'twill be a Virtue in
thee, which now will be pure Ignorance.

Hell. I perceive, good Father Captain, you design only
to make me fit for Heaven—but if on the contrary you
should quite divert me from it, and bring me back to the
World again, I should have a new Man to seek I find;
and what a grief that will be—for when I begin, I fancy
I shall love like any thing: I never try'd yet.

Will. Egad, and that's kind—Prithee, dear Creature,
give me Credit for a Heart, for faith, I'm a very honest
Fellow—Oh, I long to come first to the Banquet of Love;
and such a swinging Appetite I bring—Oh, I'm impatient.
Thy Lodging, Sweetheart, thy Lodging, or I'm a dead man.

Hell. Why must we be either guilty of Fornication or
Murder, if we converse with you Men?—And is there
no difference between leave to love me, and leave to lie
with me?

Will. Faith, Child, they were made to go together.

Lucet. Are you sure this is the Man? [*Pointing to* Blunt.

Sancho. When did I mistake your Game?

Lucet. This is a stranger, I know by his gazing; if he be brisk he'll venture to follow me; and then, if I understand my Trade, he's mine: he's *English* too, and they say that's a sort of good natur'd loving People, and have generally so kind an opinion of themselves, that a Woman with any Wit may flatter 'em into any sort of Fool she pleases.

Blunt. 'Tis so—she is taken—I have Beauties which my false Glass at home did not discover.

[*She often passes by* Blunt *and gazes on him; he struts, and cocks, and walks, and gazes on her.*

Flor. This Woman watches me so, I shall get no Opportunity to discover my self to him, and so miss the intent of my coming—But as I was saying, Sir—by this Line you should be a Lover.   [*Looking in his Hand.*

Belv. I thought how right you guess'd, all Men are in love, or pretend to be so—Come, let me go, I'm weary of this fooling.   [*Walks away.*

Flor. I will not, till you have confess'd whether the Passion that you have vow'd *Florinda* be true or false.

[*She holds him, he strives to get from her.*

Belv. Florinda!   [*Turns quick towards her.*

Flor. Softly.

Belv. Thou hast nam'd one will fix me here for ever.

Flor. She'll be disappointed then, who expects you this Night at the Garden-gate, and if you'll fail not—as let me see the other Hand—you will go near to do—she vows to die or make you happy. [*Looks on* Callis, *who observes 'em.*

Belv. What canst thou mean?

Flor. That which I say—Farewel.   [*Offers to go.*

Belv. Oh charming Sybil, stay, complete that Joy, which, as it is, will turn into Distraction!—Where must I be? at the Garden-gate? I know it—at night you say— I'll sooner forfeit Heaven than disobey.

Enter Don Pedro *and other Masquers, and pass
over the Stage.*

Call. Madam, your Brother's here.

Flor. Take this to instruct you farther.

[*Gives him a Letter, and goes off.*

Fred. Have a care, Sir, what you promise; this may be
a Trap laid by her Brother to ruin you.

Belv. Do not disturb my Happiness with Doubts.

[*Opens the Letter.*

Will. My dear pretty Creature, a Thousand Blessings
on thee; still in this Habit, you say, and after Dinner at
this Place.

Hell. Yes, if you will swear to keep your Heart, and
not bestow it between this time and that.

Will. By all the little Gods of Love I swear, I'll leave
it with you; and if you run away with it, those Deities of
Justice will revenge me.

[*Ex. all the Women except Lucetta.*

Fred. Do you know the Hand?

Belv. 'Tis *Florinda's.*

All Blessings fall upon the virtuous Maid.

Fred. Nay, no Idolatry, a sober Sacrifice I'll allow you.

Belv. Oh Friends! the welcom'st News, the softest
Letter!—nay, you shall see it; and could you now be
serious, I might be made the happiest Man the Sun shines on.

Will. The Reason of this mighty Joy.

Belv. See how kindly she invites me to deliver her from
the threaten'd Violence of her Brother—will you not
assist me?

Will. I know not what thou mean'st, but I'll make
one at any Mischief where a Woman's concern'd—but
she'll be grateful to us for the Favour, will she not?

Belv. How mean you?

Will. How should I mean? Thou know'st there's but
one way for a Woman to oblige me.

Belv. Don't prophane—the Maid is nicely virtuous.

Will. Who pox, then she's fit for nothing but a Husband; let her e'en go, Colonel.

Fred. Peace, she's the Colonel's Mistress, Sir.

Will. Let her be the Devil; if she be thy Mistress, I'll serve her—name the way.

Belv. Read here this Postcript.   [*Gives him a Letter.*

Will. [*Reads.*] *At Ten at night—at the Garden-Gate —of which, if I cannot get the Key, I will contrive a way over the Wall—come attended with a Friend or two.*—Kind heart, if we three cannot weave a String to let her down a Garden-Wall, 'twere pity but the Hangman wove one for us all.

Fred. Let her alone for that : your Woman's Wit, your fair kind Woman, will out-trick a Brother or a Jew, and contrive like a Jesuit in Chains—but see, *Ned Blunt* is stoln out after the Lure of a Damsel. [*Ex.* Blunt *and* Lucet.

Belv. So he'll scarce find his way home again, unless we get him cry'd by the Bell-man in the Market-place, and 'twou'd sound prettily—a lost *English* Boy of Thirty.

Fred. I hope 'tis some common crafty Sinner, one that will fit him; it may be she'll sell him for *Peru*, the Rogue's sturdy and would work well in a Mine; at least I hope she'll dress him for our Mirth; cheat him of all, then have him well-favour'dly bang'd, and turn'd out naked at Midnight.

Will. Prithee what Humour is he of, that you wish him so well?

Belv. Why, of an *English* Elder Brother's Humour, educated in a Nursery, with a Maid to tend him till Fifteen, and lies with his Grand-mother till he's of Age; one that knows no Pleasure beyond riding to the next Fair, or going up to *London* with his right Worshipful Father in Parliament-time; wearing gay Clothes, or making honourable Love to his Lady Mother's Landry-Maid; gets drunk at a Hunting-Match, and ten to one then gives some Proofs of his Prowess—A pox upon him, he's our

Banker, and has all our Cash about him, and if he fail we are all broke.

Fred. Oh let him alone for that matter, he's of a damn'd stingy Quality, that will secure our Stock. I know not in what Danger it were indeed, if the Jilt should pretend she's in love with him, for 'tis a kind believing Coxcomb; otherwise if he part with more than a Piece of Eight—geld him: for which offer he may chance to be beaten, if she be a Whore of the first Rank.

Belv. Nay the Rogue will not be easily beaten, he's stout enough; perhaps if they talk beyond his Capacity, he may chance to exercise his Courage upon some of them; else I'm sure they'll find it as difficult to beat as to please him.

Will. 'Tis a lucky Devil to light upon so kind a Wench!

Fred. Thou hadst a great deal of talk with thy little Gipsy, coud'st thou do no good upon her? for mine was hard-hearted.

Will. Hang her, she was some damn'd honest Person of Quality, I'm sure, she was so very free and witty. If her Face be but answerable to her Wit and Humour, I would be bound to Constancy this Month to gain her. In the mean time, have you made no kind Acquaintance since you came to Town?—You do not use to be honest so long, Gentlemen.

Fred. Faith Love has kept us honest, we have been all fir'd with a Beauty newly come to Town, the famous *Paduana Angelica Bianca.*

Will. What, the Mistress of the dead *Spanish* General?

Belv. Yes, she's now the only ador'd Beauty of all the Youth in *Naples*, who put on all their Charms to appear lovely in her sight, their Coaches, Liveries, and themselves, all gay, as on a Monarch's Birth-Day, to attract the Eyes of this fair Charmer, while she has the Pleasure to behold all languish for her that see her.

Fred. 'Tis pretty to see with how much Love the Men regard her, and how much Envy the Women.

Will. What Gallant has she?

Belv. None, she's exposed to Sale, and four Days in the Week she's yours—for so much a Month.

Will. The very Thought of it quenches all manner of Fire in me—yet prithee let's see her.

Belv. Let's first to Dinner, and after that we'll pass the Day as you please—but at Night ye must all be at my Devotion.

Will. I will not fail you.   [*Exeunt.*

ACT II.

SCENE I.   *The Long Street.*

Enter Belvile *and* Frederick *in Masquing-Habits, and* Willmore *in his own Clothes, with a Vizard in his Hand.*

Will. But why thus disguis'd and muzzl'd?

Belv. Because whatever Extravagances we commit in these Faces, our own may not be oblig'd to answer 'em.

Will. I should have chang'd my Eternal Buff too: but no matter, my little Gipsy wou'd not have found me out then : for if she should change hers, it is impossible I should know her, unless I should hear her prattle—A Pox on't, I cannot get her out of my Head : Pray Heaven, if ever I do see her again, she prove damnable ugly, that I may fortify my self against her Tongue.

Belv. Have a care of Love, for o' my conscience she was not of a Quality to give thee any hopes.

Will. Pox on 'em, why do they draw a Man in then? She has play'd with my Heart so, that 'twill never lie still till I have met with some kind Wench, that will play the Game out with me—Oh for my Arms full of soft, white, kind—Woman! such as I fancy *Angelica.*

Belv. This is her House, if you were but in stock to get admittance; they have not din'd yet; I perceive the Picture is not out.

Enter Blunt.

Will. I long to see the Shadow of the fair Substance, a Man may gaze on that for nothing.

Blunt. Colonel, thy Hand—and thine, *Fred.* I have been an Ass, a deluded Fool, a very Coxcomb from my Birth till this Hour, and heartily repent my little Faith.

Belv. What the Devil's the matter with thee *Ned?*

Blunt. Oh such a Mistress, *Fred.* such a Girl!

Will. Ha! where?   *Fred.* Ay where!

Blunt. So fond, so amorous, so toying and fine! and all for sheer Love, ye Rogue! Oh how she lookt and kiss'd! and sooth'd my Heart from my Bosom. I cannot think I was awake, and yet methinks I see and feel her Charms still—*Fred.*—Try if she have not left the Taste of her balmy Kisses upon my Lips—   [*Kisses him.*

Belv. Ha, ha, ha!   *Will.* Death Man, where is she?

Blunt. What a Dog was I to stay in dull *England* so long—How have I laught at the Colonel when he sigh'd for Love! but now the little Archer has reveng'd him, and by his own Dart, I can guess at all his Joys, which then I took for Fancies, mere Dreams and Fables—Well, I'm resolved to sell all in *Essex*, and plant here for ever.

Belv. What a Blessing 'tis, thou hast a Mistress thou dar'st boast of; for I know thy Humour is rather to have a proclaim'd Clap, than a secret Amour.

Will. Dost know her Name?

Blunt. Her Name? No, 'sheartlikins: what care I for Names?—
She's fair, young, brisk and kind, even to ravishment: and what a Pox care I for knowing her by another Title?

Will. Didst give her anything?

Blunt. Give her!—Ha, ha, ha! why, she's a Person of Quality—That's a good one, give her! 'sheartlikins dost think such Creatures are to be bought? Or are we provided for such a Purchase? Give her, quoth ye? Why she presented me with this Bracelet, for the Toy of a

Diamond I us'd to wear : No, Gentlemen, *Ned Blunt* is not every Body —She expects me again to night.

Will. Egad that's well; we'll all go.

Blunt. Not a Soul : No, Gentlemen, you are Wits; I am a dull Country Rogue, I.

Fred. Well, Sir, for all your Person of Quality, I shall be very glad to understand your Purse be secure; 'tis our whole Estate at present, which we are loth to hazard in one Bottom : come, Sir, unload.

Blunt. Take the necessary Trifle, useless now to me, that am belov'd by such a Gentlewoman—'sheartlikins Money ! Here take mine too.

Fred. No, keep that to be cozen'd, that we may laugh.

Will. Cozen'd !—Death ! wou'd I cou'd meet with one, that wou'd cozen me of all the Love I cou'd spare to night.

Fred. Pox 'tis some common Whore upon my Life.

Blunt. A Whore ! yes with such Clothes ! such Jewels ! such a House ! such Furniture, and so attended ! a Whore !

Belv. Why yes, Sir, they are Whores, tho they'll neither entertain you with Drinking, Swearing, or Baudy ; are Whores in all those gay Clothes, and right Jewels ; are Whores with great Houses richly furnisht with Velvet Beds, Store of Plate, handsome Attendance, and fine Coaches, are Whores and errant ones.

Will. Pox on't, where do these fine Whores live ?

Belv. Where no Rogue in Office yclep'd Constables dare give 'em laws, nor the Wine-inspired Bullies of the Town break their Windows ; yet they are Whores, tho this *Essex* Calf believe them Persons of Quality.

Blunt. 'Sheartlikins, y'are all Fools, there are things about this *Essex* Calf, that shall take with the Ladies, beyond all your Wits and Parts—This Shape and Size, Gentlemen, are not to be despis'd ; my Waste tolerably long, with other inviting Signs, that shall be nameless.

Will. Egad I believe he may have met with some Person of Quality that may be kind to him.

Belv. Dost thou perceive any such tempting things about him, should make a fine Woman, and of Quality, pick him out from all Mankind, to throw away her Youth and Beauty upon, nay, and her dear Heart too?—no, no, *Angelica* has rais'd the Price too high.

Will. May she languish for Mankind till she die, and be damn'd for that one Sin alone.

Enter two Bravoes, and hang up a great Picture of Angelica's, *against the Balcony, and two little ones at each side of the* .*Door.*

Belv. See there the fair Sign to the Inn, where a Man may lodge that's Fool enough to give her Price.

[*Will. gazes on the Picture.*

Blunt. 'Sheartlikins, Gentlemen, what's this?

Belv. A famous Curtezan that's to be sold.

Blunt. How! to be sold! nay then I have nothing to say to her—sold! what Impudence is practis'd in this Country?—With Order and Decency Whoring's establishd here by virtue of the Inquisition—Come let's be gone, I'm sure we're no Chapmen for this Commodity.

Fred. Thou art none, I'm sure, unless thou could'st have her in thy Bed at the Price of a Coach in the Street.

Will. How wondrous fair she is—a Thousand Crowns a Month—by Heaven as many Kingdoms were too little. A plague of this Poverty—of which I ne'er complain, but when it hinders my Approach to Beauty, which Virtue ne'er could purchase.   [*Turns from the Picture.*

Blunt. What's this?—[*Reads*] *A Thousand Crowns a Month!*
—'Sheartlikins, here's a Sum! sure 'tis a mistake.
—Hark you, Friend, does she take or give so much by the Month!

Fred. A Thousand Crowns! Why, 'tis a Portion for the *Infanta.*

Blunt. Hark ye, Friends, won't she trust?

Brav. This is a Trade, Sir, that cannot live by Credit.

Enter Don Pedro *in Masquerade, follow'd* by Stephano.

Belv. See, here's more Company, let's walk off a while.
[Pedro *Reads.*   [*Exeunt* English.

Enter Angelica *and* Moretta *in the Balcony, and draw a
Silk Curtain.*

Ped. Fetch me a Thousand Crowns, I never wish to
buy this Beauty at an easier Rate.   [*Passes off.*

Ang. Prithee what said those Fellows to thee?

Brav. Madam, the first were Admirers of Beauty only,
but no purchasers; they were merry with your Price and
Picture, laught at the Sum, and so past off.

Ang. No matter, I'm not displeas'd with their rallying;
their Wonder feeds my Vanity, and he that wishes to buy,
gives me more Pride, than he that gives my Price can
make me Pleasure.

Brav. Madam, the last I knew thro all his disguises
to be Don *Pedro*, Nephew to the General, and who was
with him in *Pampelona.*

Ang. Don *Pedro!* my old Gallant's Nephew! When
his Uncle dy'd, he left him a vast Sum of Money; it is
he who was so in love with me at *Padua*, and who us'd
to make the General so jealous.

Moret. Is this he that us'd to prance before our Window and take such care to shew himself an amorous Ass?
if I am not mistaken, he is the likeliest Man to give your
Price.

Ang. The Man is brave and generous, but of an Humour
so uneasy and inconstant, that the victory over his Heart
is as soon lost as won; a Slave that can add little to the
Triumph of the Conqueror : but inconstancy's the Sin of
all Mankind, therefore I'm resolv'd that nothing but Gold
shall charm my Heart.

Moret. I'm glad on't; 'tis only interest that Women of

our Profession ought to consider : tho I wonder what has kept you from that general Disease of our Sex so long, I mean that of being in love.

Ang. A kind, but sullen Star, under which I had the Happiness to be born ; yet I have had no time for Love ; the bravest and noblest of Mankind have purchas'd my Favours at so dear a Rate, as if no Coin but Gold were current with our Trade—But here's Don *Pedro* again, fetch me my Lute—for 'tis for him or Don *Antonio* the Vice-Roy's Son, that I have spread my Nets.

Enter at one Door Don Pedro, *and* Stephano ; *Don* Antonio *and* Diego [*his page*], *at the other Door, with People following him in Masquerade, antickly attir'd, some with Musick : they both go up to the Picture.*

Ant. A thousand Crowns ! had not the Painter flatter'd her, I should not think it dear.

Pedro. Flatter'd her ! by Heaven he cannot. I have seen the Original, nor is there one Charm here more than adorns her Face and Eyes ; all this soft and sweet, with a certain languishing Air, that no Artist can represent.

Ant. What I heard of her Beauty before had fir'd my Soul, but this confirmation of it has blown it into a flame.

Pedro. Ha !

Pag. Sir, I have known you throw away a Thousand Crowns on a worse Face, and tho y' are near your Marriage, you may venture a little Love here ; *Florinda*—will not miss it.

Pedro. Ha ! *Florinda !* Sure 'tis *Antonio*.　　　　[*aside.*

Ant. Florinda ! name not those distant Joys, there's not one thought of her will check my Passion here.

Pedro. Florinda scorn'd ! and all my Hopes defeated of the Possession of *Angelica* ! [*A noise of a Lute above.* Ant. *gazes up.*] Her Injuries by Heaven he shall not boast of.
　　　　　　　　　　　　　　　　[*Song to a Lute above.*

SONG.

When Damon *first began to love,*
He languisht in a soft Desire,
And knew not how the Gods to move,
To lessen or increase his Fire,
For Cælia *in her charming Eyes*
Wore all Love's Sweet, and all his Cruelties.

II.

But as beneath a Shade he lay,
Weaving of Flow'rs for Cælia's *Hair,*
She chanc'd to lead her Flock that way,
And saw the am'rous Shepherd there.
She gaz'd around upon the Place,
And saw the Grove (resembling Night)
To all the Joys of Love invite,
Whilst guilty Smiles and Blushes drest her Face.
At this the bashful Youth all Transport grew,
And with kind Force he taught the Virgin how
To yield what all his Sighs cou'd never do.

Ant. By Heav'n she's charming fair !
  [Angelica *throws open the Curtains, and bows to*
    Antonio, *who pulls off his Vizard, and bows and*
    blows up Kisses. Pedro *unseen looks in his Face.*
Pedro. 'Tis he, the false *Antonio!*
Ant. Friend, where must I pay my offering of Love?
                                        [*To the* Bravo.
My Thousand Crowns I mean.
  Pedro. That Offering I have design'd to make,
And yours will come too late.
  Ant. Prithee be gone, I shall grow angry else,
And then thou art not safe.
  Pedro. My Anger may be fatal, Sir, as yours ;
And he that enters here may prove this Truth.

Ant. I know not who thou art, but I am sure thou'rt worth my killing, and aiming at *Angelica.*

[*They draw and fight.*

Enter Willmore *and* Blunt, *who draw and part 'em.*

Blunt. 'Sheartlikins, here's fine doings.

Will. Tilting for the Wench I'm sure—nay gad, if that wou'd win her, I have as good a Sword as the best of ye—Put up—put up, and take another time and place, for this is design'd for Lovers only.   [*They all put up.*

Pedro. We are prevented; dare you meet me to-morrow on the *Molo?*
For I've a Title to a better quarrel,
That of *Florinda,* in whose credulous Heart
Thou'st made an Int'rest, and destroy'd my Hopes.

Ant. Dare?
I'll meet thee there as early as the Day.

Pedro. We will come thus disguis'd, that whosoever chance to get the better, he may escape unknown.

Ant. It shall be so.   [*Ex.* Pedro *and* Stephano.
Who shou'd this Rival be? unless the *English* Colonel, of whom I've often heard Don *Pedro* speak; it must be he, and time he were removed, who lays a Claim to all my Happiness.

[Willmore *having gaz'd all this while on the
Picture, pulls down a little one.*

Will. This posture's loose and negligent,
The sight on't wou'd beget a warm desire
In Souls, whom Impotence and Age had chill'd.
—This must along with me.

Brav. What means this rudeness, Sir?—restore the Picture.

Ant. Ha! Rudeness committed to the fair *Angelica!*—Restore the Picture, Sir.

Will. Indeed I will not, Sir.

Ant. By Heav'n but you shall.

Will. Nay, do not shew your Sword; if you do, by this dear Beauty—I will shew mine too.

Ant. What right can you pretend to't?

Will. That of Possession which I will maintain—you perhaps have 1000 Crowns to give for the Original.

Ant. No matter, Sir, you shall restore the Picture.

Ang. Oh, *Moretta!* what's the matter?

[Ang. *and* Moret. *above.*

Ant. Or leave your Life behind.

Will. Death! you lye—I will do neither.

Ang. Hold, I command you, if for me you fight.

[*They fight, the Spaniards join with* Antonio, Blunt *laying on like mad. They leave off and bow.*

Will. How heavenly fair she is!—ah Plague of her Price.

Ang. You Sir in Buff, you that appear a Soldier, that first began this Insolence.

Will. 'Tis true, I did so, if you call it Insolence for a Man to preserve himself; I saw your charming Picture, and was wounded: quite thro my Soul each pointed Beauty ran; and wanting a Thousand Crowns to procure my Remedy, I laid this little Picture to my Bosom— which if you cannot allow me, I'll resign.

Ang. No, you may keep the Trifle.

Ant. You shall first ask my leave, and this.

[*Fight again as before.*

Enter Belv. *and* Fred. *who join with the* English.

Ang. Hold; will you ruin me?—*Biskey, Sebastian,* part them.   [*The* Spaniards *are beaten off.*

Moret. Oh Madam, we're undone, a pox upon that rude Fellow, he's set on to ruin us: we shall never see good days, till all these fighting poor Rogues are sent to the Gallies.

Enter Belvile, Blunt *and* Willmore, *with his shirt bloody.*

Blunt. 'Sheartlikins, beat me at this Sport, and I'll ne'er wear Sword more.

Belv. The Devil's in thee for a mad Fellow, thou art always one at an unlucky Adventure.—Come, let's be gone whilst we're safe, and remember these are *Spaniards*, a sort of People that know how to revenge an Affront.

Fred. You bleed; I hope you are not wounded. [*To* Will.

Will. Not much:—a plague upon your Dons, if they fight no better they'll ne'er recover *Flanders*.—What the Devil was't to them that I took down the Picture?

Blunt. Took it! 'Sheartlikins, we'll have the great one too; 'tis ours by Conquest.—Prithee, help me up, and I'll pull it down.—

Ang. Stay, Sir, and e'er you affront me further, let me know how you durst commit this Outrage—To you I speak, Sir, for you appear like a Gentleman.

Will. To me, Madam?—Gentlemen, your Servant.

[*Belv. stays him.*

Belv. Is the Devil in thee? Do'st know the danger of entring the house of an incens'd Curtezan?

Will. I thank you for your care—but there are other matters in hand, there are, tho we have no great Temptation.—Death! let me go.

Fred. Yes, to your Lodging, if you will, but not in here.—Damn these gay Harlots—by this Hand I'll have as sound and handsome a Whore for a Patacoone.—Death, Man, she'll murder thee.

Will. Oh! fear me not, shall I not venture where a Beauty calls? a lovely charming Beauty? for fear of danger! when by Heaven there's none so great as to long for her, whilst I want Money to purchase her.

Fred. Therefore 'tis loss of time, unless you had the thousand Crowns to pay.

Will. It may be she may give a Favour, at least I shall have the pleasure of saluting her when I enter, and when I depart.

Belv. Pox, she'll as soon lie with thee, as kiss thee, and sooner stab than do either—you shall not go.

Ang. Fear not, Sir, all I have to wound with, is my Eyes.

Blunt. Let him go, 'Sheartlikins, I believe the Gentlewoman means well.

Belv. Well, take thy Fortune, we'll expect you in the next Street.—Farewell Fool,—farewell—

Will. B'ye Colonel—   [*Goes in.*

Fred. The Rogue's stark mad for a Wench. [*Exeunt.*

SCENE II.   *A Fine Chamber.*

Enter Willmore, Angelica, *and* Moretta.

Ang. Insolent Sir, how durst you pull down my Picture?

Will. Rather, how durst you set it up, to tempt poor amorous Mortals with so much Excellence? which I find you have but too well consulted by the unmerciful price you set upon't.—Is all this Heaven of Beauty shewn to move Despair in those that cannot buy? and can you think the effects of that Despair shou'd be less extravagant than I have shewn?

Ang. I sent for you to ask my Pardon, Sir, not to aggravate your Crime.—I thought I shou'd have seen you at my Feet imploring it.

Will. You are deceived, I came to rail at you, and talk such Truths, too, as shall let you see the Vanity of that Pride, which taught you how to set such a Price on Sin. For such it is, whilst that which is Love's due is meanly barter'd for.

Ang. Ha, ha, ha, alas, good Captain, what pity 'tis your edifying Doctrine will do no good upon me—*Moretta*, fetch the Gentleman a Glass, and let him survey himself, to see what Charms he has,—and guess my Business.
                              [*Aside in a soft tone.*

Moret. He knows himself of old, I believe those Breeches and he have been acquainted ever since he was beaten at *Worcester.*

Ang. Nay, do not abuse the poor Creature.—

Moret. Good Weather-beaten Corporal, will you march off? we have no need of your Doctrine, tho you have of our Charity; but at present we have no Scraps, we can afford no kindness for God's sake; in fine, Sirrah, the Price is too high i'th' Mouth for you, therefore troop, I say.

Will. Here, good Fore-Woman of the Shop, serve me, and I'll be gone.

Moret. Keep it to pay your Landress, your Linen stinks of the Gun-Room; for here's no selling by Retail.

Will. Thou hast sold plenty of thy stale Ware at a cheap Rate.

Moret. Ay, the more silly kind Heart I, but this is an Age wherein Beauty is at higher Rates.—In fine, you know the price of this.

Will. I grant you 'tis here set down a thousand Crowns a Month—Baud, take your black Lead and sum it up, that I may have a Pistole-worth of these vain gay things, and I'll trouble you no more.

Moret. Pox on him, he'll fret me to Death:—abominable Fellow, I tell thee, we only sell by the whole Piece.

Will. 'Tis very hard, the whole Cargo or nothing— Faith, Madam, my Stock will not reach it, I cannot be your Chapman.—Yet I have Countrymen in Town, Merchants of Love, like me; I'll see if they'l put for a share, we cannot lose much by it, and what we have no use for, we'll sell upon the *Friday's* Mart, at—*Who gives more?* I am studying, Madam, how to purchase you, tho at present I am unprovided of Money.

Ang. Sure, this from any other Man would anger me— nor shall he know the Conquest he has made—Poor angry Man, how I despise this railing.

Will. Yes, I am poor—but I'm a Gentleman,
And one that scorns this Baseness which you practise.
Poor as I am, I would not sell my self,
No, not to gain your charming high-priz'd Person.

Tho I admire you strangely for your Beauty,
Yet I contemn your Mind.
—And yet I wou'd at any rate enjoy you;
At your own rate—but cannot—See here
The only Sum I can command on Earth;
I know not where to eat when this is gone:
Yet such a Slave I am to Love and Beauty,
This last reserve I'll sacrifice to enjoy you.
—Nay, do not frown, I know you are to be bought,
And wou'd be bought by me, by me,
For a mean trifling Sum, if I could pay it down.
Which happy knowledge I will still repeat,
And lay it to my Heart, it has a Virtue in't,
And soon will cure those Wounds your Eyes have made.
—And yet—there's something so divinely powerful there—
Nay, I will gaze—to let you see my Strength.

        [Holds her, looks on her, and pauses and sighs.
By Heaven, bright Creature—I would not for the World
Thy Fame were half so fair as is thy Face.

          [Turns her away from him.
  Ang. His words go thro me to the very Soul.   *[Aside.*
—If you have nothing else to say to me.
  Will. Yes, you shall hear how infamous you are—
For which I do not hate thee:
But that secures my Heart, and all the Flames it feels
Are but so many Lusts,
I know it by their sudden bold intrusion.
The Fire's impatient and betrays, 'tis false—
For had it been the purer Flame of Love,
I should have pin'd and languish'd at your Feet,
E'er found the Impudence to have discover'd it.
I now dare stand your Scorn, and your Denial.
  Moret. Sure she's bewitcht, that she can stand thus
tamely, and hear his saucy railing.—Sirrah, will you be gone?
  Ang. How dare you take this liberty ?—Withdraw.

          [To Moret.

—Pray, tell me, Sir, are not you guilty of the same mercenary Crime? When a Lady is proposed to you for a Wife, you never ask, how fair, discreet, or virtuous she is; but what's her Fortune—which if but small, you cry —She will not do my business—and basely leave her, tho she languish for you.—Say, is not this as poor?

Will. It is a barbarous Custom, which I will scorn to defend in our Sex, and do despise in yours.

Ang. Thou art a brave Fellow! put up thy Gold, and know,
That were thy Fortune large, as is thy Soul,
Thou shouldst not buy my Love,
Couldst thou forget those mean Effects of Vanity,
Which set me out to sale; and as a Lover, prize
My yielding Joys.
Canst thou believe they'l be entirely thine,
Without considering they were mercenary?

Will. I cannot tell, I must bethink me first—ha,
Death, I'm going to believe her.   [*Aside.*

Ang. Prithee, confirm that Faith—or if thou canst not —flatter me a little, 'twill please me from thy Mouth.

Will. Curse on thy charming Tongue! dost thou return My feign'd Contempt with so much subtilty?   [*Aside.*
Thou'st found the easiest way into my Heart,
Tho I yet know that all thou say'st is false.
                    [*Turning from her in a Rage.*

Ang. By all that's good 'tis real,
I never lov'd before, tho oft a Mistress.
—Shall my first Vows be slighted?

Will. What can she mean?   [*Aside.*

Ang. I find you cannot credit me. [*In an angry tone.*

Will. I know you take me for an errant Ass,
An Ass that may be sooth'd into Belief,
And then be us'd at pleasure.
—But, Madam I have been so often cheated
By perjur'd, soft, deluding Hypocrites,

That I've no Faith left for the cozening Sex,
Especially for Women of your Trade.

    Ang. The low esteem you have of me, perhaps
May bring my Heart again:
For I have Pride that yet surmounts my Love.

                        [She turns with Pride, he holds her.

    Will. Throw off this Pride, this Enemy to Bliss,
And shew the Power of Love: 'tis with those Arms
I can be only vanquisht, made a Slave.

    Ang. Is all my mighty Expectation vanisht?
—No, I will not hear thee talk,—thou hast a Charm
In every word, that draws my Heart away.
And all the thousand Trophies I design'd,
Thou hast undone—Why art thou soft?
Thy Looks are bravely rough, and meant for War.
Could thou not storm on still?
I then perhaps had been as free as thou.

    Will. Death! how she throws her Fire about my Soul!
                                [Aside.

—Take heed, fair Creature, how you raise my Hopes,
Which once assum'd pretend to all Dominion.
There's not a Joy thou hast in store
I shall not then command:
For which I'll pay thee back my Soul, my Life.
Come, let's begin th' account this happy minute.

    Ang. And will you pay me then the Price I ask?

    Will. Oh, why dost thou draw me from an awful
        Worship,
By shewing thou art no Divinity?
Conceal the Fiend, and shew me all the Angel;
Keep me but ignorant, and I'll be devout,
And pay my Vows for ever at this Shrine.

                 [Kneels, and kisses her Hand.

    Ang. The Pay I mean is but thy Love for mine.
—Can you give that?

    Will. Intirely—come, let's withdraw: where I'll renew

my Vows,—and breathe 'em with such Ardour, thou shalt not doubt my Zeal.

Ang. Thou hast a Power too strong to be resisted.

[*Ex.* Will. *and* Angelica.

Moret. Now my Curse go with you—Is all our Project fallen to this? to love the only Enemy to our Trade? Nay, to love such a Shameroon, a very Beggar; nay, a Pirate-Beggar, whose Business is to rifle and be gone, a No-Purchase, No-Pay Tatterdemalion, an *English* Piccaroon; a Rogue that fights for daily Drink, and takes a Pride in being loyally lousy—Oh, I could curse now, if I durst—This is the Fate of most Whores.

> *Trophies, which from believing Fops we win,*
> *Are Spoils to those who cozen us again.*

ACT III.

SCENE I. *A Street.*

Enter Florinda, Valeria, Hellena, *in Antick different Dresses from what they were in before,* Callis *attending.*

Flor. I wonder what should make my Brother in so ill a Humour: I hope he has not found out our Ramble this Morning.

Hell. No, if he had, we should have heard on't at both Ears, and have been mew'd up this Afternoon; which I would not for the World should have happen'd—Hey ho! I'm sad as a Lover's Lute.

Val. Well, methinks we have learnt this Trade of Gipsies as readily as if we had been bred upon the Road to *Loretto:* and yet I did so fumble, when I told the Stranger his Fortune, that I was afraid I should have told my own and yours by mistake—But methinks *Hellena* has been very serious ever since.

Flor. I would give my Garters she were in love, to be reveng'd upon her, for abusing me—How is't, *Hellena?*

Hell. Ah!—would I had never seen my mad Monsieur

—and yet for all your laughing I am not in love—and yet this small Acquaintance, o'my Conscience, will never out of my Head.

Val. Ha, ha, ha—I laugh to think how thou art fitted with a Lover, a Fellow that, I warrant, loves every new Face he sees.

Hell. Hum—he has not kept his Word with me here —and may be taken up—that thought is not very pleasant to me—what the Duce should this be now that I feel?

Val. What is't like?

Hell. Nay, the Lord knows—but if I should be hanged, I cannot chuse but be angry and afraid, when I think that mad Fellow should be in love with any Body but me— What to think of my self I know not—Would I could meet with some true damn'd Gipsy, that I might know my Fortune.

Val. Know it! why there's nothing so easy; thou wilt love this wandring Inconstant till thou find'st thy self hanged about his Neck, and then be as mad to get free again.

Flor. Yes, *Valeria;* we shall see her bestride his Baggage-horse, and follow him to the Campaign.

Hell. So, so; now you are provided for, there's no care taken of poor me—But since you have set my Heart a wishing, I am resolv'd to know for what. I will not die of the Pip, so I will not.

Flor. Art thou mad to talk so? Who will like thee well enough to have thee, that hears what a mad Wench thou art?

Hell. Like me! I don't intend every he that likes me shall have me, but he that I like: I shou'd have staid in the Nunnery still, if I had lik'd my Lady Abbess as well as she lik'd me. No, I came thence, not (as my wise Brother imagines) to take an eternal Farewel of the World, but to love and to be belov'd; and I will be belov'd, or I'll get one of your Men, so I will.

Val. Am I put into the Number of Lovers?

Hell. You! my Couz, I know thou art too good natur'd

to leave us in any Design : Thou wou't venture a Cast, tho thou comest off a Loser, especially with such a Gamester —I observ'd your Man, and your willing Ears incline that way ; and if you are not a Lover, 'tis an Art soon learnt —that I find.   [*Sighs.*

Flor. I wonder how you learnt to love so easily, I had a thousand Charms to meet my Eyes and Ears, e'er I cou'd yield ; and 'twas the knowledge of *Belvile's* Merit, not the surprising Person, took my Soul—Thou art too rash to give a Heart at first sight.

Hell. Hang your considering Lover ; I ne'er thought beyond the Fancy, that 'twas a very pretty, idle, silly kind of Pleasure to pass ones time with, to write little, soft, nonsensical Billets, and with great difficulty and danger receive Answers ; in which I shall have my Beauty prais'd, my Wit admir'd (tho little or none) and have the Vanity and Power to know I am desirable ; then I have the more Inclination that way, because I am to be a Nun, and so shall not be suspected to have any such earthly Thoughts about me—But when I walk thus—and sigh thus—they'll think my Mind's upon my Monastery, and cry, how happy 'tis she's so resolv'd !—But not a Word of Man.

Flor. What a mad Creature's this !

Hell. I'll warrant, if my Brother hears either of you sigh, he cries (gravely)—I fear you have the Indiscretion to be in love, but take heed of the Honour of our House, and your own unspotted Fame ; and so he conjures on till he has laid the soft-wing'd God in your Hearts, or broke the Birds-nest—But see here comes your Lover : but where's my inconstant ? let's step aside, and we may learn something.   [*Go aside.*

Enter Belvile, Fred. *and* Blunt.

Belv. What means this ? the Picture's taken in.

Blunt. It may be the Wench is good-natur'd, and will be kind *gratis.* Your Friend's a proper handsom Fellow.

Belv. I rather think she has cut his Throat and is fled:
I am mad he should throw himself into Dangers—Pox on't,
I shall want him to night—let's knock and ask for him.

Hell. My heart goes a-pit a-pat, for fear 'tis my Man
they talk of.   [*Knock*, Moretta *above.*

Moret. What would you have?

Belv. Tell the Stranger that enter'd here about two
Hours ago, that his Friends stay here for him.

Moret. A Curse upon him for *Moretta*, would he were
at the Devil—but he's coming to you.   [*Enter* Wilmore.

Hell. I, I, 'tis he. Oh how this vexes me.

Belv. And how, and how, dear Lad, has Fortune smil'd?
Are we to break her Windows, or raise up Altars to her! hah!

Will. Does not my Fortune sit triumphant on my Brow?
dost not see the little wanton God there all gay and smiling?
have I not an Air about my Face and Eyes, that distinguish me from the Croud of common Lovers? By
Heav'n, *Cupid's* Quiver has not half so many Darts as her
Eyes—Oh such a *Bona Roba*, to sleep in her Arms is lying
in Fresco, all perfum'd Air about me.

Hell. Here's fine encouragement for me to fool on. [*Aside.*

Will. Hark ye, where didst thou purchase that rich
Canary we drank to-day? Tell me, that I may adore the
Spigot, and sacrifice to the Butt: the Juice was divine, into
which I must dip my Rosary, and then bless all things
that I would have bold or fortunate.

Belv. Well, Sir, let's go take a Bottle, and hear the Story
of your Success.

Fred. Would not *French* Wine do better?

Will. Damn the hungry Balderdash; cheerful Sack has
a generous Virtue in't, inspiring a successful Confidence,
gives Eloquence to the Tongue, and Vigour to the Soul;
and has in a few Hours compleated all my Hopes and
Wishes. There's nothing left to raise a new Desire in me
—Come let's be gay and wanton—and, Gentlemen, study,
study what you want, for here are Friends,—that will

supply, Gentlemen,—hark! what a charming sound they make—'tis he and she Gold whilst here, shall beget new Pleasures every moment.

Blunt. But hark ye, Sir, you are not married, are you?

Will. All the Honey of Matrimony, but none of the Sting, Friend.

Blunt. 'Sheartlikins, thou'rt a fortunate Rogue.

Will. I am so, Sir, let these inform you.—Ha, how sweetly they chime! Pox of Poverty, it makes a Man a Slave, makes Wit and Honour sneak, my Soul grew lean and rusty for want of Credit.

Blunt. 'Sheartlikins, this I like well, it looks like my lucky Bargain! Oh how I long for the Approach of my Squire, that is to conduct me to her House again. Why! here's two provided for.

Fred. By this light y're happy Men.

Blunt. Fortune is pleased to smile on us, Gentlemen,— to smile on us.

Enter Sancho, *and pulls* Blunt *by the Sleeve. They go aside.*

Sancho. Sir, my Lady expects you—she has remov'd all that might oppose your Will and Pleasure—and is impatient till you come.

Blunt. Sir, I'll attend you—Oh the happiest Rogue! I'll take no leave, lest they either dog me, or stay me.

[*Ex. with* Sancho.

Belv. But then the little Gipsy is forgot?

Will. A Mischief on thee for putting her into my thoughts; I had quite forgot her else, and this Night's Debauch had drunk her quite down.

Hell. Had it so, good Captain? [*Claps him on the Back.*

Will. Ha! I hope she did not hear.

Hell. What, afraid of such a Champion!

Will. Oh! you're a fine Lady of your word, are you not? to make a Man languish a whole day—

Hell. In tedious search of me.

Will. Egad, Child, thou'rt in the right, hadst thou seen what a melancholy Dog I have been ever since I was a Lover, how I have walkt the Streets like a *Capuchin*, with my Hands in my Sleeves—Faith, Sweetheart, thou wouldst pity me.

Hell. Now, if I should be hang'd, I can't be angry with him, he dissembles so heartily—Alas, good Captain, what pains you have taken—Now were I ungrateful not to reward so true a Servant.

. *Will.* Poor Soul ! that's kindly said, I see thou bearest a Conscience—come then for a beginning shew me thy dear Face.

Hell. I'm afraid, my small Acquaintance, you have been staying that swinging stomach you boasted of this morning ; I remember then my little Collation would have gone down with you, without the Sauce of a handsom Face—Is your Stomach so quesy now ?

Will. Faith long fasting, Child, spoils a Man's Appetite —yet if you durst treat, I could so lay about me still.

Hell. And would you fall to, before a Priest says Grace ?

Will. Oh fie, fie, what an old out-of-fashion'd thing hast thou nam'd ? Thou could'st not dash me more out of Countenance, shouldst thou shew me an ugly Face.

Whilst he is seemingly courting Hellena, *enter* Angelica, Moretta, Biskey, *and* Sebastian, *all in Masquerade :* Ang. *sees* Will. *and starts.*

Ang. Heavens, is't he ? and passionately fond to see another Woman ?

Moret. What cou'd you expect less from such a Swaggerer ?

Ang. Expect ! as much as I paid him, a Heart intire, Which I had pride enough to think when e'er I gave It would have rais'd the Man above the Vulgar, Made him all Soul, and that all soft and constant.

Hell. You see, Captain, how willing I am to be Friends

with you, till Time and Ill-luck make us Lovers; and ask you the Question first, rather than put your Modesty to the blush, by asking me: for alas, I know you Captains are such strict Men, severe Observers of your Vows to Chastity, that 'twill be hard to prevail with your tender Conscience to marry a young willing Maid.

Will. Do not abuse me, for fear I should take thee at thy word, and marry thee indeed, which I'm sure will be Revenge sufficient.

Hell. O' my Conscience, that will be our Destiny, because we are both of one humour; I am as inconstant as you, for I have considered, Captain, that a handsom Woman has a great deal to do whilst her Face is good, for then is our Harvest-time to gather Friends; and should I in these days of my Youth, catch a fit of foolish Constancy, I were undone; 'tis loitering by day-light in our great Journey: therefore declare, I'll allow but one year for Love, one year for Indifference, and one year for Hate—and then—go hang your self—for I profess myself the gay, the kind, and the inconstant—the Devil's in't if this won't please you.

Will. Oh most damnably!—I have a Heart with a hole quite thro it too, no Prison like mine to keep a Mistress in.

Ang. Perjur'd Man! how I believe thee now! [*Aside.*

Hell. Well, I see our Business as well as Humours are alike, yours to cozen as many Maids as will trust you, and I as many Men as have Faith—See if I have not as desperate a lying look, as you can have for the heart of you.   [*Pulls off her Vizard; he starts.*
—How do you like it, Captain?

Will. Like it! by Heav'n, I never saw so much Beauty. Oh the Charms of those sprightly black Eyes, that strangely fair Face, full of Smiles and Dimples! those soft round melting cherry Lips! and small even white Teeth! not to be exprest, but silently adored!—Oh one Look more, and strike me dumb, or I shall repeat nothing else till I am mad.

[*He seems to court her to pull off her Vizard: she refuses.*

Ang. I can endure no more—nor is it fit to interrupt him ; for if I do, my Jealousy has so destroy'd my Reason, —I shall undo him—Therefore I'll retire. And you *Sebastian* [*To one of her Bravoes*] follow that Woman, and learn who 'tis ; while you tell the Fugitive, I would speak to him instantly. [*To the other Bravo.*   [*Exit.*

[*This while* Flor. *is talking to* Belvile, *who stands sullenly.* Fred. *courting* Valeria.

Val. Prithee, dear Stranger, be not so sullen ; for tho you have lost your Love, you see my Friend frankly offers you hers, to play with in the mean time.

Belv. Faith, Madam, I am sorry I can't play at her Game.

Fred. Pray leave your Intercession, and mind your own Affair, they'll better agree apart ; he's a model Sigher in Company, but alone no Woman escapes him.

Flor. Sure he does but rally—yet if it should be true— I'll tempt him farther—Believe me, noble Stranger, I'm no common Mistress—and for a little proof on't—wear this Jewel—nay, take it, Sir, 'tis right, and Bills of Exchange may sometimes miscarry.

Belv. Madam, why am I chose out of all Mankind to be the Object of your Bounty ?

Val. There's another civil Question askt.

Fred. Pox of's Modesty, it spoils his own Markets, and hinders mine.

Flor. Sir, from my Window I have often seen you ; and Women of Quality have so few opportunities for Love, that we ought to lose none.

Fred. Ay, this is something ! here's a Woman !—When shall I be blest with so much kindness from your fair Mouth ?—Take the Jewel, Fool.   [*Aside to* Belv.

Belv. You tempt me strangely, Madam, every way.

Flor. So, if I find him false, my whole Repose is gone.
                                                        [*Aside.*

Belv. And but for a Vow I've made to a very fine Lady, this Goodness had subdu'd me.

Fred. Pox on't be kind, in pity to me be kind, for I am to thrive here but as you treat her Friend.

Hell. Tell me what did you in yonder House, and I'll unmasque.

Will. Yonder House—oh—I went to—a—to—why, there's a Friend of mine lives there.

Hell. What a she, or a he Friend?

Will. A Man upon my Honour! a Man—A She Friend! no, no, Madam, you have done my Business, I thank you.

Hell. And was't your Man Friend, that had more Darts in's Eyes than *Cupid* carries in a whole Budget of Arrows?

Will. So—

Hell. Ah such a *Bona Roba*: to be in her Arms is lying in *Fresco*, all perfumed Air about me—Was this your Man Friend too?

Will. So—

Hell. That gave you the He, and the She—Gold, that begets young Pleasures.

Will. Well, well, Madam, then you see there are Ladies in the World, that will not be cruel—there are, Madam, there are—

Hell. And there be Men too as fine, wild, inconstant Fellows as your self, there be, Captain, there be, if you go to that now—therefore I'm resolv'd—

Will. Oh!

Hell. To see your Face no more—

Will. Oh!

Hell. Till to morrow.

Will. Egad you frighted me.

Hell. Nor then neither, unless you'l swear never to see that Lady more.

Will. See her!—why! never to think of Womankind again?

Hell. Kneel, and swear. [*Kneels, she gives him her hand.*

Hell. I do, never to think—to see—to love—nor lie with any but thy self.

Hell. Kiss the Book.

Will. Oh, most religiously.   [*Kisses her Hand.*

Hell. Now what a wicked Creature am I, to damn a proper Fellow.

Call. Madam, I'll stay no longer, 'tis e'en dark. [*To* Flor.

Flor. However, Sir, I'll leave this with you—that when I'm gone, you may repent the opportunity you have lost by your modesty.   [*Gives him the Jewel, which is her Picture, and Ex. he gazes after her.*

Will. 'Twill be an Age till to morrow,—and till then I will most impatiently expect you—Adieu, my dear pretty Angel.   [*Ex. all the Women.*

Belv. Ha! *Florinda's* Picture! 'twas she her self—what a dull Dog was I? I would have given the World for one minute's discourse with her.—

Fred. This comes of your Modesty,—ah pox on your Vow, 'twas ten to one but we had lost the Jewel by't.

Belv. Willmore! the blessed'st Opportunity lost!—*Florinda*, Friends, *Florinda!*

Will. Ah Rogue! such black Eyes, such a Face, such a Mouth, such Teeth,—and so much Wit!

Belv. All, all, and a thousand Charms besides.

Will. Why, dost thou know her?

Belv. Know her! ay, ay, and a Pox take me with all my Heart for being modest.

Will. But hark ye, Friend of mine, are you my Rival? and have I been only beating the Bush all this while?

Belv. I understand thee not—I'm mad—see here—
          [*Shews the Picture.*

Will. Ha! whose Picture is this?—'tis a fine Wench.

Fred. The Colonel's Mistress, Sir.

Will. Oh, oh, here—I thought it had been another Prize—come, come, a Bottle will set thee right again.
          [*Gives the Picture back.*

Belv. I am content to try, and by that time 'twill be late enough for our Design.

Will. Agreed.

> *Love does all day the Soul's great Empire keep,*
> *But Wine at night lulls the soft God asleep.* [*Exeunt.*

SCENE II.   Lucetta's *House.*
Enter Blunt *and* Lucetta *with a Light.*

Luc. Now we are safe and free, no fears of the coming home of my old jealous Husband, which made me a little thoughtful when you came in first—but now Love is all the business of my Soul.

Blunt. I am transported—Pox on't, that I had but some fine things to say to her, such as Lovers use—I was a Fool not to learn of *Fred.* a little by Heart before I came—something I must say.—   [*Aside.*
'Sheartlikins, sweet Soul, I am not us'd to complement, but I'm an honest Gentleman, and thy humble Servant.

Luc. I have nothing to pay for so great a Favour, but such a Love as cannot but be great, since at first sight of that sweet Face and Shape it made me your absolute Captive.

Blunt. Kind heart, how prettily she talks ! Egad I'll show her Husband a *Spanish* Trick; send him out of the World, and marry her : she's damnably in love with me, and will ne'er mind Settlements, and so there's that sav'd. [*Aside.*

Luc. Well, Sir, I'll go and undress me, and be with you instantly.

Blunt. Make haste then, for 'dsheartlikins, dear Soul, thou canst not guess at the pain of a longing Lover, when his Joys are drawn within the compass of a few minutes.

Luc. You speak my Sense, and I'll make haste to provide it.   [*Exit.*

Blunt. 'Tis a rare Girl, and this one night's enjoyment with her will be worth all the days I ever past in *Essex.*— Would she'd go with me into *England*, tho to say truth, there's plenty of Whores there already.—But a pox on 'em they are such mercenary prodigal Whores, that they want such a one as this, that's free and generous, to give 'em good Examples:—Why, what a House she has! how rich and fine!

Enter Sancho.

Sancho. Sir, my Lady has sent me to conduct you to her Chamber.

Blunt. Sir, I shall be proud to follow—Here's one of her Servants too: 'dsheartlikins, by his Garb and Gravity he might be a Justice of Peace in *Essex*, and is but a Pimp here.   [*Exeunt.*

*The Scene changes to a Chamber with an Alcove-Bed in it,
    a Table, &c.* Lucetta *in Bed. Enter* Sancho *and* Blunt,
    who takes the Candle of Sancho *at the Door.*

Sanch. Sir, my Commission reaches no farther.

Blunt. Sir, I'll excuse your Complement:—what, in Bed, my sweet Mistress?

Luc. You see, I still out-do you in kindness.

Blunt. And thou shalt see what haste I'll make to quit scores—oh the luckiest Rogue!   [*Undresses himself.*

Luc. Shou'd you be false or cruel now!

Blunt. False, 'Sheartlikins, what dost thou take me for a *Jew?* an insensible Heathen,—A Pox of thy old jealous Husband: and he were dead, egad, sweet Soul, it shou'd be none of my fault, if I did not marry thee.

Luc. It never shou'd be mine.

Blunt. Good Soul, I'm the fortunatest Dog!

Luc. Are you not undrest yet?

Blunt. As much as my Impatience will permit.

[*Goes towards the Bed in his Shirt and Drawers.*

Luc. Hold, Sir, put out the Light, it may betray us else.

Blunt. Any thing, I need no other Light but that of thine Eyes!—'sheartlikins, there I think I had it. [*Aside.*

[*Puts out the Candle, the Bed descends, he
    gropes about to find it.*

—Why—why—where am I got? what, not yet?—where

are you sweetest?—ah, the Rogue's silent now—a pretty
Love-trick this—how she'll laugh at me anon!—you need
not, my dear Rogue! you need not! I'm all on a fire already
—come, come, now call me in for pity—Sure I'm enchanted! I have been round the Chamber, and can find
neither Woman, nor Bed—I lockt the Door, I'm sure she
cannot go that way; or if she cou'd, the Bed cou'd not—
Enough, enough, my pretty Wanton, do not carry the Jest
too far—Ha, betray'd! Dogs! Rogues! Pimps! help! help!
          [*Lights on a Trap, and is let down.*

Enter Lucetta, Philippo, *and* Sancho *with a Light.*

Phil. Ha, ha, ha, he's dispatcht finely.

Luc. Now, Sir, had I been coy, we had mist of this Booty.

Phil. Nay when I saw 'twas a substantial Fool, I was
mollified; but when you doat upon a Serenading Coxcomb,
upon a Face, fine Clothes, and a Lute, it makes me rage.

Luc. You know I never was guilty of that Folly, my
dear *Philippo*, but with your self—But come let's see what
we have got by this.

Phil. A rich Coat!—Sword and Hat!—these Breeches
too—are well lin'd!—see here a Gold Watch!—a Purse—
ha! Gold!—at least two hundred Pistoles! a bunch of
Diamond Rings; and one with the Family Arms!—a Gold
Box!—with a Medal of his King! and his Lady Mother's
Picture!—these were sacred Reliques, believe me!—see,
the Wasteband of his Breeches have a Mine of Gold!—
Old Queen *Bess's*. We have a Quarrel to her ever since
Eighty Eight, and may therefore justify the Theft, the
Inquisition might have committed it.

Luc. See, a Bracelet of bow'd Gold, these his Sister ty'd
about his Arm at parting—but well—for all this, I fear his
being a Stranger may make a noise, and hinder our Trade
with them hereafter.

Phil. That's our security; he is not only a Stranger to
us, but to the Country too—the Common-Shore into which

he is descended, thou know'st, conducts him into another
Street, which this Light will hinder him from ever finding
again——he knows neither your Name, nor the Street where
your House is, nay, nor the way to his own Lodgings.

Luc. And art not thou an unmerciful Rogue, not to
afford him one Night for all this ?——I should not have been
such a *Jew*.

Phil. Blame me not, *Lucetta*, to keep as much of thee
as I can to my self——come, that thought makes me wanton,
——let's to Bed,——*Sancho*, lock up these.

> *This is the Fleece which Fools do bear,*
> *Design'd for witty Men to sheer.*   [*Exeunt.*

The Scene changes, and discovers Blunt, *creeping out of a
Common Shore, his Face,* &c., *all dirty.*

Blunt. Oh Lord !   [*Climbing up.*
I am got out at last, and (which is a Miracle) without a
Clue——and now to Damning and Cursing,——but if that
would ease me, where shall I begin ? with my Fortune,
my self, or the Quean that cozen'd me——What a dog was I
to believe in Women ! Oh Coxcomb——ignorant conceited
Coxcomb ! to fancy she cou'd be enamour'd with my Person,
at the first sight enamour'd——Oh, I'm a cursed Puppy, 'tis
plain, Fool was writ upon my Forehead, she perceiv'd it,
——saw the *Essex* Calf there——for what Allurements could
there be in this Countenance ? which I can indure, because
I'm acquainted with it——Oh, dull silly Dog ! to be thus
sooth'd into a Cozening ! Had I been drunk, I might fondly
have credited the young Quean ! but as I was in my right
Wits, to be thus cheated, confirms I am a dull believing
English Country Fop.——But my Comrades ! Death and the
Devil, there's the worst of all——then a Ballad will be sung
to Morrow on the *Prado*, to a lousy Tune of the enchanted
Squire, and the annihilated Damsel——But *Fred.* that Rogue,
and the Colonel, will abuse me beyond all Christian patience
——had she left me my Clothes, I have a Bill of Exchange

at home wou'd have sav'd my Credit—but now all hope is taken from me—Well, I'll home (if I can find the way) with this Consolation, that I am not the first kind believing Coxcomb; but there are, Gallants, many such good Natures amongst ye.

> *And tho you've better Arts to hide your Follies,*
> *Adsheartlikins y'are all as errant Cullies.*

SCENE III.   *The Garden, in the Night.*

Enter Florinda *undress'd, with a Key, and a little Box.*

Flor. Well, thus far I'm in my way to Happiness; I have got my self free from *Callis*; my Brother too, I find by yonder light, is gone into his Cabinet, and thinks not of me: I have by good Fortune got the Key of the Garden Back-door,—I'll open it, to prevent *Belvile's* knocking,—a little noise will now alarm my Brother. Now am I as fearful as a young Thief. [*Unlocks the Door.*]—Hark,—what noise is that?—Oh, 'twas the Wind that plaid amongst the Boughs.—*Belvile* stays long, methinks—it's time—stay —for fear of a surprize, I'll hide these Jewels in yonder Jessamin. [*She goes to lay down the Box.*

Enter Willmore *drunk.*

Will. What the Devil is become of these Fellows, *Belvile* and *Frederick?* They promis'd to stay at the next corner for me, but who the Devil knows the corner of a full Moon?—Now—whereabouts am I?—hah—what have we here? a Garden!—a very convenient place to sleep in— hah—what has God sent us here?—a Female—by this light, a Woman; I'm a Dog if it be not a very Wench.—

Flor. He's come!—hah—who's there?

Will. Sweet Soul, let me salute thy Shoe-string.

Flor. 'Tis not my *Belvile*—good Heavens, I know him not.—Who are you, and from whence come you?

Will. Prithee—prithee, Child—not so many hard Questions—let it suffice I am here, Child—Come, come kiss me.

Flor. Good Gods ! what luck is mine ?

Will. Only good luck, Child, parlous good luck.—Come hither,—'tis a delicate shining Wench,—by this Hand she's perfum'd, and smells like any Nosegay.—Prithee, dear Soul, let's not play the Fool, and lose time,—precious time—for as Gad shall save me, I'm as honest a Fellow as breathes, tho I am a little disguis'd at present.—Come, I say,—why, thou may'st be free with me, I'll be very secret. I'll not boast who 'twas oblig'd me, not I—for hang me if I know thy Name.

Flor. Heavens ! what a filthy beast is this !

Will. I am so, and thou oughtst the sooner to lie with me for that reason,—for look you, Child, there will be no Sin in't, because 'twas neither design'd nor premeditated ; 'tis pure Accident on both sides—that's a certain thing now—Indeed should I make love to you, and you vow Fidelity—and swear and lye till you believ'd and yielded —Thou art therefore (as thou art a good Christian) oblig'd in Conscience to deny me nothing.   Now—come, be kind, without any more idle prating.

Flor. Oh, I am ruin'd—wicked Man, unhand me.

Will. Wicked! Egad, Child, a Judge, were he young and vigorous, and saw those Eyes of thine, would know 'twas they gave the first blow—the first provocation.—Come, prithee let's lose no time, I say—this is a fine convenient place.

Flor. Sir, let me go, I conjure you, or I'll call out.

Will. Ay, ay, you were best to call Witness to see how finely you treat me—do.—

Flor. I'll cry Murder, Rape, or any thing, if you do not instantly let me go.

Will. A Rape ! Come, come, you lye, you Baggage, you lye : What, I'll warrant you would fain have the World believe now that you are not so forward as I.   No, not you,—why at this time of Night was your Cobweb-door set open, dear Spider—but to catch Flies ?—Hah come—or I shall be damnably angry.—Why what a Coil is here.—

Flor. Sir, can you think——

Will. That you'd do it for nothing? oh, oh, I find what you'd be at——look here, here's a Pistole for you——here's a work indeed——here——take it, I say.——

Flor. For Heaven's sake, Sir, as you're a Gentleman——

Will. So——now——she would be wheedling me for more ——what, you will not take it then——you're resolv'd you will not.——Come, come, take it, or I'll put it up again; for, look ye, I never give more.——Why, how now, Mistress, are you so high i'th' Mouth, a Pistole won't down with you?——hah——why, what a work's here——in good time—— come, no struggling, be gone——But an y'are good at a dumb Wrestle, I'm for ye,——look ye,——I'm for ye.——

[*She struggles with him.*

Enter Belvile *and* Frederick.

Bel. The Door is open, a Pox of this mad Fellow, I'm angry that we've lost him, I durst have sworn he had follow'd us.

Fred. But you were so hasty, Colonel, to be gone.

Flor. Help, help,——Murder!——help——oh, I'm ruin'd.

Belv. Ha, sure that's *Florinda's* Voice.

[*Comes up to them.*

——A Man! Villain, let go that Lady.   [*A noise.*

[*Will.* turns *and* draws, Fred. *interposes.*

Flor. Belvile! Heavens! my Brother too is coming, and 'twill be impossible to escape.——*Belvile*, I conjure you to walk under my Chamber-window, from whence I'll give you some instructions what to do——This rude Man has undone us.   [*Exit.*

Will. Belvile!

Enter Pedro, Stephano, *and other Servants with Lights.*

Ped. I'm betray'd; run, *Stephano*, and see if *Florinda* be safe.   [*Exit Steph.*
So whoe'er they be, all is not well, I'll to *Florinda's* Chamber.   [*They fight, and* Pedro's *Party beats 'em out; going out, meets* Stephano.

Steph. You need not, Sir, the poor Lady's fast asleep, and thinks no harm : I wou'd not wake her, Sir, for fear of frightning her with your danger.

Ped. I'm glad she's there—Rascals, how came the Garden-Door open ?

Steph. That Question comes too late, Sir : some of my Fellow-Servants Masquerading I'll warrant.

Ped. Masquerading ! a leud Custom to debauch our Youth—there's something more in this than I imagine.

[*Exeunt.*

SCENE IV. *Changes to the Street.*

Enter Belvile *in Rage,* Fred. *holding him, and* Willmore *melancholy.*

Will. Why, how the Devil shou'd I know *Florinda?*

Belv. Ah plague of your ignorance ! if it had not been *Florinda,* must you be a Beast ?—a Brute, a senseless Swine ?

Will. Well, Sir, you see I am endu'd with Patience— I can bear—tho egad y're very free with me methinks,— I was in good hopes the Quarrel wou'd have been on my side, for so uncivilly interrupting me.

Belv. Peace, Brute, whilst thou'rt safe—oh, I'm distracted.

Will. Nay, nay, I'm an unlucky Dog, that's certain.

Belv. Ah curse upon the Star that rul'd my Birth ! or whatsoever other Influence that makes me still so wretched.

Will. Thou break'st my Heart with these Complaints ; there is no Star in fault, no Influence but Sack, the cursed Sack I drank.

Fred. Why, how the Devil came you so drunk ?

Will. Why, how the Devil came you so sober ?

Belv. A curse upon his thin Skull, he was always before-hand that way.

Fred. Prithee, dear Colonel, forgive him, he's sorry for his fault.

Belv. He's always so after he has done a mischief—a plague on all such Brutes.

Will. By this Light I took her for an errant Harlot.

Belv. Damn your debaucht Opinion: tell me, Sot, hadst thou so much sense and light about thee to distinguish her to be a Woman, and could'st not see something about her Face and Person, to strike an awful Reverence into thy Soul?

Will. Faith no, I consider'd her as mere a Woman as I could wish.

Belv. 'Sdeath I have no patience—draw, or I'll kill you.

Will. Let that alone till to morrow, and if I set not all right again, use your Pleasure.

Belv. To morrow, damn it.
The spiteful Light will lead me to no happiness.
To morrow is *Antonio's*, and perhaps
Guides him to my undoing;—oh that I could meet
This Rival, this powerful Fortunate.

Will. What then?

Belv. Let thy own Reason, or my Rage instruct thee.

Will. I shall be finely inform'd then, no doubt; hear me, Colonel—hear me—shew me the Man and I'll do his Business.

Belv. I know him no more than thou, or if I did, I should not need thy aid.

Will. This you say is *Angelica's* House, I promis'd the kind Baggage to lie with her to Night.   [*Offers to go in.*

Enter Antonio *and his Page.* Ant. *knocks on the Hilt of his Sword.*

Ant. You paid the thousand Crowns I directed?

Page. To the Lady's old Woman, Sir, I did.

Will. Who the Devil have we here?

Belv. I'll now plant my self under *Florinda's* Window, and if I find no comfort there, I'll die.

[*Ex.* Belv. *and* Fred.

Enter Moretta.

Moret. Page !

Page. Here's my Lord.

Will. How is this, a Piccaroon going to board my Frigate ! here's one Chase-Gun for you.

> [*Drawing his Sword, justles* Ant. *who turns and draws. They fight*, Ant. *falls.*

Moret. Oh, bless us, we are all undone !

> [*Runs in, and shuts the Door.*

Page. Help, Murder !

> [Belvile *returns at the noise of fighting.*

Belv. Ha, the mad Rogue's engag'd in some unlucky Adventure again.

Enter two or three Masqueraders.

Masq. Ha, a Man kill'd !

Will. How ! a Man kill'd ! then I'll go home to sleep.

> [*Puts up, and reels out. Ex. Masquers another way.*

Belv. Who shou'd it be ! pray Heaven the Rogue is safe, for all my Quarrel to him.   [*As* Belvile *is groping about, enter an Officer and six Soldiers.*

Sold. Who's there ?

Offic. So, here's one dispatcht—secure the Murderer.

Belv. Do not mistake my Charity for Murder :
I came to his Assistance.   [*Soldiers seize on* Belvile.

Offic. That shall be tried, Sir.—St. *Jago,* Swords drawn in the Carnival time !   [*Goes to* Antonio.

Ant. Thy Hand prithee.

Offic. Ha, Don *Antonio !* look well to the Villain there.— How is't, Sir ?

Ant. I'm hurt.

Belv. Has my Humanity made me a Criminal ?

Offic. Away with him.

Belv. What a curst Chance is this !

> [*Ex. Soldiers with* Belv.

Ant. This is the Man that has set upon me twice—

carry him to my Apartment till you have further Orders
from me.   [*To the Officer. Ex. Ant. led.*

ACT IV.
Scene I. *A fine Room.*
Discovers Belvile, *as by Dark alone.*

Belv. When shall I be weary of railing on Fortune,
who is resolv'd never to turn with Smiles upon me?—Two
such Defeats in one Night—none but the Devil and that
mad Rogue could have contriv'd to have plagued me with
—I am here a Prisoner—but where?—Heaven knows—
and if there be Murder done, I can soon decide the Fate
of a Stranger in a Nation without Mercy—Yet this is
nothing to the Torture my Soul bows with, when I think
of losing my fair, my dear *Florinda.*—Hark—my Door
opens—a Light—a Man—and seems of Quality—arm'd
too.—Now shall I die like a Dog without defence.

Enter Antonio *in a Night-Gown, with a Light ; his Arm
in a Scarf, and a Sword under his Arm : He sets the
Candle on the Table.*

Ant. Sir, I come to know what Injuries I have done
you, that could provoke you to so mean an Action, as to
attack me basely, without allowing time for my Defence.

Belv. Sir, for a Man in my Circumstances to plead
Innocence, would look like Fear—but view me well, and
you will find no marks of a Coward on me, nor any thing
that betrays that Brutality you accuse me of.

Ant. In vain, Sir, you impose upon my Sense,
You are not only he who drew on me last Night,
But yesterday before the same House, that of *Angelica.*
Yet there is something in your Face and Mein—

Belv. I own I fought to day in the defence of a Friend
of mine, with whom you (if you're the same) and your
Party were first engag'd.
Perhaps you think this Crime enough to kill me,

But if you do, I cannot fear you'll do it basely.

    Ant. No, Sir, I'll make you fit for a Defence with this.
                            [*Gives him the Sword.*

    Belv. This Gallantry surprizes me—nor know I how
to use this Present, Sir, against a Man so brave.

    Ant. You shall not need;
For know, I come to snatch you from a Danger
That is decreed against you;
Perhaps your Life, or long Imprisonment:
And 'twas with so much Courage you offended,
I cannot see you punisht.

    Belv. How shall I pay this Generosity?

    Ant. It had been safer to have kill'd another,
Than have attempted me:
To shew your Danger, Sir, I'll let you know my Quality;
And 'tis the Vice-Roy's Son whom you have wounded.

    Belv. The Vice-Roy's Son!
Death and Confusion! was this Plague reserved
To compleat all the rest?—oblig'd by him!
The Man of all the World I would destroy.   [*Aside.*

    Ant. You seem disorder'd, Sir.

    Belv. Yes, trust me, Sir, I am, and 'tis with pain
That Man receives such Bounties,
Who wants the pow'r to pay 'em back again.

    Ant. To gallant Spirits 'tis indeed uneasy;
—But you may quickly over-pay me, Sir.

    Belv. Then I am well—kind Heaven! but set us even,
That I may fight with him, and keep my Honour safe.
                            [*Aside.*
—Oh, I'm impatient, Sir, to be discounting
The mighty Debt I owe you; command me quickly—

    Ant. I have a Quarrel with a Rival, Sir,
About the Maid we love.

    Belv. Death, 'tis *Florinda* he means—
That Thought destroys my Reason, and I shall kill him—
                            [*Aside.*

Ant. My Rival, Sir.

Is one has all the Virtues Man can boast of.

Belv. Death! who shou'd this be?   [*Aside.*

Ant. He challeng'd me to meet him on the *Molo*,

As soon as Day appear'd; but last Night's quarrel

Has made my Arm unfit to guide a Sword.

Belv. I apprehend you, Sir, you'd have me kill the Man

That lays a claim to the Maid you speak of.

—I'll do't—I'll fly to do it.

Ant. Sir, do you know her?

Belv. —No, Sir, but 'tis enough she is admired by you.

Ant. Sir, I shall rob you of the Glory on't,

For you must fight under my Name and Dress.

Belv. That Opinion must be strangely obliging that
     makes

You think I can personate the brave *Antonio*,

Whom I can but strive to imitate.

Ant. You say too much to my Advantage.

Come, Sir, the Day appears that calls you forth.

Within, Sir, is the Habit.   [*Exit* Antonio.

Belv. Fantastick Fortune, thou deceitful Light,

That cheats the wearied Traveller by Night,

Tho on a Precipice each step you tread,

I am resolv'd to follow where you lead.   [*Exit.*

Scene II. *The Molo.*

Enter Florinda *and* Callis *in Masques, with* Stephano.

Flor. I'm dying with my fears; *Belvile's* not coming,

As I expected, underneath my Window,

Makes me believe that all those Fears are true.   [*Aside.*

—Canst thou not tell with whom my Brother fights?

Steph. No, Madam, they were both in Masquerade, I

was by when they challeng'd one another, and they had

decided the Quarrel then, but were prevented by some

Cavaliers; which made 'em put it off till now—but I am

sure 'tis about you they fight.

Flor. Nay then 'tis with *Belvile*, for what other Lover have I that dares fight for me, except *Antonio?* and he is too much in favour with my Brother—If it be he, for whom shall I direct my Prayers to Heaven?   [*Aside.*

Steph. Madam, I must leave you; for if my Master see me, I shall be hang'd for being your Conductor.—I escap'd narrowly for the Excuse I made for you last night i'th' Garden.

Flor. And I'll reward thee for't—prithee no more.

[*Exit.* Steph.

Enter Don Pedro *in his Masquing Habit.*

Pedro. Antonio's late to day, the place will fill, and we may be prevented.   [*Walks about.*

Flor. Antonio! sure I heard amiss.   [*Aside.*

Pedro. But who would not excuse a happy Lover.
When soft fair Arms comfine the yielding Neck;
And the kind Whisper languishingly breathes,
Must you be gone so soon?
Sure I had dwelt for ever on her Bosom.
—But stay, he's here.

Enter Belvile *drest in* Antonio's *Clothes.*

Flor. 'Tis not *Belvile*, half my Fears are vanisht.

Pedro. Antonio!—

Belv. This must be he.   [*Aside.*
You're early, Sir,—I do not use to be out-done this way.

Pedro. The wretched, Sir, are watchful, and 'tis enough
You have the advantage of me in *Angelica.*

Belv. Angelica!
Or I've mistook my Man! Or else *Antonio,*
Can he forget his Interest in *Florinda,*
And fight for common Prize?   [*Aside.*

Pedro. Come, Sir, you know our terms—

Belv. By Heaven, not I.   [*Aside.*
—No talking, I am ready, Sir.

[*Offers to fight.* Flor. *runs in.*

Flor. Oh, hold! whoe'er you be, I do conjure you hold.
If you strike here—I die—   [*To* Belv.
    Pedro. Florinda!
    Belv. Florinda imploring for my Rival!
    Pedro. Away, this Kindness is unseasonable.

> [*Puts her by, they fight; she runs in just
>   as* Belv. *disarms* Pedro.

    Flor. Who are you, Sir, that dare deny my Prayers?
    Belv. Thy Prayers destroy him; if thou wouldst pre-
serve him.
Do that thou'rt unacquainted with, and curse him.

                                    [*She holds him.*

    Flor. By all you hold most dear, by her you love,
I do conjure you, touch him not.
    Belv. By her I love!
See—I obey—and at your Feet resign
The useless Trophy of my Victory.

                    [*Lays his sword at her Feet.*

    Pedro. Antonio, you've done enough to prove you love
Florinda.
    Belv. Love *Florinda!*
Does Heaven love Adoration, Pray'r, or Penitence?
Love her! here Sir,—your Sword again.

            [*Snatches up the Sword, and gives it him.*

Upon this Truth I'll fight my Life away.
    Pedro. No, you've redeem'd my Sister, and my Friend-
ship.
    Belv. Don *Pedro!*

        [*He gives him* Flor. *and pulls off his Vizard to
          shew his Face, and puts it on again.*

    Pedro. Can you resign your Claims to other Women,
And give your Heart intirely to *Florinda?*
    Belv. Intire, as dying Saints Confessions are.
I can delay my happiness no longer.
This minute let me make *Florinda* mine:
    Pedro. This minute let it be—no time so proper,

This Night my Father will arrive from *Rome*,
And possibly may hinder what we propose.

    Flor. Oh Heavens! this Minute!

                         [*Enter Masqueraders, and pass over.*

    Belv. Oh, do not ruin me!

    Pedro. The place begins to fill; and that we may not
be observ'd, do you walk off to St. *Peter's* Church, where
I will meet you, and conclude your Happiness.

    Belv. I'll meet you there—if there be no more Saints
Churches in *Naples*.   [*Aside.*

    Flor. Oh stay, Sir, and recall your hasty Doom:
Alas I have not yet prepar'd my Heart
To entertain so strange a Guest.

    Pedro. Away, this silly Modesty is assum'd too late.

    Belv. Heaven, Madam! what do you do?

    Flor. Do! despise the Man that lays a Tyrant's Claim
To what he ought to conquer by Submission.

    Belv. You do not know me—move a little this way.

                         [*Draws her aside.*

    Flor. Yes, you may even force me to the Altar,
But not the holy Man that offers there
Shall force me to be thine.

                [*Pedro talks to Callis this while.*

    Belv. Oh do not lose so blest an opportunity!
See—'tis your *Belvile*—not *Antonio*,
Whom your mistaken Scorn and Anger ruins.

                  [*Pulls off his Vizard.*

    Flor. Belvile!
Where was my Soul it cou'd not meet thy Voice,
And take this knowledge in?

        [*As they are talking, enter* Willmore *finely drest,
and* Frederick.

    Will. No Intelligence! no News of *Belvile* yet—well I
am the most unlucky Rascal in Nature—ha!—am I deceiv'd
—or is it he—look, *Fred.*—'tis he—my dear *Belvile*.

   [Runs and embraces him. Belv. *Vizard falls out on's Hand.*

Belv. Hell and Confusion seize thee!

Pedro. Ha! *Belvile!* I beg your Pardon, Sir.

                              [Takes Flor. *from him.*

Belv. Nay, touch her not, she's mine by Conquest, Sir.
I won her by my Sword.

Will. Did'st thou so—and egad, Child, we'll keep her
by the Sword.   *[Draws on* Pedro, Belv. *goes between.*

Belv. Stand off.
Thou'rt so profanely leud, so curst by Heaven,
All Quarrels thou espousest must be fatal.

Will. Nay, an you be so hot, my Valour's coy,
And shall be courted when you want it next.

                                [Puts up his Sword.

Belv. You know I ought to claim a Victor's Right,

                                [To Pedro.

But you're the Brother to divine *Florinda,*
To whom I'm such a Slave—to purchase her,
I durst not hurt the Man she holds so dear.

Pedro. 'Twas by *Antonio's,* not by *Belvile's* Sword,
This Question should have been decided, Sir:
I must confess much to your Bravery's due,
Both now, and when I met you last in Arms.
But I am nicely punctual in my word,
As Men of Honour ought, and beg your Pardon.
—For this Mistake another Time shall clear.
—This was some Plot between you and *Belvile:*
But I'll prevent you.   *[Aside to* Flor. *as they are going out.*

          *[Belv. looks after her, and begins to walk up and
              down in a Rage.*

Will. Do not be modest now, and lose the Woman:
but if we shall fetch her back, so—

Belv. Do not speak to me.

Will. Not speak to you!—Egad, I'll speak to you, and
will be answered too.

Belv. Will you, Sir?

Will. I know I've done some mischief, but I'm so dull a Puppy, that I am the Son of a Whore, if I know how, or where—prithee inform my Understanding.——

Belv. Leave me I say, and leave me instantly.

Will. I will not leave you in this humour, nor till I know my Crime.

Belv. Death, I'll tell you, Sir—

> [*Draws and runs at* Will. *he runs out ;* Belv. *after him,* Fred. *interposes.*

Enter Angelica, Moretta, *and* Sebastian.

Ang. Ha—*Sebastian*—Is not that *Willmore?* haste, haste, and bring him back.

Fred. The Colonel's mad—I never saw him thus before; I'll after 'em, lest he do some mischief, for I am sure *Willmore* will not draw on him.   [*Exit.*

Ang. I am all Rage! my first desires defeated
For one, for ought he knows, that has no
Other Merit than her Quality,—
Her being Don *Pedro's* Sister—He loves her :
I know 'tis so—dull, dull, insensible—
He will not see me now tho oft invited ;
And broke his Word last night—false perjur'd Man !
—He that but yesterday fought for my Favours,
And would have made his Life a Sacrifice
To've gain'd one Night with me,
Must now be hired and courted to my Arms.

Moret. I told you what wou'd come on't, but *Moretta's* an old doating Fool—Why did you give him five hundred Crowns, but to set himself out for other Lovers? You shou'd have kept him poor, if you had meant to have had any good from him.

Ang. Oh, name not such mean Trifles.—Had I given him all
My Youth has earn'd from Sin,

I had not lost a Thought nor Sigh upon't.
But I have given him my eternal Rest,
My whole Repose, my future Joys, my Heart;
My Virgin Heart. *Moretta!* oh 'tis gone!

Moret. Curse on him, here he comes;
How fine she has made him too!

Enter Willmore *and* Sebast. Ang. *turns and walks away.*

Will. How now, turn'd Shadow?
Fly when I pursue, and follow when I fly!

> *Stay gentle Shadow of my Dove,*   [Sings.
>   *And tell me e'er I go,*
> *Whether the Substance may not prove*
>   *A fleeting Thing like you.*

There's a soft kind Look remaining yet.
                    [*As she turns she looks on him.*
Ang. Well, Sir, you may be gay; all Happiness, all Joys
pursue you still, Fortune's your Slave, and gives you every
hour choice of new Hearts and Beauties, till you are cloy'd
with the repeated Bliss, which others vainly languish for
—But know, false Man, that I shall be reveng'd.
                    [*Turns away in a Rage.*
Will. So, 'gad, there are of those faint-hearted Lovers,
whom such a sharp Lesson next their Hearts would make
as impotent as Fourscore—pox o' this whining—my
Bus'ness is to laugh and love—a pox on't; I hate your sullen Lover, a Man shall lose as much time to put you in
Humour now, as would serve to gain a new Woman.

Ang. I scorn to cool that Fire I cannot raise,
Or do the Drudgery of your virtuous Mistress.

Will. A virtuous Mistress! Death, what a thing thou
hast found out for me! why what the Devil should I do
with a virtuous Woman?—a fort of ill-natur'd Creatures,
that take a Pride to torment a Lover. Virtue is but an
Infirmity in Women, a Disease that renders even the

handsom ungrateful; whilst the ill-favour'd, for want of
Sollicitations and Address, only fancy themselves so.—I
have lain with a Woman of Quality, who has all the while
been railing at Whores.

Ang. I will not answer for your Mistress's Virtue,
Tho she be young enough to know no Guilt:
And I could wish you would persuade my Heart,
'Twas the two hundred thousand Crowns you courted.

Will. Two hundred thousand Crowns! what Story's
this?—what Trick?—what Woman?—ha.

Ang. How strange you make it! have you forgot the
Creature you entertain'd on the Piazza last night?

Will. Ha, my Gipsy worth two hundred thousand
Crowns!—oh how I long to be with her—pox, I knew
she was of Quality.   [*Aside.*

Ang. False Man, I see my Ruin in thy Face.
How many vows you breath'd upon my Bosom,
Never to be unjust—have you forgot so soon?

Will. Faith no, I was just coming to repeat 'em—but
here's a Humour indeed—would make a Man a Saint—
Wou'd she'd be angry enough to leave me, and command
me not to wait on her.   [*Aside.*

      Enter Hellena, *drest in Man's Clothes.*

Hell. This must be *Angelica*, I know it by her mumping
Matron here—Ay, ay, 'tis she: my mad Captain's with
her too, for all his swearing—how this unconstant Humour
makes me love him:—pray, good grave Gentlewoman, is
not this *Angelica?*

Moret. My too young Sir, it is—I hope 'tis one from
Don *Antonio.*   [*Goes to* Angelica.

Hell. Well, something I'll do to vex him for this. [*Aside.*

Ang. I will not speak with him; am I in humour to
receive a Lover?

Will. Not speak with him! why I'll be gone—and
wait your idler minutes—Can I shew less Obedience to
the thing I love so fondly?   [*Offers to go.*

Ang. A fine Excuse this—stay—

Will. And hinder your Advantage : should I repay your Bounties so ungratefully ?

Ang. Come hither, Boy,—that I may let you see
How much above the Advantages you name
I prize one Minute's Joy with you.

Will. Oh, you destroy me with this Endearment.

[Impatient to be gone.

—Death, how shall I get away?—Madam, 'twill not be fit I should be seen with you—besides, it will not be convenient—and I've a Friend—that's dangerously sick.

Ang. I see you're impatient—yet you shall stay.

Will. And miss my Assignation with my Gipsy.

[Aside, and walks about impatiently.

Hell. Madam,   [*Moretta brings Hellena, who addresses*
You'l hardly pardon my Intrusion,   (*her self to* Angelica.
When you shall know my Business;
And I'm too young to tell my Tale with Art :
But there must be a wondrous store of Goodness
Where so much Beauty dwells.

Ang. A pretty Advocate, whoever sent thee,
—Prithee proceed—Nay, Sir, you shall not go.

[To Will. *who is stealing off.*

Will. Then shall I lose my dear Gipsy for ever.
—Pox on't, she stays me out of spite.   *[Aside.*

Hell. I am related to a Lady, Madam,
Young, rich, and nobly born, but has the fate
To be in love with a young *English* Gentleman.
Strangely she loves him, at first sight she lov'd him,
But did adore him when she heard him speak ;
For he, she said, had Charms in every word,
That fail'd not to surprize, to wound, and conquer—

Will. Ha, Egad I hope this concerns me.   *[Aside.*

Ang. 'Tis my false Man, he means—wou'd he were gone.
This Praise will raise his Pride and ruin me—Well,

Since you are so impatient to be gone,
I will release you, Sir.   [*To* Will.

Will. Nay, then I'm sure 'twas me he spoke of, this
cannot be the Effects of Kindness in her.   [*Aside.*
—No, Madam, I've consider'd better on't,
And will not give you cause of Jealousy.

Ang. But, Sir, I've—business, that—

Will. This shall not do, I know 'tis but to try me.

Ang. Well, to your Story, Boy,—tho 'twill undo me.
                                        [*Aside.*

Hell. With this Addition to his other Beauties,
He won her unresisting tender Heart,
He vow'd and sigh'd, and swore he lov'd her dearly ;
And she believ'd the cunning Flatterer,
And thought her self the happiest Maid alive :
To day was the appointed time by both,
To consummate their Bliss ;
The Virgin, Altar, and the Priest were drest,
And whilst she languisht for the expected Bridegroom,
She heard, he paid his broken Vows to you.

Will. So, this is some dear Rogue that's in love with me,
and this way lets me know it ; or if it be not me, she means
some one whose place I may supply.   [*Aside.*

Ang. Now I perceive
The cause of thy Impatience to be gone,
And all the business of this glorious Dress.

Will. Damn the young Prater, I know not what he
means.

Hell. Madam,
In your fair Eyes I read too much concern
To tell my farther Business.

Ang. Prithee, sweet Youth, talk on, thou may'st perhaps
Raise here a Storm that may undo my Passion,
And then I'll grant thee any thing.

Hell. Madam, 'tis to intreat you, (oh unreasonable !)
You wou'd not see this Stranger ;

For if you do, she vows you are undone,
Tho Nature never made a Man so excellent;
And sure he'ad been a God, but for Inconstancy.

Will. Ah, Rogue, how finely he's instructed! [*Aside.*
—'Tis plain some Woman that has seen me *en passant.*

Ang. Oh, I shall burst with Jealousy! do you know
the Man you speak of?—

Hell. Yes, Madam, he us'd to be in Buff and Scarlet.

Ang. Thou, false as Hell, what canst thou say to this?
[*To* Will.

Will. By Heaven—

Ang. Hold, do not damn thy self—

Hell. Nor hope to be believ'd.   [*He walks about,
they follow.*

Ang. Oh, perjur'd Man!
Is't thus you pay my generous Passion back?

Hell. Why wou'd you, Sir, abuse my Lady's Faith?

Ang. And use me so inhumanly?

Hell. A Maid so young, so innocent—

Will. Ah, young Devil!

Ang. Dost thou not know thy Life is in my Power?

Hell. Or think my Lady cannot be reveng'd?

Will. So, so, the Storm comes finely on.   [*Aside.*

Ang. Now thou art silent, Guilt has struck thee dumb.
Oh, hadst thou still been so, I'd liv'd in safety.
[*She turns away and weeps.*

Will. Sweetheart, the Lady's Name and House—
quickly: I'm impatient to be with her.—
[*Aside to* Hellena, *looks towards* Angel. *to watch her turning; and as she comes towards them, he meets her.*

Hell. So now is he for another Woman.   [*Aside.*

Will. The impudent'st young thing in Nature!
I cannot persuade him out of his Error, Madam.

Ang. I know he's in the right,—yet thou'st a Tongue
That wou'd persuade him to deny his Faith.   [*In Rage
walks away.*

Will. Her Name, her Name, dear Boy— [*Said softly to*

Hell. Have you forgot it, Sir ?   Hell.

Will. Oh, I perceive he's not to know I am a Stranger
to his Lady.   [*Aside.*

—Yes, yes, I do know—but—I have forgot the—

[*Angel. turns.*

—By Heaven, such early confidence I never saw.

Ang. Did I not charge you with this Mistress, Sir ?
Which you denied, tho I beheld your Perjury.
This little Generosity of thine has render'd back my Heart.

[*Walks away.*

Will. So, you have made sweet work here, my little
      mischief ;
Look your Lady be kind and good-natur'd now, or
I shall have but a cursed Bargain on't.   [*Ang. turns to-*
—The Rogue's bred up to Mischief,   *wards them.*
Art thou so great a Fool to credit him ?

Ang. Yes, I do ; and you in vain impose upon me.

—Come hither, Boy—Is not this he you speak of ?

Hell. I think—it is ; I cannot swear, but I vow he has
just such another lying Lover's look.

[*Hell. looks in his Face, he gazes on her.*

Will. Hah ! do not I know that Face ?—
By Heaven, my little Gipsy ! what a dull Dog was I ?
Had I but lookt that way, I'd known her.
Are all my hopes of a new Woman banisht ?   [*Aside.*
—Egad, if I don't fit thee for this, hang me.
—Madam, I have found out the Plot.

Hell. Oh Lord, what does he say ? am I discover'd now ?

Will. Do you see this young Spark here ?

Hell. He'll tell her who I am.

Will. Who do you think this is ?

Hell. Ay, ay, he does know me.—Nay, dear Captain,
I'm undone if you discover me.

Will. Nay, nay, no cogging ; she shall know what a
precious Mistress I have.

Hell. Will you be such a Devil?

Will. Nay, nay, I'll teach you to spoil sport you will not make.—This small Ambassador comes not from a Person of Quality, as you imagine, and he says; but from a very errant Gipsy, the talkingst, pratingst, cantingst little Animal thou ever saw'st.

Ang. What news you tell me! that's the thing I mean.

Hell. Wou'd I were well off the place.—If ever I go a Captain-hunting again.—   [*Aside.*

Will. Mean that thing? that Gipsy thing? thou may'st as well be jealous of thy Monkey, or Parrot as her: a *German* Motion were worth a dozen of her, and a Dream were a better Enjoyment, a Creature of Constitution fitter for Heaven than Man.

Hell. Tho I'm sure he lyes, yet this vexes me. [*Aside.*

Ang. You are mistaken, she's a *Spanish* Woman
Made up of no such dull Materials.

Will. Materials! Egad, and she be made of any that will either dispense, or admit of Love, I'll be bound to continence.

Hell. Unreasonable Man, do you think so?
                        [*Aside to him.*

Will. You may Return, my little Brazen Head, and tell your Lady, that till she be handsom enough to be belov'd, or I dull enough to be religious, there will be small hopes of me.

Ang. Did you not promise then to marry her?

Will. Not I, by Heaven.

Ang. You cannot undeceive my fears and torments, till you have vow'd you will not marry her.

Hell. If he swears that, he'll be reveng'd on me indeed for all my Rogueries.

Ang. I know what Arguments you'll bring against me, Fortune and Honour.

Will. Honour! I tell you, I hate it in your Sex; and those that fancy themselves possest of that Foppery, are

the most impertinently troublesom of all Woman-kind,
and will transgress nine Commandments to keep one : and
to satisfy your Jealousy I swear—

Hell. Oh, no swearing, dear Captain— [*Aside to him.*

Will. If it were possible I should ever be inclin'd to
marry, it should be some kind young Sinner, one that has
Generosity enough to give a favour handsomely to one that
can ask it discreetly, one that has Wit enough to manage
an Intrigue of Love—oh, how civil such a Wench is, to
a Man than does her the Honour to marry her.

Ang. By Heaven, there's no Faith in any thing he says.

Enter Sebastian.

Sebast. Madam, *Don Antonio*—

Ang. Come hither.

Hell. Ha, *Antonio!* he may be coming hither, and he'll
certainly discover me, I'll therefore retire without a Ceremony.　　　　　　　　　　　　　　　　　[*Exit* Hellena.

Ang. I'll see him, get my Coach ready.

Sebast. It waits you, Madam.

Will. This is lucky : what, Madam, now I may be
gone and leave you to the enjoyment of my Rival ?

Ang. Dull Man, that canst not see how ill, how poor
That false dissimulation looks—Be gone,
And never let me see thy cozening Face again,
Lest I relapse and kill thee.

Will. Yes, you can spare me now,—farewell till you
are in a better Humour—I'm glad of this release—
Now for my Gipsy :
For tho to worse we change, yet still we find
New Joys, New Charms, in a new Miss that's kind.
　　　　　　　　　　　　　　　　　　　　[*Ex.* Will.

Ang. He's gone, and in this Ague of My Soul
The shivering Fit returns ;
Oh with what willing haste he took his leave,
As if the long'd for Minute were arriv'd,

Of some blest Assignation.
In vain I have consulted all my Charms,
In vain this Beauty priz'd, in vain believ'd
My eyes cou'd kindle any lasting Fires.
I had forgot my Name, my Infamy,
And the Reproach that Honour lays on those
That dare pretend a sober passion here.
Nice Reputation, tho it leave behind
More Virtues than inhabit where that dwells,
Yet that once gone, those virtues shine no more.
—Then since I am not fit to belov'd,
I am resolv'd to think on a Revenge
On him that sooth'd me thus to my undoing.   [*Exeunt.*

Scene III.   *A Street.*

Enter Florinda *and* Valeria *in Habits different from
what they have been seen in.*

Flor. We're happily escap'd, yet I tremble still.

Val. A Lover and fear! why, I am but half a one, and
yet I have Courage for any Attempt. Would *Hellena*
were here. I wou'd fain have had her as deep in this
Mischief as we, she'll fare but ill else I doubt.

Flor. She pretended a Visit to the *Augustine* Nuns, but
I believe some other design carried her out, pray Heavens
we light on her.

—Prithee what didst do with *Callis?*

Val. When I saw no Reason wou'd do good on her, I
follow'd her into the Wardrobe, and as she was looking
for something in a great Chest, I tumbled her in by the
Heels, snatcht the Key of the Apartment where you were
confin'd, lockt her in, and left her bauling for help.

Flor. 'Tis well you resolve to follow my Fortunes, for
thou darest never appear at home again after such an Action.

Val. That's according as the young Stranger and I shall
agree—But to our business—I deliver'd your Letter, your

Note to *Belvile*, when I got out under pretence of going to Mass, I found him at his Lodging, and believe me it came seasonably; for never was Man in so desperate a Condition. I told him of your Resolution of making your escape to day, if your Brother would be absent long enough to permit you; if not, die rather than be *Antonio's*.

Flor. Thou shou'dst have told him I was confin'd to my Chamber upon my Brother's suspicion, that the Business on the *Molo* was a Plot laid between him and I.

Val. I said all this, and told him your Brother was now gone to his Devotion, and he resolves to visit every Church till he find him; and not only undeceive him in that, but caress him so as shall delay his return home.

Flor. Oh Heavens! he's here, and *Belvile* with him too.   [*They put on their Vizards.*

Enter Don Pedro, Belvile, Willmore; Belvile *and Don* Pedro *seeming in serious Discourse.*

Val. Walk boldly by them, I'll come at a distance, lest he suspect us. [*She walks by them, and looks back on them.*

Will. Ha! A Woman! and of an excellent Mien!

Ped. She throws a kind look back on you.

Will. Death, tis a likely Wench, and that kind look shall not be cast away—I'll follow her.

Belv. Prithee do not.

Will. Do not! By Heavens to the Antipodes, with such an Invitation.   [*She goes out, and* Will. *follows her.*

Belv. 'Tis a mad Fellow for a Wench.

Enter Fred.

Fred. Oh Colonel, such News.

Belv. Prithee what?

Fred. News that will make you laugh in spite of Fortune.

Belv. What, *Blunt* has had some damn'd Trick put upon him, cheated, bang'd, or clapt?

Fred. Cheated, Sir, rarely cheated of all but his Shirt and Drawers; the unconscionable Whore too turn'd him

out before Consummation, so that traversing the Streets
at Midnight, the Watch found him in this *Fresco*, and
conducted him home: By Heaven 'tis such a slight, and
yet I durst as well have been hang'd as laugh at him, or
pity him; he beats all that do but ask him a Question,
and is in such an Humour——

Ped. Who is't has met with this ill usage, Sir?

Belv. A Friend of ours, whom you must see for Mirth's
sake. I'll imploy him to give *Florinda* time for an escape.
[Aside.

Ped. Who is he?

Belv. A young Countryman of ours, one that has been
educated at so plentiful a rate, he yet ne'er knew the want
of Money, and 'twill be a great Jest to see how simply
he'll look without it. For my part I'll lend him none, and
the Rogue knows not how to put on a borrowing Face, and
ask first. I'll let him see how good 'tis to play our parts
whilst I play his——Prithee, *Fred.* do go home and keep him
in that posture till we come. *[Exeunt.*

Enter Florinda *from the farther end of the Scene, looking
behind her.*

Flor. I am follow'd still——hah——my Brother too advancing this way, good Heavens defend me from being seen
by him. *[She goes off.*

Enter Willmore, *and after him* Valeria, *at a little distance.*

Will. Ah! There she sails, she looks back as she were
willing to be boarded, I'll warrant her Prize.
[He goes out, Valeria *following.*

Enter Hellena, *just as he goes out, with a Page.*

Hell. Hah, is not that my Captain that has a Woman
in chase?——'tis not *Angelica.* Boy, follow those People
at a distance, and bring me an Account where they go in.
——I'll find his Haunts, and plague him every where.——
ha——my Brother! *[Exit Page.*
[Bel. Wil. Ped. cross the Stage: Hell. *runs off.*

Scene changes to another Street.   Enter Florinda.

Flor. What shall I do, my Brother now pursues me.
Will no kind Power protect me from his Tyranny?
—Hah, here's a Door open, I'll venture in, since nothing
can be worse than to fall into his Hands, my Life and
Honour are at stake, and my Necessity has no choice.

[*She goes in.*

Enter Valeria, *and* Hellena's *Page peeping after* Florinda.

Pag. Here she went in, I shall remember this House.

[*Exit Boy.*

Val. This is *Belvile's* Lodgings; she's gone in as readily
as if she knew it—hah—here's that mad Fellow again, I
dare not venture in—I'll watch my Opportunity.

[*Goes aside.*

Enter Willmore, *gazing about him.*

Will. I have lost her hereabouts—Pox on't she must
not scape me so.   [*Goes out.*

Scene changes to Blunt's *Chamber, discovers him sitting
on a Couch in his Shirt and Drawers, reading.*

Blunt. So, now my Mind's a little at Peace, since I
have resolv'd Revenge—A Pox on this Taylor tho, for
not bringing home the Clothes I bespoke; and a Pox of
all poor Cavaliers, a Man can never keep a spare Suit for
'em; and I shall have these Rogues come in and find me
naked; and then I'm undone; but I'm resolv'd to arm my
self—the Rascals shall not insult over me too much.

[*Puts on an old rusty Sword and Buff-Belt.*

—Now, how like a Morrice-Dancer I am equipt—a fine
Lady-like Whore to cheat me thus, without affording me
a Kindness for my Money, a Pox light on her, I shall
never be reconciled to the Sex more, she has made me as
faithless as a Physician, as uncharitable as a Churchman,
and as ill-natur'd as a Poet. O how I'll use all Women-
kind hereafter! what wou'd I give to have one of 'em

within my reach now! any Mortal thing in Petticoats,
kind Fortune, send me; and I'll forgive thy last Night's
Malice—Here's a cursed Book too, (a Warning to all young
Travellers) that can instruct me how to prevent such
Mischiefs now 'tis too late. Well 'tis a rare convenient
thing to read a little now and then, as well as hawk and
hunt.   [*Sits down again and reads.*

Enter to him Florinda.

Flor. This House is haunted sure, 'tis well furnisht and
no living thing inhabits it—hah—a Man! Heavens how
he's attir'd! sure 'tis some Rope-dancer, or Fencing-
Master; I tremble now for fear, and yet I must venture
now to speak to him—Sir, if I may not interrupt your
Meditations—   [*He starts up and gazes.*

Blunt. Hah—what's here? Are my wishes granted?
and is not that a she Creature? Adsheartlikins 'tis! what
wretched thing art thou—hah!

Flor. Charitable Sir, you've told your self already what
I am; a very wretched Maid, forc'd by a strange unlucky
Accident, to seek a safety here, and must be ruin'd, if you
do not grant it.

Blunt. Ruin'd! Is there any Ruin so inevitable as that
which now threatens thee? Dost thou know, miserable
Woman, into what Den of Mischiefs thou art fall'n?
what a Bliss of Confusion?—hah—dost not see something
in my looks that frights thy guilty Soul, and makes thee
wish to change that Shape of Woman for any humble
Animal, or Devil? for those were safer for thee, and less
mischievous.

Flor. Alas, what mean you, Sir? I must confess your
Looks have something in 'em makes me fear; but I be-
seech you, as you seem a Gentleman, pity a harmless
Virgin, that takes your House for Sanctuary.

Blunt. Talk on, talk on, and weep too, till my faith
return. Do, flatter me out of my Senses again—a harmless

Virgin with a Pox, as much one as t'other, adsheartlikins.
Why, what the Devil can I not be safe in my House for you?
not in my Chamber? nay, even being naked too cannot
secure me. This is an Impudence greater than has invaded
me yet.—Come, no Resistance.   [*Pulls her rudely.*

Flor. Dare you be so cruel?

Blunt. Cruel, adsheartlikins as a Gally-slave, or a *Spanish*
Whore: Cruel, yes, I will kiss and beat thee all over;
kiss, and see thee all over; thou shalt lie with me too, not
that I care for the Injoyment, but to let you see I have
ta'en deliberated Malice to thee, and will be revenged on
one Whore for the Sins of another; I will smile and deceive
thee, flatter thee, and beat thee, kiss and swear, and lye to
thee, imbrace thee and rob thee, as she did me, fawn on
thee, and strip thee stark naked, then hang thee out at my
Window by the Heels, with a Paper of scurvey Verses
fasten'd to thy Breast, in praise of damnable Women——
Come, come along.

Flor. Alas, Sir, must I be sacrific'd for the Crimes of
the most infamous of my Sex? I never understood the Sins
you name.

Blunt. Do, persuade the Fool you love him, or that one
of you can be just or honest; tell me I was not an easy
Coxcomb, or any strange impossible Tale: it will be
believ'd sooner than thy false Showers or Protestations.
A Generation of damn'd Hypocrites, to flatter my very
Clothes from my back! dissembling Witches! are these
the Returns you make an honest Gentleman that trusts,
believes, and loves you?—But if I be not even with you
—Come along, or I shall—   [*Pulls her again.*

Enter Frederick.

Fred. Hah, what's here to do?

Blunt. Adsheartlikins, *Fred.* I am glad thou art come,
to be a Witness of my dire Revenge.

Fred. What's this, a Person of Quality too, who is upon

the Ramble to supply the Defects of some grave impotent Husband?

Blunt. No, this has another Pretence, some very unfortunate Accident brought her hither, to save a Life pursued by I know not who, or why, and forc'd to take Sanctuary here at Fools Haven. Adsheartlikins to me of all Mankind for Protection? Is the Ass to be cajol'd again, think ye? No, young one, no Prayers or Tears shall mitigate my Rage; therefore prepare for both my Pleasure of Enjoyment and Revenge, for I am resolved to make up my Loss here on thy Body, I'll take it out in kindness and in beating.

Fred. Now, Mistress of mine, what do you think of this?

Flor. I think he will not—dares not be so barbarous.

Fred. Have a care, *Blunt*, she fetch'd a deep Sigh, she is inamour'd with thy Shirt and Drawers, she'll strip thee even of that. There are of her Calling such unconscionable Baggages, and such dexterous Thieves, they'll flea a Man, and he shall ne'er miss his Skin, till he feels the Cold. There was a Country-man of ours robb'd of a Row of Teeth whilst he was sleeping, which the Jilt made him buy again when he wak'd—You see, Lady, how little Reason we have to trust you.

Blunt. 'Dsheartlikins, why, this is most abominable.

Flor. Some such Devils there may be, but by all that's holy I am none such, I entered here to save a Life in danger.

Blunt. For no goodness I'll warrant her.

Fred. Faith, Damsel, you had e'en confess the plain Truth, for we are Fellows not to be caught twice in the same Trap: Look on that Wreck, a tight Vessel when he set out of Haven, well trim'd and laden, and see how a Female Piccaroon of this Island of Rogues has shatter'd him, and canst thou hope for any Mercy?

Blunt. No, no, Gentlewoman, come along, adsheartlikins we must be better acquainted—we'll both lie with her, and then let me alone to bang her.

Fred. I am ready to serve you in matters of Revenge, that has a double Pleasure in't.

Blunt. Well said.   You hear, little one, how you are condemn'd by publick Vote to the Bed within, there's no resisting your Destiny, Sweetheart.   [*Pulls her.*

Flor. Stay, Sir, I have seen you with *Belvile,* an *English* Cavalier, for his sake use me kindly ; you know how, Sir.

Blunt. Belvile! why, yes, Sweeting, we do know *Belvile,* and wish he were with us now, he's a Cormorant at Whore and Bacon, he'd have a Limb or two of thee, my Virgin Pullet : but 'tis no matter, we'll leave him the Bones to pick.

Flor. Sir, if you have any Esteem for that *Belvile,* I conjure you to treat me with more Gentleness ; he'll thank you for the Justice.

Fred. Hark ye, *Blunt,* I doubt we are mistaken in this matter.

Flor. Sir, If you find me not worth *Belvile's* Care, use me as you please ; and that you may think I merit better treatment than you threaten—pray take this Present—
                    [*Gives him a Ring: He looks on it.*

Blunt. Hum—A Diamond ! why, 'tis a wonderful Virtue now that lies in this Ring, a mollifying Virtue ; adsheartlikins there's more persuasive Rhetorick in't, than all her Sex can utter.

Fred. I begin to suspect something ; and 'twou'd anger us vilely to be truss'd up for a Rape upon a Maid of Quality, when we only believe we ruffle a Harlot.

Blunt. Thou art a credulous Fellow, but adsheartlikins I have no Faith yet ; why, my Saint prattled as parlously as this does, she gave me a Bracelet too, a Devil on her : but I sent my Man to sell it to day for Necessaries, and it prov'd as counterfeit as her Vows of Love.

Fred. However let it reprieve her till we see *Belvile.*

Blunt. That's hard, yet I will grant it.

                    Enter a Servant.

Serv. Oh, Sir, the Colonel is just come with his new

Friend and a *Spaniard* of Quality, and talks of having you to Dinner with 'em.

Blunt. 'Dsheartlikins, I'm undone—I would not see 'em for the World: Harkye, *Fred.* lock up the Wench in your Chamber.

Fred. Fear nothing, Madam, whate'er he threatens, you're safe whilst in my Hands.   [*Ex.* Fred. *and* Flor.

Blunt. And, Sirrah—upon your Life, say—I am not at home—or that I am asleep—or—or any thing—away—I'll prevent them coming this way. [*Locks the Door and Exeunt.*

ACT V.

SCENE I.   *Blunt's Chamber.*

After a great knocking as at his Chamber-door, enter Blunt *softly, crossing the Stage in his Shirt and Drawers, as before.*

Ned, Ned Blunt, Ned Blunt.   [*Call within.*
   Blunt. The Rogues are up in Arms, 'dsheartlikins, this villainous *Frederick* has betray'd me, they have heard of my blessed Fortune.
Ned Blunt, Ned, Ned—   [*and knocking within.*
   Belv. Why, he's dead, Sir, without dispute dead, he has not been seen to day; let's break open the Door—here—Boy—
   Blunt. Ha, break open the Door! 'dsheartlikins that mad Fellow will be as good as his word.
   Belv. Boy, bring something to force the Door.
                     [*A great noise within at the Door again.*
   Blunt. So, now must I speak in my own Defence, I'll try what Rhetorick will do—hold—hold, what do you mean, Gentlemen, what do you mean?
   Belv. Oh Rogue, art alive? prithee open the Door, and convince us.
   Blunt. Yes, I am alive, Gentlemen—but at present a little busy.

Belv. How! *Blunt* grown a man of Business! come, come, open, and let's see this Miracle.   [*within.*

Blunt. No, no, no, no, Gentlemen, 'tis no great Business —but—I am—at—my Devotion,—'dsheartlikins, will you not allow a man time to pray?

Belv. Turn'd religious! a greater Wonder than the first, therefore open quickly, or we shall unhinge, we shall.
          [*within.*

Blunt. This won't do—Why, hark ye, Colonel; to tell you the plain Truth, I am about a necessary Affair of Life.—I have a Wench with me—you apprehend me? the Devil's in't if they be so uncivil as to disturb me now.

Will. How, a Wench! Nay, then we must enter and partake; no Resistance,—unless it be your Lady of Quality, and then we'll keep our distance.

Blunt. So, the Business is out.

Will. Come, come, lend more hands to the Door,— now heave altogether—so, well done, my Boys—
          [*Breaks open the Door.*

Enter Belvile, Willmore, Fred. Pedro *and* Belvile's *Page :*
     Blunt *looks simply, they all laugh at him, he lays his hand*
     on his Sword, and comes up to Willmore.

Blunt. Hark ye, Sir, laugh out your laugh quickly, d'ye hear, and be gone, I shall spoil your sport else; 'dsheartlikins, Sir, I shall—the Jest has been carried on too long, —a Plague upon my Taylor—   [*Aside.*

Will. 'Sdeath, how the Whore has drest him! Faith, Sir, I'm sorry.

Blunt. Are you so, Sir? keep't to your self then, Sir, I advise you, d'ye hear? for I can as little endure your Pity as his Mirth.   [*Lays his Hand on's Sword.*

Belv. Indeed, *Willmore,* thou wert a little too rough with *Ned Blunt's* Mistress; call a Person of Quality Whore, and one so young, so handsome, and so eloquent!—ha, ha, ha.

Blunt. Hark ye, Sir, you know me, and know I can be angry; have a care—for 'dsheartlikins I can fight too—I can, Sir,—do you mark me—no more.

Belv. Why so peevish, good *Ned?* some Disappointments, I'll warrant—What! did the jealous Count her Husband return just in the nick?

Blunt. Or the Devil, Sir,—d'ye laugh? [*They laugh.*] Look ye, settle me a good sober Countenance, and that quickly too, or you shall know *Ned Blunt* is not—

Belv. Not every Body, we know that.

Blunt. Not an Ass, to be laught at, Sir.

Will. Unconscionable Sinner, to bring a Lover so near his Happiness, a vigorous passionate Lover, and then not only cheat him of his Moveables, but his Desires too.

Belv. Ah, Sir, a Mistress is a Trifle with *Blunt*, he'll have a dozen the next time he looks abroad; his Eyes have Charms not to be resisted: There needs no more than to expose that taking Person to the view of the Fair, and he leads 'em all in Triumph.

Ped. Sir, tho I'm a stranger to you, I'm ashamed at the rudeness of my Nation; and could you learn who did it, would assist you to make an Example of 'em.

Blunt. Why, ay, there's one speaks sense now, and handsomly; and let me tell you Gentlemen, I should not have shew'd my self like a Jack-Pudding, thus to have made you Mirth, but that I have revenge within my power; for know, I have got into my possession a Female, who had better have fallen under any Curse, than the Ruin I design her: 'dsheartlikins, she assaulted me here in my own Lodgings, and had doubtless committed a Rape upon me, had not this Sword defended me.

Fred. I knew not that, but o' my Conscience thou hadst ravisht her, had she not redeem'd her self with a Ring— let's see't, *Blunt.*   [*Blunt shews the Ring.*

Belv. Hah!—the Ring I gave *Florinda* when we exchang'd our Vows!—hark ye, *Blunt*—

[*Goes to whisper to him.*

Will. No whispering, good Colonel, there's a Woman in the case, no whispering.

Belv. Hark ye, Fool, be advis'd, and conceal both the Ring and the Story, for your Reputation's sake ; don't let People know what despis'd Cullies we *English* are : to be cheated and abus'd by one Whore, and another rather bribe thee than be kind to thee, is an Infamy to our Nation.

Will. Come, come, where's the Wench ? we'll see her, let her be what she will, we'll see her.

Ped. Ay, ay, let us see her, I can soon discover whether she be of Quality, or for your Diversion.

Blunt. She's in *Fred's* Custody.

Will. Come, come, the Key.

       [*To* Fred. *who gives him the Key, they are going.*

Belv. Death ! what shall I do ?—stay, Gentlemen—yet if I hinder 'em, I shall discover all—hold, let's go one at once—give me the Key.

Will. Nay, hold there, Colonel, I'll go first.

Fred. Nay, no Dispute, *Ned* and I have the property of her.

Will. Damn Property—then we'll draw Cuts.

       [Belv. *goes to whisper* Will.

Nay, no Corruption, good Colonel : come, the longest Sword carries her.—   [*They all draw, forgetting Don* Pedro, *being a* Spaniard, *had the longest.*

Blunt. I yield up my Interest to you Gentlemen, and that will be Revenge sufficient.

Will. The Wench is yours—(*To* Ped.) Pox of his *Toledo*, I had forgot that.

Fred. Come, Sir, I'll conduct you to the Lady.

       [*Ex.* Fred. *and* Ped.

Belv. To hinder him will certainly discover—[*Aside.*] Dost know, dull Beast, what Mischief thou hast done ?

      [Will. *walking up and down out of Humour.*

Will. Ay, ay, to trust our Fortune to Lots, a Devil on't, 'twas madness, that's the Truth on't.

Belv. Oh intolerable Sot !

Enter Florinda, *running masqu'd,* Pedro *after her,* Will. *gazing round her.*

Flor. Good Heaven, defend me from discovery. [*Aside.*

Pedro. 'Tis but in vain to fly me, you are fallen to my Lot.

Belv. Sure she is undiscover'd yet, but now I fear there is no way to bring her off.

Will. Why, what a Pox is not this my Woman, the same I follow'd but now ?

   [Ped. *talking to* Florinda, *who walks up and down.*

Ped. As if I did not know ye, and your Business here.

Flor. Good Heaven ! I fear he does indeed— [*Aside.*

Ped. Come, pray be kind, I know you meant to be so when you enter'd here, for these are proper Gentlemen.

Will. But, Sir—perhaps the Lady will not be impos'd upon, she'll chuse her Man.

Ped. I am better bred, than not to leave her Choice free.

Enter Valeria, *and is surpriz'd at the Sight of Don* Pedro.

Val. Don *Pedro* here ! there's no avoiding him. [*Aside.*

Flor. Valeria ! then I'm undone—   [*Aside.*

Val. Oh ! have I found you, Sir—

      [*To* Pedro, *running to him.*
—The strangest Accident—if I had breath—to tell it.

Ped. Speak—is *Florinda* safe ? *Hellena* well?

Val. Ay, ay, Sir—*Florinda*—is safe—from any fears of you.

Ped. Why, where's *Florinda* ?—speak.

Val. Ay, where indeed, Sir ? I wish I could inform you, —But to hold you no longer in doubt—

Flor. Oh, what will she say !   [*Aside.*

Val. She's fled away in the Habit of one of her Pages, Sir—but *Callis* thinks you may retrieve her yet, if you make haste away ; she'll tell you, Sir, the rest—if you can find her out.   [*Aside.*

Ped. Dishonourable Girl, she has undone my Aim—
Sir—you see my necessity of leaving you, and I hope you'll
pardon it : my Sister, I know, will make her flight to you ;
and if she do, I shall expect she should be render'd back.

Belv. I shall consult my Love and Honour, Sir.

[*Ex.* Ped.

Flor. My dear Preserver, let me imbrace thee. [*To* Val.

Will. What the Devil's all this ?

Blunt. Mystery by this Light.

Val. Come, come, make haste and get your selves
married quickly, for your Brother will return again.

Belv. I am so surpriz'd with Fears and Joys, so amaz'd
to find you here in safety, I can scarce persuade my Heart
into a Faith of what I see—

Will. Harkye, Colonel, is this that Mistress who has cost
you so many Sighs, and me so many Quarrels with you ?

Belv. It is—Pray give him the Honour of your Hand.

[*To* Flor.

Will. Thus it must be receiv'd then.

[*Kneels and kisses her Hand.*

And with it give your Pardon too.

Flor. The Friend to *Belvile* may command me anything.

Will. Death, wou'd I might, 'tis a surprizing Beauty.

[*Aside.*

Belv. Boy, run and fetch a Father instantly. [*Ex.* Boy.

Fred. So, now do I stand like a Dog, and have not a
Syllable to plead my own Cause with : by this Hand,
Madam, I was never thorowly confounded before, nor
shall I ever more dare look up with Confidence, till you
are pleased to pardon me.

Flor. Sir, I'll be reconcil'd to you on one Condition,
that you'll follow the Example of your Friend, in marrying
a Maid that does not hate you, and whose Fortune (I
believe) will not be unwelcome to you.

Fred. Madam, had I no Inclinations that way, I shou'd
obey your kind Commands.

Belv. Who, *Fred.* marry; he has so few Inclinations for Womankind, that had he been possest of Paradise, he might have continu'd there to this Day, if no Crime but Love cou'd have disinherited him.

Fred. Oh, I do not use to boast of my Intrigues.

Belv. Boast! why thou do'st nothing but boast; and I dare swear, wer't thou as innocent from the Sin of the Grape, as thou art from the Apple, thou might'st yet claim that right in *Eden* which our first Parents lost by too much loving.

Fred. I wish this Lady would think me so modest a Man.

Val. She shou'd be sorry then, and not like you half so well, and I shou'd be loth to break my Word with you; which was, That if your Friend and mine are agreed, it shou'd be a Match between you and I.

[She gives him her Hand.

Fred. Bear witness, Colonel, 'tis a Bargain.

[Kisses her Hand.

Blunt. I have a Pardon to beg too; but adsheartlikins I am so out of Countenance, that I am a Dog if I can say any thing to purpose.   [*To* Florinda.

Flor. Sir, I heartily forgive you all.

Blunt. That's nobly said, sweet Lady—*Belvile*, prithee present her her Ring again, for I find I have not Courage to approach her my self.

[Gives him the Ring, he gives it to Florinda.

Enter Boy.

Boy. Sir, I have brought the Father that you sent for.

Belv. 'Tis well, and now my dear *Florinda*, let's fly to compleat that mighty Joy we have so long wish'd and sigh'd for.—Come, *Fred.* you'll follow?

Fred. Your Example, Sir, 'twas ever my Ambition in War, and must be so in Love.

Will. And must not I see this juggling Knot ty'd?

Belv. No, thou shalt do us better Service, and be our

Guard, lest Don *Pedro's* sudden Return interrupt the Ceremony.

Will. Content; I'll secure this Pass.

       [*Ex.* Bel. Flor. Fred. *and* Val.

      Enter Boy.

Boy. Sir, there's a Lady without wou'd speak to you.
            [*To* Will.

Will. Conduct her in, I dare not quit my Post.

Boy. And, Sir, your Taylor waits you in your Chamber.

Blunt. Some comfort yet, I shall not dance naked at the Wedding.   [*Ex.* Blunt *and* Boy.

Enter again the Boy, *conducting in* Angelica *in a masquing Habit and a Vizard,* Will. *runs to her.*

Will. This can be none but my pretty Gipsy—Oh, I see you can follow as well as fly—Come, confess thy self the most malicious Devil in Nature, you think you have done my Bus'ness with *Angelica*—

Ang. Stand off, base Villain— [*She draws a Pistol
           and holds to his Breast.*

Will. Hah, 'tis not she : who art thou? and what's thy Business?

Ang. One thou hast injur'd, and who comes to kill thee for't.

Will. What the Devil canst thou mean?

Ang. By all my Hopes to kill thee—
     [*Holds still the Pistol to his Breast, he
      going back, she following still.*

Will. Prithee on what Acquaintance? for I know thee not.

Ang. Behold this Face !—so lost to thy Remembrance ! And then call all thy Sins about thy Soul, [*Pulls off her
And let them die with thee.   Vizard.*

Will. Angelica !

Ang. Yes, Traitor.

Does not thy guilty Blood run shivering thro thy Veins?

Hast thou no Horrour at this Sight, that tells thee,
Thou hast not long to boast thy shameful Conquest?

Will. Faith, no Child, my Blood keeps its old Ebbs and
Flows still, and that usual Heat too, that cou'd oblige thee
with a Kindness, had I but opportunity.

Ang. Devil! dost wanton with my Pain—have at thy
Heart.

Will. Hold, dear Virago! hold thy Hand a little,
I am not now at leisure to be kill'd—hold and hear me—
Death, I think she's in earnest.　　　　　　　*[Aside.*

Ang. Oh if I take not heed,
My coward Heart will leave me to his Mercy.
　　　　　　　　　　　　[Aside, turning from him.
—What have you, Sir, to say?—but should I hear thee,
Thoud'st talk away all that is brave about me:
　　　　　　[Follows him with the Pistol to his Breast.
And I have vow'd thy Death, by all that's sacred.

Will. Why, then there's an end of a proper handsom
Fellow, that might have liv'd to have done good Service
yet:—That's all I can say to't.

Ang. Yet—I wou'd give thee—time for Penitence.
　　　　　　　　　　　　　　　　　[Pausingly.

Will. Faith, Child, I thank God, I have ever took care
to lead a good, sober, hopeful Life, and am of a Religion
that teaches me to believe, I shall depart in Peace.

Ang. So will the Devil: tell me
How many poor believing Fools thou hast undone;
How many Hearts thou hast betray'd to ruin!
—Yet these are little Mischiefs to the Ills
Thou'st taught mine to commit: thou'st taught it Love.

Will. Egad, 'twas shreudly hurt the while.

Ang. —Love, that has robb'd it of its Unconcern,
Of all that Pride that taught me how to value it,
And in its room a mean submissive Passion was convey'd,
That made me humbly bow, which I ne'er did
To any thing but Heaven.

—Thou, perjur'd Man, didst this, and with thy Oaths,
Which on thy Knees thou didst devoutly make,
Soften'd my yielding Heart—And then, I was a Slave—
Yet still had been content to've worn my Chains,
Worn 'em with Vanity and Joy for ever,
Hadst thou not broke those Vows that put them on.
—'Twas then I was undone.

[*All this while follows him with a Pistol to his Breast.*

Will. Broke my Vows! why, where hast thou lived?
Amongst the Gods! For I never heard of mortal Man,
That has not broke a thousand Vows.

Ang. Oh, Impudence!

Will. Angelica! that Beauty has been too long tempting,
Not to have made a thousand Lovers languish,
Who in the amorous Favour, no doubt have sworn
Like me; did they all die in that Faith? still adoring?
I do not think they did.

Ang. No, faithless Man: had I repaid their Vows, as
I did thine, I wou'd have kill'd the ungrateful that had
abandon'd me.

Will. This old General has quite spoil'd thee, nothing
makes a Woman so vain, as being flatter'd; your old Lover
ever supplies the Defects of Age, with intolerable Dotage,
vast Charge, and that which you call Constancy; and
attributing all this to your own Merits, you domineer, and
throw your Favours in's Teeth, upbraiding him still with
the Defects of Age, and cuckold him as often as he deceives
your Expectations. But the gay, young, brisk Lover, that
brings his equal Fires, and can give you Dart for Dart,
he'll be as nice as you sometimes.

Ang. All this thou'st made me know, for which I hate
      thee.
Had I remain'd in innocent Security,
I shou'd have thought all Men were born my Slaves;
And worn my Pow'r like Lightning in my Eyes,
To have destroy'd at Pleasure when offended.

—But when Love held the Mirror, the undeceiving Glass
Reflected all the Weakness of my Soul, and made me know,
My richest Treasure being lost, my Honour,
All the remaining Spoil cou'd not be worth
The Conqueror's Care or Value.
——Oh how I fell like a long worship'd Idol,
Discovering all the Cheat!
Wou'd not the Incense and rich Sacrifice,
Which blind Devotion offer'd at my Altars,
Have fall'n to thee?
Why woud'st thou then destroy my fancy'd Power?
   Will. By Heaven thou art brave, and I admire thee
     strangely.
I wish I were that dull, that constant thing,
Which thou woud'st have, and Nature never meant me:
I must, like chearful Birds, sing in all Groves,
And perch on every Bough,
Billing the next kind She that flies to meet me;
Yet after all cou'd build my Nest with thee,
Thither repairing when I'd lov'd my round,
And still reserve a tributary Flame.
—To gain your Credit, I'll pay you back your Charity,
And be oblig'd for nothing but for Love.
                 [Offers her a Purse of Gold.
   Ang. Oh that thou wert in earnest!
So mean a Thought of me,
Wou'd turn my Rage to Scorn, and I shou'd pity thee,
And give thee leave to live;
Which for the publick Safety of our Sex,
And my own private Injuries, I dare not do.
Prepare—   *[Follows still, as before.*
—I will no more be tempted with Replies.
   Will. Sure—
   Ang. Another Word will damn thee! I've heard thee
     talk too long.   *[She follows him with a Pistol ready*
                   to shoot: he retires still amaz'd.

Enter Don Antonio, *his Arm in a Scarf, and lays hold
on the Pistol.*

Ant. Hah! *Angelica!*

Ang. Antonio! What Devil brought thee hither?

Ant. Love and Curiosity, seeing your Coach at Door.
Let me disarm you of this unbecoming Instrument of
Death.—   [*Takes away the Pistol.*
Amongst the Number of your Slaves, was there not one
worthy the Honour to have fought your Quarrel?
—Who are you, Sir, that are so very wretched
To merit Death from her?

Will. One, Sir, that cou'd have made a better End of
an amorous Quarrel without you, than with you.

Ant. Sure 'tis some Rival—hah—the very Man took
down her Picture yesterday—the very same that set on me
last night—Blest opportunity—   [*Offers to shoot him.*

Ang. Hold, you're mistaken, Sir.

Ant. By Heaven the very same!
—Sir, what pretensions have you to this Lady?

Will. Sir, I don't use to be examin'd, and am ill at all
Disputes but this—   [*Draws,* Anton. *offers to shoot.*

Ang. Oh, hold! you see he's arm'd with certain Death :
[*To* Will.

—And you, *Antonio,* I command you hold,
By all the Passion you've so lately vow'd me.

Enter Don Pedro, *sees* Antonio, *and stays.*

Ped. Hah, *Antonio!* and *Angelica!*   [*Aside.*

Ant. When I refuse Obedience to your Will,
May you destroy me with your mortal Hate.
By all that's Holy I adore you so,
That even my Rival, who has Charms enough
To make him fall a Victim to my Jealousy,
Shall live, nay, and have leave to love on still.

Ped. What's this I hear?   [*Aside.*

Ang. Ah thus, 'twas thus he talk'd, and I believ'd.
[*Pointing to* Will.

—*Antonio*, yesterday,
I'd not have sold my Interest in his Heart,
For all the Sword has won and lost in Battle.
—But now to show my utmost of Contempt,
I give thee Life—which if thou would'st preserve,
Live where my Eyes may never see thee more,
Live to undo some one, whose Soul may prove
So bravely constant to revenge my Love.

> [*Goes out*, Ant. *follows, but* Ped. *pulls him back.*

Ped. Antonio—stay.

Ant. Don *Pedro*—

Ped. What Coward Fear was that prevented thee
From meeting me this Morning on the *Molo*?

Ant. Meet thee?

Ped. Yes me; I was the Man that dar'd thee to't.

Ant. Hast thou so often seen me fight in War,
To find no better Cause to excuse my Absence?
—I sent my Sword and one to do thee Right,
Finding my self uncapable to use a Sword.

Ped. But 'twas *Florinda's* Quarrel that we fought,
And you to shew how little you esteem'd her,
Sent me your Rival, giving him your Interest.
—But I have found the Cause of this Affront,
But when I meet you fit for the Dispute,
—I'll tell you my Resentment.

Ant. I shall be ready, Sir, e'er long to do you Reason.

> [*Exit* Ant.

Ped. If I cou'd find *Florinda*, now whilst my Anger's
high, I think I shou'd be kind, and give her to *Belvile* in
Revenge.

Will. Faith, Sir, I know not what you wou'd do, but
I believe the Priest within has been so kind.

Ped. How! my Sister married?

Will. I hope by this time she is, and bedded too, or he
has not my longings about him.

Ped. Dares he do thus? Does he not fear my Pow'r?

Will. Faith not at all. If you will go in, and thank him for the Favour he has done your Sister, so ; if not, Sir, my Power's greater in this House than yours ; I have a damn'd surly Crew here, that will keep you till the next Tide, and then clap you an board my Prize ; my Ship lies but a League off the *Molo*, and we shall show your Donship a damn'd *Tramontana* Rover's Trick.

Enter Belvile.

Belv. This Rogue's in some new Mischief—hah, *Pedro* return'd !

Ped. Colonel *Belvile*, I hear you have married my Sister.

Belv. You have heard truth then, Sir.

Ped. Have I so ? then, Sir, I wish you Joy.

Belv. How !

Ped. By this Embrace I do, and I glad on't.

Belv. Are you in earnest ?

Ped. By our long Friendship and my Obligations to thee, I am. The sudden Change I'll give you Reasons for anon. Come lead me into my Sister, that she may know I now approve her Choice.   [*Exit* Bel. *with* Ped.

          [Will. *goes to follow them. Enter* Hellena *as before in Boy's Clothes, and pulls him back.*

Will. Ha ! my Gipsy—Now a thousand Blessings on thee for this Kindness. Egad, Child, I was e'en in despair of ever seeing thee again ; my Friends are all provided for within, each Man his kind Woman.

Hell. Hah ! I thought they had serv'd me some such Trick.

Will. And I was e'en resolv'd to go aboard, condemn my self to my lone Cabin, and the Thoughts of thee.

Hell. And cou'd you have left me behind ? wou'd you have been so ill-natur'd ?

Will. Why, 'twou'd have broke my Heart, Child—but since we are met again, I defy foul Weather to part us.

Hell. And wou'd you be a faithful Friend now, if a Maid shou'd trust you ?

Will. For a Friend I cannot promise, thou art of a Form so excellent, a Face and Humour too good for cold dull Friendship; I am parlously afraid of being in love, Child, and you have not forgot how severely you have us'd me.

Hell. That's all one, such Usage you must still look for, to find out all your Haunts, to rail at you to all that love you, till I have made you love only me in your own Defence, because no body else will love.

Will. But hast thou no better Quality to recommend thy self by?

Hell. Faith none, Captain—Why, 'twill be the greater Charity to take me for thy Mistress, I am a lone Child, a kind of Orphan Lover; and why I shou'd die a Maid, and in a Captain's Hands too, I do not understand.

Will. Egad, I was never claw'd away with Broad-Sides from any Female before, thou hast one Virtue I adore, good-Nature; I hate a coy demure Mistress, she's as troublesom as a Colt, I'll break none; no, give me a mad Mistress when mew'd, and in flying on[e] I dare trust upon the Wing, that whilst she's kind will come to the Lure.

Hell. Nay, as kind as you will, good Captain, whilst it lasts, but let's lose no time.

Will. My time's as precious to me, as thine can be; therefore, dear Creature, since we are so well agreed, let's retire to my Chamber, and if ever thou were treated with such savory Love—Come—My Bed's prepar'd for such a Guest, all clean and sweet as thy fair self; I love to steal a Dish and a Bottle with a Friend, and hate long Graces—Come, let's retire and fall to.

Hell. 'Tis but getting my Consent, and the Business is soon done; let but old Gaffer *Hymen* and his Priest say Amen to't, and I dare lay my Mother's Daughter by as proper a Fellow as your Father's Son, without fear or blushing.

Will. Hold, hold, no Bugg Words, Child, Priest and *Hymen*: prithee add Hangman to 'em to make up the onsort—No, no, we'll have no Vows but Love, Child, nor Witness but the Lover; the kind Diety injoins naught but love and enjoy. *Hymen* and *Priest* wait still upon Portion, and Joynture; Love and Beauty have their own Ceremonies. Marriage is as certain a Bane to Love, as lending Money is to Friendship: I'll neither ask nor give a Vow, tho I could be content to turn Gipsy, and become a Left-hand Bridegroom, to have the Pleasure of working that great Miracle of making a Maid a Mother, if you durst venture; 'tis upse Gipsy that, and if I miss, I'll lose my Labour.

Hell. And if you do not lose, what shall I get? A Cradle full of Noise and Mischief, with a Pack of Repentance at my Back? Can you teach me to weave Incle to pass my time with? 'Tis upse Gipsy that too.

Will. I can teach thee to weave a true Love's Knot better.

Hell. So can my Dog.

Will. Well, I see we are both upon our Guard, and I see there's no way to conquer good Nature, but by yielding —here—give me thy Hand—one Kiss and I am thine—

Hell. One Kiss! How like my Page he speaks; I am resolv'd you shall have none, for asking such a sneaking Sum—He that will be satisfied with one Kiss, will never die of that Longing; good Friend single-Kiss, is all your talking come to this? A Kiss, a Caudle! farewel, Captain single-Kiss.   [*Going out he stays her*.

Will. Nay, if we part so, let me die like a Bird upon a Bough, at the Sheriff's Charge. By Heaven, both the *Indies* shall not buy thee from me. I adore thy Humour and will marry thee, and we are so of one Humour, it must be a Bargain—give me thy Hand—   [*Kisses her hand*. And now let the blind ones (Love and Fortune) do their worst.

Hell. Why, God-a-mercy, Captain!

Will. But harkye—The Bargain is now made; but is it not fit we should know each other's Names? That when

we have Reason to curse one another hereafter, and People
ask me who 'tis I give to the Devil, I may at least be able
to tell what Family you came of.

Hell. Good reason, Captain; and where I have cause,
(as I doubt not but I shall have plentiful) that I may know at
whom to throw my—Blessings—I beseech ye your Name.

Will. I am call'd *Robert the Constant.*

Hell. A very fine Name! pray was it your Faulkner or
Butler that christen'd you? Do they not use to whistle
when then call you?

Will. I hope you have a better, that a Man may name
without crossing himself, you are so merry with mine.

Hell. I am call'd *Hellena the Inconstant.*

Enter Pedro, Belvile, Florinda, Fred. Valeria.

Ped. Hah! *Hellena!*

Flor. *Hellena!*

Hell. The very same—hah my Brother! now, Captain,
shew your Love and Courage; stand to your Arms, and
defend me bravely, or I am lost for ever.

Ped. What's this I hear? false Girl, how came you
hither, and what's your Business? Speak.

[*Goes roughly to her.*

Will. Hold off, Sir, you have leave to parly only.

[*Puts himself between.*

Hell. I had e'en as good tell it, as you guess it. Faith,
Brother, my Business is the same with all living Creatures
of my Age, to love, and be loved, and here's the Man.

Ped. Perfidious Maid, hast thou deceiv'd me too, deceiv'd
thy self and Heaven?

Hell. 'Tis time enough to make my Peace with that:
Be you but kind, let me alone with Heaven.

Ped. *Belvile*, I did not expect this false Play from you;
was't not enough you'd gain *Florinda* (which I pardon'd)
but your leud Friends too must be inrich'd with the Spoils
of a noble Family?

Belv. Faith, Sir, I am as much surpriz'd at this as you can be : Yet, Sir, my Friends are Gentlemen, and ought to be esteem'd for their Misfortunes, since they have the Glory to suffer with the best of Men and Kings; 'tis true, he's a Rover of Fortune, yet a Prince aboard his little wooden World.

Ped. What's this to the maintenance of a Woman or her Birth and Quality?

Will. Faith, Sir, I can boast of nothing but a Sword which does me Right where-e'er I come, and has defended a worse Cause than a Woman's : and since I lov'd her before I either knew her Birth or Name, I must pursue my Resolution, and marry her.

Ped. And is all your holy Intent of becoming a Nun debauch'd into a Desire of Man?

Hell. Why—I have consider'd the matter, Brother, and find the Three hundred thousand Crowns my Uncle left me (and you cannot keep from me) will be better laid out in Love than in Religion, and turn to as good an Account —let most Voices carry it, for Heaven or the Captain?

All cry, a Captain, a Captain.

Hell. Look ye, Sir, 'tis a clear Case.

Ped. Oh I am mad—if I refuse, my Life's in Danger—
　　　　　　　　　　　　　　　　　　　　[*Aside.*

—Come—There's one motive induces me—take her—I shall now be free from the fear of her Honour ; guard it you now, if you can, I have been a Slave to't long enough.
　　　　　　　　　　　　　　　　　　[*Gives her to him.*

Will. Faith, Sir, I am of a Nation, that are of opinion a Woman's Honour is not worth guarding when she has a mind to part with it.

Hell. Well said, Captain.

Ped. This was your Plot, Mistress, but I hope you have married one that will revenge my Quarrel to you—
　　　　　　　　　　　　　　　　　　　　[*To Valeria.*

Val. There's no altering Destiny, Sir.

Ped. Sooner than a Woman's Will, therefore I forgive you all—and wish you may get my Father's Pardon as easily; which I fear.

Enter Blunt *drest in a* Spanish *Habit, looking very ridiculously; his Man adjusting his Band.*

Man. 'Tis very well, Sir.

Blunt. Well, Sir, 'dsheartlikins I tell you 'tis damnable ill, Sir—a Spanish Habit, good Lord! cou'd the Devil and my Taylor devise no other Punishment for me, but the Mode of a Nation I abominate?

Belv. What's the matter, *Ned*?

Blunt. Pray view me round, and judge—[*Turns round.*

Belv. I must confess thou art a kind of an odd Figure.

Blunt. In a Spanish Habit with a Vengeance! I had rather be in the Inquisition for Judaism, than in this Doublet and Breeches; a Pillory were an easy Collar to this, three Handfuls high; and these Shoes too are worse than the Stocks, with the Sole an Inch shorter than my Foot: In fine, Gentlemen, methinks I look altogether like a Bag of Bays stuff'd full of Fools Flesh.

Belv. Methinks 'tis well, and makes thee look *en Cavalier*: Come, Sir, settle your Face, and salute our Friends, Lady—

Blunt. Hah! Say'st thou so, my little Rover? [*To* Hell. Lady—(if you be one) give me leave to kiss your Hand, and tell you, adsheartlikins, for all I look so, I am your humble Servant—A Pox of my *Spanish* Habit.

Will. Hark—what's this?   [*Musick is heard to Play.*

Enter Boy.

Boy. Sir, as the Custom is, the gay People in Masquerade, who make every Man's House their own, are coming up.

Enter several Men and Women in masquing Habits, with Musick, they put themselves in order and dance.

Blunt. Adsheartlikins, wou'd 'twere lawful to pull off their false Faces, that I might see if my Doxy were not amongst 'em.

Belv. Ladies and Gentlemen, since you are come so *a propos*, you must take a small Collation with us.

[*To the Masquers.*

Will. Whilst we'll to the Good Man within, who stays to give us a Cast of his Office.   [*To* Hell.

—Have you no trembling at the near approach?

Hell. No more than you have in an Engagement or a Tempest.

Will. Egad, thou'rt a brave Girl, and I admire thy Love and Courage.

Lead on, no other Dangers they can dread,
Who venture in the Storms o'th' Marriage-Bed.

[*Exeunt.*

EPILOGUE.

THE banisht Cavaliers! a Roving Blade!
A popish Carnival! a Masquerade!
The Devil's in't if this will please the Nation,
In these our blessed Times of Reformation,
When Conventicling is so much in Fashion.
And yet—
That mutinous Tribe less Factions do beget,
Than your continual differing in Wit;
Your Judgment's (as your Passions) a Disease:
Nor Muse nor Miss your Appetite can please;
You're grown as nice as queasy Consciences,
Whose each Convulsion, when the Spirit moves,
Damns every thing that Maggot disapproves.

With canting Rule you wou'd the Stage refine,
And to dull Method all our Sense confine.
With th' Insolence of Common-wealths you rule,
Where each gay Fop, and politick brave Fool
On Monarch Wit impose without controul.
As for the last who seldom sees a Play,
Unless it be the old Black-Fryers way,

Shaking his empty Noddle o'er Bamboo,
He crys—Good Faith, these Plays will never do.
—Ah, Sir, in my young days, what lofty Wit,
What high-strain'd Scenes of Fighting there were writ:
These are slight airy Toys.   But tell me, pray,
What has the House of Commons *done to day?*
Then shews his Politicks, to let you see
Of State Affairs he'll judge as notably,
As he can do of Wit and Poetry.

  The younger Sparks, who hither do resort,
Cry—
Pox o' your gentle things, give us more Sport;
—Damn me, I'm sure 'twill never please the Court.

  Such Fops are never pleas'd, unless the Play
Be stuff'd with Fools, as brisk and dull as they:
Such might the Half-Crown spare, and in a Glass
At home behold a more accomplisht Ass,
Where they may set their Cravats, Wigs and Faces,
And practice all their Buffoonry Grimaces;
See how this—Huff becomes—this Dammy—flare—
Which they at home may act, because they dare,
But—must with prudent Caution do elsewhere.
Oh that our Nokes, *or* Tony Lee *could show*
A Fop but half so much to th' Life as you.

POST-SCRIPT.

THIS Play had been sooner in Print, but for a Report about the Town (made by some either very Malitious or very Ignorant) that 'twas Thomaso *alter'd; which made the Book-sellers fear some trouble from the Proprietor of that Admirable Play, which indeed has Wit enough to stock a Poet, and is not to be piec't or mended by any but the Excellent Author himself; That I have stol'n some hints from it may be a proof, that I valu'd it more than to pretend to alter it: had I had the Dexterity of some Poets who are not more expert in stealing than in the Art of Concealing, and who even that way out-do the* Spartan-Boyes *I might have appropriated all to myself, but I, vainly proud of my Judgment hang out the Sign of* ANGELICA *(the only Stol'n Object) to give Notice where a great part of the Wit dwelt; though if the Play of the* Novella *were as well worth remembring as* Thomaso, *they might (bating the Name) have as well said, I took it from thence: I will only say the Plot and Bus'ness (not to boast on't) is my own: as for the Words and Characters, I leave the Reader to judge and compare 'em with* Thomaso, *to whom I recommend the great Entertainment of reading it, tho' had this succeeded ill, I shou'd have had no need of imploring that Justice from the Critics, who are naturally so kind to any that pretend to usurp their Dominion, they wou'd doubtless have given me the whole Honour on't. Therefore I will only say in* English *what the famous* Virgil *does in* Latin: *I make Verses and others have the Fame.*

THE WIDOW RANTER.

THE WIDOW RANTER:

Or, the History of Bacon in *Virginia*.

PROLOGUE,

By Mr. *Dryden*.

HEAVEN save ye, Gallants; and this hopeful Age,
Y' are welcome to the downfal of the Stage:
The Fools have labour'd long in their Vocation;
And Vice (the Manufacture of the Nation)
O'er-stocks the Town so much, and thrives so well,
That Fops and Knaves grow Drugs, and will not sell.
In vain our Wares on Theaters are shown,
When each has a Plantation of his own.
His Cruse ne'er fails; for whatsoe'er he spends,
There's still God's plenty for himself and Friends.
Shou'd Men be rated by Poetick Rules,
Lord, what a Poll would there be rais'd from Fools!
Mean time poor Wit prohibited must lie,
As if 'twere made some French Commodity.
Fools you will have, and rais'd at vast expence;
And yet as soon as seen, they give offence.
Time was, when none would cry that Oaf was me,
But now you strive about your Pedigree:
Bauble and Cap no sooner are thrown down,
But there's a Muss of more than half the Town.
Each one will challenge a Child's part at least,
A sign the Family is well increas'd.
Of Foreign Cattle there's no longer need,
When we're supply'd so fast with English Breed,

Well! Flourish, Countrymen; drink, swear and roar,
Let every free-born Subject keep his Whore;
And wandring in the Wilderness about,
At end of Forty Years not wear her out.
But when you see these Pictures, let none dare
To own beyond a Limb or single share:
For where the Punk is common, he's a Sot,
Who needs will father what the Parish got.

DRAMATIS PERSONÆ.

MEN.

Indian King called *Cavernio*,   Mr. *Bowman.*

Bacon, General of the *English*,   Mr. *Williams.*

Colonel *Wellman*, Deputy Governor,   Mr. *Freeman.*

Col. *Downright*, a loyal honest Colonel, Mr. *Harris.*

Hazard, } Two Friends known to one another { Mr. *Alexander,*
Friendly, }   many Years in *England,*   { Mr. *Powell.*

Daring, }   { Mr. *Sandford,*
Fearless, } Lieutenant Generals to *Bacon,* { Mr. *Cudworth.*

Dullman, a Captain,   Mr. *Bright.*

Timorous Cornet, }   { Mr. *Underbill,*
Whimsey, } Justices of the Peace, and very { Mr. *Trefuse,*
Whiff, }   great Cowards,   { Mr. *Bowen,*
Boozer, }   { Mr. *Barns.*

Brag, a Captain.

Grubb, { One complain'd of by Capt. *Whiff*, for
       { calling his Wife Whore.

A Petitioner against *Brag*,   Mr. *Blunt.*

Parson *Dunce*, formerly a Farrier, fled from } Mr. *Baker.*
  England, and Chaplain to the Governour, }

Jeffery, Coachman to *Widow Ranter.*

Cavaro, an *Indian*, Confidant to the *Indian King.*

Jack, a Sea-Boy.

Clerk; Boy; An Officer; Messenger; Seaman; 2nd Seaman;
             A Highlander.

WOMEN.

Indian Queen, call'd *Semernia*, belov'd by *Bacon*, Mrs. *Bracegirdle.*

Madam *Surelove*, belov'd by *Hazard*,   Mrs. *Knight.*

Mrs. *Chrisante*, Daughter to Colonel *Downright*, Mrs. *Jordon.*

Widow Ranter, in love with *Daring*,   Mrs. *Currer.*

Mrs. *Flirt*, a Tapstress,   Mrs. *Cory.*

Mrs. *Whimsey.*

Mrs. *Whiff.*

Jenny, Maid to *Widow Ranter.*

Nell, Maid at the Inn.

Anaria, Confidante to the *Indian Queen.*

Maid to Madam *Surelove.*

Priests, Indians, Bailiffs, Soldiers, Rabble, Negroes, with
other Attendants.

SCENE, *Virginia :* in *Bacon's* Camp, *James-Town* and the surrounding Country.

ACT I.

Scene I. *A Room with several Tables.*

Enter Hazard *in a travelling Habit, and* Jack, *a Sea-Boy, carrying his Portmantle.*

Haz. What Town's this, Boy?

Boy. James-Town, Master.

Haz. Take care my Trunk be brought ashore to night, and there's for your Pains.

Boy. God bless you, Master.

Haz. What do you call this House?

Boy. Mrs. *Flirt's*, Master, the best House for Commendation in all *Virginia*.

Haz. That's well, has she any handsome Ladies, Sirrah?

Boy. Oh! she's woundy handsome her self, Master, and the kindest Gentlewoman—look, here she comes, Master.—

Enter Flirt *and* Nell.

God bless you, Mistress, I have brought you a young Gentleman here.

Flirt. That's well, honest *Jack*.—Sir, you are most heartily welcome.

Haz. Madam, your Servant.   [*Salutes her.*

Flirt. Please you walk into a Chamber, Sir?

Haz. By and by, Madam; but I'll repose here awhile for the coolness of the Air.

Flirt. This is a Publick Room, Sir, but 'tis at your service.

Haz. Madam, you oblige me.

Flirt. A fine spoken Person. A Gentleman, I'll warrant him: come, *Jack*, I'll give thee a Cogue of Brandy for old acquaintance.   [*Exeunt Landlady and Boy.*

[*Hazard pulls out Pen, Ink and Paper, and goes to write.*

Enter Friendly.

Friend. Here, *Nell*, a Tankard of cool Drink, quickly.

Nell. You shall have it, Sir.

Friend. Hah! who's that Stranger? he seems to be a Gentleman.

Haz. If I should give credit to mine Eyes, that should be *Friendly*.

Friend. Sir, you seem a Stranger; may I take the liberty to present my Service to you?   [*Exit* Nell.

Haz. If I am not mistaken, Sir, you are the only Man in the World whom I would soonest pledge; you'll credit me, if three Year's absence has not made you forget *Hazard*.

Friend. *Hazard*, my Friend! come to my Arms and Heart.

Haz. This unexpected Happiness o'erjoys me. Who could have imagin'd to have found thee in *Virginia*? I thought thou hadst been in *Spain* with thy Brother.

Friend. I was so till ten Months since, when my Uncle Colonel *Friendly* dying here, left me a considerable Plantation; and, faith, I find Diversions not altogether to be despis'd; the God of Love reigns here with as much power as in Courts or popular Cities. But prithee what Chance (fortunate to me) drove thee to this part of the new World.

Haz. Why, faith, ill Company, and that common Vice of the Town, Gaming, soon run out my younger Brother's Fortune: for imagining, like some of the luckier Gamesters, to improve my Stock at the Groom Porter's, I ventur'd on, and lost all. My elder Brother, an errant Jew, had neither Friendship nor Honour enough to support me; but at last being mollified by Persuasions, and the hopes of being for ever rid of me, sent me hither with a small Cargo to seek my Fortune—

Friend. And begin the World withal.

Haz. I thought this a better Venture than to turn sharping Bully, Cully in Prentices and Country Squires, with my Pocket full of false Dice, your high and low Flats and

Bars; or turn Broker to young Heirs; take up Goods to pay tenfold at the Death of their Fathers, and take Fees on both sides; or set up all night at the Groom-Porter's, begging his Honour to go a Guinea the better of the lay. No, *Friendly*, I had rather starve abroad, than live pity'd and despis'd at home.

Friend. Thou art in the right, and art come just in the nick of time to make thy Fortune.——Wilt thou follow my Advice?

Haz. Thou art too honest to command any thing that I shall refuse.

Friend. You must know then, there is about a Mile from *James-Town* a young Gentlewoman——no matter for her Birth, her Breeding's the best this World affords, she is married to one of the richest Merchants here; he is old and sick, and now gone into *England* for the recovery of his Health, where he'll e'en give up the Ghost: he has writ her word he finds no Amendment, and resolves to stay another Year. The letter I accidentally took up, and have about me; 'tis easily counterfeited, and will be of great use to us.

Haz. Now do I fancy I conceive thee.

Friend. Well, hear me first, you shall get another Letter writ like this Character, which shall say, you are his Kinsman, that is come to traffick in this Country, and 'tis his will you should be received into his House as such.

Haz. Well, and what will come of this?

Friend. Why, thou art young and handsome, she young and desiring; 'twere easy to make her love thee; and if the old Gentleman chance to die, you guess the rest, you are no Fool.

Haz. Ay, but if he shou'd return——

Friend. If——Why, if she love you, that other will be but a slender Bar to thy Happiness; for if thou canst not marry her, thou mayst lie with her: and, Gad, a younger Brother may pick out a pretty Livelihood here that way,

as well as in *England*. Or if this fail, thou wilt find a
perpetual Visiter, the Widow *Ranter*, a Woman bought
from the ship by old Colonel *Ranter ;* she served him half
a Year, and then he marry'd her, and dying in a Year
more, left her worth fifty thousand Pounds Sterling, besides
Plate and Jewels: She's a great Gallant, but assuming
the humour of the Country Gentry, her Extravagancy is
very pleasant, she retains something of her primitive
Quality still, but is good-natur'd and generous.

Haz. I like all this well.

Friend. But I have a further End in this matter ; you
must know there is in the same House a young Heiress,
one Colonel *Downright's* Daughter, whom I love, I think
not in vain : her Father indeed has an implacable Hatred
to me, for which reason I can but seldom visit her, and
in this Affair I have need of a Friend in that House.

Haz. Me you're sure of.

Friend. And thus you'll have an opportunity to manage
both our Amours: Here you will find occasion to shew
your Courage, as well as express your Love ; for at this
time the *Indians*, by our ill Management of Trade, whom
we have armed against our selves, very frequently make
War upon us with our own Weapons ; though often
coming by the worst, they are forced to make Peace with
us again, but so, as upon every turn they fall to massacring
us wherever we lie exposed to them.

Haz. I heard the News of this in *England*, which
hastens the new Governour's arrival here, who brings
you fresh Supplies.

Friend. Would he were landed, we hear he is a noble
Gentleman.

Haz. He has all the Qualities of a Gallant Man:
besides, he is nobly born.

Friend. This Country wants nothing but to be peopled
with a well-born Race, to make it one of the best Colonies
in the World ; but for want of a Governour we are ruled

by a Council, some of whom have been perhaps transported Criminals, who having acquired great Estates, are
now become your Honour and Right Worshipful, and
possess all Places of Authority; there are amongst them
some honest Gentlemen, who now begin to take upon
'em, and manage Affairs as they ought to be.

Haz. *Bacon* I think was one of the Council.

Friend. Now you have named a Man indeed above the
common Rank, by Nature generous, brave, resolv'd and
daring; who studying the Lives of the *Romans* and great
Men, that have raised themselves to the most elevated
Fortunes, fancies it easy for ambitious Men to aim at any
pitch of Glory. I've heard him often say, Why cannot I
conquer the Universe as well as *Alexander?* or like another
Romulus, form a new *Rome*, and make my self ador'd?

Haz. Why might he not? Great Souls are born in
common Men sometimes, as well as Princes.

Friend. This Thirst of Glory cherish'd by sullen Melancholy, I believe, was the first motive that made him in
love with the young *Indian* Queen, fancying no Hero
ought to be without his Princess. And this was the reason
why he so earnestly press'd for a Commission, to be made
General against the *Indians*, which long was promis'd him;
but they fearing his Ambition, still put him off, till the
Grievances grew so high, that the whole Country flock'd
to him, and beg'd he would redress them.—He took the
opportunity, and led them forth to fight, and vanquishing
brought the Enemy to fair Terms; but now instead of
receiving him as a Conqueror, we treat him as a Traitor.

Haz. Then it seems all the Crime this brave Fellow
has committed, is serving his Country without Authority.

Friend. 'Tis so, and however I admire the Man, I am
resolv'd to be of the contrary Party, that I may make an
Interest in our new Governor. Thus stand Affairs, so that
after you have seen Madam *Surelove*, I'll present you to
the Council for a Commission.

Haz. But my Kinsman's Character——

Friend. He was a *Leicestershire* younger Brother, came over with a small Fortune, which his Industry has increas'd to a thousand Pounds a year; and he is now Colonel *John Surelove*, and one of the Council.

Haz. Enough.

Friend. About it then, Madam *Flirt* to direct you.

Haz. You are full of your Madams here.

Friend. Oh! 'tis the greatest Affront imaginable to call a Woman Mistress, though but a retail Brandy-monger. Adieu.——One thing more, to morrow is our Country-Court, pray do not fail to be there, for the rarity of the Entertainment: but I shall see you anon at *Surelove's*, where I'll salute thee as my first meeting, and as an old Acquaintance in *England*——here's Company, farewel.

[*Exit* Friend.

Enter Dullman, Timorous *and* Boozer.
Hazard *sits at a Table and writes.*

Dull. Here, *Nell*——Well, Lieutenant *Boozer*, what are you for?

Enter Nell.

Booz. I am for cooling *Nants*, Major.

Dull. Here, *Nell*, a Quart of *Nants*, and some Pipes and Smoke.

Tim. And do ye hear, *Nell*, bid your Mistress come in to joke a little with us; for, adzoors, I was damnable drunk last Night, and I am better at the Petticoat than the Bottle to day.   [*Exit* Nell.

Dull. Drunk last Night, and sick to Day! how comes that about, Mr. Justice? you use to bear your Brandy well enough.

Tim. Ay, your shier Brandy I'll grant you; but I was drunk at Col. *Downright's* with your high Burgundy Claret.

Dull. A Pox of that paulter Liquor, your *English French* Wine, I wonder how the Gentlemen do to drink it.

Tim. Ay, so do I, 'tis for want of a little *Virginia* Breeding : how much more like a Gentleman 'tis, to drink as we do, brave edifying Punch and Brandy.—But they say, the young Noblemen now, and Sparks in *England*, begin to reform, and take it for their Mornings draught, get drunk by Noon, and despise the lousy Juice of the Grape.

Enter Mrs. Flirt, *and* Nell, *with drink, pipes, etc.*

Dull. Come, Landlady, come, you are so taken up with Parson *Dunce*, that your old Friends can't drink a Dram with you.—What, no smutty Catch now, no Gibe or Joke to make the Punch go down merrily, and advance Trading ? Nay, they say, Gad forgive ye, you never miss going to Church when Mr. *Dunce* preaches.—but here's to you.
                                                                    [*Drinks.*

Flirt. Lords, your Honours are pleas'd to be merry— but my service to your Honour.   [*Drinks.*

Haz. Honours ! who the Devil have we here ? some of the wise Council at least, I'd sooner take 'em for Hoggerds.   [*Aside.*

Flirt. Say what you please of the Doctor, but I'll swear he's a fine Gentleman, he makes the prettiest Sonnets, nay, and sings 'em himself to the rarest Tunes.

Tim. Nay, the Man will serve for both Soul and Body ; for they say he was a Farrier in *England*, but breaking, turn'd Life-guard-man, and his Horse dying, he counterfeited a Deputation from the Bishop, and came over here a substantial Orthodox. But come, where stands the Cup? Here, my service to you, Major.

Flirt. Your Honours are pleased,—but methinks Doctor *Dunce* is a very edifying Person, and a Gentleman, and I pretend to know a Gentleman ; for I my self am a Gentlewoman : my Father was a Baronet, but undone in the late Rebellion, and I am fain to keep an Ordinary now, Heaven help me.

Tim. Good lack, why, see how Virtue may be bely'd. We heard your Father was a Taylor, but trusting for old *Oliver's* Funeral broke, and so came hither to hide his Head.—But my service to you; what, you are never the worse?

Flirt. Your Honour knows this is a scandalous place, for they say your Honour was but a broken Excise-Man, who spent the King's Money to buy your Wife fine Petti-coats; and at last not worth a Groat, you came over a poor Servant, though now a Justice of the Peace, and of the Honourable Council.

Tim. Adz zoors, if I knew who 'twas said so, I'd sue him for *Scandalum Magnatum*.

Dull. Hang 'em, Scoundrels, hang 'em, they live upon Scandal, and we are Scandal-proof.—They say too, that I was a Tinker, and running the Country, robb'd a Gentleman's House there, was put into *Newgate*, got a Reprieve after Condemnation, and was transported hither; —and that you, *Boozer*, was a common Pick-pocket, and being often flogg'd at the Carts-tale, afterwards turn'd Evidence, and when the Times grew honest was fain to flie.

Booz. Ay, ay, Major, if Scandal would have broke our Hearts, we had not arriv'd to the Honour of being Privy-Counsellors.—But come, Mrs. *Flirt*, what, never a Song to entertain us?

Flirt. Yes, and a Singer too newly come ashore.

Tim. Adz zoors, let's have it then.

Enter a Girl who sings, they bear the Bob.

Haz. Here, Maid, a Tankard of your Drink.

Flirt. Quickly, *Nell*, wait upon the Gentleman.

Dull. Please you, Sir, to taste of our Liquor.—My service to you. I see you are a Stranger, and alone; please you to come to our Table? [*He rises and comes.*

Flirt. Come, Sir, pray sit down here; these are very honourable Persons, I assure you : This is Major *Dullman*,

Major of his Excellency's own Regiment, when he
arrives; this Mr. *Timorous*, Justice a Peace in *Corum;*
this Captain *Boozer*, all of the honourable Council.

Haz. With your leave, Gentlemen.   [*Sits.*

Tim. My service to you, Sir.   [*Drinks.*
What, have you brought over any Cargo, Sir? I'll be
your Customer.

Booz. Ay, and cheat him too, I'll warrant him. [*Aside.*

Haz. I was not bred to Merchandizing, Sir, nor do
intend to follow the drudgery of Trading.

Dull. Men of Fortune seldom travel hither, Sir, to see
Fashions.

Tim. Why, Brother, it may be the Gentleman has
a mind to be a Planter; will you hire your self to make
a Crop of Tobacco this Year?

Haz. I was not born to work, Sir.

Tim. Not work, Sir! Zoors, your Betters have workt,
Sir. I have workt my self, Sir, both set and stript
Tobacco, for all I am of the honourable Council. Not
work, quoth a!—I suppose, Sir, you wear your Fortune
upon your Back, Sir?

Haz. Is it your Custom here, Sir, to affront Strangers?
I shall expect Satisfaction.   [*Rises.*

Tim. Why, does any body here owe you any thing?

Dull. No, unless he means to be paid for drinking
with us,—ha, ha, ha.

Haz. No, Sir, I have money to pay for what I drink:
here's my Club, my Guinea,   [*Flings down a Guinea.*
I scorn to be oblig'd to such Scoundrels.

Booz. Hum—call Men of Honour Scoundrels.

                                        [*Rise in huff.*
Tim. Let him alone, let him alone, Brother; how
should he learn Manners? he never was in *Virginia*
before.

Dull. He's some Covent-Garden Bully.

Tim. Or some broken Citizen turned Factor.

Haz. Sir, you lye, and you are a Rascal.

        [*Flings the Brandy in his Face.*

Tim. Adz zoors, he has spil'd all the Brandy.

  [*Tim. runs behind the Door*, Dull. *and* Booz. *strike*
   Hazard.

Haz. I understand no Cudgel-play, but wear a Sword
to right myself.   [*Draws, they run off.*

Flirt. Good Heavens! what, quarelling in my House?

Haz. Do the Persons of Quality in this Country treat
Strangers thus?

Flirt. Alas, Sir, 'tis a familiar way they have, Sir.

Haz. I'm glad I know it.——Pray, Madam, can you
inform one how I may be furnish'd with a Horse and
a Guide to Madam *Surelove's*?

Flirt. A most accomplish'd Lady, and my very good
Friend, you shall be immediately—— [*Exeunt.*

SCENE II. *The Council-Table.*

Enter Wellman, Downright, Dunce, Whimsey, Whiff,
and others.

Well. Come, Mr. *Dunce*, though you are no Counsellor,
yet your Counsel may be good in time of Necessity, as now.

Dun. If I may give worthy Advice, I do not look upon
our Danger to be so great from the *Indians*, as from young
Bacon, whom the People have nick-nam'd *Fright-all*.

Whim. Ay, ay, that same *Bacon*, I would he were
well hang'd: I am afraid that under pretence of killing
all the *Indians* he means to murder us, lie with our Wives,
and hang up our little Children, and make himself Lord
and King.

Whiff. Brother *Whimsey*, not so hot; with leave of the
honourable Board, my Wife is of opinion, that *Bacon*
came seasonably to our Aid, and what he has done was
for our Defence, the *Indians* came down upon us, and
ravish'd us all, Men, Women, and Children.

Well. If these Grievances were not redrest, we had our Reasons for it; it was not that we were insensible, Captain *Whiff*, of what we suffer'd from the Insolence of the *Indians;* but all knew what we must expect from *Bacon*, if that by lawful Authority he had arrived to so great a Command as General; nor would we be hufft out of our Commissions.

Down. 'Tis most certain that *Bacon* did not demand a Commission out of a design of serving us, but to satisfy his Ambition and his Love; it being no secret that he passionately admires the *Indian* Queen, and under the pretext of a War, intends to kill the King her Husband, establish himself in her Heart, and on all occasions make himself a more formidable Enemy than the Indians are.

Whim. Nay, nay, I ever foresaw he would prove a Villain.

Whiff. Nay, and he be thereabout, my *Nancy* shall have no more to do with him.

Well. But, Gentlemen, the People daily flock to him, so that his Army is too considerable for us to oppose by any thing but Policy.

Down. We are sensible, Gentlemen, that our Fortunes, our Honours, and our Lives are at stake; and therefore you are call'd together to consult what's to be done in this Grand Affair, till our Governour and Forces arrive from *England:* the Truce he made with the *Indians* will be out to morrow.

Whiff. Ay, and then he intends to have another bout with the *Indians.* Let's have patience, I say, till he has thrumb'd their Jackets, and then to work with your Politicks as soon as you please.

Down. Colonel *Wellman* has answer'd that point, good Captain *Whiff*; 'tis the Event of this Battel we ought to dread; and if won or lost, will be equally fatal for us, either from the *Indians* or from *Bacon*.

Dun. With the Permission of the honourable Board, I think I have hit upon an Expedient that may prevent this Battel: your Honours shall write a Letter to *Bacon*, where you shall acknowledge his Services, invite him kindly home, and offer him a Commission for General—

Whiff. Just my *Nancy's* Counsel—Dr. *Dunce* has spoken like a Cherubin, he shall have my Voice for General; what say you, Brother *Whimsey*?

Down. I say he is a Noble Fellow, and fit for a General.

Dun. But conceive me right, Gentlemen; as soon as he shall have render'd himself, seize him, and strike off his Head at the Fort.

Whiff. Hum! his Head—Brother.

Whim. Ay, ay, Dr. *Dunce* speaks like a Cherubin.

Well. Mr. *Dunce*, your Counsel in extremity, I confess, is not amiss; but I should be loth to deal dishonourably with any Man.

Down. His Crimes deserve Death, his Life is forfeited by Law, but shall never be taken by my consent by Treachery: If by any Stratagem we could take him alive, and either send him for *England* to receive there his Punishment, or keep him Prisoner here till the Governour arrive, I should agree to it; but I question his coming in upon our Invitation.

Dun. Leave that to me.

Whim. Come, I'll warrant him, the Rogue's as stout as *Hector*, he fears neither Heaven nor Hell.

Down. He's too brave and bold to refuse our Summons, and I am for sending him for *England*, and leaving him to the King's Mercy.

Dun. In that you'll find more difficulty, Sir; to take him off here will be more quick and sudden: for the People worship him.

Well. I'll never yield to so ungenerous an Expedient. The seizing him I am content in the Extremity wherein we are to follow. What say you, Colonel *Downright*? shall we send him a Letter now, while this two days Truce lasts, between him and the *Indians*?

Down. I approve it.

All. And I, and I, and I.

Dun. If your Honours please to make me the Messenger, I'll use some Arguments of my own to prevail with him.

Well. You say well, Mr. *Dunce,* and we'll dispatch you presently.   [*Ex.* Well. Down. *and all but*
                                   Whim. Whiff. *and* Dunce.

Whiff. Ah, Doctor, if you could but have persuaded Colonel *Wellman* and Colonel *Downright* to have hanged him—

Whim. Why, Brother *Whiff,* you were for making him a General but now.

Whiff. The Counsels of wise States-men, Brother *Whimsey,* must change as Causes do, d'ye see.

Dun. Your Honours are in the right; and whatever those two leading Counsellors say, they would be glad if *Bacon* were dispatch'd : but the punctilio of Honour is such a thing.

Whim. Honour, a Pox on't; what is that Honour that keeps such a bustle in the World, yet never did good as I heard of ?

Dun. Why, 'tis a foolish word only, taken up by great Men, but rarely practis'd.—But if you wou'd be great Men indeed—

Whiff. If we wou'd, Doctor, name, name the way.

Dun. Why, you command each of you a Company— when *Bacon* comes from the Camp, as I am sure he will, (and full of this silly thing call'd Honour, will come unguarded too) lay some of your Men in Ambush along those Ditches by the *Sevana,* about a Mile from the Town; and as he comes by, seize him, and hang him up upon the next Tree.

Whiff. Hum—hang him ! a rare Plot.

Whim. Hang him !—we'll do't, we'll do't, Sir, and I doubt not but to be made General for the Action—I'll take it all upon my self.   [*Aside.*

Dun. If you resolve upon this, you must about instantly—Thus I shall at once serve my Country, and revenge my self on the Rascal for affronting my Dignity once at the Council-Table, by calling me Farrier. [*Ex.* Dr.

Whiff. Do you know, Brother, what we are to do?

Whim. To do! yes, to hang a General, Brother, that's all.

Whiff. All! but is it lawful to hang any General?

Whim. Lawful, yes, that 'tis lawful to hang any General that fights against Law.

Whiff. But in what he has done, he has serv'd the King and our Country, and preserv'd our Lives and Fortunes.

Whim. That's all one, Brother; if there be but a Quirk in the Law offended in this Case, though he fought like *Alexander*, and preserv'd the whole World from Perdition, yet if he did it against Law, 'tis lawful to hang him; why, what, Brother, is it fit that every impudent Fellow that pretends to a little Honour, Loyalty, and Courage, should serve his King and Country against the Law? no, no, Brother, these things are not to be suffer'd in a civil Government by Law establish'd,—wherefore let's about it.   [*Exeunt.*

SCENE III.   Surelove's *House.*

Enter Ranter *and* Jeffery *her Coachman.*

Ran. Here, *Jeffery*, ye drunken Dog, set your Coach and Horses up, I'll not go till the cool of the Evening, I love to ride in *Fresco.*

Enter a Boy.

Coach. Yes, after hard drinking—[*Aside.*] It shall be done, Madam.   [*Exit.*

Ran. How now, Boy, is Madam *Surelove* at home?

Boy. Yes, Madam.

Ran. Go tell her I am here, Sirrah.

Boy. Who are you pray forsooth?

Ran. Why, you Son of a Baboon, don't you know me?

Boy. No, Madam, I came over but in the last Ship.

Ran. What, from *Newgate* or *Bridewell?* from shoveing the Tumbler, Sirrah, lifting or filing the Cly?

Boy. I don't understand this Country Language, forsooth, yet.

Ran. You Rogue, 'tis what we transport from *England* first—go, ye Dog, go tell your Lady the Widow *Ranter* is come to dine with her—[*Exit* Boy.] I hope I shall not find that Rogue *Daring* here sniveling after Mrs. *Chrisante:* If I do, by the Lord, I'll lay him thick. Pox on him, why shou'd I love the Dog, unless it be a Judgment upon me.

Enter Surelove *and* Chrisante.

—My dear Jewel, how do'st do? — as for you, Gentlewoman, you are my Rival, and I am in Rancour against you till you have renounc'd my *Daring.*

Chris. All the Interest I have in him, Madam, I resign to you.

Ran. Ay, but your House lying so near the Camp, gives me mortal Fears—but prithee how thrives thy Amour with honest *Friendly?*

Chris. As well as an Amour can that is absolutely forbid by a Father on one side, and pursued by a good Resolution on the other.

Ran. Hay Gad, I'll warrant for *Friendly's* Resolution, what though his Fortune be not answerable to yours, we are bound to help one another.—Here, Boy, some Pipes and a Bowl of Punch; you know my Humour, Madam, I must smoak and drink in a Morning, or I am maukish all day.

Sure. But will you drink Punch in a Morning?

Ran. Punch! 'tis my Morning's Draught, my Tabledrink, my Treat, my Regalio, my every thing; ah, my dear *Surelove*, if thou wou'd but refresh and cheer thy

Heart with Punch in a Morning, thou wou'dst not look thus cloudy all the day.

Enter Pipes and a great Bowl, she falls to smoaking.

Sure. I have reason, Madam, to be melancholy, I have receiv'd a Letter from my Husband, who gives me an account that he is worse in *England* than when he was here, so that I fear I shall see him no more, the Doctors can do no good on him.

Ran. A very good hearing. I wonder what the Devil thou hast done with him so long? an old fusty weather-beaten Skeleton, as dried as Stock-fish, and much of the Hue.—Come, come, here's to the next, may he be young, Heaven, I beseech thee.   [*Drinks.*

Sure. You have reason to praise an old Man, who dy'd and left you worth fifty thousand Pound.

Ran. Ay, Gad—and what's better, Sweetheart, dy'd in good time too, and left me young enough to spend this fifty thousand Pound in better Company—rest his Soul for that too.

Chris. I doubt 'twill be all laid out in *Bacon's* mad Lieutenant General *Daring.*

Ran. Faith, I think I could lend it the Rogue on good Security.

Chris. What's that, to be bound Body for Body?

Ran. Rather that he should love no body's Body besides my own; but my fortune is too good to trust the Rogue, my Money makes me an Infidel.

Chris. You think they all love you for that.

Ran. For that, ay, what else? if it were not for that, I might sit still and sigh, and cry out, a Miracle! a Miracle! at sight of a Man within my Doors.

Enter Maid.

Maid. Madam, here's a young Gentleman without wou'd speak with you.

Sure. With me? sure thou'rt mistaken; is it not *Friendly?*

Maid. No, Madam, 'tis a Stranger.

Ran. 'Tis not *Daring*, that Rogue, is it?

Maid. No, Madam.

Ran. Is he handsome? does he look like a Gentleman?

Maid. He's handsome, and seems a Gentleman.

Ran. Bring him in then, I hate a Conversation without a Fellow,—hah,—a good handsome Lad indeed.

Enter Hazard *with a Letter.*

Sure. With me, Sir, would you speak?

Haz. If you are Madam *Surelove.*

Sure. So I am call'd.

Haz. Madam, I am newly arriv'd from *England*, and from your Husband my Kinsman bring you this.—

[*Gives a Letter.*

Ran. Please you to sit, Sir.

Haz. She's extremely handsome.   [*Aside—sits down.*

Ran. Come, Sir, will you smoke a Pipe?

Haz. I never do, Madam.

Ran. Oh, fie upon't, you must learn then, we all smoke here, 'tis a part of good Breeding.—Well, well, what Cargo, what Goods have ye? any Points, Lace, rich Stuffs, Jewels; if you have, I'll be your Chafferer, I live hard by, any body will direct you to the Widow *Ranter's.*

Haz. I have already heard of you, Madam.

Ran. What, you are like all the young Fellows, the first thing they do when they come to a strange Place, is to enquire what Fortunes there are.

Haz. Madam, I had no such Ambition.

Ran. Gad, then you're a Fool, Sir; but come, my service to you; we rich Widows are the best Commodity this Country affords, I'll tell you that.

[*This while* Sure. *reads the Letter.*

Sure. Sir, my Husband has recommended you here in a most particular manner, by which I do not only find the esteem he has for you, but the desire he has of gaining you mine, which on a double score I render you, first for his sake, next for those Merits that appear in your self.

Haz. Madam, the endeavours of my Life shall be to express my Gratitude for this great Bounty.

Enter Maid.

Maid. Madam, Mr. *Friendly*'s here.

Sure. Bring him in.

Haz. Friendly! —I had a dear Friend of that name, who I hear is in these Parts.—Pray Heaven it may be he.

Ran. How now, *Charles.*

Enter Friendly.

Friend. Madam, your Servant—Hah! should not I know you for my dear friend *Hazard.* [*Embracing him.*

Haz. Or you're to blame, my *Friendly.*

Friend. Prithee what calm brought thee ashore?

Haz. Fortune *de la guerre,* but prithee ask me no Questions in so good Company, where a Minute lost from this Conversation is a Misfortune not to be retriev'd.

Friend. Dost like her, Rogue—   [*Softly aside.*

Haz. Like her! have I sight, or sense?—Why, I adore her.

Friend. Mrs. *Chrisante,* I heard your Father would not be here to day, which made me snatch this opportunity of seeing you.

Ran. Come, come, a Pox of this whining Love, it spoils good Company.

Friend. You know, my dear Friend, these Opportunities come but seldom, and therefore I must make use of them.

Ran. Come, come, I'll give you a better Opportunity at my House to morrow, we are to eat a Buffalo there, and I'll secure the old Gentleman from coming.

Friend. Then I shall see *Chrisante* once more before I go.

Chris. Go—Heavens—whither, my *Friendly?*

Friend. I have received a Commission to go against the *Indians, Bacon* being sent for home.

Ran. But will he come when sent for?

Friend. If he refuse we are to endeavour to force him.

Chris. I do not think he will be forc'd, not even by *Friendly.*

Friend. And, faith, it goes against my Conscience to lift my Sword against him, for he is truly brave, and what he has done, a Service to the Country, had it but been by Authority.

Chris. What pity 'tis there should be such false Maxims in the World, that noble Actions, however great, must be criminal for want of a Law to authorise 'em.

Friend. Indeed 'tis pity that when Laws are faulty they should not be mended or abolish'd.

Ran. Hark ye, *Charles*, by Heaven, if you kill my *Daring* I'll pistol you.

Friend. No, Widow, I'll spare him for your sake.

[*They join with* Surelove.

Haz. Oh, she's all divine, and all the Breath she utters serves but to blow my Flame.

Enter Maid.

Maid. Madam, Dinner's on the Table—

Sure. Please you, Sir, to walk in—come, Mr. *Friendly.*

[*She takes* Hazard.

Ran. Prithee, good Wench, bring in the Punch-Bowl.

[*Exeunt.*

ACT II.

SCENE I. *A Pavilion.*

Discovers the Indian King *and* Queen *sitting in State, with Guards of* Indians, *Men and Women attending: To them* Bacon *richly dress'd, attended by* Daring, Fearless *and other Officers; he bows to the* King *and* Queen, *who rise to receive him.*

King. I am sorry, Sir, we meet upon these Terms, we who so often have embrac'd as Friends.

Bac. How charming is the Queen! [*Aside.*] War, Sir, is not my Business nor my Pleasure: Nor was I bred in Arms, my Country's Good has forc'd me to assume a Soldier's Life; and 'tis with much regret that I employ the first Effects of it against my Friends: yet whilst I may —whilst this Cessation lasts, I beg we may exchange those Friendships, Sir, we have so often paid in happier Peace.

King. For your part, Sir, you've been so noble, that I repent the fatal Difference that makes us meet in Arms. Yet though I'm young, I'm sensible of Injuries; and oft have heard my Grandsire say, That we were Monarchs once of all this spacious World, till you, an unknown People, landing here, distress'd and ruin'd by destructive Storms, abusing all our charitable Hospitality, usurp'd our Right, and made your Friends your Slaves.

Bac. I will not justify the Ingratitude of my Fore-fathers, but finding here my Inheritance, I am resolv'd still to maintain it so, and by my Sword which first cut out my Portion, defend each Inch of Land, with my last drop of Blood.

Queen. Even his Threats have Charms that please the Heart.   [*Aside.*

King. Come, Sir, let this ungrateful Theme alone, which is better disputed in the Field.

Queen. Is it impossible there might be wrought an understanding betwixt my Lord and you? 'Twas to that end I first desired this Truce, my self proposing to be Mediator, to which my Lord *Cavernio* shall agree, could you but condescend—I know you are noble: And I have heard you say our tender Sex could never plead in vain.

Bac. Alas! I dare not trust your pleading, Madam: a few soft Words from such a charming Mouth would make me lay the Conqueror at your Feet, as a Sacrifice for all the Ills he has done you.

Queen. How strangely am I pleas'd to hear him talk.
                                                        [*Aside.*

King. Semernia, see, the Dancers do appear;
Sir, will you take your Seat?   [*To* Bacon.
                [*He leads the* Queen *to a Seat, they sit and talk.*
Bac. Curse on his Sports that interrupted me, my very
Soul was hovering at my Lip, ready to have discover'd all
its Secrets. But oh! I dread to tell her of my pain, and
when I wou'd an awful trembling seizes me, and she can
only from my dying Eyes read all the Sentiments of my
captive Heart.   [*Sits down, the rest wait.*

Enter Indians *that dance Anticks: after the Dance the*
King *seems in discourse with* Bacon, *the* Queen
rises and comes forth.

Queen. The more I gaze upon this *English* Stranger,
the more Confusion struggles in my Soul: Oft I have
heard of Love, and oft this Gallant Man (when Peace
had made him pay his idle Visits) has told a thousand
Tales of dying Maids; and ever when he spoke, my
panting Heart, with a prophetick Fear in Sighs reply'd,
I shall fall a Victim to his Eyes.

Enter an Indian.

Indian. Sir, here's a Messenger from the *English* Council
desires admittance to the General.   [*To the* King.
Bac. With your Permission he may advance.
                                    [*To the* King.

Re-enter Indian *with* Dunce. *A Letter.*

Dun. All Health and Happiness attend your Honour,
this from the honourable Council. [*Gives him a Letter.*
King. I'll leave you till you have dispatch'd the Messenger,
and then expect your presence in the Royal Tent.
                [*Exeunt* King, Queen, *and* Indians.
Bac. Lieutenant, read the Letter.   [*To* Daring.

Daring *reads.*

SIR, the necessity of what you have acted makes it pardon-
able, and we could wish we had done the Country and our

*selves so much Justice as to have given you that Commission
you desired.—We now find it reasonable to raise more Forces,
to oppose these Insolences, which possibly yours may be too weak
to accomplish, to which end the Council is ordered to meet this
Evening, and desiring you will come and take your place there,
and be pleas'd to accept from us a Commission to command in
Chief in this War.—Therefore send those Soldiers under your
Command to their respective Houses, and haste, Sir, to your
affectionate Friends—*

Fear. Sir, I fear the Hearts and Pen did not agree
when this was writ.

Dar. A plague upon their shallow Politicks! Do they
think to play the old Game twice with us?

Bac. Away, you wrong the Council, who of themselves are honourable Gentlemen; but the base coward
Fear of some of them, puts the rest on tricks that suit not
with their Nature.

Dun. Sir, 'tis for noble ends you are sent for, and for
your safety I'll engage my Life.

Dar. By Heaven, and so you shall;—and pay it too
with all the rest of your wise-headed Council.

Bac. Your Zeal is too officious now; I see no Treachery,
and can fear no Danger.

Dun. Treachery! now Heavens forbid, are we not
Christians, Sir, all Friends and Countrymen? believe me,
Sir, 'tis Honour calls you to increase your Fame, and he
who would dissuade you is your Enemy.

Dar. Go cant, Sir, to the Rabble—for us, we know you.

Bac. You wrong me when you but suspect for me;
let him that acts dishonourably fear. My innocence and
my good Sword's my Guard.

Dar. If you resolve to go, we will attend you.

Bac. What, go like an invader! No, *Daring*, the Invitation's friendly, and as a Friend attended only by my
menial Servants, I'll wait upon the Council, that they

may see that when I could command it, I came an humble
Suppliant for their Favour.—You may return, and tell
'em I'll attend.

   Dun. I kiss your Honour's Hands——   [*Goes out.*

   Dar. 'Sdeath, will you trust the faithless Council, Sir,
who have so long held you in hand with Promises, that
Curse of States-men, that unlucky Vice that renders even
Nobility despis'd?

   Bac. Perhaps the Council thought me too aspiring, and
would not add Wings to my ambitious Flight.

   Dar. A pox of their considering Caps, and now they
find that you can soar alone, they send for you to knip
your spreading Wings.
Now, by my Soul, you shall not go alone.

   Bac. Forbear, lest I suspect you for a Mutineer; I am
resolv'd to go.

   Fear. What, and send your Army home; a pretty fetch.

   Dar. By Heaven, we'll not disband, not till we see
how fairly you are dealt with : If you have a Commission
to be General, here we are ready to receive new Orders :
If not, we'll ring them such a thundering Peal shall beat
the Town about their treacherous Ears.

   Bac. I do command you not to stir a Man, till you're
inform'd how I am treated by 'em.—leave me, all.

                   [*Exeunt Officers.*

   [*While* Bacon *reads the Letter again, to him the* Indian
        Queen *with Women waiting.*

   Queen. Now while my Lord's asleep in his Pavilion,
I'll try my Power with the General for an Accommodation
of a Peace : The very dreams of War fright my soft
Slumbers that us'd to be employ'd in kinder Business.

   Bac. Ha !—the Queen—what Happiness is this presents
it self which all my Industry could never gain?

   Queen. Sir——   [*Approaching him.*

   Bac. Prest with the great extremes of Joy and Fear,
I trembling stand, unable to approach her.

Queen. I hope you will not think it Fear in me, though timorous as a Dove by nature fram'd : Nor that my Lord, whose Youth's unskill'd in War, can either doubt his Courage, or his Forces, that makes me seek a Reconciliation on any honourable Terms of Peace.

Bac. Ah Madam ! if you knew how absolutely you command my Fate, I fear but little Honour would be left me, since whatsoe'er you ask me I should grant.

Queen. Indeed I would not ask your Honour, Sir, that renders you too brave in my esteem. Nor can I think that you would part with that. No, not to save your Life.

Bac. I would do more to serve your least commands than part with trivial Life.

Queen. Bless me, Sir, how came I by such a Power ?

Bac. The Gods and Nature gave it you in your Creation, form'd with all the Charms that ever grac'd your Sex.

Queen. Is't possible ? am I so beautiful ?

Bac. As Heaven, or Angels there.

Queen. Supposing this, how can my Beauty make you so obliging ?

Bac. Beauty has still a Power over great Souls, and from the moment I beheld your Eyes, my stubborn Heart melted to compliance, and from a nature rough and turbulent, grew soft and gentle as the God of Love.

Queen. The God of Love ! what is the God of Love ?

Bac. 'Tis a resistless Fire, that's kindled thus——at every
                    [*Takes her by the Hand and gazes on her.*
gaze we take from such fine Eyes, from such bashful Looks, and such soft Touches——it makes us sigh,——and pant as I do now, and stops the breath when e'er we speak of Pain.

Queen. Alas for me if this should be Love !   [*Aside.*

Bac. It makes us tremble when we touch the fair one ; and all the Blood runs shivering through the Veins, the Heart's surrounded with a feeble Languishment, the Eyes are dying, and the Cheeks are pale, the Tongue is faltring, and the Body fainting.

Queen. Then I'm undone, and all I feel is Love. [*Aside.*
If Love be catching, Sir, by Looks and Touches, let us
at distance parley—or rather let me fly, for within view
is too near—   [*Aside.*

Bac. Ah! she retires—displeas'd I fear with my pre-
sumptuous Love,—Oh, pardon, fairest Creature. [*Kneels.*

Queen. I'll talk no more, our Words exchange our
Souls, and every Look fades all my blooming Honour, like
Sun-beams on unguarded Roses—Take all our Kingdoms
—make our People Slaves, and let me fall beneath your
conquering Sword: but never let me hear you talk again,
or gaze upon your Eyes.—   [*Goes out.*

Bac. She loves! by Heaven, she loves! and has not Art
enough to hide her Flame, though she have cruel Honour
to suppress it. However, I'll pursue her to the Banquet.
                                                  [*Exit.*

SCENE II. *The Widow* Ranter's *Hall.*

Enter Surelove *fan'd by two Negroes, followed by* Hazard.

Sure. This Madam *Ranter* is so prodigious a Treater
—oh! I hate a Room that smells of a great Dinner, and
what's worse, a desert of Punch and Tobacco—what!
are you taking leave so soon, Cousin?

Haz. Yes, Madam, but 'tis not fit I should let you know
with what regret I go,—but Business will be obey'd.

Sure. Some Letters to dispatch to *English* Ladies you
have left behind—come, Cousin, confess.

Haz. I own I much admire the *English* Beauties but
never yet have put their Fetters on.

Sure. Never in love! oh, then you have pleasure to come.

Haz. Rather a Pain when there's no Hope attends it.

Sure. Oh, such Diseases quickly cure themselves.

Haz. I do not wish to find it so; for even in Pain
I find a Pleasure too.

Sure. You are infected then, and come abroad for Cure.

Haz. Rather to receive my Wounds, Madam.

Sure. Already, Sir,—whoe'er she be, she made good haste to conquer, we have few here boast that Dexterity.

Haz. What think you of *Chrisante*, Madam?

Sure. I must confess your Love and your Despair are there plac'd right, of which I am not fond of being made a Confident, since I am assur'd she can love none but *Friendly*.   [*Coldly.*

Haz. Let her love on as long as Life shall last, let *Friendly* take her, and the Universe, so I had my next wish——   [*Sighs.*
Madam, it is yourself that I adore—I should not be so vain to tell you this, but that I know you have found the Secret out already from my Sighs.

Sure. Forbear, Sir, and know me for your Kinsman's Wife, and no more.

Haz. Be scornful as you please, rail at my Passion, and refuse to hear it; yet I'll love on, and hope in spite of you; my Flame shall be so constant and submissive, it shall compel your Heart to some return.

Sure. You're very confident of your Power, I perceive; but if you chance to find yourself mistaken, say your Opinion and your Affectation were misapply'd, and not that I was cruel.   [*Ex.* Surelove.

Haz. Whate'er denials dwell upon your Tongue, your Eyes assure me that your Heart is tender.   [*Goes out.*

Enter the Bagpiper, playing before a great Bowl of Punch, carry'd between two Negroes, a Highlander dancing after it; the Widow Ranter *led by* Timorous; Chrisante *by* Dullman; *Mrs.* Flirt *and* Friendly, *all dancing after it; they place it on the Table.*

Dull. This is like the noble Widow all over, i'faith.

Tim. Ay, ay, the Widow's Health in a full Ladle, Major.   [*Drinks.*

—But a Pox on't, what made that young Fellow here, that affronted us yesterday, Major?

[While they drink about.

Dull. Some damned Sharper that would lay his Knife aboard your Widow, Cornet.

Tim. Zoors, if I thought so, I'd arrest him for Salt and Battery, lay him in Prison for a swinging Fine, and take no Bail.

Dull. Nay, had it not been before my Mistress here, Mrs. *Chrisante*, I had swinged him for his Yesterday's Affront;—ah, my sweet Mistress *Chrisante*—if you did but know what a power you have over me——

Chris. Oh, you're a great Courtier, Major.

Dull. Would I were any thing for your sake, Madam.

Ran. Thou art anything, but what thou shouldst be; prithee, Major, leave off being an old Buffoon, that is, a Lover turn'd ridiculous by Age, consider thy self a mere rouling Tun of *Nantz*,—a walking Chimney, ever smoaking with nasty Mundungus, and then thou hast a Countenance like an old worm-eaten Cheese.

Dull. Well, Widow, you will joke, ha, ha, ha——

Tim. Gad' Zoors, she's pure company, ha, ha——

Dull. No matter for my Countenance,—Col. *Downright* likes my Estate, and is resolved to have it a match.

Friend. Dear Widow, take off your damned Major, for if he speak another word to *Chrisante*, I shall be put past all my patience, and fall foul upon him.

Ran. S'life, not for the world—Major, I bar Love-making within my Territories, 'tis inconsistent with the Punch-Bowl, if you'l drink, do, if not, be gone.

Tim. Nay, Gad's Zooks, if you enter me at the Punch-Bowl you enter me in Politicks—well, 'tis the best Drink in Christendom for a Statesman.

[They drink about, the Bagpipe playing.

Ran. Come, now you shall see what my High-land Valet can do.　　　　　　　　[*A* Scots *Dance.*

Dull. So—I see, let the World go which way it will, Widow, you are resolv'd for mirth,—but come—to the conversation of the Times.

Ran. The Times! why, what a Devil ails the Times? I see nothing in the Times but a Company of Coxcombs that fear without a Cause.

Tim. But if these Fears were laid, and *Bacon* were hanged, I look upon *Virginia* to be the happiest part of the World, gads zoors,—why, there's *England*—'tis nothing to't,—I was in *England* about six Years ago, and was shewed the Court of Aldermen, some were nodding, some saying nothing, and others very little to purpose; but how could it be otherwise, for they had neither Bowl of Punch, Bottles of Wine or Tobacco before 'em, to put Life and Soul into 'em as we have here: then for the young Gentlemen—their farthest Travels is to *France* or *Italy*, they never come hither.

Dull. The more's the pity, by my troth.   [*Drinks.*

Tim. Where they learn to swear Mor-blew, Mor-dee—

Friend. And tell you how much bigger the *Louvre* is than *Whitehall*; buy a suit a-la-mode, get a swinging Clap of some *French* Marquise, spend all their Money, and return just as they went.

Dull. For the old Fellows, their business is Usury, Extortion, and undermining young Heirs.

Tim. Then for young Merchants, their Exchange is the Tavern, their Ware-house the Play-house, and their Bills of Exchange Billet-Douxs, where to sup with their Wenches at the other end of the Town,—now judge you what a condition poor *England* is in: for my part I look upon it as a lost Nation, gads zoors.

Dull. I have considered it, and have found a way to save all yet.

Tim. As how, I pray?

Dull. As thus: we have Men here of great Experience and Ability—now I would have as many sent into *England*, as would supply all Places and Offices, both Civil and Military, d'ye see; their young Gentry should all travel hither for breeding, and to learn the mysteries of State.

Friend. As for the old covetous Fellows, I would have the Tradesmen get in their Debts, break and turn Troopers.

Tim. And they'd be soon weary of Extortion, gad zoors.

Dull. Then for the young Merchants, there should be a Law made, none should go beyond *Ludgate*.

Friend. You have found out the only way to preserve that great Kingdom.

[*Drinking all this while sometimes.*

Tim. Well, gad zoors, 'tis a fine thing to be a good Statesman.

Friend. Ay, Cornet, which you had never been had you staid in Old *England*.

Dull. Why, Sir, we were somebody in *England*.

Friend. So I heard, Major.

Dull. You heard, Sir! what have you heard? he's a Kidnapper that says he heard any thing of me—and so my service to you.—I'll sue you, Sir, for spoiling my Marriage here by your Scandals with Mrs. *Chrisante*: but that shan't do, Sir, I'll marry her for all that, and he's a Rascal that denies it.

Friend. S'death, you lye, Sir—I do.

Tim. Gad zoors, Sir, lye to a Privy-Counsellor, a Major of Horse! Brother, this is an Affront to our Dignities: draw and I'll side with you.

[*They both draw on* Friendly, *the Ladies run off*.

Friend. If I disdain to draw, 'tis not that I fear your base and cowardly Force, but for the respect I bear you as Magistrates, and so I leave you.   [*Goes out.*

Tim. An arrant Coward, gad zoors.

Dull. A mere Paultroon, and I scorn to drink in his Company.   [*Exeunt, putting up their Swords.*

SCENE III. *A Sevana, or large Heath.*

Enter Whimsey, Whiff, *and* Boozer, *with some Soldiers arm'd.*

Whim. Stand—stand—and hear the word of Command —do ye see yon Cops, and that Ditch that runs along Major *Dullman's* Plantation?

Booz. We do.

Whim. Place your Men there, and lie flat on your Bellies, and when *Bacon* comes, (if alone) seize him, d'ye see.

Whiff. Observe the Command now (if alone) for we are not for blood-shed.

Booz. I'll warrant you for our parts.

[*Exeunt all but* Whim. *and* Whiff.

Whim. Now we have ambusht our Men, let's light our Pipes, and sit down and take an encouraging dram of the Bottle. [*Pulls a Bottle of Brandy out of his Pocket—they sit.*

Whiff. Thou art a Knave, and hast emptied half the Bottle in thy Leathern Pockets; but come, here's young *Frightall's* Health.

Whim. What, wilt drink a Man's Health thou'rt going to hang?

Whiff. 'Tis all one for that, we'll drink his Health first, and hang him afterwards, and thou shalt pledge me, d'ye see, and though 'twere under the Gallows.

Whim. Thou'rt a Traitor for saying so, and I defy thee.

Whiff. Nay, since we are come out like loving Brothers to hang the General, let's not fall out among our selves; and so here's to you, [*Drinks.*] though I have no great Maw to this Business.

Whim. Prithee, Brother *Whiff*, do not be so villainous a Coward, for I hate a Coward.

Whiff. Nay, 'tis not that—but, my *Whiff*, my *Nancy* dreamt to night she saw me hanged.

Whim. 'Twas a cowardly Dream, think no more on't;

but as Dreams are expounded by contraries, thou shalt hang the General.

Whiff. Ay—but he was my Friend, and I owe him at this time a hundred Pounds of Tobacco.

Whim. Nay, then I am sure thou'dst hang him if he were thy Brother.

Whiff. But hark—I think I hear the Neighing of Horses, where shall we hide our selves? for if we stay here, we shall be mawled damnably.

[*Exeunt both behind a Bush, peeping.*

Enter Bacon, Fearless, *and* 3 *or* 4 *Footmen.*

Bac. Let the Groom lead the Horses o'er the *Sevana;* we'll walk it on Foot, 'tis not a quarter of a Mile to the Town; and here the Air is cool.

Fear. The Breezes about this time of the Day begin to take wing, and fan refreshment to the Trees and Flowers.

Bac. And at these Hours how fragrant are the Groves!

Fear. The Country's well, were but the people so.

Bac. But come, lets on—   [*They pass to the Entrance.*

Whim. There, Boys—

[*The Soldiers come forth and fall on* Bacon.

Bac. Hah! Ambush—

[*Draws,* Fearless *and Footmen draw, the Soldiers after a while fighting, take* Bacon *and* Fearless, *they having laid* 3 *or* 4 *dead.*

Whiff. So, so, he's taken; now we may venture out.

Whim. But are you sure he's taken?

Whiff. Sure! can't you believe your Eyes, come forth; I hate a Coward—Oh, Sir, have we caught your Mightiness.

Bac. Are you the Authors of this valiant Act? None but such villainous Cowards durst have attempted it.

Whim. Stop his railing Tongue.

Whiff. No, no, let him rail, let him rail now his Hands are ty'd, ha, ha. Why, good General *Frightall,* what, was no body able d'ye think to tame the roaring Lyon?

Bac. You'll be hanged for this.

Whim. Come, come, away with him to the next
Tree.

Bac. What mean you, Villains?

Whiff. Only to hang your Honour a little, that's all.
We'll teach you, Sir, to serve your Country against Law.

As they go off, enter Daring *with Soldiers.*

Dar. Hah—my General betray'd!—this I suspected.
  [*His Men come in, they fall on, release* Bacon *and*
    Fearless, *and his Man, and get Swords.* Whimsey's
    Party put Whim. *and* Whiff *before 'em striking 'em
    as they endeavour to run on this side or that, and
    forcing 'em to bear up, they are taken after some
    fighting.*

Fear. Did not the General tell you Rogues, you'd be
all hang'd?

Whiff. Oh, *Nancy, Nancy,* how prophetick are thy
Dreams!

Bac. Come, lets on—

Dar. S'death, what mean you, Sir?

Bac. As I designed—to present my self to the Council.

Dar. By Heavens, we'll follow then to save you from
their Treachery, 'twas this that has befallen you that
I feared, which made me at a distance follow you.

Bac. Follow me still, but still at such a distance as
your Aids may be assisting on all occasions.—*Fearless,*
go back and bring your Regiment down; and *Daring,*
let your Sergeant with his Party guard these Villains to
the Council.

                              [*Ex.* Bac. Dar. *and* Fearless.
Whiff. A Pox on your Worship's Plot.

Whim. A Pox of your forwardness to come out of the
Hedge.

                              [*Ex. Officers, with* Whim. *and* Whiff.

SCENE IV. *The Council-Table.*

Enter Col. Wellman, *Col.* Downright, Dullman, Timorous,
and about seven or eight more seat themselves.

Well. You heard Mr. *Dunce's* opinion, Gentlemen,
concerning *Bacon's* coming upon our Invitation. He believes
he will come, but I rather think, though he be himself
undaunted, yet the persuasions of his two Lieutenant-
Generals, *Daring* and *Fearless,* may prevent him—Colonel,
have you order'd our Men to be in Arms?

Enter a Soldier.

Down. I have, and they'l attend further order on the
Sevana.

Sold. May it please your Honours, *Bacon* is on his way,
he comes unattended by any but his Footmen, and Col.
Fearless.

Down. Who is this Fellow?

Well. A Spy I sent to watch *Bacon's* Motions.

Sold. But there is a Company of Soldiers in Ambush on
this side of the *Sevana* to seize him as he passes by.

Well. That's by no order of the Council.

Omnes. No, no, no order.

Well. Nay, 'twere a good design if true.

Tim. Gad zoors, wou'd I had thought on't for my
Troop.

Down. I am for no unfair dealing in any extremity.

Enter Brag *in haste.*

Brag. An't please your Honours, the saddest News—
an Ambush being laid for *Bacon,* they rush'd out upon
him on the *Sevana,* and after some fighting took him and
Fearless—

Tim. Is this your sad News—zoors, wou'd I had had
a hand in't.

Brag. When on a sudden, *Daring* and his Party fell

in upon us, turn'd the tide—kill'd our Men, and took
Captain *Whimsey*, and Captain *Whiff* Pris'ners; the rest
run away, but *Bacon* fought like fury.

Tim. A bloody Fellow!

Down. Whimsey and *Whiff*? they deserve Death for
acting without order.

Tim. I'm of the Colonel's Opinion, they deserve to
hang for't.

Dull. Why, Brother, I thought you had wish'd that
the Plot had been yours but now.

Tim. Ay, but the Case is alter'd since that, good Brother.

Well. Now he's exasperated past all hopes of a Reconciliation.

Dull. You must make use of the Statesman's Refuge,
wise Dissimulation.

Brag. For all this, Sir, he will not believe but that you
mean honourably, and no Persuasions could hinder him
from coming, so he has dismiss'd all his Soldiers, and is
entring the Town on foot.

Well. What pity 'tis a brave Man should be guilty of
an ill Action.

Brag. But the noise of his danger has so won the
Hearts of the Mobile, that they increase his Train as he
goes, and follow him in the Town like a Victor.

Well. Go wait his coming.   [*Exit* Brag.
He grows too popular and must be humbled.

Tim. I was ever of your mind, Colonel.

Well. Ay, right or wrong—but what's your Counsel
now?

Tim. E'en as it used to be, I leave it to wiser Heads.

Enter Brag.

Brag. Bacon, Sir, is entring.

Tim. Gad zoors, wou'd I were safe in bed.

Dull. Colonel, keep in your Heat, and treat calmly
with him.

Well. I rather wish you would all follow me, I'd meet him at the head of all his noisy Rabble, and seize him from the Rout.

Down. What, Men of Authority dispute with Rakehells! 'tis below us, Sir.

Tim. To stake our Lives and Fortunes against their nothing.

Enter Bacon, *after him the Rabble with Staves and Clubs, bringing in* Whim. *and* Whiff *bound.*

Well. What means this Insolence?—What, Mr. *Bacon,* do you come in Arms?

Bac. I'd need, Sir, come in Arms, when Men that should be honourable can have so poor Designs to take my Life.

Well. Thrust out his following Rabble.

1st Rab. We'll not stir till we have the General safe back again.

Bac. Let not your Loves be too officious—but retire—

1st Rab. At your Command we vanish.—

[*The Rabble retire.*

Bac. I hope you'll pardon me, if in my own defence I seized on these two Murderers.

Down. You did well, Sir, 'twas by no order they acted —stand forth and hear your Sentence—in time of War we need no formal Tryals to hang Knaves that act without order.

Whiff. Oh, Mercy, Mercy, Colonel—'twas Parson *Dunce's* Plot.

Down. Issue out a Warrant to seize *Dunce* immediately —you shall be carry'd to the Fort to pray.

Whim. Oh, good your Honour, I never pray'd in all my Life.

Down. From thence drawn upon a Sledge to the place of Execution—where you shall hang till you are dead— and then be cut down and—

Whim. Oh, hold—hold—we shall never be able to endure half this.   [*Kneeling.*

Well. I think the Offence needs not so great Punishment; their Crime, Sir, is but equal to your own, acting without Commission.

Bac. 'Tis very well explained, Sir,—had I been murder'd by Commission then, the Deed had been approved, and now perhaps I am beholding to the Rabble for my Life.

Well. A fine Pretence to hide a popular Fault, but for this once we pardon them and you.

Bac. Pardon! for what? by Heaven, I scorn your Pardon, I've not offended Honour nor Religion.

Well. You have offended both in taking Arms.

Bac. Should I stand by and see my Country ruin'd, my King dishonour'd, and his Subjects murder'd, hear the sad Crys of Widows and of Orphans? you heard it loud, but gave no pitying care to't, and till the War and Massacre was brought to my own door, my Flocks and Herds surprized, I bore it all with Patience. Is it unlawful to defend my self against a Thief that breaks into my Doors?

Well. And call you this defending of your self?

Bac. I call it doing of my self that right, which upon just demand the Council did refuse me; if my Ambition, as you're pleased to call it, made me demand too much, I left my self to you.

Well. Perhaps we thought it did.

Bac. Sir, you affront my Birth—I am a Gentleman, and yet my Thoughts were humble—I would have fought under the meanest of your Parasites.

Tim. There's a Bob for us, Brother.   [*To* Dull.

Bac. But still you put me off with Promises—and when compell'd to stir in my Defence I call'd none to my aid, and those that came, 'twas their own Wrongs that urg'd them.

Down. 'Tis fear'd, Sir, under this Pretence, you aim at Government.

Bac. I scorn to answer to so base an Accusation; the height of my Ambition is to be an honest Subject.

Well. An honest Rebel, Sir—

Bac. You know you wrong me, and 'tis basely urg'd —but this is trifling—here are my Commissions.

               [Throws down Papers, Down. *reads.*

Down. To be General of the Forces against the *Indians,* and blank Commissions for his Friends.

Well. Tear them in pieces—are we to be imposed upon? Do ye come in hostile manner to compel us?

Down. Be not too rough, Sir, let us argue with him.

Well. I am resolv'd I will not.

Tim. Then we are all dead Men, Gudzoors! he will not give us time to say our Prayers.

Well. We every day expect fresh force from *England,* till then, we of our selves shall be sufficient to make defence against a sturdy Traitor.

Bac. Traitor! S'death, Traitor—I defy ye, but that my Honour's yet above my Anger, I'd make you answer me that Traitor dearly.   *[Rises.*

Well. Hah—am I threatned—Guards, secure the Rebel.

                   [Guards seize him.

Bac. Is this your honourable Invitation? Go—triumph in your short-liv'd Victory, the next turn shall be mine.

                 [Exeunt Guards with Bac.

A Noise of Fighting—Enter Bacon, Wellman's *Guards beat back by the Rabble,* Bacon *snatches a Sword from one, and keeps back the Rabble,* Tim. *gets under the Table.*

Down. What means this Insolence?

Rab. We'll have our General, and knock that Fellow's Brains out, and hang up Colonel *Wellman.*

All. Ay, ay, hang up *Wellman.*

       [The Rabble seize Well. *and* Dull. *and the rest.*

Dull. Hold, hold, Gentlemen, I was always for the General.

Rab. Let's barbicu this fat Rogue.

Bac. Be gone, and know your distance to the Council.

[*The Rabble let 'em go.*

Well. I'd rather perish by the meanest Hand, than owe my safety poorly thus to *Bacon.*   [*In Rage.*

Bac. If you persist still in that mind I'll leave you, and conquering make you happy 'gainst your will.

[*Ex.* Bacon *and Rabble, hollowing a* Bacon, *a* Bacon.

Well. Oh villanous Cowards! who will trust his Honour with Sycophants so base? Let us to Arms—by Heaven, I will not give my Body rest, till I've chastised the boldness of this Rebel.

[*Exeunt* Well. Down. *and the rest, all but* Dull.
Tim. *peeps from under the Table.*

Tim. What, is the roistering Hector gone, Brother?

Dull. Ay, ay, and the Devil go with him.

[*Looking sadly,* Tim. *comes out.*

Tim. Was there ever such a Bull of *Bashan!* Why, what if he should come down upon us and kill us all for Traitors.

Dull. I rather think the Council will hang us all for Cowards—ah—oh—a Drum—a Drum—oh. [*He goes out.*

Tim. This is the Misery of being great.

We're sacrific'd to every turn of State.   [*Exit.*

ACT III.

SCENE I. *The Country Court, a great Table, with Papers, a* Clerk *writing.*

Enter a great many People of all sorts, then Friendly, *after him* Dullman.

Friend. How now, Major; what, they say *Bacon* scar'd you all out of the Council yesterday; What say the People?

Dull. Say? they curse us all, and drink young *Frightall's* Health, and swear they'll fight through Fire and Brimstone for him.

Friend. And to morrow will hollow him to the Gallows, if it were his chance to come there.

Dull. 'Tis very likely : Why, I am forced to be guarded to the Court now, the Rabble swore they would *De-Wit* me, but I shall hamper some of 'em. Wou'd the Governour were here to bear the brunt on't, for they call us the evil Counsellors.

Enter Hazard, *goes to* Friendly.

Here's the young Rogue that drew upon us too, we have Rods in Piss for him, i'faith.

Enter Timorous *with* Bailiffs, *whispers to* Dullman, *after which to the* Bailiffs.

Tim. Gadzoors, that's he, do your Office.

Bail. We arrest you, Sir, in the King's Name, at the suit of the honourable Justice *Timorous.*

Haz. Justice *Timorous!* who the Devil's he?

Tim. I am the man, Sir, d'ye see, for want of a better ; you shall repent, Guds zoors, your putting of tricks upon Persons of my Rank and Quality.

　　　[After he has spoke, he runs back as afraid of him.

Haz. Your Rank and Quality!

Tim. Ay, Sir, my Rank and Quality ; first I am one of the honourable Council, next, a Justice of Peace in *Quorum*, Cornet of a Troop of Horse, d'ye see, and Church-warden.

Friend. From whence proceeds this, Mr. Justice? you said nothing of this at Madam *Ranter's* yesterday ; you saw him there, then you were good Friends.

Tim. Ay, however I have carried my Body swimmingly before my Mistress, d'ye see, I had Rancour in my Heart, Gads zoors.

Friend. Why, this Gentleman's a Stranger, and but lately come ashore.

Haz. At my first landing I was in company with this

Fellow and two or three of his cruel Brethren, where I was affronted by them, some Words pass'd, and I drew——

Tim. Ay, ay, Sir, you shall pay for't,—why—what, Sir, cannot a civil Magistrate affront a Man, but he must be drawn upon presently?

Friend. Well, Sir, the Gentleman shall answer your Suit, and I hope you'll take my Bail for him.

Tim. 'Tis enough—I know you to be a civil Person.

Timorous and Dullman *take their Places on a long Bench placed behind the Table, to them* Whimsey *and* Whiff, *they seat themselves, then* Boozer *and two or three more; who seat themselves: Then enter two, bearing a Bowl of Punch and a great Ladle or two in it; the rest of the Stage being fill'd with People.*

Whiff. Brothers, it hath often been mov'd at the Bench, that a new Punch-Bowl shou'd be provided, and one of a larger Circumference; when the Bench sits late about weighty Affairs, oftentimes the Bowl is emptied before we end.

Whim. A good Motion; Clerk, set it down.

Clerk. Mr. Justice *Boozer*, the Council has order'd you a Writ of Ease, and dismiss your Worship from the Bench.

Booz. Me from the Bench, for what?

Whim. The Complaint is, Brother *Boozer*, for drinking too much Punch in the time of hearing Tryals.

Whiff. And that you can neither write nor read, nor say the Lord's Prayer.

Tim. That your Warrants are like a Brewer's Tally, a Notch on a Stick; if a special Warrant, then a couple. Gods zoors, when his Excellency comes he will have no such Justices.

Booz. Why, Brother, though I can't read my self, I have had *Dalton's* Country-Justice read over to me two or three times, and understand the Law. This is your Malice, Brother *Whiff*, because my Wife does not come to your

Warehouse to buy her Commodities,—but no matter,
to show I have no Malice in my Heart, I drink your
Health.—I care not this, I can turn Lawyer, and plead
at the Board.   [*Drinks, all pledge him, and hum.*

Dull. Mr. Clerk, come to the Tryals on the Dockett.
                              [*Clerk reads.*

Cler. The first is between his Worship Justice *Whiff*
and one *Grubb*.

Dull. Ay, that *Grubb*'s a common Disturber, Brother,
your Cause is a good Cause if well manag'd, here's to't.
                              [*Drinks.*

Whiff. I thank you, Brother *Dullman*—read my Petition.
                              [*Drinks.*

Cler. The Petition of Captain *Thomas Whiff*, sheweth,
That whereas *Gilbert Grubb* calls his Worship's Wife
Ann Whiff Whore, and said he would prove it; your
Petitioner desires the Worshipful Bench to take it into
Consideration, and your Petitioner shall ever pray, &c.—
Here's two Witnesses have made Affidavit *viva voce*,
an't like your Worships.

Dull. Call *Grubb*.

Cler. Gilbert Grubb, come into the Court.

Grub. Here.

Whim. Well, what can you say for your self, Mr. *Grubb*.

Grub. Why, an't like your Worship, my Wife invited
some Neighbours Wives to drink a Cagg of Syder; now
your Worship's Wife, Madam *Whiff*, being there fuddled,
would have thrust me out of doors, and bid me go to my
old Whore Madam *Whimsey*, meaning your Worship's
Wife.   [*To* Whimsey.

Whim. Hah! My Wife called Whore, she's a Jade, and
I'll arrest her Husband here—in an Action of Debts.

Tim. Gad zoors, she's no better than she should be,
I'll warrant her.

Whiff. Look ye, Brother *Whimsey*, be patient; you
know the humour of my *Nancy*, when she's drunk; but

when she's sober, she's a civil Person, and shall ask your pardon.

Whim. Let this be done, and I am satisfied. And so here's to you.   [*Drinks.*

Dull. Go on to the Trial.

Grub. I being very angry, said indeed, I would prove her a greater Whore than Madam *Whimsey.*

Cler. An't like your Worships, he confesses the Words in open Court.

Grub. Why, an't like your Worships, she has had two Bastards, I'll prove it.

Whiff. Sirrah, Sirrah, that was when she was a Maid, not since I marry'd her; my marrying her made her honest.

Dull. Let there be an order of Court to sue him for *Scandalum magnatum.*

Tim. Mr. Clerk, let my Cause come next.

Cler. The Defendant's ready, Sir.

                            [*Hazard comes to the Board.*

Tim. Brothers of the Bench, take notice, that this Hector here coming into Mrs. *Flirt's* Ordinary, where I was with my Brother *Dullman* and Lieutenant *Boozer;* we gave him good Counsel to fall to work : Now my Gentleman here was affronted at this, forsooth, and makes no more to do but calls us Scoundrels, and drew his Sword on us; and had I not defended my self by running away, he had murdered me, and assassinated my two Brothers.

Whiff. What Witness have you, Brother?

Tim. Here's Mrs. *Flirt* and her Maid *Nell,*—besides, we may be Witness for one another, I hope, our Words may be taken.

Cler. Mrs. *Flirt* and *Nell* are sworn. [*They stand forth.*

Whim. By the Oaths that you have taken, speak nothing but the truth.

Flirt. An't please your Worships, your Honours came to my House, where you found this young Gentleman :

and your Honours invited him to drink with your Honours;
Where after some opprobrious Words given him, Justice
Dullman, and Justice *Boozer* struck him over the Head;
and after that indeed the Gentleman drew.

Tim. Mark that, Brother, he drew.

Haz. If I did, it was *se defendendo*.

Tim. Do you hear that, Brothers, he did it in defiance.

Haz. Sir, you ought not to sit Judge and Accuser too.

Whiff. The Gentleman's i'th' right, Brother, you
cannot do't according to Law.

Tim. Gads zoors, what new tricks, new querks?

Haz. Gentlemen, take notice, he swears in Court.

Tim. Gads zoors, what's that to you, Sir?

Haz. This is the second time of his swearing.

Whim. What, do you think we are deaf, Sir? Come,
come, proceed.

Tim. I desire he may be bound to his Good Behaviour,
fin'd, and deliver up his Sword, what say you, Brother?
　　　　　　　　　　　　　　　　[*Jogs* Dull. *who nods.*

Whim. He's asleep, drink to him and waken him,—
you have miss'd the Cause by sleeping, Brother.
　　　　　　　　　　　　　　　　　　　　　[*Drinks.*

Dull. Justice may nod, but never sleeps, Brother—
you were at—Deliver his Sword—a good Motion, let it
be done.　　　　　　　　　　　　　　　　　　[*Drinks.*

Haz. No, Gentlemen, I wear a Sword to right my self.

Tim. That's fine, i'faith, Gads zoors, I've worn a Sword
this dozen Year, and never cou'd right my self.

Whiff. Ay, 'twou'd be a fine World if Men should
wear Swords to right themselves; he that's bound to the
Peace shall wear no Sword.

Whim. I say, he that's bound to the Peace ought to
wear no Peruke, they may change 'em for black or white,
and then who can know them.

Haz. I hope, Gentlemen, I may be allowed to speak
for my self.

Whiff. Ay, what can you say for your self, did you not draw your Sword, Sirrah?

Haz. I did.

Tim. 'Tis sufficient, he confesses the Fact, and we'll hear no more.

Haz. You will not hear the Provocation given.

Dull. 'Tis enough, Sir, you drew—

Whim. Ay, ay, 'tis enough, he drew—let him be fin'd.

Friend. The Gentleman should be heard, he's Kinsman too to Colonel *John Surelove.*

Tim. Hum—Colonel *Surelove's* Kinsman.

Whiff. Is he so? nay, then all the reason in the World he should be heard, Brothers.

Whim. Come, come, Cornet, you shall be Friends with the Gentleman; this was some drunken bout, I'll warrant you.

Tim. Ha, ha, ha, so it was, Gads zoors.

Whiff. Come, drink to the Gentleman, and put it up.

Tim. Sir, my service to you, I am heartily sorry for what's pass'd, but it was in my drink.   [*Drinks.*

Whim. You hear his Acknowledgments, Sir, and when he's sober he never quarrels. Come, Sir, sit down, my Service to you.

Haz. I beg your excuse, Gentlemen—I have earnest business.

Dull. Let us adjourn the Court, and prepare to meet the Regiments on the *Sevana.*

          [*All go but* Friend. *and* Hazard.

Haz. Is this the best Court of Judicature your Country affords?

Friend. To give it its due, it is not. But how does thy Amour thrive?

Haz. As well as I can wish in so short a time.

Friend. I see she regards thee with kind Eyes, Sighs and Blushes.

Haz. Yes, and tells me I am so like a Brother she had

—to excuse her kind concern,—then blushes so prettily, that, Gad, I cou'd not forbear making a discovery of my Heart.

Friend. Have a care of that, come upon her by slow degrees, for I know she is virtuous;—but come, let's to the *Sevana*, where I'll present you to the two Colonels, *Wellman* and *Downright*, the Men that manage all till the arrival of the Governour.　　　　　　［*Exeunt.*

SCENE II. *The* Sevana *or Heath*.

Enter Wellman, Downright, Boozer, *and Officers*.

Well. Have you dispatch'd the Scouts, to watch the Motions of the Enemies? I know that *Bacon* is violent and haughty, and will resent our vain Attempts upon him; therefore we must be speedy in prevention.

Down. What Forces have you raised since our last order?

Booz. Here's a List of 'em, they came but slowly in, till we promised every one a Bottle of Brandy.

Enter Officer *and* Dunce.

Offi. We have brought Mr. *Dunce* here, as your Honour commanded us; after strict search we found him this Morning in bed with Madam *Flirt*.

Down. No matter, he'll exclaim no less against the Vices of the Flesh the next Sunday.

Dun. I hope, Sir, you will not credit the Malice of my Enemies.

Well. No more, you are free, and what you counsell'd about the Ambush, was both prudent and seasonable, and perhaps I now wish it had taken effect.

Enter Friendly *and* Hazard.

Friend. I have brought an *English* Gentleman to kiss your Hands, Sir, and offer you his Service, he is young and brave, and Kinsman to Colonel *Surelove*.

Well. Sir, you are welcome; and to let you see you

are so, we will give you your Kinsman's Command, Captain of a Troop of Horse-Guards, and which I'm sure will be continued to you when the Governour arrives.

Haz. I shall endeavour to deserve the Honour, Sir.

Enter Dull. Tim. Whim. *and* Whiff, *all in Buff, Scarf, and Feather.*

Down. So, Gentlemen, I see you're in a readiness.

Tim. Readiness! What means he, I hope we are not to be drawn out to go against the Enemy, Major.

Dull. If we are, they shall look a new Major for me.

Well. We were debating, Gentlemen, what course were best to pursue against this powerful Rebel.

Friend. Why, Sir, we have Forces enough, let's charge him instantly, Delays are dangerous.

Tim. Why, what a damn'd fiery Fellow is this?

Down. But if we drive him to extremities, we fear his siding with the *Indians.*

Dull. Colonel *Downright* has hit it; why should we endanger our Men against a desperate Termagant; If he love Wounds and Scars so well, let him exercise on our Enemies—but if he will needs fall upon us, 'tis then time enough for us to venture our Lives and Fortunes.

Tim. How, we go to *Bacon!* under favour, I think 'tis his duty to come to us, an you go to that, Gads zoors.

Friend. If he do, 'twill cost you dear, I doubt, Cornet. —I find by our List, Sir, we are four thousand Men.

Tim. Gads zoors, not enough for a Breakfast for that insatiate *Bacon,* and his two Lieutenant Generals, *Fearless* and *Daring.*

[Whiff *sits on the Ground with a Bottle of Brandy.*

Whim. A Morsel, a Morsel.

Well. I am for an attack, what say you, Gentlemen, to an attack?—What, silent all? What say you, Major?

Dull. I say, Sir, I hope my Courage was never in dispute. But, Sir, I am going to marry Colonel *Downright's*

Daughter here—and should I be slain in this Battle 'twould break her Heart;—besides, Sir, I should lose her Fortune.   [*Speaks big.*

Well. I'm sure here's a Captain will never flinch.
                                    [*To* Whim.

Whim. Who, I, an't like your Honour?

Well. Ay, you.

Whim. Who, I? ha, ha, ha: Why, did your Honour think that I would fight?

Well. Fight! yes; why else do you take Commissions?

Whim. Commissions! Oh Lord, O Lord, take Commissions to fight! ha, ha, ha; that's a jest, if all that take Commissions should fight—

Well. Why do you bear Arms then?

Whim. Why, for the Pay; to be called Captain, noble Captain, to show, to cock and look big, and bluff as I do: to be bow'd to thus as we pass, to domineer and beat our Soldiers: Fight, quoth a, ha, ha, ha.

Friend. But what makes you look so simply, Cornet?

Tim. Why, a thing that I have quite forgot, all my Accounts for *England* are to be made up, and I'm undone if they be neglected—else I wou'd not flinch for the stoutest he that wears a Sword—   [*Looking big.*

Down. What say you, Captain *Whiff*?
                                    [Whiff *almost drunk.*

Whiff. I am trying, Colonel, what Mettle I'm made on; I think I am valiant, I suppose I have Courage, but I confess 'tis a little of the D— breed, but a little inspiration from the Bottle, and the leave of my *Nancy*, may do wonders.

Enter a Seaman *in haste.*

Sea. An't please your Honours, *Frightall's* Officers have seiz'd all the Ships in the River, and rid now round the Shore, and had by this time secur'd the sandy Beach, and landed Men to fire the Town, but that they are high in drink aboard the Ship call'd the Good-Subject; the Master of her sent me to let your Honours know, that a few Men sent to his assistance will surprize them and retake the Ships.

Well. Now, Gentlemen, here is a brave occasion for Emulation—why writ not the Master?

Dull. Ay, had he writ, I had soon been amongst them, i'faith; but this is some Plot to betray us.

Sea. Keep me here, and kill me if it be not true.

Down. He says well—there's a Brigantine and a Shallop ready, I'll embark immediately.

Friend. No, Sir, your Presence is here more necessary, let me have the Honour of this Expedition.

Haz. I'll go your Volunteer, *Charles.*

Well. Who else offers to go?

Whim. A mere Trick to kidnap us, by *Bacon,*—if the Captain had writ.

Tim. Ay, ay, if he had writ—

Well. I see you're all base Cowards, and here cashier ye from all Commands and Offices.

Whim. Look ye, Colonel, you may do what you please, but you lose one of the best dress'd Officers in your whole Camp, Sir.

Tim. And in me, such a Head-piece.

Whiff. I'll say nothing, but let the State want me.

Dull. For my part I am weary of weighty Affairs.

[*In this while* Well. Down. Friend. *and* Haz. *talk.*

Well. Command what Men you please, but Expedition makes you half a Conqueror. [*Ex.* Friend. *and* Haz.

Enter another Seaman *with a Letter, gives it to* Downright, *he and* Wellman *read it.*

Down. Look ye now, Gentlemen, the Master has writ.

Dull. Has he—he might have writ sooner, while I was in Command,—if he had—

Whim. Ay, Major—if he had—but let them miss us.

Well. Colonel, haste with your Men, and reinforce the Beach, while I follow with the Horse;—Mr. *Dunce,* pray let that Proclamation be read concerning *Bacon,* to the Soldiers.   [*Ex.* Down. *and* Well.

Dun. It shall be done, Sir. Gentlemen, how simply you look now.

The Scene opens and discovers a Body of Soldiers.

Tim. Why, Mr. Parson, I have a scruple of Conscience upon me, I am considering whether it be lawful to kill, though it be in War; I have a great aversion to't, and hope it proceeds from Religion.

Whiff. I remember the Fit took you just so when the *Dutch* besieged us, for you cou'd not then be persuaded to strike a stroke.

Tim. Ay, that was because they were Protestants as we are; but, Gads zoors, had they been *Dutch* Papists I had maul'd them: but Conscience—

Whim. I have been a Justice of Peace this six Years, and never had a Conscience in my Life.

Tim. Nor I neither, but in this damn'd thing of fighting.

Dun. Gentlemen, I am commanded to read the Declaration of the honourable Council to you.   [*To the Soldiers.*

All. Hum, hum, hum—

Booz. Silence—silence—   [*Dunce reads.*

Dun. By an order of Council, dated *May* the 10th, 1670. To all Gentlemen Soldiers, Merchants, Planters, and whom else it may concern. Whereas *Bacon,* contrary to Law and Equity, has, to satisfy his own Ambition, taken up Arms with a pretence to fight the *Indians,* but indeed to molest and enslave the whole Colony, and to take away their Liberties and Properties; this is to declare, that whoever shall bring this Traitor dead or alive to the Council, shall have three hundred pounds Reward. And so God save the King.

All. A Council, a Council! Hah—   [*Hollow.*

Enter a Soldier *hastily.*

Sold. Stand to your Arms, Gentlemen, stand to your Arms, *Bacon* is marching this way.

Dun. Hah—what Numbers has he?

Sold. About a hundred Horse, in his march he has surpriz'd Colonel *Downright*, and taken him Prisoner.

All. Let's fall on *Bacon*—let's fall on *Bacon*, hay.

[*Hollow.*

Booz. We'll hear him speak first—and see what he can say for himself.

All. Ay, ay, we'll hear *Bacon* speak.

[*Dunce pleads with them.*

Tim. Well, Major, I have found a Stratagem shall make us Four the greatest Men in the Colony, we'll surrender our selves to *Bacon*, and say we disbanded on purpose.

Dull. Good—

Whiff. Why, I had no other design in the World in refusing to fight.

Whim. Nor I, d'ye think I wou'd have excus'd it with the fear of disordering my Cravat-String else.

Dun. Why, Gentlemen, he designs to fire *James* Town, murder you all, and then lie with your Wives; and will you slip this opportunity of seizing him?

Booz. Here's a termagant Rogue, Neighbours—we'll hang the Dog.

All. Ay, ay, hang *Bacon*, hang *Bacon*.

Enter Bacon *and* Fearless, *some Soldiers leading in* Downright *bound;* Bacon *stands and stares a while on the Regiments, who are silent all.*

Bac. Well, Gentlemen, in order to your fine Declaration, you see I come to render my self.

Dun. How came he to know of our Declaration?

Whiff. Rogues, Rogues among our selves, that inform.

Bac. What, are ye silent all,—not a Man to lift his Hand in Obedience to the Council, to murder this Traytor

that has exposed his Life so often for you? Hah, what,
not for three hundred Pound?—You see I've left my
Troops behind, and come all wearied with the Toils
of War, worn out by Summers heats, and Winters cold,
march'd tedious Days and Nights through Bogs and
Fens as dangerous as your Clamours, and as faithless,—
what though 'twas to preserve you all in Safety, no matter,
you shou'd obey the grateful Council, and kill this honest
Man that has defended you.

All. Hum, hum, hum.

Whiff. The General speaks like a Gorgon.

Tim. Like a Cherubin, Man.

Bac. All silent yet—where's that mighty Courage, that
cried so loud but now, A Council, a Council? where is your
Resolution? cannot three hundred Pound excite your
Valour to seize that Traitor *Bacon* who has bled for you?

All. A *Bacon*, a *Bacon*, a *Bacon*.   [*Hollow.*

Down. Oh villainous Cowards!—Oh the faithless
Multitude!

Bac. What say you, Parson?—you have a forward Zeal.

Dun. I wish my Coat, Sir, did not hinder me from
acting as becomes my Zeal and Duty.

Whim. A plaguy rugged Dog,—that Parson—

Bac. Fearless, seize me that canting Knave from out
the Herd, and next those honourable Officers.

> [*Points to* Dull, Whim, Whiff, *and* Tim. *Fearless
> seizes them, and gives them to the Soldiers, and takes
> the Proclamation from* Dunce, *and shews* Bacon;
> *they read it.*

Dull. Seize us, Sir, you shall not need, we laid down our
Commissions on purpose to come over to your Honour.

Whiff. We ever lov'd and honour'd your Honour.

Tim. So intirely, Sir—that I wish I were safe in *James*
Town for your sake, and your Honour were hang'd. [*Aside.*

Bac. This fine Piece is of your penning, Parson,—
though it be countenanc'd by the Council's Names.—Oh

Ingratitude! Burn, burn the treacherous Town, fire it immediately.—

Whim. We'll obey you, Sir.

Whiff. Ay, ay, we'll make a Bonfire on't, and drink your Honour's health round about it. [*They offer to go.*

Bac. Yet hold, my Revenge shall be more merciful, I ordered that all the Women of Rank shall be seiz'd and brought to my Camp. I'll make their Husbands pay their Ransoms dearly; they'd rather have their Hearts bleed than their Purses.

Fear. Dear General, let me have the seizing of Colonel *Downright*'s Daughter; I would fain be plundering for a Trifle call'd a Maiden-head.

Bac. On pain of Death treat them with all respect; assure them of the safety of their Honour. Now, all that will follow me, shall find a welcome, and those that will not, may depart in Peace.

All. Hay, a General, a General, a General.

[*Some Soldiers go off: Some go to the side of* Bacon.

Enter Daring *and Soldiers, with* Chrisante, Surelove, *Mrs.* Whim. *and Mrs.* Whiff, *and several other Women.*

Bac. Successful *Daring*, welcome, what Prizes have ye?

Dar. The fairest in the World, Sir; I'm not for common Plunder.

Down. Hah, my Daughter and my Kinswoman!—

Bac. 'Tis not with Women, Sir, nor honest men like you, that I intend to combat; not their own Parents shall be more indulgent, nor better Safe-guard to their Honours, Sir: But 'tis to save the expence of Blood I seize on their most valued Prizes.

Down. But, Sir, I know your wild Lieutenant General has long lov'd my *Chrisante*, and perhaps, will take this time to force her to consent.

Dar. I own I have a Passion for *Chrisante*, yet by my General's Life, or her fair self, what now I act is on the score of War, I scorn to force the Maid I do adore.

Bac. Believe me, Ladies, you shall have honourable Treatment here.

Chris. We do not doubt it, Sir, either from you or *Daring*; if he love me, that will secure my Honour; or if he do not, he's too brave to injure me.

Dar. I thank you for your just opinion of me, Madam.

Chris. But, Sir, 'tis for my Father I must plead; to see his reverend Hands in servile Chains; and then perhaps, if stubborn to your Will, his Head must fall a Victim to your Anger.

Down. No, my good pious Girl, I cannot fear ignoble usage from the General; and if thy Beauty can preserve thy Fame, I shall not mourn in my Captivity.

Bac. I'll ne'er deceive your kind opinion of me— Ladies, I hope you're all of that Opinion too.

Sure. If seizing us, Sir, can advance your Honour, or be of any use considerable to you, I shall be proud of such a Slavery.

Mrs. *Whim.* I hope, Sir, we shan't be ravish'd in your Camp.

Dar. Fie, Mrs. *Whimsey*, do Soldiers use to ravish?

Mrs. *Whiff.* Ravish! marry, I fear 'em not, I'd have 'em know, I scorn to be ravish'd by any Man.

Fear. Ay, o' my Conscience, Mrs. *Whiff*, you are too good-natur'd.

Dar. Madam, I hope you'll give me leave to name Love to you, and try by all submissive ways to win your Heart.

Chris. Do your worst, Sir: I give you leave, if you assail me only with your Tongue.

Dar. That's generous and brave, and I'll requite it.

Enter Soldier *in haste.*

Sold. The Truce being ended, Sir, the *Indians* grow so insolent as to attack us even in our Camp, and have killed several of our Men.

Bac. 'Tis time to check their Boldness; *Daring*, haste,
draw up our Men in order to give 'em Battel, I rather
had expected their submission.

> *The Country now may see what they're to fear,*
> *Since we that are in Arms are not secure.*

> [*Exeunt, leading the Ladies.*

ACT IV.

SCENE I. *A Temple, with an* Indian *God placed upon it,*
Priests and Priestesses attending: Enter Indian King *on one*
side attended by Indian *Men; the* Queen *enters on the other*
with Women. All bow to the Idol, and divide on each side of the
Stage. Then the Musick playing louder, the Priests and Priest-
esses dance about the Idol with ridiculous Postures, and crying
(as for Incantations) thrice repeated, Agah Yerkin,
Agah Boah, Sulen Tawarapah, Sulen Tawarapah.

After this soft Musick plays again: then they sing something
fine: after which the Priests lead the King *to the Altar, and*
the Priestesses the Queen *; they take off little Crowns*
from their Heads, and offer them at the Altar.

King. Invoke the God of our Quiocto to declare what
the Event shall be of this our last War against the *English*
General.   [*Soft Musick ceases.*

> [*The Musick changes to confused Tunes, to which the*
> *Priests and Priestesses dance, antickly singing between,*
> *the same Incantation as before; and then dance again,*
> *and so invoke again alternately: Which Dance ended,*
> *a Voice behind the Altar cries, while soft Musick plays,*

The *English* General shall be
A Captive to his Enemy;
And you from all your Toils be freed,
When by your Hand the Foe shall bleed:
And e'er the Sun's swift course be run,
This mighty Conquest shall be won.

King. I thank the Gods for taking care of us; prepare new Sacrifice against the Evening, when I return a Conqueror, I will my self perform the Office of a Priest.

Queen. Oh, Sir, I fear you'll fall a Victim first.

King. What means *Semernia?* why are thy Looks so pale?

Queen. Alas, the Oracles have double meanings, their Sense is doubtful, and their Words Enigmas: I fear, Sir, I cou'd make a truer Interpretation.

King. How, *Semernia!* by all thy Love I charge thee, as you respect my Life, to let me know your Thoughts.

Queen. Last Night I dream'd a Lyon fell with hunger, spite of your Guards, slew you, and bore you hence.

King. This is thy Sex's fear, and no Interpretation of the Oracle.

Queen. I cou'd convince you farther.

King. Hast thou a Secret thou canst keep from me? thy Soul a Thought that I must be a Stranger to? This is not like the Justice of *Semernia:* Come unriddle me the Oracle.

Queen. The *English* General shall be a Captive to his Enemy; he is so, Sir, already, to my Beauty, he says he languishes for Love of me.

King. Hah! the General my Rival—but go on—

Queen. And you from all your War be freed: Oh, let me not explain that fatal Line, for fear it mean, you shall be freed by Death.

King. What, when by my Hand the Foe shall bleed? —away—it cannot be—

Queen. No doubt, my Lord, you'll bravely sell your Life, and deal some Wounds where you'll receive so many.

King. 'Tis Love, *Semernia,* makes thee dream while waking:
I'll trust the Gods, and am resolv'd for Battel.

Enter an Indian.

Ind. Haste, haste, great Sir, to Arms; *Bacon* with all his Forces is prepar'd, and both the Armies ready to engage.

King. Haste to my General, bid him charge 'em instantly; I'll bring up the Supplies of stout *Teroomians*, those so well skill'd in the envenom'd Arrow. [*Ex.* Indian.
—*Semernia*—Words but poorly do express the Griefs of parting Lovers—'tis with dying Eyes, and a Heart trembling—thus—   [*Puts her Hand on his Heart.*
they take a heavy leave;—one parting Kiss, and one Love pressing sigh, and then farewel:—but not a long farewel; I shall return victorious to thy Arms—commend me to the Gods, and still remember me.   [*Exit.*

Queen. Alas! What pity 'tis I saw the General, before my Fate had given me to the King—But now—like those that change their Gods, my faithless Mind betwixt my two Opinions wavers; while to the Gods my Monarch I commend; my wandring Thoughts in pity of the General makes that Zeal cold, declin'd—ineffectual.— If for the General I implore the Deities, methinks my Prayers should not ascend the Skies, since Honour tells me 'tis an impious Zeal.

> *Which way soever my Devotions move,*
> *I am too wretched to be heard above.*
>   [*Goes in.   All exeunt.*

SCENE II. *Shows a Field of Tents, seen at some distance through the Trees of a Wood, Drums, Trumpets and the noise of Battel, with hollowing. The* Indians *are seen with Battel-Axes to retreat fighting from the* English, *and all go off; when they re-enter immediately beating back the* English, *the* Indian King *at the head of his Men, with Bows and Arrows;*
Daring *being at the head of the* English: *They fight off; the Noise continues less loud as more at distance.*

Enter Bacon *with his Sword drawn, meets* Fearless *with his Sword drawn.*

Fear. Haste, haste, Sir, to the Entrance of the Wood, *Daring's* engaged past hope of a Retreat, venturing too far, pursuing of the Foe; the King in Ambush, with his poison'd Archers, fell on, and now we are dangerously distrest.

Bac. *Daring* is brave, but he's withal too rash, come on and follow me to his Assistance——   [*Go out.*

> [*A hollowing within, the Fight renews; enter the* Indians *beaten back by* Bacon, Daring *and* Fearless; *they fight off; the noise of Fighting continues a while, this still behind the Wood.*

Enter Indians *flying over the Stage, pursu'd by the* King.

King. Turn, turn, ye fugitive Slaves, and face the Enemy; Oh Villains, Cowards, deaf to all Command: by Heaven, I had my Rival in my view, and aim'd at nothing but my conquering him—now like a Coward I must fly with Cowards, or like a desperate Madman fall, thus singly, midst the numbers. [*Follows the* Indians.

Enter Bacon *inraged with his Sword drawn,* Fearless *and* Daring *following him.*

Bac. —Where is the King, oh ye perfidious Slaves? how, have you hid him from my just Revenge?—search all the Brakes, the Furzes and the Trees, and let him not escape on pain of Death.

Dar. We cannot do wonders, Sir.

Bac. But you can run away.——

Dar. Yes, when we see occasion—yet—shou'd any but my General tell me so—by Heaven, he should find I were no starter.

Bac. Forgive me, I'm mad—the King's escaped, hid like a trembling Slave in some close Ditch, where he will sooner starve than fight it out.

Re-enter Indians *running over the Stage, pursued by the* King, *who shoots them as they fly; some few follow him.*

King. All's lost—the Day is lost—and I'm betray'd; —Oh Slaves, that even Wounds can't animate. [*In Rage.*

Bac. The King!

King. The General here ! by all the Powers, betray'd by my own Men !

Bac. Abandon'd as thou art, I scorn to take thee basely ; you shall have Soldiers chance, Sir, for your Life, since Chance so luckily has brought us hither ; without more Aids we will dispute the Day : This Spot of Earth bears both our Armies Fates ; I'll give you back the Victory I have won, and thus begin a-new on equal Terms.

King. That's nobly said !—the Powers have heard my Wish. You, Sir, first taught me how to use a Sword, which heretofore has served me with Success : But now —'tis for *Semernia* that it draws, a Prize more valued than my Kingdom, Sir—

Bac. Hah, *Semernia* !

King. Your Blushes do betray your Passion for her.

Dar. 'Sdeath, have we fought for this, to expose the Victor to the conquer'd Foe ?

Fear. What, fight a single Man—our Prize already.

King. Not so, young Man, while I command a Dart.

Bac. Fight him ! by Heaven, no reason shall dissuade me, and he that interrupts me is a Coward ; whatever be my Fate, I do command ye to let the King pass freely to his Tents.

Dar. The Devil's in the General.

Fear. 'Sdeath, his Romantick Humour will undo us.
                              [*They fight and pause.*

King. You fight as if you meant to outdo me this way, as you have done in Generosity.

Bac. You're not behind-hand with me, Sir, in courtesy : Come, here's to set us even—   [*Fight again.*

King. You bleed apace.

Bac. You've only breath'd a Vein, and given me new Health and Vigour by it.

    [*They fight again, Wounds on both sides, the* King *staggers ;
        Bacon takes him in his Arms ; the* King *drops his Sword.*
How do you, Sir ?

King. Like one—that's hovering between Heaven and Earth; I'm—mounting—somewhere—upwards—but giddy with my flight,—I know not where.

Bac. Command my Surgeons,—instantly—make haste; Honour returns, and Love all bleeding's fled.

[*Ex.* Fearless.

King. Oh, *Semernia*, how much more Truth had thy Divinity than the Predictions of the flattering Oracles! Commend me to her—I know you'll—visit—your fair Captive, Sir, and tell her—oh—but Death prevents the rest.   [*Dies.*

Enter Fearless.

Bac. He's gone—and now, like *Cæsar*, I could weep over the Hero I my self destroyed.

Fear. I'm glad for your repose I see him there—'twas a mad hot-brain'd Youth, and so he died.

Bac. Come bear him on your Shoulders to my Tent. from whence with all the solemn State we can, we will convey him to his own Pavilion.

Enter a Soldier.

Sold. Some of our Troops pursuing of the Enemy even to their Temples, which they made their Sanctuary, finding the Queen at her Devotion there with all her *Indian* Ladies, I'd much ado to stop their violent Rage from setting fire to the holy Pile.

Bac. Hang 'em immediately that durst attempt it, while I my self will fly to rescue her.

[*Goes out, they bear off the* King's *Body; Ex. all.*

Enter Whimsey, *pulling in* Whiff, *with a Halter about his Neck.*

Whim. Nay, I'm resolved to keep thee here till his Honour the General comes.—What, to call him Traitor, and run away after he had so generously given us our freedom, and listed us Cadees for the next Command that fell in his Army—I'm resolved to hang thee—

Whiff. Wilt thou betray and peach thy Friend? thy
Friend taht kept thee Company all the while thou wert
a Prisoner—drinking at my own charge—

Whim. No matter for that, I scorn Ingratitude, and
therefore will hang thee—but as for thy drinking with
me—I scorn to be behind-hand with thee in Civility, and
therefore here's to thee.

> [*Takes a Bottle of Brandy out of his Pocket, Drinks.*
Whiff. I can't drink.

Whim. A certain sign thou wo't be hang'd.

Whiff. You us'd to be o' my side when a Justice, let
the Cause be how it wou'd.   [*Weeps.*

Whim. Ay—when I was a Justice I never minded
Honesty, but now I'll be true to my General, and hang
thee to be a great Man.—

Whiff. If I might but have a fair Trial for my Life—

Whim. A fair Trial!—come, I'll be thy Judge—and
if thou canst clear thy self by Law, I'll acquit thee:
Sirrah, Sirrah, what canst thou say for thy self for calling
his Honour Rebel?   [*Sits on a Drum-head.*

Whiff. 'Twas when I was drunk, an't like your Honour.

Whim. That's no Plea; for if you kill a Man when
you are sober, you must be hanged when you are drunk.
Hast thou any thing else to say for thy self why Sentence
may not pass upon thee?

Whiff. I desire the Benefit of the Clergy.

Whim. The Clergy! I never knew any body that ever
did benefit by 'em; why, thou canst not read a word.

Whiff. Transportation then—

Whim. It shall be to *England* then—but hold—who's
this?   [Dullman *creeping from a Bush.*

Dull. So the Danger's over, I may venture out—Pox
on't, I wou'd not be in this fear again, to be Lord Chief
Justice of our Court. Why, how now, Cornet?—what,
in dreadful Equipage? Your Battle-Ax bloody, with Bow
and Arrows.

Enter Timorous *with Battle-Ax, Bow and Arrows, and Feathers on his Head.*

Tim. I'm in the posture of the times, Major—I cou'd not be idle where so much Action was; I'm going to present my self to the General, with these Trophies of my Victory here—

Dull. Victory—what Victory—did not I see thee creeping out of yonder Bush, where thou wert hid all the Fight—stumble on a dead *Indian,* and take away his Arms?

Tim. Why, didst thou see me?

Dull. See thee, ay—and what a fright thou wert in, till thou wert sure he was dead.

Tim. Well, well, that's all one—Gads zoors, if every Man that passes for valiant in a Battel, were to give an account how he gained his Reputation, the World wou'd be but thinly stock'd with Heroes; I'll say he was a great War-Captain, and that I kill'd him hand to hand, and who can disprove me?

Dull. Disprove thee—why, that pale Face of thine, that has so much of the Coward in't.

Tim. Shaw, that's with loss of Blood—Hah, I am overheard I doubt—who's yonder—[*Sees* Whim. *and* Whiff.] how, Brother *Whiff* in a Hempen Cravat-string?

Whim. He call'd the General Traitor, and was running away, and I'm resolv'd to peach.

Dull. Hum—and one Witness will stand good in Law, in case of Treason—

Tim. Gads zoors, in case of Treason, he'll be hang'd if it be proved against him, were there ne'er a Witness at all; but he must be tried by a Council of War, Man—Come, come, let's disarm him—

[*They take away his Arms, and pull a Bottle of Brandy out of his Pocket.*

Whiff. What, I hope you will not take away my Brandy, Gentlemen, my last comfort.

Tim. Gads zoors, it's come in good time—we'll drink it off, here, Major—   [*Drinks*, Whiff *takes him aside.*

Whiff. Hark ye, Cornet—you are my good Friend, get this matter made up before it come to the General.

Tim. But this is Treason, Neighbour.

Whiff. If I hang—I'll declare upon the Ladder how you kill'd your War-Captain.

Tim. Come, Brother *Whimsey*—we have been all Friends and loving Magistrates together, let's drink about, and think no more of this Business.

Dull. Ay, ay, if every sober Man in the Nation should be called to account of the Treason he speaks in's Drink, the Lord have mercy upon us all.—Put it up—and let us, like loving Brothers, take an honest Resolution to run away together; for this same *Frightall* minds nothing but Fighting.

Whim. I'm content, provided we go all to the Council, and tell them (to make our Peace) we went in obedience to the Proclamation, to kill *Bacon*, but the Traitor was so strongly guarded we could not effect it: but mum—who's here?—

To them, enter Ranter *and* Jenny, *as Man and Footman.*

Ran. Hah, our four reverend Justices—I hope the Blockheads will not know me—Gentlemen, can you direct me to Lieutenant General *Daring's* Tents?

Whiff. Hum, who the Devil's this?—that's he you see coming this way. 'Sdeath, yonder's *Daring*—let's slip away before he advances. [*Exeunt all but* Ran. *and* Jen.

Jen. I am scar'd with those dead Bodies we have pass'd over; for God's sake, Madam, let me know your design in coming.

Ran. Why, now I tell thee—my damn'd mad Fellow *Daring*, who has my Heart and Soul, loves *Chrisante*, has stolen her, and carried her away to his Tents; she hates him, while I am dying for him.

Jem. Dying, Madam! I never saw you melancholy.

Ran. Pox on't, no; why should I sigh and whine, and make my self an Ass, and him conceited? no, instead of snivelling I am resolved——

Jen. What, Madam?

Ran. Gad, to beat the Rascal, and bring off *Chrisante*.

Jen. Beat him, Madam! what, a Woman beat a Lieutenant-General?

Ran. Hang 'em, they get a name in War from Command, not Courage; but how know I but I may fight? Gad, I have known a Fellow kick'd from one end of the Town to t'other, believing himself a Coward; at last forced to fight, found he could; got a Reputation, and bullied all he met with; and got a Name, and a great Commission.

Jen. But if he should kill you, Madam.

Ran. I'll take care to make it as comical a Duel as the best of 'em; as much in love as I am, I do not intend to die its Martyr.

Enter Daring *and* Fearless.

Fear. Have you seen *Chrisante* since the Fight?

Dar. Yes, but she is still the same, as nice and coy as Fortune when she's courted by the wretched; yet she denies me so obligingly, she keeps my Love still in its humble Calm.

Ran. Can you direct me, Sir, to one *Daring's* Tent?
                                                    [*Sullenly.*

Dar. One *Daring!*——he has another Epithet to his Name.

Ran. What's that, Rascal, or Coward?

Dar. Hah, which of thy Stars, young Man, has sent thee hither, to find that certain Fate they have decreed?

Ran. I know not what my Stars have decreed, but I shall be glad if they have ordain'd me to fight with *Daring*:——by thy concern thou shou'dst be he?

Dar. I am, prithee who art thou?

Ran. Thy Rival, though newly arrived from *England*, and came to marry fair *Chrisante*, whom thou hast ravish'd, for whom I hear another Lady dies.

Dar. Dies for me?

Ran. Therefore resign her fairly——or fight me fairly——

Dar. Come on, Sir——but hold——before I kill thee, prithee inform me who this dying Lady is?

Ran. Sir, I owe ye no Courtesy, and therefore will do you none by telling you——come, Sir, for *Chrisante*——draw.

[*They offer to fight*, Fearless *steps in.*

Fear. Hold——what mad Frolick's this?——Sir, you fight for one you never saw [*to* Ranter.] and you for one that loves you not.   [*To* Dar.

Dar. Perhaps she'll love him as little.

Ran. Gad, put it to the Trial, if you dare——if thou be'st generous, bring me to her, and whom she does neglect shall give the other place.

Dar. That's fair, put up thy Sword——I'll bring thee to her instantly.   [*Exeunt.*

Scene III.   *A Tent.*

Enter Chrisante *and* Surelove.

Chris. I'm not so much afflicted for my Confinement, as I am that I cannot hear of *Friendly*.

Sure. Art not persecuted with *Daring*?

Chris. Not at all; though he tells me daily of his Passion, I rally him, and give him neither Hope nor Despair,——he's here.

Enter Daring, Fear. Rant. *and* Jenny.

Dar. Madam, the Complaisance I show in bringing you my Rival, will let you see how glad I am to oblige you every way.

Ran. I hope the Danger I have exposed my self to for

the Honour of kissing your Hand, Madam, will render
me something acceptable—here are my Credentials—

                                  [Gives her a Letter.

Chrisante reads.

*Dear Creature, I have taken this Habit to free you from
an impertinent Lover, and to secure the damn'd Rogue*
Daring *to my self: receive me as sent by Colonel* Surelove
from England *to marry you—favour me—no more—*

                                   Yours, Ranter.

—Hah, *Ranter?* [*Aside.*] —Sir, you have too good a
Character from my Cousin Colonel *Surelove,* not to
receive my Welcome.   [*Gives* Surelove *the Letter.*

Ran. Stand by, General—

    [*Pushes away* Daring, *looks big, and takes* Chrisante
    by the Hand, and kisses it.

Dar. 'Sdeath, Sir, there's room enough—at first sight
so kind! Oh Youth, Youth and Impudence, what Temptations are you to Villanous Woman?

Chris. I confess, Sir, we Women do not love these
rough fighting Fellows, they're always scaring us with
one Broil or other.

Dar. Much good may it do you with your tame Coxcomb.

Ran. Well, Sir, then you yield the Prize?

Dar. Ay, Gad, were she an Angel, that can prefer
such a callow Fop as thou before a Man—take her and
domineer.   [*They all laugh.*
—'Sdeath, am I grown ridiculous?

Fear. Why hast thou not found the Jest? by Heaven, 'tis
Ranter, 'tis she that loves you; carry on the humour. [*Aside.*
Faith, Sir, if I were you, I wou'd devote my self to
Madam *Ranter.*

Chris. Ay, she's the fittest Wife for you, she'll fit your
Humour.

Dar. Ranter—Gad, I'd sooner marry a she-Bear,

unless for a Penance for some horrid Sin; we should be eternally challenging one another to the Field, and ten to one she beats me there; or if I should escape there, she wou'd kill me with drinking.

Ran. Here's a Rogue—does your Country abound with such Ladies?

Dar. The Lord forbid, half a dozen wou'd ruin the Land, debauch all the Men, and scandalize all the Women.

Fear. No matter, she's rich.

Dar. Ay, that will make her insolent.

Fear. Nay, she's generous too.

Dar. Yes, when she's drunk, and then she'll lavish all.

Ran. A pox on him, how he vexes me.

Dar. Then such a Tongue—she'll rail and smoke till she choke again; then six Gallons of Punch hardly recovers her, and never but then is she good-natur'd.

Ran. I must lay him on—

Dar. There's not a Blockhead in the Country that has not—

Ran. What—

Dar. Been drunk with her.

Ran. I thought you had meant something else, Sir.

[*In huff.*

Dar. Nay—as for that—I suppose there is no great difficulty.

Ran. 'Sdeath, Sir, you lye—and you are a Son of a Whore.

[*Draws and fences with him, and he runs back round the Stage.*

Dar. Hold—hold, Virago—dear Widow, hold, and give me thy hand.

Ran. Widow!

Dar. 'Sdeath, I knew thee by instinct, Widow, though I seemed not to do so, in Revenge for the Trick you put on me in telling me a Lady dy'd for me.

Ran. Why, such an one there is, perhaps she may dwindle forty or fifty years—or so—but will never be her own Woman again, that's certain.

Sure. This we are all ready to testify, we know her.

Chris. Upon my Life, 'tis true.

Dar. Widow, I have a shreud Suspicion, that you your self may be this dying Lady.

Ran. Why so, Coxcomb?

Dar. Because you took such Pains to put your self into my hands.

Ran. Gad, if your Heart were but half so true as your Guess, we should conclude a Peace before *Bacon* and the Council will—besides, this thing whines for *Friendly*, and there's no hopes.   [*To* Chrisante.

Dar. Give me thy Hand, Widow, I am thine—and so entirely, I will never—be drunk out of thy Company :— *Dunce* is in my Tent,—prithee let's in and bind the Bargain.

Ran. Nay, faith, let's see the Wars at an end first.

Dar. Nay, prithee take me in the humour, while thy Breeches are on—for I never lik'd thee half so well in Petticoats.

Ran. Lead on, General, you give me good incouragement to wear them.   [*Exeunt.*

ACT V.

SCENE I. *The* Sevana *in sight of the Camp; the Moon rises.*

Enter Friendly, Hazard *and* Boozer, *and a Party of Men.*

Friend. We are now in sight of the Tents.

Booz. Is not this a rash Attempt, Gentlemen, with so small Force to set upon *Bacon's* whole Army?

Haz. Oh, they are drunk with Victory and Wine; there will be nought but revelling to night.

Friend. Would we could learn in what Quarter the

Ladies are lodg'd, for we have no other business but to
release them—But hark—who comes here?

Booz. Some Scouts, I fear, from the Enemy.

Enter Dull. Tim. Whim. *and* Whiff, *creeping as in
the dark.*

Friend. Let's shelter ourselves behind yonder Trees—
lest we be surpriz'd.

Tim. Wou'd I were well at home—Gad zoors, if e'er
you catch me a Cadeeing again, I'll be content to be set
in the fore-front of the Battle for Hawks-Meat.

Whim. Thou'rt afraid of every Bush.

Tim. Ay, and good reason too: Gad zoors, there may
be Rogues hid—prithee, Major, do thou advance.

Dull. No, no, go on—no matter of Ceremony in these
cases of running away.   [*They advance.*

Friend. They approach directly to us, we cannot escape
them—their numbers are not great—let us advance.
                              [*They come up to them.*

Tim. Oh! I am annihilated.

Whiff. Some of *Frightall*'s Scouts, we are lost Men.
                        [*They push each other foremost.*

Friend. Who goes there?

Whim. Oh, they'll give us no Quarter; 'twas long
of you, Cornet, that we ran away from our Colours.

Tim. Me—'twas the Major's Ambition here—to make
himself a great Man with the Council again.

Dull. Pox o' this Ambition, it has been the ruin of
many a gallant Fellow.

Whiff. If I get home again, the height of mine shall
be to top Tobacco; would I'd some Brandy.

Tim. Gads zoors, would we had, 'tis the best Armour
against Fear—hum—I hear no body now—prithee
advance a little.

Whim. What, before a Horse-Officer?

Friend. Stand, on your Lives—

Tim. Oh, 'tis impossible—I'm dead already.

Friend. What are ye?—speak—or I'll shoot.

Whim. Friends to thee,—who the Devil are we Friends to?

Tim. E'en who please you, Gad zoors.

Friend. Hah—Gad zoors—who's there, *Timorous?*

Tim. Hum—I know no such Scoundrel—[*Gets behind.*

Dull. Hah—that's *Friendly's* Voice.

Friend. Right—thine's that of *Dullman*—who's with you?

Dull. Only *Timorous, Whimsey* and *Whiff,* all valiantly running away from the Arch-Rebel that took us Prisoners.

Haz. Can you inform us where the Ladies are lodg'd?

Dull. In the hither Quarter, in *Daring's* Tent; you'll know them by Lanthorns on every corner—there was never better time to surprize them—for this day *Daring's* married, and there's nothing but Dancing and Drinking.

Haz. Married! to whom?

Dull. That I ne'er enquir'd.

Friend. 'Tis to *Chrisante,* Friend—and the Reward of my Attempt is lost. Oh, I am mad, I'll fight away my Life, and my Despair shall yet do greater Wonders, than even my Love could animate me to. Let's part our Men, and beset his Tents on both sides.

[*Friendly goes out with a Party.*

Haz. Come, Gentlemen, let's on—

Whiff. On, Sir,—we on, Sir?—

Haz. Ay, you on, Sir—to redeem the Ladies.

Whiff. Oh, Sir, I am going home for Money to redeem my *Nancy.*

Whim. So am I, Sir.

Tim. I thank my Stars I am a Batchelor.—Why, what a Plague is a Wife?

Haz. Will you march forward?

Dull. We have atchiev'd Honour enough already, in having made our Campaign here—   [*Looking big.*

Haz. 'Sdeath, but you shall go—put them in the front, and prick them on—if they offer to turn back, run them thro.

Tim. Oh, horrid—

      [*The Soldiers prick them on with their Swords.*

Whiff. Oh, *Nancy*, thy Dream will yet come to pass.

Haz. Will you advance, Sir?   [*Pricks* Whiff.

Whiff. Why, so we do, Sir; the Devil's in these fighting Fellows.   [*Exeunt.*

    An Alarm at a distance.

Within. To Arms, to Arms, the Enemy's upon us.

    [*A Noise of Fighting, after which enters* Friendly *with his Party, retreating and fighting from* Daring *and some Soldiers,* Ranter *fighting like a Fury by his side, he putting her back in vain; they fight out. Re-enter* Daring *and* Friendly *all bloody. Several Soldiers enter with Flambeaux.*

Dar. Now, Sir—what Injury have I ever done you, that you should use this Treachery against me?

Friend. To take advantage any way in War, was never counted Treachery—and had I murder'd thee, I had not paid thee half the Debt I owe thee.

Dar. You bleed too much to hold too long a Parley— come to my Tent, I'll take a charitable care of thee.

Friend. I scorn thy Courtesy, who against all the Laws of Honour and of Justice, hast ravish'd innocent Ladies.

Dar. Sir, your upbraiding of my Honour shall never make me forfeit it, or esteem you less—Is there a Lady here you have a Passion for?

Friend. Yes, on a nobler score than thou darest own.

Dar. To let you see how you're mistaken, Sir, whoe'er that Lady be whom you affect, I will resign, and give you both your Freedoms.

Friend. Why, for this Courtesy, which shews thee brave, in the next fight I'll save thy Life to quit the Obligation.

Dar. I thank you, Sir ;—come to my Tent,—and when we've dress'd your Wounds, and yielded up the Ladies, I'll give you my Pass-port for your Safe-Conduct back, and tell your Friends i'th' Town, we'll visit them i'th' Morning.

Friend. They'll meet you on your way, Sir—

Dar. Come, my young Soldier, now thou'st won my Soul.   [*Exeunt.*

> [*An Alarm beats: Enter at another Passage* Boozer *with all the Ladies; they pass over the Stage, while* Hazard *and* Downright *beat back a Party of Soldiers.* Dull. Tim. Whim. *and* Whiff, *prick'd on by their Party to fight, lay about them like Madmen.* Bacon, Fearless *and* Daring *come in, rescue their Men, and fight out the other Party, some falling dead.* Bacon, Fearless *and* Daring *return tired, with their Swords drawn. Enter* Soldier *running.*

Sold. Return, Sir, where your Sword will be more useful—a Party of *Indians*, taking advantage of the Night, have set fire on your Tents, and borne away the Queen.

Bac. Hah, the Queen ! By Heaven, this Victory shall cost them dear ; come, let us fly to rescue her. [*All go out.*

SCENE II. *Changes to* Wellman's *Tent.*

Enter Wellman, Brag, Grubb, *and Officers.*

Well. I cannot sleep, my Impatience is so great to engage this haughty Enemy, before they have reposed their weary Limbs—Is not yon ruddy Light the Morning's dawn ?

Brag. 'Tis, and please your Honour.

Well. Is there no News of *Friendly* yet, and *Hazard?*

Brag. Not yet—'tis thought they left the Camp to night, with some design against the Enemy.

Well. What Men have they ?

Brag. Only *Boozer's* Party, Sir.

Well. I know they are brave, and mean to surprize me with some handsome Action.

Enter Friendly.

Friend. I ask a thousand Pardons, Sir, for quitting the Camp without your leave.

Well. Your conduct and your Courage cannot err; I see thou'st been in action by thy Blood.

Friend. Sir, I'm ashamed to own these slender Wounds, since without more my luck was to be taken, while *Hazard* did alone effect the Business, the rescuing of the Ladies.

Well. How got ye Liberty?

Friend. By *Daring's* Generosity, who sends ye word he'll visit you this Morning.

Well. We are prepared to meet him.

Enter Down. Hazard, *Ladies*, Whim. Whiff, Dullman, Tim. *looking big.* Well. *embraces* Down.

Well. My worthy Friend, how am I joyed to see you?

Down. We owe our Liberties to these brave Youths, who can do Wonders when they fight for Ladies.

Tim. With our assistance, Ladies.

Whim. For my part I'll not take it as I have done; Gad, I find, when I am damnable angry, I can beat both Friend and Foe.

Whiff. When I fight for my *Nancy* here—adsfish, I'm a Dragon.

Mrs. *Whiff.* Lord, you need not have been so hasty.

Friend. Do not upbraid me with your Eyes, *Chrisante*; but let these Wounds assure you I endeavour'd to serve you, though *Hazard* had the Honour on't.

Well. But, Ladies, we'll not expose you in the Camp, —a Party of our Men shall see you safely conducted to Madam *Surelove's;* 'tis but a little Mile from our Camp.

Friend. Let me have that honour, Sir.

Chris. No, I conjure you let your Wounds be dress'd ; obey me if you love me, and *Hazard* shall conduct us home.

Well. He had the Toil, 'tis fit he have the Recompence.

Whiff. He the Toil, Sir! what, did we stand for Cyphers?

Whim. The very appearance I made in the front of the Battel, aw'd the Enemy.

Tim. Ay, ay, let the Enemy say how I maul'd 'em— but Gads zoors, I scorn to brag.

Well. Since you've regain'd your Honour so gloriously, I restore you to your Commands you lost by your seeming Cowardice.

Dull. Valour is not always in humour, Sir.

Well. Come, Gentlemen, since they've resolv'd to engage us, let's set our Men in order to receive 'em.

[*Exeunt all but the four Justices.*

Tim. Our Commissions again—you must be bragging, and see what comes on't; I was modest ye see, and said nothing of my Prowess.

Whiff. What a Devil does the Colonel think we are made of Iron, continually to be beat on the Anvil?

Whim. Look, Gentlemen, here's two Evils—if we go we are dead Men; if we stay we are hang'd—and that will disorder my Cravat-string :—therefore the least Evil is to go—and set a good Face on the Matter, as I do—

[*Goes out singing. All exeunt.*

Scene III. *A thick Wood.*

Enter Queen *dress'd like an* Indian *Man, with a Bow in her Hand, and Quiver at her Back ;* Anaria *her Confident disguis'd so too; and about a dozen* Indians *led by* Cavaro.

Queen. I tremble yet, dost think we're safe, *Cavaro?*

Cav. Madam, these Woods are intricate and vast, and 'twill be difficult to find us out—or if they do, this Habit will secure you from the fear of being taken.

Queen. Dost think if *Bacon* find us, he will not know me? Alas, my Fears and Blushes will betray me.

Ana. 'Tis certain, Madam, if we stay we perish; for all the Wood's surrounded by the Conqueror.

Queen. Alas, 'tis better we should perish here, than stay to expect the Violence of his Passion, to which my Heart's too sensibly inclin'd.

Ana. Why do you not obey its Dictates then? why do you fly the Conqueror?

Queen. Not fly—not fly the Murderer of my Lord?

Ana. What World, what Resolution can preserve you? and what he cannot gain by soft submission, Force will at last o'ercome.

Queen. I wish there were in Nature one excuse, either by Force or Reason to compel me:—For Oh, *Anaria*—I adore this General;—take from my Soul a Truth—till now conceal'd—at twelve Years old—at the *Pauwomungian* Court, I saw this Conqueror. I saw him young and gay as new-born Spring, glorious and charming as the Mid-day's Sun; I watch'd his Looks, and listned when he spoke, and thought him more than mortal.

Ana. He has a graceful Form.

Queen. At last a fatal Match concluded was between my Lord and me; I gave my Hand, but oh, how far my Heart was from consenting, the angry Gods are Witness.

Ana. 'Twas pity.

Queen. Twelve tedious Moons I pass'd in silent Languishment; Honour endeavouring to destroy my Love, but all in vain; for still my Pain return'd whenever I beheld my Conqueror; but now when I consider him as Murderer of my Lord—[*Fiercely.*] I sigh and wish—some other fatal Hand had given him his Death.—But now there's a necessity, I must be brave and overcome my Heart; What if I do? ah, whither shall I fly? I have no *Amazonian* Fire about me, all my Artillery is Sighs

and Tears, the Earth my Bed, and Heaven my Canopy.
　　　　[*Weeps.*　　　[*After Noise of Fighting.*
Hah, we are surpriz'd; Oh, whither shall I fly? And
yet methinks a certain trembling Joy, spite of my Soul,
spite of my boasted Honour, runs shivering round my
Heart.

Enter an Indian.

Ind. Madam, your Out-guards are surpriz'd by *Bacon*,
who hews down all before him, and demands the Queen
with such a Voice, and Eyes so fierce and angry, he kills
us with his Looks.

Cav. Draw up your poison'd Arrows to the head, and
aim them at his Heart, sure some will hit.

Queen. Cruel *Cavaro*,—wou'd 'twere fit for me to contradict thy Justice.　　　　　　　　　　　　　　[*Aside.*

Bac. [*Within.*] The Queen, ye Slaves, give me the
Queen, and live!

He enters furiously, beating back some Indians; Cavaro's
　　　Party going to shoot, the Queen *runs in.*

Queen. Hold, hold, I do command ye.
　　　　[Bacon *flies on 'em as they shoot and miss him, fights*
　　　　like a Fury, and wounds the Queen *in the Disorder;*
　　　　beats them all out.
—hold thy commanding Hand, and do not kill me, who
wou'd not hurt thee to regain my Kingdom—
　　　　　　　　　[*He snatches her in his Arms, she reels.*

Bac. Hah—a Woman's Voice,—what art thou? Oh
my Fears!

Queen. Thy Hand has been too cruel to a Heart—
whose Crime was only tender Thoughts for thee.

Bac. The Queen! What is't my sacrilegious Hand
has done!

Queen. The noblest Office of a gallant Friend, thou'st
sav'd my Honour, and hast given me Death.

Bac. Is't possible! ye unregarding Gods, is't possible?

Queen. Now I may love you without Infamy, and please my dying Heart by gazing on you.

Bac. Oh, I am lost—for ever lost—I find my Brain turn with the wild confusion.

Queen. I faint—oh, lay me gently on the Earth.

[*Lays her down.*

Bac. Who waits—   [*Turns in Rage to his Men.*
Make of the Trophies of the War a Pile, and set it all on fire, that I may leap into consuming Flames—while all my Tents are burning round about me.   [*Wildly.*
Oh thou dear Prize, for which alone I toil'd!

[*Weeps, and lies down by her.*

Enter Fearless *with his Sword drawn.*

Fear. Hah, on the Earth—how do you, Sir?

Bac. What wou'dst thou?

Fear. Wellman with all the Forces he can gather, attacks us even in our very Camp; assist us, Sir, or all is lost.

Bac. Why, prithee let him make the World his Prize, I have no business with the Trifle now; it contains nothing that's worth my care, since my fair Queen—is dead—and by my hand.

Queen. So charming and obliging is thy Moan, that I cou'd wish for Life to recompense it; but oh, Death falls—all cold upon my Heart, like Mildews on the Blossoms.

Fear. By Heaven, Sir, this Love will ruin all—rise, rise, and save us yet.

Bac. Leave me, what e'er becomes of me—lose not thy share of Glory—prithee leave me.

Queen. Alas, I fear thy Fate is drawing on, and I shall shortly meet thee in the Clouds; till then—farewel—even Death is pleasing to me, while thus—I find it in thy Arms—   [*Dies.*

Bac. There ends my Race of Glory and of Life.

[*An Alarm at distance—continues a while.*

Bac. Hah—Why should I idly whine away my Life, since there are nobler ways to meet with Death? Up, up, and face him then—Hark—there's the Soldier's Knell—and all the Joys of Life—with thee I bid farewel—

[*Goes out. The* Indians *bear off the Body of the* Queen.

The Alarm continues: Enter Downright, Wellman, *and others, Swords drawn.*

Well. They fight like Men possest—I did not think to have found them so prepar'd.

Down. They've good Intelligence—but where's the Rebel?

Well. Sure he's not in the Fight; Oh, that it were my happy chance to meet him, that while our Men look on, we might dispatch the business of the War—Come, let's fall in again, now we have taken breath.

[*They go out.*

Enter Daring *and* Fearless *hastily, with their Swords drawn; meet* Whim. Whiff, *with their Swords drawn, running away.*

Dar. How now, whither away? [*In anger.*

Whim. Hah, *Daring* here—we are pursuing of the Enemy, Sir; stop us not in the pursuit of Glory.

[*Offers to go.*

Dar. Stay!—I have not seen you in my Ranks to day.

Whiff. Lord, does your Honour take us for Starters?

Fear. Yes, Sirrah, and believe you are now rubbing off—confess, or I'll run you through.

Whiff. Oh, mercy, Sir, mercy, we'll confess.

Whim. What will you confess? we were only going behind yon Hedge to untruss a point; that's all.

Whiff. Ay, your Honours will smell out the truth, if you keep us here long.

Dar. Here, carry them Prisoners to my Tent.

[*Ex. Soldiers with* Whim. *and* Whiff.

Enter Ranter *without a Hat, and Sword drawn,*
    Daring *angrily goes the other way.*

Ran. A pox of all ill luck, how came I to lose *Daring*
in the fight? Ha—who's here? *Dullman* and *Timorous*
dead—the Rogues are Counterfeits.—I'll see what Moveables they have about them, all's lawful Prize in War.
            [*Takes their Money, Watches and Rings; goes out.*
    Tim. What, rob the dead?—why, what will this
villanous World come to?
            [*Clashing of Swords, just as they were going to rise.*

        Enter Hazard *bringing in* Ranter.

Haz. Thou cou'dst expect no other Fate, young Man;
thy Hands are yet too tender for a Sword.
    Ran. Thou look'st like a good-natur'd Fellow, use me
civilly, and *Daring* shall ransom me.
    Haz. Doubt not a generous Treatment. [*They go out.*
    Dull. So the Coast is clear, I desire to move my
Quarters to some place of more safety—
                        [*They rise and go off.*

        Enter Wellman *and Soldiers hastily.*

Well. 'Twas this way *Bacon* fled.
Five hundred Pound for him who finds the Rebel. [*Go out.*

SCENE IV. *Changes to another part of the Wood.*

Enter Bacon *and* Fearless *with their Swords drawn,*
            all bloody.

Bac. 'Tis just, ye Gods! that when ye took the Prize for
which I fought, Fortune and you should all abandon me.
    Fear. Oh, fly, Sir, to some place of safe retreat, for
there's no mercy to be hop'd if taken. What will you
do? I know we are pursu'd, by Heaven, I will not die a
shameful Death.
    Bac. Oh, they'll have pity on thy Youth and Bravery,
but I'm above their Pardon.   [*A noise is heard.*

Within. This way—this way—hay halloo.

Fear. Alas, Sir, we're undone—I'll see which way they take.   *[Exit.*

Bac. So near! Nay, then to my last shift.
                         [Undoes the Pomel of his Sword.
Come, my good Poison, like that of *Hannibal;* long I have born a noble Remedy for all the Ills of Life.
                                    [Takes Poison.
I have too long surviv'd my Queen and Glory, those two bright Stars that influenc'd my Life are set to all Eternity.
                                    [Lies down.

Enter Fearless, *runs to* Bacon, *and looks on his Sword.*

Fear. —Hah—what have ye done?

Bac. Secur'd my self from being a publick Spectacle upon the common Theatre of Death.

Enter Daring *and Soldiers.*

Dar. Victory, Victory! they fly, they fly, where's the victorious General?

Fear. Here,—taking his last Adieu.

Dar. Dying! Then wither all the Laurels on my Brows, for I shall never triumph more in War; where are the Wounds?

Fear. From his own Hand, by what he carried here, believing we had lost the Victory.

Bac. And is the Enemy put to flight, my Hero?
                                  [Grasps his Neck.

Dar. All routed Horse and Foot; I plac'd an Ambush, and while they were pursuing you, my Men fell on behind, and won the day.

Bac. Thou almost makest me wish to live again, if I cou'd live now fair *Semernia's* dead.—But oh—the baneful Drug is just and kind, and hastens me away—Now while you are Victors, make a Peace—with the *English* Council, and never let Ambition,—Love,—or Interest, make you

forget, as I have done, your Duty and Allegiance—
Farewel—a long Farewel— [*Dies embracing their Necks.*

Dar. So fell the *Roman Cassius*, by mistake—

Enter Soldiers with Dunce, Tim. *and* Dullman.

Sold. An't please your Honour, we took these Men
running away.

Dar. Let 'em loose—the Wars are at an end, see where
the General lies—that great-soul'd Man, no private Body
e'er contain'd a nobler; and he that cou'd have conquered
all *America*, finds only here his scanty length of Earth.
Go, bear the Body to his own Pavilion—

[*Soldiers go out with the Body.*

though we are Conquerors we submit to treat, and yield
upon Condition : You, Mr. *Dunce*, shall bear our Articles
to the Council.

Dun. With Joy I will obey you.

Tim. Good General, let us be put in the Agreement.

Dar. You shall be obliged—

[*Ex.* Dar. Dun. Dull. *and* Tim. *as* Fear. *goes out a
Soldier meets him.*

Sold. What does your Honour intend to do with *Whimsey*
and *Whiff*, who are condemn'd by a Council of War ?

Enter Daring, Dullman, Tim. Fearless, *and Officers.*

Dar. You come too late, Gentlemen, to be put into
the Articles; nor am I satisfy'd you're worthy of it.

Dull. Why, did not you, Sir, see us lie dead in the
Field ?

Dar. Yes, but I see no Wound about you.

Tim. We were stun'd with being knock'd down;
Gads zoors, a Man may be kill'd with the but-end of a
Musquet, as soon as with the point of a Sword.

Enter Dunce.

Dun. The Council, Sir, wishes you Health and Happiness, and sends you these sign'd by their Hands—

[*Gives Papers.*

Dar. reads.

That you shall have a general Pardon for your self and Friends; that you shall have all new Commissions, and Daring *to command as General; that you shall have free leave to inter your dead General in* James Town. *And to ratify this, we will meet you at Madam* Surelove's *House, which stands between the Armies, attended only by our Officers.*

The Council's noble, and I'll wait upon them. [*Exeunt.*

SCENE V. *A Grove near Madam* Surelove's.

Enter Surelove *weeping,* Well. Chrisante, *Mrs.* Flirt, Ranter *as before,* Down. Haz. Friend. Booz. Brag.

Well. How long, Madam, have you heard the News of Col. *Surelove's* Death?

Sure. By a Vessel last Night arriv'd.

Well. You shou'd not grieve when Men so old pay their debt to Nature; you are too fair not to have been reserved for some young Lover's Arms.

Haz. I dare not speak,—but give me leave to hope.

Sure. The way to oblige me to't, is never more to speak to me of Love till I shall think it fit—

[Wellman *speaks to* Down.

Well. Come, you shan't grant it—'tis a hopeful Youth.

Down. You are too much my Friend to be denied—*Chrisante,* do you love *Friendly?* nay, do not blush—till you have done a fault, your loving him is none—Here, take her, young Man, and with her all my Fortune—when I am dead, Sirrah—not a Groat before—unless to buy ye Baby-Clouts.

Friend. He merits not this Treasure, Sir, can wish for more.

Enter Daring, Fearless, Dunce, *Officers, and the rest, they meet* Well. *and* Down. *who embrace 'em.* Dull. *and* Tim. *stand.*

Dar. Can you forgive us, Sir, our Disobedience?

Well. Your offering Peace while yet you might command it, has made such kind impressions on us, that now you may command your Propositions; your Pardons are all seal'd and new Commissions.

Dar. I'm not ambitious of that Honour, Sir, but in obedience will accept your Goodness; but, Sir, I hear I have a young Friend taken Prisoner by Captain *Hazard*, whom I intreat you will render me.

Haz. Sir—here I resign him to you. [*Gives him* Ran.

Ran. Faith, General, you left me but scurvily in Battle.

Dar. That was to see how well you cou'd shift for your self; now I find you can bear the brunt of a Campaign, you are a fit Wife for a Soldier.

All. A Woman—*Ranter*—

Haz. Faith, Madam, I should have given you kinder Quarter, if I had known my happiness.

Flirt. I have an humble Petition to you, Sir.

Sure. In which we all join.

Flirt. An't please you, Sir, Mr. *Dunce* has long made Love to me, and on promise of Marriage has—[*Simpers.*

Down. What has he, Mistress? What has he, Mrs. *Flirt?*

Flirt. Only been a little familiar with my Person, Sir—

Well. Do you hear, Parson—you must marry Mrs. *Flirt.*

Dun. How, Sir, a Man of my Coat, Sir, marry a Brandy-monger?

Well. Of your Calling you mean, a Farrier and no Parson—   [*Aside to him.*
She'll leave her Trade, and spark it above all the Ladies at Church: No more—take her, and make her honest.

Enter Whim. *and* Whiff *stript.*

Chris. Bless me, what have we here?

Whim. Why, an't like your Honours, we were taken by the Enemy—hah, *Daring* here, and *Fearless?*

Fear. How now, Gentlemen, were not you two condemn'd to be shot for running from your Colours.

Down. From your Colours!

Fear. Yes, Sir, they were both listed in my Regiment.

Down. Then we must hang them for deserting us.

Whim. So, out of the Frying Pan—you know where, Brother—

Whiff. Ay, he that's born to be hang'd—you know the rest; a Pox of these Proverbs.

Well. I know ye well—you're all rank Cowards; but once more we forgive ye; your Places in the Council shall be supplied by these Gentlemen of Sense and Honour. The Governor when he comes, shall find the Country in better hands than he expects to find it.

Whim. A very fair Discharge.

Whiff. I'm glad 'tis no worse, I'll home to my *Nancy*.

Dull. Have we expos'd our Lives and Fortunes for this?

Tim. Gad zoors, I never thriv'd since I was a Statesman, left Planting, and fell to promising and lying; I'll to my old Trade again, bask under the shade of my own Tobacco, and drink my Punch in Peace.

Well. *Come, my brave Youths, let all our Forces meet,*
To make this Country happy, rich and great;
Let scanted Europe *see that we enjoy*
Safer Repose, and larger Worlds, than they.

EPILOGUE.

GALLANTS, you have so long been absent hence,
That you have almost cool'd your Diligence:
For while we study or revive a Play,
You like good Husbands in the Country stay,
There frugally wear out your Summer-Suit,
And in Frize Jerkin after Beagles toot,
Or in Mountero Caps at Fel-fares shoot:
Nay, some are so obdurate in their Sin,
That they swear never to come up again;
But all their charge of Clothes and Treat retrench.
To Gloves and Stockings for some Country-Wench.
Even they who in the Summer had Mishaps,
Send up to Town for Physick, for their Claps.
The Ladies too, are as resolv'd as they,
And having Debts unknown to them, they stay,
And with the gain of Cheese and Poultry pay.
Even in their Visits, they from Banquets fall,
To entertain with Nuts and Bottle-Ale;
And in Discourse with secrecy report
Stale News that past a Twelve-month since at Court.
Those of them who are most refin'd and gay,
Now learn the Songs of the last Summer's Play:
While the young Daughter does in private mourn
Her Love's in Town, and hopes not to return.
These Country-Grievances too great appear;
But, cruel Ladies, we have greater here;
You come not sharp, as you were wont, to Plays;
But only on the first and second Days:
This made our Poet in his Visits look
What new strange Courses for your Time you took;

And to his great regret he found too soon,
Basset *and* Ombre *spent the Afternoon:*
So that we cannot hope to see you here
Before the little Net-work Purse be clear.
Suppose you should have luck:—
Yet sitting up so late as I am told,
You'll lose in Beauty what you win in Gold;
And what each Lady of another says,
Will make you new Lampoons, and us new Plays.

THE FALSE COUNT.

THE FALSE COUNT:

or, A New Way to play an old Game.

PROLOGUE.

Spoken by Mr. *Smith*.

KNOW all ye Whigs and Tories of the Pit,
(Ye furious Guelphs and Gibelins of Wit,
Who for the Cause, and Crimes of Forty One
So furiously maintain the Quarrel on)
Our Author, as you'll find it writ in Story,
Has hitherto been a most wicked Tory;
But now, to th' joy o'th' Brethren be it spoken,
Our Sister's vain mistaken Eyes are open;
And wisely valuing her dear Interest now,
All-powerful Whigs, converted is to you.
'Twas long she did maintain the Royal Cause,
Argu'd, disputed, rail'd with great Applause;
Writ Madrigals and Doggerel on the Times,
And charg'd you all with your Fore-fathers Crimes;
Nay, confidently swore no Plot was true,
But that so slily carried on by you:
Rais'd horrid Scandals on you, hellish Stories,
In Conventicles how you eat young Tories;
As Jew *did heretofore eat* Christian *Suckling;*
And brought an Ödium on your pious Gutling:
When this is all Malice it self can say,
You for the good Old Cause devoutly eat and pray.
Though this one Text were able to convert ye,
Ye needy Tribe of Scriblers to the Party;
Yet there are more advantages than these,
For write, invent, and make what Plots you please,

The wicked Party keep your Witnesses;
Like frugal Cuckold-makers you beget
Brats that secur'd by others fires shall sit.
Your Conventicling Miracles out-do
All that the Whore of Babylon *e'er knew:*
By wondrous art you make Rogues honest Men,
And when you please transform 'em Rogues again.
To day a Saint, if he but hang a Papist,
Peach a true Protestant, your Saint's turn'd Atheist:
And dying Sacraments do less prevail,
Than living ones, though took in Lamb's-Wool-Ale.
Who wou'd not then be for a Common-weal,
To have the Villain cover'd with his Zeal?
A Zeal, who for Convenience can dispense
With Plays provided there's no Wit nor Sense.
For Wit's profane, and Jesuitical,
And Plotting's Popery, and the Devil and all.
We then have fitted you with one to day,
'Tis writ as 'twere a Recantation Play;
Renouncing all that has pretence to witty,
T' oblige the Reverend Brumighams *o'th' City:*
No smutty Scenes, no Jests to move your Laughter,
Nor Love that so debauches all your Daughters.
But shou'd the Torys now, who will desert me,
Because they find no dry bobs on your Party,
Resolve to hiss, as late did Popish Crew,
By Yea and Nay, she'll throw her self on you,
The grand Inquest of Whigs, to whom she's true.
Then let 'em rail and hiss, and damn their fill,
Your Verdict will be Ignoramus *still.*

DRAMATIS PERSONÆ.

MEN.

Don *Carlos*, Governour of *Cadiz*, young and rich, in love with *Julia*,   Mr. *Smith*.

Antonio, a Merchant, young and rich, Friend to *Carlos*, in love with *Clara*, but promis'd to *Isabella*,   Mr. *Wiltshire*.

Francisco, old and rich, Husband to *Julia*, and Father to *Isabella*,   Mr. *Nokes*.

Baltazer, Father to *Julia* and *Clara*,   Mr. *Bright*.

Sebastian, Father to *Antonio*,   Mr. *Freeman*.

Guzman, Gentlemen to *Carlos*,   Mr. *Underhill*.

Guiliom, a Chimney-Sweeper; the False Count,   Mr. *Lee*.

Two overgrown Pages to the False Count. A little Page to the False Count.

Petro, Cashier to *Antonio*.

Page to Don *Carlos*.

Captain of a Gally.

Two Seamen.

Lopez, Servant to *Baltazer*.

Several disguis'd like *Turks*.

WOMEN.

Julia, Wife to *Francisco*, young and handsom, in love with *Carlos*,   Mrs. *Davis*.

Clara, Sister to *Julia*, in love with *Antonio*,   Mrs. *Petty*.

Isabella, Daughter to *Francisco*; proud, vain and foolish, despising all Men under the degree of Quality, and falls in love with *Guiliom*,   Mrs. *Corror*.

Jacinta, Woman to *Julia*,   Mrs. *Osborne*.

Wife to *Petro*.

Dancers, Singers, &c.

ACT I.

SCENE I. *The Street.*

Enter Carlos, Antonio *and* Guzman.

Car. By all that's good, I'm mad, stark raving mad,
To have a Woman young, rich, beautiful,
Just on the point of yielding to my Love,
Snatcht from my Arms by such a Beast as this;
An old ridiculous Buffoon, past Pleasure,
Past Love, or any thing that tends that way;
Ill-favour'd, ill-bred, and ill-qualify'd,
With more Diseases than a Horse past Service;
And only blest with Fortune and my *Julia*;
For him, I say, this Miser, to obtain her,
After my tedious nights and days of Love,
My midnight Watchings, Quarrels, Wounds and Dangers;
—My Person not unhandsom too,
By Heav'n, 'twas wondrous strange !

Ant. And old *Francisco*, without the expence of an hour's
Courtship, a *Billet-Doux*, or scarce a sight of her, could
gain her in a day; and yet 'tis wonder, your Fortune and
your Quality, should be refus'd by Don *Baltazer* her Father.

Car. A Pox upon't, I went the wrong way to work,
and courted the Daughter; but indeed my Father, the late
Governour of *Cadiz*, whose Estate and Honour I now
enjoy, was then living; and, fearing he would not consent
to my Passion, I endeavoured to keep it secret, though
sacred Vows had past between us two.

Ant. Did she not tell you of this Marriage with old
Francisco?

Car. The night before, she did; but only by a Letter

from her Window dropt; which when by the help of a
dark Lanthorn, I had read, I was struck dead with Grief.
                              [*Gives him the Letter.*

   Ant. [reads.]
*Expect to morrow night to hear I'm dead, since the next Sun
will guide me to a fatal Marriage with old* Francisco.
                                          Your Julia.

   Car. Judge, dear *Antonio*, my Surprize and Grief;
A-while I stood unmov'd, thoughtless, and silent,
But soon Rage wak'd me to new Life again;
But what I said and did, I leave to raging Lovers,
Like disappointed me, to guess and judge;
She heard—and only answer'd me in Tears,
Nor could I beg one tender Word from her,
She sigh'd, and shut the Window too, and vanish'd.

   Ant. And she accordingly next day was married.

   Car. She was—and I have since endeavoured all the
Arts and Ways I can to cuckold him; 'tis now two months
since the Wedding, and I hear he keeps her as close as a
Relict, jealous as Age and Impotence can make him. She
hitherto has been absent at *Sevil*, but Expectation of her
Daughter-in-law's Wedding with you has brought 'em
hither,—and, I ask your Pardon, *Antonio*, for raillying
your Father-in-law that shall be, old *Francisco*.

   Ant. I hope you are mistaken, Sir.

   Car. How, are you not to marry his Daughter, *Isabella*?

   Ant. Not if I can help it, Sir,—the Honour you have
done me in your Friendship to me, a Person so much
above me in Title and Birth, makes me think it my Duty
to conceal no part of my Heart to you,—Know then this
Isabella, Daughter to old *Francisco*, and your Cuckold that
shall be I hope, is, though fair, most ridiculously proud,
vain and fantastical; as all of her Birth and Education,
grown rich, are.

   Car. Prithee, what was her Birth?

   Ant. Why, her Father, old *Francisco*, was in his youth

an English Cordwainer, that is to say, a Shoemaker, which
he improv'd in time to a Merchant ; and the Devil and his
Knavery helping him to a considerable Estate, he set up
for Gentleman ; and being naturally a stingey, hide-bound
Rascal, and in the Humour of Jealousy even out-doing
the most rigid of us *Spaniards*, he came over into *Spain*,
to settle with his whole Family, where his Wife dying, to
heighten the Vice, marries this young *Julia*, your Mistress,
Sir ;—and now this Daughter of his having wholly forgot
her original Dunghill, sets up for a Viscountess at least,
though her Father has design'd me the Blessing ; but I
have fixt my Heart and Eyes else-where, *Clara*, the young
Sister of your Mistress, Sir, commands my Liberty.

Car. I've seen her, she has Youth and Beauty capable
to make a Conquest any where,—but does she know
your Love ?

Ant. She does, and makes me think my Love return'd.

Car. Then know, *Antonio*, I must be your Rival.

Ant. How, Sir !

Car. You said but now you were my Friend, *Antonio ;*
If true, you must assist in my design.

Ant. I listen, Sir, impatiently.

Car. Then thus ; before I knew she was your Mistress,
I had resolv'd upon Addresses to her, in order to't, have
treated with her Father about a Marriage.

Ant. How ! and wou'd the false, forsworn, receive
your Vows ?

Car. No ; but with Tears implores her Father daily,
whene'er he speaks to her about my Passion ; nor can I
undeceive her, for indeed I have but feign'd a Love, (she
living in the same house with *Julia* whilst here at *Cadiz*)
to get an opportunity with that dear, charming Creature ;
for, coming as a Brother, sure they'll admit me kindly ;
nor will *Francisco*, who has heard of what has past 'twixt
me and *Julia*, suspect me any more.

Ant. I knew I had a Rival, Sir, whom *Clara* lov'd

not; but ne'er cou'd get it from her who he was, for fear
of mischief: I have often the Liberty to see her, under
the name and pretence of *Isabella's* Lover.

Car. And I visit her only to get a sight of *Julia*, which
hitherto has been impossible, though I have oft endeavour'd
it. I beg you'll not be jealous; for this, by Heav'n, is only
my Design.

Ant. I'll trust my Life, my Honour and my Mistress
in so good hands at any time.

Car. You oblige me; but though I find your *Clara*
cold and cruel, *Isabella* would invite me to her Love, and
makes so many kind advances to me—

Ant. So would she for your Title, were you deform'd,
and had no shape of Man about you; but me, because a
little Citizen and Merchant, she so reviles, calling me base
Mechanick, saucy Fellow; and wonders where I got the
Impudence to speak of Love to her—in fine, I am resolved
to be reveng'd on all her Pride and Scorn; by Heav'n, I
will invent some dire Revenge:—I'm bent upon't, and
will about it instantly.

Car. And would you do it home and handsomly, and
have a good occasion of being disengaged from her, and
make her self the instrument?

Ant. Ay, such a Plot were worth the Prosecution.

Car. And such a one I have in my head: *Guzman*, my
Servant, knows a fellow here in *Cadiz*, whom for his
pleasant humour I have oft observ'd, as I have past the
Streets, but too mean to be convers'd with, by almost any
human thing, by Trade a Chimney-Sweeper.

Ant. On, Sir, I beseech you.

Car. This Fellow's of a quick Wit and good Apprehen-
sion, though possibly he cannot act the Don so well, yet
that which makes up the best part of our young Gallants
now a-days, he shall not want; that is, good Clothes,
Money, and an Equipage,—and a little Instruction will
serve turn.

Ant. I'm ravisht with the Fancy;—let me see—he shall be an *English* Lord, or a *French* Count.

Car. Either, we'll furnish him with Bills on Signior Don *Francisco*,—Men and Baggage, and the business is done—he shall make Love to her.

Ant. Most excellent.

Car. Guzman, have you not observ'd this Fellow I am speaking of.

Guz. Observ'd him, Sir! I know him particularly, I'll fetch him to you now, Sir; he always stands for new Imployment with the rest of his Gang under St. *Jago's* Church-wall.

Car. Bring him anon to my Lodgings, where we'll prepare him for the Adventure.

Ant. And if the proud *Isabella* bite not at so gay a bait, I'll be bound to be married to her.

Car. And if she do not, possibly that may be your Fate—but in return, you must let *Clara* know the Design I have, and, undeceiving her opinion of my Love, make her of our Party.

Ant. Trust my Friendship, Sir, and Management. I'll to her instantly, that is, make a visit to *Isabella*, and get an opportunity to speak with *Clara*.

Car. And I must write a Letter to *Julia*, to undeceive her Fears too, could I but get it to her.

Guz. For that let me alone. [*Exeunt severally, bowing.*

SCENE II. *A Chamber.*

Enter Julia *and* Jacinta.

Jac. Lord, Madam, you are as melancholy as a sick Parrot.

Jul. And can you blame me, *Jacinta?* have I not many Reasons to be sad? first have I not lost the only Man on earth in Don *Carlos*, that I cou'd love? and worse than that, am married to a Thing, fit only for his Tomb; a

Brute, who wanting sense to value me, treats me more like a Prisoner than a Wife?—and his Pretence is, because I should not see nor hear from Don *Carlos*.

Jac. Wou'd I were in your room, Madam, I'd cut him out work enough, I'd warrant him; and if he durst impose on me, i'faith, I'd transform both his Shape and his Manners; in short, I'd try what Woman-hood cou'd do. And indeed, the Revenge wou'd be so pleasant, I wou'd not be without a jealous Husband for all the World; and really, Madam, Don *Carlos* is so sweet a Gentleman.

Jul. Ay, but the Sin, *Jacinta!*

Jac. O' my Conscience, Heav'n wou'd forgive it; for this match of yours, with old *Francisco*, was never made there.

Jul. Then if I wou'd, alas, what opportunities have I, for I confess since his first Vows made him mine—

Jac. Right—that lying with old *Francisco* is flat Adultery.

Jul. I might, with some excuse, give my self away to *Carlos*—But oh, he's false, he takes unjustly all the Vows he paid me, and gives 'em to my Sister *Clara* now.

Jac. Indeed that's something uncivil, Madam, if it be true.

Jul. True! my Father has with joy consented to it, and he has leave to visit her; and can I live to see't? No, Mischief will ensue, my Love's too high, too nicely true to brook Affronts like that.

Jac. Yet you first broke with him.

Jul. Not I; be witness, Heav'n, with what reluctancy I forc'd my breaking heart; and can I see that charming Body in my Sister's Arms! that Mouth that has so oft sworn Love to me kist by another's Lips! no, *Jacinta*, that night that gives him to another Woman, shall see him dead between the Charmer's Arms. My Life I hate, and when I live no more for *Carlos*, I'll cease to be at all; it is resolv'd.

Jac. Faith, Madam, I hope to live to see a more comical end of your Amours—but see where your amiable Spouse comes with Don *Baltazer* your Father.

Enter Francisco *and* Baltazer.

Fran. So—you two are damnable close together, 'tis for no goodness I'll warrant, you have your trade betimes.

Jac. Meaning me, Sir?

Fran. Yes, you, one of my Wife's evil Counsellors,—go, get you up both to your respective Chambers, go—

[*Ex. both.*

Bal. Barring your Compliments, good Son, give me leave to speak.

Fran. Shaw, I know as well as your self what you wou'd say now; you wou'd assure me I am sole Master of your House, and may command; that you are heartily glad to see me at *Cadiz*, and that you desire I wou'd resolve upon a Week's stay, or so; that you'll spare nothing for my entertainment: why, I know all this, and therefore pray take my word, good Father-in-Law, without any more ado.

Bal. Well, Sir, pray answer me one question, what drew you to *Cadiz?*

Fran. Why, I'll tell you; in the first place, a Pox of all Lovers, I say; for my Daughter *Isabella* is to be married, as you know, to *Antonio*, a young rich Merchant of this Town; in the second place, my Wife, with a Vengeance, must be gadding to visit you and her Sister, whom we heard also was to be married to the young Governor Don *Carlos*; 'tis shrewdly against my will, Heav'n knows, for my Wits are in an uproar already about this business—your Gallants, Father, your young Gallants,—I wish my Wife were secure at home again.

Bal. Pray, why so?

Fran. Alas, I see the Trick, Sir, a mere Trick put upon a Man, a married Man, and a married Man to a handsome young Woman,—you apprehend me.

Bal. Not I, Sir.

Fran. Not you, Sir! why, look ye, your young Governor who now is, made most desperate love to her who is now my Wife, d'ye mind me?—but you, being a Man of an exact Judgment, to her great grief, gave her to me, who best deserv'd her, both for my civil Behaviour, and comely Personage, d'ye understand me? but now this *Carlos*, by his Father's death, being made Governor, d'ye see? is to marry me your other daughter *Clara*, and to exasperate me, wou'd never let me be at quiet till he had got both of us hither to *Cadiz*, to grace his Wedding; a Pox of his Invitation, was I so civil to invite him to mine?

Bal. If this be your Affliction, you may avoid it.

Fran. No, no, I'll try to force Nature a little, and be civil, or so; but as soon as the Ceremony's over, I'll steal out of Town, whip a way, presto, i'faith.

Bal. But shou'd you do so rude a thing to your new Brother, your Wife wou'd think you were jealous of her. No, dissemble that Fault, I beseech you, 'twill make you odious to her and all the world, when 'tis needless, 'tis natural for Women to hate what they fear.

Fran. Say you so, then I will hide it as much as I can in words, I can dissemble too upon occasion.

Bal. Let her remain awhile amongst us.

Fran. The Devil a bit she shall, good Father mine, no, no, I have more years than you, Sir Father, and understand what Women are, especially when married to ancient Men, and have the Conversation of young Men—whose Eyes like Basilisks destroy Modesty with looking on 'em; the very Thought on't has rais'd a Bump in my Forehead already.

Bal. I am sorry you should suspect my Daughter's Virtue.

Fran. May be you are, Sir—but Youth you know— Opportunity—Occasion—or so—there are Winks, and Nods, and Signs, and Twirs—and—well—in short I am satisfied, and they that are not may go whistle: and so I'll to my Wife, whom I have left too long alone, evil thoughts will grow upon her—Wife, Love—Duckling—
[*Calls her.*

Enter Julia *and* Jacinta.

Bal. Wou'd I had never married her to this Sot.

Jul. Your pleasure, Sir.

Fran. Only to see thee, Love.

Jul. I have a Suit to you.

Fran. What is't, my Chicken.

Jul. I wou'd go make a Visit to my Aunt, my Sister *Clara's* there, and I'll go fetch her home.

Fran. Hum—perhaps the Governor's there too?

Jul. What if he be? we ought to make him a visit too, who so kindly sent for us to *Cadiz*.

Fran. How! Make a visit to the Governor? What have I to do with the Governor, or what have you to do with the Governor? you are no Soldier, Love. As for a Visit to your Aunt, there's some reason in't; but for the Governor, think no more upon him, I say no more.

Jul. Since he's to marry my Sister, why shou'd you refuse him that Civility.

Fran. Your Sister, so much the worse.

Jul. So much the worse?

Fran. I, so much the worse, I tell you; for mark me, you have been Lovers lately; and old Stories may arise that are not yet forgotten; and having under the Cloke of a Husband both Sisters at command, one for a Wife, t'other for a Mistress, hoyte toyte, there will be mad work, i'faith; What a mixture of Brother by the Father's side, and Uncle by the Mother's side there will be; Aunt by the Mother's side, and Sister by the Father's side; a man may find as good kindred amongst a kennel of Beagles.—No, no, no Visits to the Governor, I beseech you, fair Madam.

Bal. So, you are at your Jealousy again.

Fran. Come, come, I love plain dealing; besides, when she named the Governor, Flesh and Blood could not contain.

Jul. I spoke in reference to his Quality.

Fran. A Pox of your Civility; I tell you, I scorn my Wife should be civil. Why, what a Coil's here about a Governor! I'll stand to't, a Man had better have a Mule to his Wife than a Woman, and 'twere easier govern'd.

Bal. But hear reason, Son.

Fran. What, from a Woman and a Wife? Lord, Lord, where are your Wits, good Father-in-Law? Why, what a Devil, shall I be made ridiculous, a Coxcomb, Cuckold, to shew my Wife? No, no, there's no Necessity of your Civility, Mistress; leave that to me who understand the due Punctilios of it.

Bal. Harkye, Son, Harkye!

Fran. Father mine, every Man to his business, I say, therefore say no more of this; for I'll give my Mother's Son to the Devil, when any Wife of mine ever makes a Visit to the Governor; and there's an end on't. Was ever so horrid a Plot contriv'd against her own lawful Husband? Visit the Governor with a Pox!

Bal. 'Tis an Honour due to all Men of his Rank.

Fran. I care not for that, my opinion is, my Wife's my Slave, and let him keep his Rank to himself.

Enter Guzman.

[*Fran. gets his Wife behind him, and fences her with his Cloke.*

Guz. He's here, and with his Wife; how shall I do to deliver my Letter to her;—Sir, by the order of my Master, Don *Carlos*, the Governour, I am commanded to come hither to the end that, going from hence, and returning to my Master, I may be able to inform him—

Fran. That I am in health,—very well, I was afraid he wou'd have been harping upon my Wife in the first place—the Devil take her, she looks for't.

[*Makes signs to have her gone.*

Guz. Farther, Sir, he kisses your hand, with a more than ordinary friendship.

Fran. A Pox of his Compliments.—   [*Aside.*

Guz. But he charg'd me, Sir, most passionately to present his Service to your Lady.

Fran. Yes, yes; I thought as much.

Guz. —In a more particular manner.

Fran. Friend, my Wife, or Lady, has no need of his Service in a more particular manner, and so you may return it.

Jac. Indeed, but she has great need of his service in a very particular manner.

Guz. Sir, I meant no hurt, but 'tis always the fashion of your true bred Courtier, to be more ceremonious in his Civilities to Ladies than Men ;—and he desires to know how she does.

Fran. How strong this *Carlos* smells of the Devil— Friend, tell your Master she's very well, but since she was married, she has forgot her gentile Civility and good Manners, and never returns any Compliments to Men.

Guz. —How shall I get it to her ?—Sir, the Governor hopes he shall have the honour of entertaining you both at his House. He's impatient of your coming, and waits at home on purpose.

Fran. Friend, let your Master know we are here in very good quarters already, and he does us both too much honour ; and that if we have notice of the Wedding-day, and I have nothing else to do, we'll certainly wait on him, and the next morning we intend to take our leaves, which I send him word of beforehand to prevent surprize.

Guz. But, Sir—

                    [*Approaching him, he puts his Wife farther.*

Fran. Go, Sir, and deliver your Message.

Guz. But I have order, Sir—

Fran. There's no such thing in this World.

Guz. I'm resolv'd to teaze him, if I can do nothing else, in revenge ;—But, Sir, he most earnestly desires to entertain your fair Lady in his own house.

Fran. Yes, yes; I know he does; but I'll give him to the Devil first.—Troth, Sir, this *Cadiz* Air does not agree with my fair Lady, she has ventured out but once, and has got an Ague already.

Guz. Agues, Sir, are kind Diseases, they allow of Truces and Cessations.

Fran. No, no; she has no Cessation, Friend, her Ague takes her night and day, it shakes her most unmercifully, and it shall shake her till the Wedding-day.

Guz. Were this Fellow to be tried by a Jury of Women, I would not be in his Coat to lie with his Lady.—What shall I do to deliver this Letter?—Well, Sir, since I see you are so averse to what the Governor desires, I'll return —but, Sir, I must tell you as a Friend, a Secret; that to a man of your temper may concern you;—Sir,—he's resolv'd when he comes next to visit his Mistress, to make another visit to your Apartment, to your Lady too.

    [*Goes to whisper him, and gives* Julia *the Letter over his Shoulder.*

Fran. Is he so, pray tell him he need not take that pains; there's no occasion for't; besides 'twill be but in vain; for the Doctors have prescribed her Silence and Loneliness, 'tis good against the Fit; how this damn'd Fellow of a Rival torments me! honest Friend, adieu.

Guz. Now is this Fellow so afraid of being made a Cuckold that he fears his own Shadow, and dares not go into his Wife's Chamber if the Sun do but shine into the room—   [*Ex.* Guz.

Fran. So, your *Mercury's* gone; Lord, how simply you look now, as if you knew nothing of the matter!

Jul. Matter! what matter? I heard the civil Message the Governor sent, and the uncivil Answer you return'd back.

Fran. Very good; did that grieve your heart? alas, what pity 'twas I carried you not in my hand, presented you to him my self, and beg'd him to favour me so much to do my office a little for me, or the like; hah,—

Jul. And there's need enough, and the truth were known.

Jac. Well said, Madam.

Fran. Peace, thou wicked Limb of *Satan*—but for you, Gentlewoman, since you are so tarmagant, that your own natural Husband cannot please you, who, though I say it, am as quiet a Bed-fellow, and sleep as sweetly, for one of my years, as any in *Spain*—I'll keep you to hard meat, i'faith.

Jul. I find no fault with your sleeping, 'tis the best quality you have a-bed.

Fran. Why so then, is the Devil in an unmerciful Woman? Come, come, 'tis a good Tenant that pays once a quarter.

Jac. Of an hour do you mean, Sir?—

Fran. Peace, I say—thou damnable Tormentor, this is the Doctrine you preach to your Mistress, but you shall do't it private, for I'm resolv'd to lock ye both up, and carry the Keys in my Pocket.

Jul. Well, I am a wicked Creature to teaze thee so, Dear; but I'll do what thou wilt; come, come, be friends, I vow, I care not for the Governor, not I, no more than I do for my—own Soul.

Fran. Why so, this is something; Come, come your ways in,—who have we here? a Man! ad's my life, away, away.

Jul. Yes, up to my Chamber, to write an answer to this dear Letter.   [*Ex* Julia.

Enter Isabella.

Fran. No, 'tis not a Man, but my Daughter *Isabella*.

Jac. Now will I stay, and set her on to teaze the Dotard: wou'd I could teaze him to Death, that my Mistress might be rid of him.

Fran. How now, what makes you look so scurvily to day? Sure the Devil rides once a day through a Woman, that she may be sure to be inspired with some ill Qualities —what wou'd you have now?

Isa. Something.

Fran. Something? what thing? have I not provided you a Husband whom you are to marry within a day or two.

Isa. There's a Husband indeed, pray keep him to your

self, if you please; I'll marry none of him, I'll see him
hanged first.

Fran. Hey day;—what, is he not young and handsome
enough, forsooth?

Isa. Young and handsome; is there no more than that
goes to the making up of a Husband—Yes, there's Quality.

Fran. Quality!—Why, is he not one of the richest
Merchants of his standing in all *Cadiz.*

Isa. Merchant! a pretty Character! a Woman of my
Beauty, and five Thousand Pound, marry a Merchant—
a little, petty, dirty-heel'd Merchant; faugh, I'd rather
live a Maid all the days of my life, or be sent to a Nunnery, and that's Plague enough I'm sure.

Jac. Have a care of a Nunnery, lest he take you at
your word.

Isa. I would not for the world; no, *Jacinta,* when ever
thou seest me in holy Orders, the World will be at an end.

Fran. Merchant! why, what Husband do you expect?

Isa. A Cavalier at least, if not a Nobleman.

Fran. A Nobleman, marry come up, your Father,
Huswife, meaning my self, was a Leather-seller at first,
till, growing rich, I set up for a Merchant, and left that
mechanick Trade; and since turned Gentleman; and
Heav'n blest my Endeavours so as I have an Estate for a
Spanish Grandee; and, are you so proud, forsooth, that a
Merchant won't down with you, but you must be gaping
after a Cap and Feather, a Silver Sword with a more dreadful Ribbon at the hilt?—Come, come, I fear me, Huswise,
you are one that puffs her up with Pride thus;—but lay
thy hand upon thy Conscience now.—   [*To* Jacinta.

Jac. Who, I, Sir? No, no, I am for marrying her out
of hand to any reasonable Husband, except a Merchant;
for Maids will long, and that's *Probatum est* against the
prevailing distemper of Longing. Hitherto I dare answer
for her, but Batteries will be made, and I dare not be
always responsible for frail Mortality.

Fran. Well, I have provided her one that I like, but if she be so squeamish, let her fast, with a Murrain to her.

Isa. Dear Father.

Fran. Dear me no Dears: wou'd your old Mother were alive, she wou'd have strapt your Just-au-corps, for puleing after Cavaliers and Nobleman, i'faith, that wou'd she; a Citizen's Daughter, and would be a *Madona*—in good time.

Isa. Why, Father, the Gentry and Nobility now-a-days frequently marry Citizens Daughters.

Fran. Come, come, Mistress, I got by the City, and I love and honour the City; I confess 'tis the Fashion now-a-days, if a Citizen get but a little Money, one goes to building Houses, and brick Walls; another must buy an Office for his Son, a third hoists up his Daughter's Top-sail, and flaunts it away, much above her breeding; and these things make so many break, and cause the decay of Trading: but I am for the honest *Dutch* way of breeding their Children, according to their Fathers Calling.

Isa. That's very hard, because you are a laborious, ill-bred Tradesman, I must be bound to be a mean Citizen's Wife.

Fran. Why, what are you better than I, forsooth, that you must be a Lady, and have your Petticoats lac'd four Stories high; wear your false Towers, and cool your self with your *Spanish* Fan? Come, come, Baggage, wear me your best Clothes a Sunday, and brush 'em up a Monday Mornings, and follow your Needle all the Week after; that was your good old Mother's way, and your Grand-mother's before her; and as for the Husband, take no care about it, I have designed it *Antonio*, and *Antonio* you are like to wed, or beat the hoof, Gentlewoman, or turn poor *Clare*, and die a begging Nun, and there's an end on't—see where he comes—I'll leave you to ponder upon the business.   [*Exit.*

Enter Antonio. Isabella *weeps.*

Ant. What, in Tears, *Isabella?* what is't can force that tribute from your Eyes?

Isa. A Trifle, hardly worth the naming, your self.—

Ant. Do I? pray, for what Sin of mine must your fair Eyes be punish'd?

Isa. For the Sin of your odious Addresses to me, I have told you my mind often enough, methinks your Equals should be fitter for you, and sute more with your Plebeian Humour.

Ant. My Equals! 'Tis true, you are fair; but if there be any Inequality in our births, the advantage is on my side.

Isa. Saucy Impertinent, you shew your City breeding; you understand what's due to Ladys! you understand your Pen and Ink, how to count your dirty Money, trudge to and fro chaffering of base commodities, and cozening those you deal with, till you sweat and stink again like an o'er heated Cook, faugh, I smell him hither.

Ant. I must confess I am not perfum'd as you are, to stifle Stinks you commonly have by Nature; but I have wholesom, cleanly Linen on; and for my Habit wore I but a Sword, I see no difference between your Don and me, only, perhaps, he knows less how to use it.

Isa. Ah, name not a Don, the very sound from the Mouth of a little Cit is disagreeable—Bargain and Sale, Bills, Money, Traffick, Trade, are words become you better.

Jac. Well said, use him scurvily that Mrs. *Clara* may have him.   [*Aside.*

Ant. The best of those you think I should not name, dare hardly tell me this.

Isa. Good Lord, you think your self a very fine Fellow now, and finical your self up to be thought so; but there's as much difference between a Citizen and a true bred Cavalier—

Ant. As between you and a true bred Woman of Honour.

Isa. Oh, Sir, you rail, and you may long enough, before you rail me out of my Opinion, whilst there are Dons with Coaches and fine Lackeys, and I have Youth and Beauty, with a Fortune able to merit one, so farewel, Cit.   [*Ex.*

Ant. Farewel, proud Fool.

Jac. Sir, be this Evening at the Door, Donna *Clara* has something to say to you.

Ant. Bless thee for this Tidings, dear *Jacinta*.

[*Ex.* Jacinta.

—I find let Man be brave, or good, or wise,
His Virtue gains no Smiles from Woman's Eyes;
'Tis the gay Fool alone that takes the Heart,
Foppery and Finery still guide the Dart.   [*Ex.*

ACT II.

Scene I. *A Chamber.*

Enter Jacinta *with a Light, and* Julia.

Jac. Well, Madam, have you writ to Don *Carlos*?

Jul. No, nor is it possible I shou'd, this Devil haunts me so from room to room, like my evil Genius to prevent that Good; oh, for an opportunity of one kind Minute to return Acknowledgments for this kind Letter he has sent me.

Jac. I'm glad you find me a Sybil: Madam, I ever prophesy'd a happier end of that Amour than your ill Fortune his hitherto promised,—but what said the lovely Cavalier?

Jul. All that a Man inspir'd with Love cou'd say, all that was soft and charming.

Jac. Nay, I believe his Art.

Jul. Judge then what my Heart feels, which like a Fire but lightly cover'd o'er with the cold Ashes of Despair, with the least blast breaks out into a Flame; I burn, I burn, *Jacinta*, and only charming *Carlos* can allay my Pain—but how? Ay, there's the question.

Jac. Some way I will contrive to speak with him, for he has lost his old wont if he traverse not the Street where you live: but see Donna *Clara*.—   [*Enter* Clara.

Jul. Hah, my Sister, whom yet my jealous heart can

scarce be reconciled to; so deeply was my fear of Rivalship fixt there,—so sad, my Sister, and so near the happy day with *Carlos?*

Cla. 'Tis pity she that thinks it so shou'd want him; the Blessing's thrown away on me, but we are both unhappy to be match'd to those we cannot love. *Carlos,* though young, gay, handsom, witty, rich, I hate as much as you the old *Francisco;* for since I cannot marry my *Antonio,* both Youth and Beauty are but lost on me, and Age decrepid would be equal torment.

Jul. Wou'd *Carlos* knew your heart, sure he'd decline; for he has too much Honor to compel a Maid to yield that loves him not.

Cla. 'Tis true, he is above me every way, and the Honor my Father thinks to do our Family by this Match, makes him resolve upon't; but I have given my Vows to young *Antonio.*

Jul. And young *Antonio* you are like to have, for any thing that *Carlos* cares; for know, to thy eternal joy, my *Clara,* he has but feigned to thee, as much as thy *Antonio* to *Isabella.*

Cla. But are you sure of this?

Jul. Most certain; this Night if you can let *Antonio* see you, he'll tell you all the Cheat, and beg your Pardon.

Cla. Which he will soon obtain, and in return, what Service I can render him in your behalf he shall not want.

Jul. *Antonio* will engage you they are Friends.

Cla. You amaze me.

Jac. I have appointed him this night to wait, and, if possible, I would get him a Minute's time with you.

Cla. Dear *Jacinta,* thou art the kindest Maid.——

Jac. Hang't, why should we young Woman pine and languish for what our own natural Invention may procure us; let us three lay our Heads together, and if *Machiavel* with all his Politicks can out-wit us, 'tis pity but we all lead Apes in Hell, and die without the *Jewish* Blessing of Consolation.

Jul. No more, here comes the Dragon.

Enter Francisco.

Fran. So, together consulting and contriving.

Jac. What, are you jealous of the Petticoat?

Fran. Petticoat! Come, come, Mistress *Pert*, I have known as much danger hid under a Petticoat, as a pair or Breeches. I have heard of two Women that married each other—oh abominable, as if there were so prodigious a scarcity of Christian Mans Flesh.

Jac. No, the Market's well enough stored, thanks be praised, might every Woman be afforded a reasonable Allowance.

Fran. Peace, I say, thou Imp of Lucifer; wou'd thou hadst thy Bellyful, that I might be fairly rid of thee—go get you up to your Chamber, and, d'ye hear, stir not from thence, on pain of our severe displeasure, for I am sent for in all haste, to Signior Don *Sebastian's*, 'tis but hard by, I shall soon return;—what, are you here?

Enter Isabella.

I have a high commendation of your fine Behaviour, Gentlewoman, to *Antonio*; his Father has sent for me, and I shall know all anon, this shall but hasten your Wedding, Huswise, I tell you that, and so farewel to you—

　　　　　　　　　　　　　　[*Ex.* Isabella *crying.*

Cla. Say you so, then 'tis time for me to look about me.

Jul. But will you go out so late, Love? indeed some hurt will come to thee.

Fran. No, look ye, I go arm'd.

　　　　　　　　　[*Shews his Girdle round with Pistols.*

Go, get you to your Chambers.　[*He goes out, they go in.*

SCENE II. *Changes to the Street.*

Enter Carlos, Antonio.

Car. I wonder where this Man of mine should be, whom I sent this Evening with my Letter to *Julia*. What art thou?　[*Enter* Guzman, *runs against* Carlos.

Guz. My Lord, 'tis I, your trusty Trojan, *Guzman.*
—what makes you here, Sir, so near the Door of your
Mistress?

Car. To wait my Doom; what Tidings hast thou,
Guzman?

Guz. Why, Sir, I went as you directed me, to Don
Baltazer's.

Car. And didst thou deliver it?

Guz. And the first thing I met with was old *Francisco.*

Car. So.

Guz. To whom I civilly addrest my self—told him,
you presented your Service to him,—sent to know how
his Lady and he did. Which word Lady I no sooner
named, but I thought he would have saluted me with a
Cudgel,—in fine, observing her behind him, whom he
shelter'd all he could with his Cloke, I taking an occasion
to whisper him, gave it her over his shoulder, whilst she
return'd some Smiles and Looks of Joy,—but for an answer,
'twas impossible to get the least sign of one.

Car. No matter, that joy was evident she wisht me one,
and by the first opportunity my diligent waiting will be
recompensed; but where hast thou been all this while?

Guz. Finding out the Chimney-sweeper you spoke of,
Sir, and whom you ordered me to bring this Evening.

Car. And hast thou found him?

Guz. He's here, at the corner of the Street, I'll call
him.   [*Ex.* Guz.

Car. I have, *Antonio,* besides your particular Revenge,
one of my own to act by this deceit, since all my Industry
to see the charming *Julia* has hitherto been vain, I have
resolv'd upon a new project, if this False Count pass upon
'em, as I doubt not but he will, and that he gets admittance into the House, I'll pass for one of his Domesticks.

Enter Guzman *and* Guiliom. Page *holding his lanthorn
to his face.*

Guz. Here's the Fellow, Sir.

Ant. Fellow! he may be the Devil's Fellow by his countenance.

Car. Come nearer, Friend; dost think thou canst manage a Plot well?

Guil. As any Man in *Cadiz*, Sir, with good instructions.

Car. That thou shalt have, thou art apprehensive.

Guil. So, so, I have a pretty memory for mischief.

Ant. Hast thou Assurance and Courage?

Guil. To kill the honestest Man in *Spain*, if I be well paid.

Car. That thou shalt be.

Guil. I'll do't, say no more, I'll do't.

Car. But canst thou swear stoutly, and lye handsomely.

Guil. Prettily, by Nature, Sir, but with good instructions I shall improve; I thank Heaven I have Docity, or so.

Car. Thou want'st not Confidence.

Guil. No, nor Impudence neither; how should a man live in this wicked world without that Talent?

Ant. Then know our Design is only comical, though if you manage not Matters well, it may prove tragical to you; in fine, dost think thou canst personate a Lord?

Guil. A Lord! marry, that's a hard question: but what sort of a Lord?

Car. Why, any Lord.

Guil. That I cannot do, but I can do some sort of a Lord, as some Lords are wiser than other-some; there is your witty Lord,—him I defie; your wise Lord, that is to say, your knavish Lord, him I renounce; then there's your Politick Lord, him I wou'd have hang'd; then there's your Foolish Lord, let him follow the Politician; then there's your brisk, pert, noisy Lord, and such a small insignificant Fiend I care not if I am possest with; I shall deal well enough with a Devil of his capacity.

Car. Very well, then there needs no more but that you go along with my man to my house, my Authority shall secure you from all the injuries that shall accrue from a discovery, but I hope none will happen: Equipage, Clothes

and Money we'll furnish you with.—Go home with him,
and dress, and practise the Don till we come, who will
give you ample instructions what to do.

Guil. And if I do not fit you with a Don better than
Don Del Phobos, or *Don Quixote*, let me be hang'd up for
the Sign of the Black Boy on my own Poles at a *Spanish*
Inn door.

Ant. We'll be with you presently.

Guil. And if you find me not en Cavalier, say Clothes,
Garniture, Points, and Feathers have lost their Power of
making one.   [*Ex.* Guz. *and* Page, *and* Guil.

Enter, opening the door, Jacinta.

Car. Hah, the Door opens, and surely 'tis a Woman
that advances: dear *Antonio*, wait a little farther;—who's
there?

Jac. Hah, if it should be old *Franicsco* now.

Car. Let it be who it will, I'll tell my name, it cannot injure either;—I'm *Carlos*, who are you?

Jac. A thing that looks for him you name—*Jacinta;*
—are you alone?

Car. Never since *Julia* did possess my heart; what
news, my dearest Messenger of Love? what may I hope?—

Enter Julia.

Jul. All that the kindest Mistress can bestow,
If *Carlos* loves, and still will keep his Vows.

Car. *Julia*, my Life, my Soul, what happy Stars
Conspir'd to give me this dear lucky minute?

Jul. Those that conducted old *Francisco* out,
And will too soon return him back again;
I dare not stay to hear thy love or chiding,
Both which have power to charm, since both proceed
From a kind heart, that's mine.

Car. Oh, take not this dear Body from my Arms,
For if you do, my Soul will follow it.

Jul. What would'st thou have me do?

Car. Be wondrous kind, be lavish of thy Heart,
Be generous in thy Love, and give me all.

Jul. Oh Heavens! what mean you? I shall die with fear.

Car. Fear! let coward Lovers fear, who love by halves,
We that intirely love are bold in Passion,
Like Soldiers fir'd with glory dread no Danger.

Jul. But should we be unthrifty in our Loves,
And for one Moment's joy give all away,
And be hereafter damn'd to pine at distance?

Car. Mistaken Miser, Love like Money put
Into good hands increases every day,
Still as you trust me, still the Sum amounts:
Put me not off with promise of to morrow,
To morrow will take care for new delights,
Why shou'd that rob us of a present one?

Jul. Ah, *Carlos!*
How fondly do I listen to thy words,
And fain would chide, and fain wou'd boast my Virtue,
But mightier Love laughs at those poor delays;
And I should doubtless give you all your *Julia,*
Did not my fear prevent my kinder business;
—And should *Francisco* come and find me absent,
Or take thee with me, we were lost, my *Carlos.*

Car. When then, my *Julia,* shall we meet again?

Jul. You *Spaniards* are a jealous Nation,
But in this *English Spaniard* Old *Francisco,*
That mad Passion's doubled; wholly deprives him of his
Sense, and turns his Nature Brute; wou'd he but trust
me only with my Woman, I wou'd contrive some way
to see my *Carlos.*

Car. 'Tis certain, *Julia,* that thou must be mine.

Jul. Or I must die, my *Carlos.* [*Ant. listning advances.*

Ant. —I'm sure 'tis *Carlos's* voice, and with a Woman;
And though he be my Rival but in Jest,
I have a natural curiosity to see who 'tis he entertains.

Jul. Oh Heavens! Sir, here's *Francisco;* step aside,
Lest mischief shou'd befall you.   [*Runs in.*

Car. Now Love and wild Desire prompt me to kill
this happy Rival,—he's old, and can't be long in his Arrears
to Nature.—What if I paid the debt? [*Draws half way.*
One single push wou'd do't, and *Julia's* mine;—but, hang't,
Adultery is a less sin than Murder, and I will wait my
Fortune.—

Ant. Where are you,—Don *Carlos?*

Car. Who's there, *Antonio?* I took thee for my Rival,
and ten to one but I had done thy business.

Ant. I heard ye talking and believ'd you safe, and came
in hopes to get a little time to speak to *Clara* in;—hah!
—*Jacinta*—

Jac. Who's there, *Antonio?*   [*Peeping out of the door.*

Ant. The same; may I not speak with *Clara?*

Jac. Come in, she's here.—

Car. And prithee, dear *Jacinta,* let me have one word
with *Julia* more, she need not fear surprize; just at the
door let me but kiss her hand.   [*Going in.*

Jac. I'll see if I can bring her.—

Enter Francisco.

Fran. A proud ungracious Flirt,—a Lord with a Pox!
here's a fine business, i'faith, that she should be her own
Carver,—well I'll home, and thunder her together with
a vengeance.

Car. Who's here? sure this is he indeed; I'll step aside,
lest my being seen give him an occasion of jealousy, and
make him affront his Wife.

                    [*Goes aside as* Fran. *was going in.*

Enter Julia.

Fran. Hum, what have we here, a Woman?

Jul. Heavens! what, not gone yet, my Dear?

Fran. So, so, 'tis my confounded Wife, who expecting
some body wou'd have me gone now.

Jul. Are you not satisfied with all I've said,
With all the Vows I've made,
Which here anew, in sight of Heaven, I breathe?

Fran. Yes, yes, you can promise fair, but hang him that trusts ye.

Jul. Go, go, and pray be satisfyed with· my eternal Love.—

Fran. How fain she'd have me gone now; ah, subtle Serpent! is not this plain demonstration,—I shall murder her, I find the Devil great with me. *[Aside still.*

Jul.—What is't thou pausest on?

Fran. The wicked Dissimulation of villainous Woman.
[Aloud to her.

Jul. Francisco!

Fran. Oh thou Monster of Ingratitude, have I caught thee? You'd have me gone, wou'd ye? ay, to Heaven, I believe, like a wicked Woman as you are, so you were rid of me. Go,—and be satisfyed of my eternal love —ah, Gipsey,—no, Gentlewoman, I am a tuff bit, and will hold you tugging till your heart ake.

Jul. Why, was there such hurt in desiring you to go that you might make haste back again,—Oh, my fears!

Fran. That you might receive a Lover,—'tis plain —and my Indignation's high.

Jul. Heav'n knows I meant—

Fran. Only to cuckold me a little,—get you in,—where I will swear thee by Bell, Book and Candle,—get you in, I say,—go, go,—I'll watch for your Lover, and tell him how unkind he was to stay so long, I will.—

[Ex. Julia, *he stands just in the door,* Carlos *advances.*

Car. I hear no noise, sure 'twas he,—and he's gone in— To reap those Joys he knows not how to value,
And I must languish for; I'll stay a little—perhaps *Jacinta* may return again, for anything belonging to my *Julia* is dear, even to my Soul.

[Goes just to the door, Fran. *bolts out on him.*

Fran. Who's there?—what wou'd you have?—who wou'd you speak to?—who do you come from?—and what's your business?

Car. Hah, 'tis the Sot himself;—my name is *Carlos.*

Fran. Carlos! what Father of *Belzebub* sent him hither? —a plain case;—I'll murder her out of hand.

Car. —And I wou'd speak to any body, Friend, that belongs to the fair *Clara,*—if you are any of this house.

Fran. Only the Cuckold of the house, that's all;—my name, Sir, is *Francisco*; but you, perhaps, are better acquainted with my Wife.

Car. Francisco, let me embrace you, my noble Brother, and chide you, that you wou'd not visit me.

[*Going to embrace him, he flies off.*

Fran. And bring my Wife along with me.

Car. Both had been welcome—and all I have, you shou'd command.

Fran. For my Wife's sake—what if I shou'd pistol him now;—and I am damnably provok'd to't, had I but Courage to shoot off one.   [*Aside.*

Car. Methinks you make not so kind returns as my Friendship to you, and the Alliance shall be between us, deserves.

Fran. I am something ill-bred, I confess, Sir;—'tis dark, and if I shou'd do't no body wou'd know 'twas I.

[*Aside.*

Car. I fear there's some Misunderstanding between us, pray let us go in a while, I'll talk you from your error.

[*Offers to go, he gets between him and the door.*

Fran. Between us, Sir! oh Lord, not in the least, Sir, I love and honour you so heartily—I'd be content to give you to the Devil, but the noise of the Pistol wou'd discover the business.   [*Aside.*

Car. Come, let's in, and talk a while.

Fran. I'm sorry I cannot do't, Sir, we are something incommoded being not at our own house.

Car. Brother, I am afraid you are a little inclined to be jealous, that will destroy all Friendship.——

Fran. So, how finely the Devil begins to insinuate!

Car. That makes a Hell of the Heav'n of Love, and those very Pains you fear, are less tormenting than that Fear; what say you, Brother, is't not so with you?

Fran. I find you wou'd have me turn a Husband of the Mode, a fine convenient Tool, one of the modern Humour, a civil Person, that understands Reason, or so; and I doubt not but you wou'd be as modish a Gallant.

Car. Ha, ha, ha.

Fran. What, do you laugh, Sir?

Car. Who can chuse, to hear your Suspicions, your needless Fears. Come, come, trust your Wife's Discretion, and Modesty—and I doubt not but you will find your self——

Fran. In the Road to Heaven, whither they say all Cuckolds go—I thank you for your advice; I perceive you wou'd willingly help me onwards of my Journey.

Car. I'm glad I know you, Sir,—farewel to you——
[*Goes out.*

Fran. No matter for that, so you know not my Wife— and so farewel to you, Sir, and, the Devil take all Cuckold-makers.
[*Exit.*

SCENE III. *The inside of the House.*

Enter Clara, Julia, Antonio, Jacinta *running to 'em.*

Jac. He has seen Don *Carlos*, and they have been in great discourse together, I cou'd not hear one word, but you'll have it at both ears anon, I'll warrant you. Ha, he's coming.

Enter Francisco.

Cla. Heavens, he must not see you here. [*To* Ant.

Jac. Here, step into *Clara's* Bed-chamber.—[*He goes in.*

Fran. So the Plot's at last discover'd,—he was a Cavalier of his Parole.

Jul. Who speak you of?

Fran. Only the Governor, the fine young Governor, I deliver'd him the message, told him my mind and the like.

Jul. So kind to visit us, and have you sent him away already?

Fran. Ah, Witch; already! why, have I any lodging for him?

Jul. But I am glad you brought him not in, I being so unready.

Fran. But you are always ready for him, my dear victorious Man-slayer.

Jul. What means he, sure he has a Gad-bee in his Brain.

Fran. Satan's she Advocate—peace, I say;—so, you look as innocently now, as a little Devil of two years old, I'll warrant;—come, come, look me full in the face—thus,— turn your nose just to mine—so—now tell me whose damnable Plot this was, to send your Gallant with his Eloquence, Querks and Conundrums, to tutor me into better manners?

Jul. Send him! I'll answer no such idle questions.

Fran. He has taken a world of pains about your particular Chapter, and no doubt but he preach'd according to instructions;—what say you for your self, that Judgment may not pass?

Jul. I say you're an old jealous Fool; have I seen Don *Carlos*, or heard from Don *Carlos*, or sent to Don *Carlos*? here's a-do indeed.

Fran. What made you at the door against my positive commands,—the very Street-door,—in the night,—alone, —and undrest,—this is a matter of Fact, Gentlewoman; you hastened me away,—a plain case,—and presently, after Don *Carlos* comes to the door,—positive proof,—sees me and falls right down upon my Jealousy,—clear conviction,—'twas pity but I had follow'd his counsel, yes, when the Devil turns student in Divinity;—but no matter, I'll see your back fairly turn'd upon this Town to morrow; I'll marry my Daughter in the morning to *Antonio*, and a fair wind or not, we'll home; the Gally lies ready in the Harbour—therefore prepare, pack up your tools, for you are no woman of this world.

Ant. How! marry me to morrow to his daughter;—and carry his Wife from my Friend; this misfortune must be prevented.   [*Aside peeping.*

Fran. And so, Mistress, come your ways to your Chamber.

Jul. And study how to prevent this cruel separation.
                    [*Aside, goes out with him and* Jacinta.

Cla. Ah, *Antonio*, I find by that sad look of yours, you have over-heard our hasty Doom.

Ant. I have, and am a little surpriz'd at the suddenness of it; and I my self am the unlucky occasion of it,—to break it off, I told my Father how scurvily *Isabella* treated me,—he thereupon sends for old *Francisco*, tells him of my complaint, and instead of disengaging my self, I find my self more undone.

Cla. What shall we do? I'm sure thou wilt not marry her, thou canst not do't and hope to go to Heaven.

Ant. No, I have one prevention left, and if that fail, I'll utterly refuse to marry her, a thing so vainly proud; no Laws of Nature or Religion, sure, can bind me to say yes; and for my Fortune, 'tis my own, no Father can command it.

Cla. I know thou wilt be true, and I'll not doubt it.

                    Enter Jacinta.

Jac. Ah! Madam, the saddest news—

Cla. Hah! what?

Jac. Poor Gentleman, I pity you of all things in the World,—you must be forc'd—how can I utter it,—to the most lamentable torment that ever Lover endur'd—to remain all night in your Mistress's Chamber.

Ant. Alas, how shall I endure so great an Affliction?

Cla. And I.

Jac. Ha, ha, ha, how I am griev'd to think on it; ha, ha,

ha, that you shou'd both be so hardly put to it; ha, ha, ha,
for the old Gentleman has lock'd all the doors, and took
the keys to bed to him,—go, get you in,—ha, ha, ha.—

Ant. Oh, my dear *Clara*, this is a blessing I could not
hope.

Cla. *So large a Freedom shall my Virtue prove,*
        I'll trust my Honour with Antonio's *Love.*

                                [*They go in.*
                        [*Ex.* Jacinta *laughing.*

ACT III.

Scene I. *Don* Carlos' *house.*

Enter Don Carlos *in his Night-gown*, Antonio, *and* Guzman
                with Clothes.

Car. All night with *Clara* say'st thou? that was lucky;
But was she kind, my friend?

Ant. As I desir'd, or Honour wou'd permit her;
Nor wou'd I press her farther.

Car. A very moderate Lover.

Ant. For some part of my Virtue, Sir, I owe to you;
in midst of all my Love, even in the kindest moments of
Delight, my Joys were broken by concern for you.
—*Julia* this day, or very suddenly, leaves *Cadiz.*

Car. By Heaven, and so will *Carlos* then; for I'm so
resolutely bent to possess that dear Creature,
That I will do't with hazard of my Life,
Expence of Fortune, or what's dear to me.

Guz. And how wou'd you reward that politick head,
that shou'd contrive the means to bring this handsomly
about; not for an a hour, or a night, but even as long as you
please, with freedom; without the danger of venturing
your honourable neck, in showing Feats of Activity three
stories high, with a Dagger in one hand, and a Pistol in
t'other, like a Ropedancer?

Car. But how? Thou talkest of Impossibilities.

Ant. Dost think she'll e'er consent to quit her Husband?

Guz. No, Heaven forbid, I am too good a Christian to part Man and Wife; but being naturally inclined to works of Charity, I will with one project I have in this noddle of mine,—make old *Francisco* a Cuckold, accommodate my Lord and *Julia*, serve you, Sir,—and give our selves a good Scene of Mirth.

Car. Thou amazest me.

Guz. If I do't not, send me to the Galleys; nay, and so far cure the Jealousy of the old Fellow, that from a rigid suspicious troublesom Fool, he shall become so tame and gentle a Husband,—that he shall desire you to favour him so much as to lie with his dear Wife.

Car. By what strange Witchcraft shall this be brought to pass?

Guz. E'en honest Invention, Sir, good Faith, listen and believe :—When he goes, he certainly goes by Sea, to save the charges of Mules.

Ant. Right, I heard him say so; in the Galley that lies in the Port.

Guz. Good, there is a Galley also, in the Harbour, you lately took from the *Turks;* Habits too were taken in her enough to furnish out some forty or fifty as convenient *Turks* as a man wou'd wish at the Devil.

Car. Ah, Rogue, I begin to apprehend already.

Guz. Our *Turkish* Galley thus man'd, I'll put to Sea, and about a League from Land, with a sham-fight set on that of Old *Francisco*, take it, make 'em all Slaves, clap the Old Fellow under hatches, and then you may deal with the fair Slave his Wife, as *Adam* did with *Eve.*

Car. I'm ravish'd with the thought.

Ant. But what will be the event of this?

Car. I will not look so far, but stop at the dear Joys, and fear no Fate beyond 'em.

Guz. Nay, with a little cudgelling this dull Brain of mine I shall advance it farther for the Jest-sake ;—as I

take it, Signior Don *Antonio*, you have a fine Villa, within
a Bow-shot of this City belonging to your self.

Ant. I have with pleasant Gardens, Grotto's, Water-
works.——

Car. A most admirable Scene for Love and our Designs.

Ant. 'Tis yours, Sir.

Guz. Then, Sir, when we have taken this old Fool, on
whom the grossest cheat wou'd pass, much more this,
which shall carry so seeming a Truth in't, he being clapt
under hatches in the Dark, we'll wind round a League or
two at Sea, turn in, and land at this Garden, Sir, of yours,
which we'll pretend to be a *Seraglio*, belonging to the
Grand Seignior; whither, in this hot part o'th' year, he
goes to regale himself with his She-Slaves.

Car. But the distance of Place and Time allow not such
a Fallacy.

Guz. Why he never read in's life; knows neither
Longitude nor Latitude, and *Constantinople* may be in the
midst of *Spain* for any thing he knows; besides, his Fear
will give him little leisure for thinking.

Ant. But how shall we do with the Seamen of this
other Gally?

Guz. There's not above a Dozen, besides the Slaves
that are chain'd to the Oar, and those Dozen, a Pistole
apiece wou'd not only make 'em assist in the design, but
betray it in earnest to the *Grand Seignior*;—for them I'll
undertake, the Master of it being *Pier de Sala*, your Father's
old Servant, Sir.   [*To* Carlos.

Ant. But possibly his mind may alter upon the Arrival
of this False Count of ours?

Car. No matter, make sure of those Seamen however;
that they may be ready upon occasion.

Ant. 'Tis high time for me that your Count were arriv'd,
for this morning is destin'd the last of my Liberty.

Car. This Morning—Come, haste and dress me—[*To*
Guz.]—*Guzman*, where's our Count?

Enter Guiliom *drest fine, two great* Pages *and a little one following.*

Guz. Coming to give you the good morrow, Sir ;
And shew you how well he looks the Part.

Car. Good day to your Lordship—   [*Bowing.*

Guil. Morrow, morrow, Friend.

Ant. My Lord, your most humble Servant.

Guil. Thank you, Friend, thank you; Page, Boy—
what's a-Clock, Sirrah?

Page. About Eight, my Lord.

Ant. Your Lordship's early up.

Guil. My Stomach was up before me, Friend ; and I'm
damnably hungry; 'tis strange how a man's Appetite
increases with his Greatness; I'll swinge it away now I'm
a Lord,—then I will wench without Mercy ; I'm resolv'd
to spare neither Man, Woman, nor Child, not I; hey,
Rogues, Rascals, Boys, my Breakfast, quickly, Dogs—let
me see, what shall I have now that's rare?

Page. What will your Honour please to have?

Guil. A small rasher of delicate Bacon, Sirrah—of
about a Pound, or two, with a small Morsel of Bread—
round the Loaf, d'ye hear, quickly, Slaves.

Ant. That's gross meat, Sir, a pair of Quails—or—

Guil. I thank you for that, i'faith, take your Don
again, an you please, I'll not be starv'd for ne'er a Don
in Christendom.

Ant. But you must study to refine your Manners a little.

Guil. Manners! you shall pardon me for that ; as if a
Lord had not more privilege to be more saucy, more
rude, impertinent, slovenly and foolish than the rest of his
Neighbours, or Mankind.

Car. Ay, ay, 'tis great.

Guil. Your saucy Rudeness, in a Grandee, is Freedom;
your Impertinence, Wit ; your Sloven, careless ; and your
Fool, good natur'd ; as least they shall pass so in me, I'll
warrant ye.

Car. Well, you have your full Instructions; your Baggage, Bills and Letters, from *Octavio* the *Sevilian* Merchant.

Guz. All, all, Sir, are ready, and his Lordship's breakfast waits.

Car. Which ended, we advance,
Just when *Aurora* rose from *Thetis*' Bed,
Where he had wantoned a short Summer's night,
Harness'd his bright hoov'd Horses to begin
His gilded course above the Firmament,
Out sallied Don *Gulielmo Rodorigo de Chimney Sweperio*, and so forth. Gad, this adventure of ours will be worthy to be sung in Heroick Rhime Doggerel, before we have finisht it; Come—   [*Goes out.*

Guil. Hey, Rogues, Rascals, Boys, follow me just behind.   [*Exeunt.*

SCENE II. Francisco's *house.*

Enter Clara *and* Jacinta.

Jac. Nay, I knew he would be civil, Madam, or I would have borne you Company; but neither my Mistress nor I, cou'd sleep one wink all Night, for fear of a Discovery in the Morning; and to save the poor Gentleman a tumbling Cast from the Window, my Mistress, just at day-break, feigned her self wondrous sick,—I was called, desired to go to Signior *Spadilio's* the Apothecary's, at the next Door, for a Cordial; and so he slipt out;—but the Story of this false Count pleases me extremely, and, if it should take, Lord, what mirth we shall have. Ha, ha, ha, I can't forbear with the thoughts on't.

Cla. And to see the Governor his Man?

Jac. Ah, what a Jest that would be too—Ha, ha, ha! but here comes *Isabella*; let's puff up her Pride with Flatteries on her Beauty.

Enter Isabella *looking in a Glass, and seeing her Face.*

Isa. Ah, Heavens, those Eyes—that Look,—that pretty

Leer,—that my Father shou'd be so doating an old Fool to
think these Beauties fit for a little Merchandize ; a Mar-
chioness wou'd so much better become me. [*Looks again.*
—Ah, what a Smile's there—and then that scornful Look
—'tis great—Heavens, who's here ?   [*Sees them.*

Cla. Only those Friends that wish you better Fortune
than this day promises.

Jac. Look on that Face ; are there not Lines that foretel
a world of Greatness, and promise much Honour ?

Cla. Her Face, her Shape, her Mein, her every part
declares her Lady—or something more.

Isa. Why, so, and yet this little Creature of a Father,
ridiculously and unambitious, would spoil this Lady, to
make up a simple Citizen's Wife—in good time.

Jac. That very look had some presaging Grandeur.

Isa. Do you think so, *Jacinta?* Ha, ha, ha.

Jac. That Laugh again, oh Heavens, how it charms !

Cla. And how graceful 'tis !

Jac. Ah, nothing but a great gilt Coach will become it.

Cla. With six *Spanish* Mares.—

Jac. And embroidered Trappings.

Cla. With four Lackeys.

Jac. And a Page at the tail on't.

Cla. She's evidently design'd for a Person of Quality.

Isa. Besides I have so natural an Inclination for a Don,
that if my Father do force me to marry this small Creature
of a Merchant, I shall make an Intrigue with some body
of Quality.

Cla. Cou'd you but manage it well, and keep it from
Antonio.

Isa. Keep it from *Antonio,*—is it think you for a little
silly Cit, to complain when a Don does him the Honour
to visit his Lady ? Marry, that were pretty.

              Enter Francisco, *and* Lopez.

Fran. How, a Count to speak with me ! with me, I
say,—here at *Cadiz.*

Lop. A Count, Sir, and to speak with you.

Fran. Art sure 'tis not the Governor?—I'll go lock up my Wife.

Lop. Governor, Sir! No, no, 'tis a mere Stranger, Sir, a rare Count whom I never saw all days of my life before.

Fran. And with me wou'd he speak? I hope he comes not to my Wife.

Enter Julia.

Jul. Oh Husband, the delicatest fine Person of Quality, just alighted at the Door, Husband.

Fran. What, have you seen him then? the Devil's in these Women, and there be but a Loop-hole to peep out of they'll spy a man,—I'm resolved to see this thing,—go, retire, you Women, here's Men coming up.

Isa. And will Men eat us?

Fran. No, but they may do worse, they may look on ye, and Looking breeds Liking; and Liking, Love; and Love a damn'd thing, call'd Desire; and Desire begets the Devil and all of Mischief to young Wenches—Get ye gone in, I say—here's a Lord coming—and Lords are plaguy things to Women.

Isa. How, a Lord! oh, heavens! *Jacinta*, my Fan, and set my Hair in order, oh, the Gods! I would not but see a Lord for all the World! how my Heart beats already —keep your Distance behind, *Jacinta*,—bless me, how I tremble—a little farther, *Jacinta*.

Fran. Come, come, Huswife, you shall be married anon, and then let your Husband have the plague of you—but for my Gentlewoman,—Oh Lord—they're here.

Enter Guiliom, Carlos, *and* Pages, &c.

Guil. How now, Fellow, where's this old Don *Francisco*?

Fran. I'm the Person, Sir.

Isa. Heavens, what an Air he has!

Guil. Art thou he? Old Lad, how dost thou do? Hah!

Fran. I don't know.

Guil. Thou knowest me not it seems, old Fellow, hah !

Fran. Know you—no, nor desire to do,—on what acquaintance, pray ?

Guil. By Instinct; such as you ought to know a Person of Quality, and pay your Civilities naturally; in *France,* where I have travel'd, so much good manners is used, your Citizen pulls off his hat, thus—to every Horse of Quality, and every Coach of Quality; and do you pay my proper Person no more respect, hah !

Isa. What a Dishonour's this to me, to have so dull a Father, that needs to be instructed in his Duty.

Guil. But, Sir, to open the eyes of your understanding —here's a Letter to you, from your Correspondent a Merchant of *Sevil.*

[*Gives him a dirty Letter which he wipes on his Cloke and reads, and begins to pull off his hat, and reading on bows lower and lower till he have finisht it.*

Fran. Cry Mercy, my Lord,—and yet I wou'd he were a thousand Leagues off.

Guil. I have Bills of Exchange too, directed to thee, old Fellow, at *Sevil;* but finding thee not there, and I (as most Persons of my Quality are) being something idle, and never out of my way, came to this Town, to seek thee, Fellow—being recommended as thou seest here, old Vermin—here—   [*Gives him Bills.*

Isa. Ah, what a graceful Mein he has ! how fine his Conversation ! ah, the difference between him and a filthy Citizen !

Jul.—*Clara* has told me all.— [*Jac. whispering to* Jul.

Car. That's she in the middle; stand looking on her languishingly,—your head a little on one side,—so,—fold your Arms,—good,—now and then heave your breast with a sigh,—most excellent.—   [*He groans.*

Fran. Bills for so many thousands.

Jac. He has you in his eye already.

Isa. Ah, *Jacinta,* thou flatterest me.

Jac. Return him some kind looks in pity.

[*She sets her Eyes, and bows*, &c.

Car. That other's my Mistress,—couldst thou but keep this old Fellow in discourse whilst I give her the sign to retire a little.—

Guil. I'll warrant you I'll banter him till you have cuckolded him, if you manage matters as well as I.

Fran. My Lord, I ask your pardon for my rudeness in not knowing you before, which I ought to have done in good manners I confess ; who the Devil does he stare at so ?— Wife, I command you to withdraw, upon pain of our high displeasure.—my Lord, I shall dispatch your affairs,—he minds me not,—Ay, 'tis my Wife, I say, Minion, be gone,— your Bills, my Lord, are good, and I accept 'em ;—why a Devil he minds me not yet, [Julia *goes to t'other side to* Carlos.]—and though I am not at my proper home,— I am where I can command Money,—hum,—sure 'tis my Daughter,—Ay, ay,—'tis so, how if he should be smitten now ; the plaguy Jade had sure the Spirit of Prophecy in her ; 'tis so—'tis she—my Lord.

Guil. Prithee, old Fellow, Peace,—I am in love.

Fran. In love,—what, shall I be the Father of a Lord ? wou'd it become me, think ye ?—he's mighty full of Cogitabund—my Lord,—sure his Soul has left the Tenement of his Body—I have his Bills here, and care not if it never return more.   [*Looks over the Bills.*

Car. Dear *Julia*, let's retire, our time's but short.

Jul. I dare not with you, the venture wou'd be too bold in a young beginner in the Thefts of Love.

Guil. Her Eyes are Suns, by *Jove.*

Car. Oh, nothing is so ventrous as Love, if it be true.

Guil. Or else, two Morning Stars,
All other Beauties are but Soot to her.

Jul. But shou'd my Husband—

Car. He's safe for one dear half hour, I'll warrant you, come.

Fran. Um—my Wife here still, must I begin to thunder.

Jul. Lord, and you be so froward, I'll be gone.—

Car. So, her Husband, kind heart, lest she should be cruel, has himself given me the dear opportunity.— [*Aside.* —Be sure you keep the old Fellow in discourse awhile.

Guil. Be you as sure to cuckold him.—[*Ex.* Car. *and* Jul. —Old Fellow,—prithee what Person of Quality is that?

Fran. Person of Quality! alas, my Lord, 'tis a silly Citizen's Daughter.

Guil. A Citizen's! what clod of Earth cou'd bring forth such a Beauty?

Fran. Alas, my Lord, I am that clod of Earth, and to Earth, if you call it so, she must return again, for she's to be married to a Citizen this Morning.

Guil. Oh! I am doubly wounded, first with her harmonious Eyes,

Who've fir'd my Heart to that degree,

No Chimney ever burnt like me.

Fair Lady,—suffer the Broom of my Affection to sweep all other Lovers from your heart.

Isa. Ah, my Lord, name it not, I'm this day to be married.

Guil. To day! name me the Man; Man did I say? the Monster, that dares lay claim to her I deign to love, —none answer me,—I'll make him smoak, by *Vulcan*— and all the rest of the Goddesses.

Fran. Bless me, what a furious thing this Love is?

Guil. By this bright Sword, that is so used to slaughter, he dies; [*Draws.*] old Fellow, say—the Poltroon's name.

Fran. Oh, fearful—alas, dread Sir!

Isa. Ah! sheath your Sword, and calm your generous Rage.

Guil. I cannot brook a Rival in my Love, the rustling Pole of my Affection is too strong to be resisted.

[*Runs raging up and down the Stage with his Sword in his hand.*

Isa. I cannot think, my Lord, so mean a Beauty can so suddenly charm a Heart so great as yours.

Guil. Oh! you're mistaken, as soon as I cast my eyes upon the Full-moon of your Countenance, I was struck blind and dumb.

Fran. Ay, and deaf too, I'll be sworn, he cou'd neither hear, see nor understand; this Love's a miraculous thing.

Guil. And that Minute, the most renoun'd Don *Gulielmo Roderigo de Chimeny Sweperio*, became your Gally-Slave, —I say no more, but that I do love,—and I will love,— and that if you are but half so willing as I, I will dub you, Viscountess *de Chimeny Sweperio*.

Isa. I am in Heaven, ah! I die, *Jacinta*. How can I credit this, that am so much unworthy?

Guil. I'll do't, say no more, I'll do't.

Fran. Do't, but, my Lord, and with what face can I put off Signior *Antonio*, hum.

Guil. Antonio,—hy, Pages, give order that *Antonio* be instantly run through the Lungs—d'ye hear?

Fran. Oh, hold, hold, my Lord! run through the Lungs!

Page. It shall be done, my Lord! but what *Antonio*?

Guil. Why, any *Antonio*; all the *Antonio*'s that you find in *Cadiz*.

Fran. Oh, what bloody-minded Monsters these Lords are!—But, my Lord, I'll ne'er give you the trouble of killing him, I'll put him off with a handsom Compliment; as thus,—Why, look ye, Friend *Antonio*, the business is this, my Daughter *Isabella* may marry a Lord, and you may go fiddle.—

Guil. Ay, that's civil,—and if he do not desist, I'll unpeople *Spain* but I'll kill him; for, Madam, I'll tell you what happened to me in the Court of *France*—there was a Lady in the Court in love with me,—she took a liking to my Person which—I think,—you will confess—

Isa. To be the most accomplisht in the World.

Guil. I had some sixscore Rivals, they all took Snuff;

that is, were angry—at which I smiled;—they were incensed; at which I laught, ha, ha, ha,—i'faith; they rag'd, I—when I met 'em,—Cockt, thus—*en passant*—justled 'em—thus,— [*Overthrows* Fran.] They turn'd and frown'd,—thus,—I drew.—

Fran. What, on all the sixscore, my Lord?

Guil. All, all; sa, sa, quoth I, sa, sa, sa, sa, sa, sa.

[*Fences him round the Stage.*

Fran. Hold, hold, my Lord, I am none of the sixscore.

Guil. And run 'em all through the Body!

Fran. Oh Heavens! and kill'd 'em all.

Guil. Not a Man,—only run 'em through the body a little, that's all, my two Boys were by, my Pages here.

Isa. Is it the fashion, Sir, to be attended by Pages so big?

Guil. Pages of Honour always;—these were stinted at nurse, or they had been good proper Fellows.

Fran. I am so frighted with this relation, that I must up to my Wife's Chamber for a little of that strong Cordial that recovered her this morning.

[*Going out* Guil. *stays him.*

Guil. Why, I'll tell you, Sir, what an odd sort of a Wound I received in a Duel the other day,—nay, Ladies, I'll shew it you; in a very odd place—in my back parts.

[*Goes to untuck his Breeches, the Ladies squeak.*

Isa. Ah.

Page. Shew a Wound behind, Sir! the Ladies will think you are a Coward.

Guil. Peace, Child, peace, the Ladies understand Dueling as little as my self; but, since you are so tender-hearted, Ladies, I'll not shew you my wound; but faith, it spoiled my dancing. [*Page comes in.*

Page. My Lord, now you talk of dancing, here's your Baggage brought from a-board the Gally by your Seamen, who us'd to entertain you with their rustick Sports.

Guil. Very well; Sir, with your permission, I am resolved whether you will or no, to give the Ladies some

divertisement,—bid 'em come in; nay, Sir, you stir not.
                                        [*Ex*. Page.
'Tis for your delight, Sir, I do't; for, Sir, you must understand, a Man, if he have any thing in him, Sir, of Honour,
for the case, Sir, lies thus, 'tis not the business of an Army
to droll upon an Enemy—truth is, every man loves a
whole skin;—but 'twas the fault of the best Statesmen
in Christendom to be loose in the hilts,—you conceive me.

Fran. Very well, my Lord, I'll swear he's a rare spoken
man;—why, what a Son-in-law shall I have? I have a
little business, my Lord, but I'll wait on you presently.
                                        [*Going out.*

Guil. Sir, there is nothing like your true jest; a thing
once well done, is twice done, and I am the happiest Man
in the World in your Alliance; for, Sir, a Nobleman if
he have any tolerable parts,—is a thing much above the
Vulgar;—oh,—here comes the Dancers.

Enter Dancers.

Come, sit down by me.
    Fran. 'Tis my duty to stand, my Lord.
    Guil. Nay, you shall sit.   [*They dance.*

Enter Antonio.

Ant. Good day, Sir, I hope you will not chide my
tardiness, I have a little overslept my self, and am ashamed
to see my lovely Bride, and all this worthy Company attend.
—But you, fair Creature—   [*To* Isabella.
    Isa. No marrying to day, Sir.
    Fran. No, Sir, no marrying to day.
    Ant. How, do I dream, or hear this from *Francisco*?
    Guil. How now, Fellow, what art thou?
    Ant. The Husband of that proud disdainful Woman.
    Guil. Another word like that—and thou art—
    Ant. What, Sir?
    Fran. Oh, hold, hold, my Lord! *Antonio*, I must tell
you, you're uncivil.

Guil. Dost know, dull Mortal, that I am a Lord,
And *Isabella* my adopted Lady.

Ant. I beg your pardon, Sir, if it be so, poor Mortals
can but grieve in silence.

Guil. Alas, poor Mortal!

Ant. But, for you, *Francisco.*

Fran. Ah, dear *Antonio,* I vow and swear I cannot chuse
but weep to lose thee; but my Daughter was born for a
Lady, and none can help their destiny.

Ant. And is it possible thou canst use me thus? [*To Isa.*

Isa. Take away that little Fellow; in pity of your life,
I deign to bid you withdraw and be safe.

Guil. D'ye hear, hah?—this Lady has beg'd your life.

Ant. Beg'd my Life!

Guil. Vile Wretch, dar'st thou retort?

[*Draws, the Women hold him.*

Fran. Oh, hold, hold, my noble Son-in-law, he shall
do any thing;—dear *Antonio,* consider, I was never Father
to a Lord all days of my Life before:—my Lord, be
pacified, my Daughter shall be a Lady.

Isa. For my sake spare him, and be Friends with him,
as far as you may deign to be with a little Citizen.

Guil. Fellow, I forgive thee,—here's my hand to kiss
in sign and token I am appeased.

[*Gives him his hand to kiss, 'tis all black.*

Ant. A Pox of his honourable hand, 't had like to have
spoiled all,—well, since it must be so, I am content.

Guil. So, now Peace is concluded on, on all sides, what
shall we do to day besides eating and drinking in abundance; for to morrow I shall get my self in order for my
Marriage.

Cla. What thinks your Honour of taking the Air upon
the Sea, in a Galley, a League or two?

Guil. With Fiddles, Drums and Trumpets, Westphalia
hams and Pidgeons, and the like: Hey, Rogues, Scoundrels,
Dogs.

Isa. Ah, how fine is every Action of a great Man!

Guil. Command a Galley to attend us presently.

—You shall along, old Boy.   [*To* Fran.

Fran. Alas, I must stay at home with my Wife, my Lord.

Guil. A Wife! have I a Mother-in-law too?—she must along with us, and take a frisk,—no denial.

Enter Carlos.

—Oh, are you come?   [*Aside.*

Car. Yes, and thank thee for the best moment of my Life—

Hast thou contrived the Voyage then?

Guil. Take no care—come, haste on board—our Honour will not lose the Fresco of the Morning,—Follow me, Pages.

Page. At your heels, my Lord—   [*Exeunt.*

ACT IV.

SCENE I.

Enter, as aboard the Ship, Guiliom, Isabella, Francisco, Julia, Antonio, Clara, Jacinta, Pedro *and his Wife,* Pages.

Guil. Ladies and Gentlemen, you are very welcome aboard—Come, put off to Sea, Rogues, Scoundrels, Tarpaulins, to your Business, and then, every man his Bottle, —hey, Page, Rogues, where are my Men? Come, spread the Table—for we are very hungry.

Isa. Heav'ns, what a peculiar Grace there is in every word that comes from the Mouth of a Cavalier.

Guil. By *Mars*, the God of Love!

Page. By *Cupid*, Sir.   [*Aside to him.*

Guil. Cupid, Sirrah! I say, I'll have it *Mars*, there's more Thunder in the Sound: I say, by *Mars*, these Gallies are pretty neat convenient Tenements—but a— I see ne'er a Chimney in 'em :—Pox on't, what have I to do with a Chimney now?

Isa. He is a delicate fine Person, *Jacinta* ; but, methinks he does not make Love enough to me.

Jac. Oh, Madam, Persons of his Quality never make Love in Words, the greatness of their Actions show their Passion.

Jac Ay, 'tis true all the little Fellows talk of Love.

Guil. Come, Ladies, set ; Come, *Isabella*, you are melancholy,—Page—Fill my Lady a Beer-glass.

Isa. Ah, Heav'ns, a Beer-glass.

Guil. O, your Viscountess never drinks under your Beer-glass, your Citizens Wives simper and sip, and will be drunk without doing Credit to the Treater ; but in their Closets, they swinge it away, whole Slashes, i'faith, and egad, when a Woman drinks by her self, Glasses come thick about : your Gentlewoman, or your little Lady, drinks half way, and thinks in point of good manners, she must leave some at the bottom ; but your true bred Woman of Honour drinks all, *Supernaculum*, by *Jove*.

Isa. What a misfortune it was, that I should not know this before, but shou'd discover my want of so necessary a piece of Grandeur.

Jac. And nothing, but being fuddled, will redeem her Credit.

Guil. Come—fall to, old Boy,—thou art not merry ; what, have we none that can give us a Song ?

Ant. Oh Sir, we have an Artist aboard I'll assure you ; Signior *Cashier*, shall I beg the favour of you to shew your Skill ?

Pet. Sir, my Wife and I'm at your service.

Guil. Friend, what Language can you sing ?

Pet. Oh, Sir, your Singers speak all Languages.

Guil. Say'st thou so, prithee then let's have a touch of Heathen *Greek*.

Pet. That you shall, Sir, Sol la me fa sol, &c.

Fran. Hum, I think this is indeed Heathen *Greek*, I'm sure 'tis so to me.

Guil. Ay, that may be, but I understand every word on't.

Fran. Good lack, these Lords are very learned Men.

Pet. Now, Sir, you shall hear one of another Language from my Wife and I.   [*Sing a Dialogue in* French.

Enter the Captain.

Capt. Well, Gentlemen, though the news be something unpleasant that I bring, yet to noble minds 'tis sport and pastime.

Guil. Hah, Fellow! What's that that's sport and pastime to noble minds.

Fran. Oh Lord, no goodness, I'll warrant.

Capt. But, Gentlemen, pluck up your Spirits, be bold and resolute.

Fran. Oh Lord, bold and resolute! why, what's the matter, Captain?

Capt. You are old, Signior, and we expect no good from you but Prayers to Heaven?

Fran. Oh Lord, Prayers to Heaven! Why, I hope, Captain, we have no need to think of Heaven.

Capt. At your own Peril be it then, Signior, for the *Turks* are coming upon us.

Fran. Oh Lord, *Turks, Turks!*   [*Ex.* Cap.

Guil. Turks, oh, is that all?   [*Falls to eating.*

Fran. All—why, they'll make Eunuchs of us, my Lord, Eunuchs of us poor men, and lie with all our Wives.

Guil. Shaw, that's nothing, 'tis good for the Voice.— how sweetly we shall sing, ta, la, ta la la, ta la, *&c.*

Fran. Ay, 'twill make you sing another note, I'll warrant you.

Enter a Seaman.

Sea. For Heaven's sake, Sirs, do not stand idle here; Gentlemen, if you wou'd save your lives,—draw and defend 'em.   [*Exit.*

Fran. Draw! I never drew any thing in my Life, but

my Purse, and that most damnably against my will; oh, what shall I do?

Enter Captain.

Capt. Ah, my Lord, they bear up briskly to us, with a fresh Gale and full Sails.

Fran. Oh, dear Captain, let us tack about and go home again.

Capt. 'Tis impossible to scape, we must fight it out.

Fran. Fight it out! oh, I'm not able to indure it,— why, what the Devil made me a ship-board? [*Ex.* Cap.

Guil. Why, where be these *Turks?* set me to 'em, I'll make 'em smoke, Dogs, to dare attack a man of Quality.

Isa. Oh, the Insolence of these *Turks!* do they know who's aboard? for Heaven's sake, my Lord, do not expose your noble Person.

Guil. What, not fight?—Not fight! A Lord, and not fight? Shall I submit to Fetters, and see my Mistress ravish'd by any great *Turk* in Christendom, and not fight?

Isa. I'd rather be ravish'd a thousand times, than you should venture your Person.   [*Seamen shout within.*

Fran. Ay, I dare swear.

Enter Seaman.

Sea. Ah, Sirs, what mean you? Come on the Deck for shame.

Ant. My Lord, let us not tamely fall, there's danger near.   [*Draws.*

Guil. Ay, ay, there's never smoke, but there's some fire—Come, let's away—ta la, tan ta la, la la, &c. [*Draws.*
       [*Exit singing, and* Antonio *and* Pet.

Fran. A Pox of all Lords, I say, you must be janting in the Devil's name, and God's dry Ground wou'd not serve your turn.   [*Shout here.*

Oh, how they thunder! What shall I do?—oh, for some Auger-hole to thrust my head into, for I could never indure the noise of Cannons,—oh, 'tis insupportable,—intolerable —and not to be indur'd. [*Running as mad about the Stage.*

Isa. Dear Father, be not so frighted.   [*Weeps.*

Fran. Ah, Crocodile, wou'd thou hadst wept thy Eyes out long ago, that thou hadst never seen this Count; then he had never lov'd thee, and then we had never been invited a ship-board.   [*A noise of fighting.*

Enter Guiliom, Pet. *and* Antonio, *driven in fighting by* Guzman *and other* Turks.

Ant. Ah, Sir, the *Turks* have boarded us, we're lost, we're lost.

Fran. Oh, I am slain, I'm slain.   [*Falls down.*

Guil. Hold, hold, I say, you are now in the presence of Ladies, and 'tis uncivil to fight before Ladies.

Guz. Yield then, you are our Slaves.

Guil. Slaves, no Sir, we're Slaves to none but the Ladies.
[*Offers to fight.*

Isa. Oh, hold, rude man,—d'ye know whom you encounter?

Guz. What's here—one dead—[*Looking on* Francisco.

Fran. Oh, Lord!

Guz. Or, if he be not, he's old, and past service, we'll kill the Christian Dog out of the way.

Fran. Oh, hold, hold, I'm no Christian, Gentlemen; but as errant a Heathen as your selves.

Guz. Bind him strait, neck and heels, and clap him under hatches.

Jul. Oh, spare him, Sir, look on his Reverend Age.

Guz. For your sake, Lady, much may be done, we've need of handsom Women.
[*Gives her to some* Turks *that are by.*

Fran. Hah,—my Wife! My Wife ravish'd—oh, I'm dead.

Jul. Fear not, my dear, I'll rather die than do thee wrong.

Fran. Wou'd she wou'd, quickly,—then there's her Honour sav'd, and her Ransom, which is better.

Guz. Down with the muttering Dog;   [*He descends.*
—And takes the Ladies to several Cabins.
                              [*The* Turks *take hold of the Men.*
Isa. Must we be parted then?—ah, cruel Destiny!
                                                    [*Weeps.*
Guil. Alas! this Separation's worse than Death.

Isa. You possibly may see some *Turkish* Ladies, that
may insnare your Heart, and make you faithless;—but I,
ah Heavens! if ever I change my Love, may I become
deformed, and lose all hopes of Title or of Grandure.

Guil. But should the *Grand Seignior* behold thy Beauty,
thou wou'dst despise thine own dear hony Viscount to be
a *Sultana.*

Isa. A *Sultana,* what's that?

Guil. Why, 'tis the great *Turk,* a Queen of *Turkey.*

Isa. These dear expressions go to my Heart. [*Weeps.*
And yet a *Sultana* is a tempting thing—   [*Aside smiling.*
—And you shall find your *Isabella* true,—though the
Grand Seignior wou'd lay his Crown at my feet,—wou'd
he wou'd try me though—Heavens! to be Queen of
Turkey.   [*Aside.*

Guil. May I believe thee,—but when thou seest the
difference, alas, I am but a Chimney—hum, nothing to a
great *Turk.*

Isa. Is he so rare a thing?—Oh, that I were a she
great *Turk.*   [*Aside.*

Guz. Come, come, we can't attend your amorous
Parleys.   [*Parts 'em.*

Jul. Alas, what shall we poor Women do? [*Ex. Men.*

Isa. We must e'en have patience, Madam, and be
ravisht.

Cla. Ravisht! Heavens forbid.

Jac. An please the Lord, I'll let my nails grow against
that direful day.

Isa. And so will I, for I'm resolv'd none should ravish
me but the great *Turk.*

Guz. Come, Ladies, you are Dishes to be serv'd up to the board of the *Grand Seignior*.

Isa. Why, will he eat us all?

Guz. A slice of each, perhaps, as he finds his Appetite inclin'd.

Isa. A slice, uncivil Fellow,—as if this Beauty were for a bit and away;—Sir, a word,—if you will do me the favour, to recommend me to be first served up to the *Grand Seignior*, I shall remember the Civility when I am great.

Guz. Lady, he is his own Carver, a good word by the bye, or so, will do well, and I am—a Favorite—

Isa. Are you so? here, take this Jewel,—in earnest of greater Favours—   [*Gives him a Jewel.*
        [*Exeunt all.*

SCENE II. *A Garden.*

Enter Don Carlos *and* Lopez.

Car. But, why so near the Land? by Heaven, I saw each action of the Fight, from yonder grove of Jessamine; and doubtless all beheld it from the Town.

Lop. The Captain, Sir, design'd it so, and at the Harbour gave it out those two Galleys were purposely prepared to entertain the Count and the Ladies with the representation of a Sea-fight; lest the noise of the Guns should alarm the Town, and, taking it for a real fight, shou'd have sent out Supplies, and so have ruin'd our Designs.

Car. Well, have we all things in readiness?

Lop. All, Sir, all.

Enter Page.

Page. My Lord, a Barge from the Galley is just arriv'd at the Garden-Stairs.

Enter Guzman.

Car. I'll retire then, and fit me for my part of this Farce.

Guz. My Lord, you must retire, they're just bringing the Old Gentleman ashore.

Car. Prithee how does he take his Captivity?

Guz. Take it, Sir! he has cast himself into a Fit, and has lain like one in a Trance this half hour; 'tis impossible for him to speak Sense this fortnight; I'll secure his Reason a play-day for so long at least; your Servants, in *Turkish* habits, are now his Guards, who will keep him safe enough from hindering your designs with *Julia*.

Car. Whatever you do, have a care you do not over-fright the Coxcomb, and make a Tragedy of our Comedy.

Guz. I'll warrant you, Sir, mind your Love-affairs,—he's coming in,—retire, Sir.—

[*Ex.* Car. *and* Page *and* Lop.

Enter some Turks *with the body of* Francisco *in chains, and lay him down on a Bank.*

1 *Turk.* Christian, so ho ho, Slave, awake.—

[*Rubbing and calling him.*

Fran. Hah! where am I?—my Wife,—my Wife—where am I?—hah! what are you?—Ghosts,—Devils,—Mutes,—no answer?—hah, bound in chains,—Slaves, where am I?

1 *Turk.* They understand not your Language; but I, who am a *Renegado Spaniard*, understand you when you speak civilly, which I advise you to do.

Fran. Do you know me, Friend?

1 *Turk.* I know you to be a Slave, and the Great *Turk's* Slave too.

Fran. The Great *Turk*,—the Great Devil, why, where am I, Friend?

1 *Turk.* Within the Territories of the *Grand Seignior*, and this a Palace of Pleasure, where he recreates himself with his Mistresses.

Fran. And how far is that from *Cadiz?*—but what care I? my Wife, Friend, my own Wife.

1 *Turk.* Your own,—a true Musselman cou'd have said no more; but take no care for her, she's provided for.

Fran. Is she dead? That wou'd be some comfort.

1 *Turk.* No, she's alive, and in good hands.

Fran. And in good hands! oh, my head! and, oh, my heart! ten thousand tempests burst the belly of this day, wherein old *Francisco* ventur'd Life and Limbs, Liberty and Wife to the mercy of these Heathen *Turks*.

1 *Turk.* Friend, you need not thus complain; a good round Ransom redeems ye.

Fran. A round Ransom! I'll rot in my chains first, before I'll part with a round ransom.

1 *Turk.* You have a fair Wife, and need not fear good usage, if she knows how to be kind. You apprehend me.

Fran. Patience, good Lord.

1 *Turk.* Perhaps the *Grand Seignior* may like her, and to be favour'd by him in such a Glory—

Fran. As the Devil take me if I desire.

1 *Turk.* And then you may in triumph laugh at all the rest of your Brother Cuckolds.

Fran. Hum, and has the Devil serv'd me thus?—but no matter, I must be gadding, like an old Coxcomb, to *Cadiz*,—and then, jaunting to Sea, with a Pox, to take pains to be a Cuckold, to bring my Wife into a strange Land, amongst Unbelievers, with a vengeance, as if we had not honest Christian Cuckold-makers enough at home; Sot that I was, not to consider how many Merchants have been undone by trusting their Commodities out at Sea; why, what a damn'd ransom will the Rogues exact from me, and more for my Wife, because she's handsome; and then, 'tis ten to one, I have her turned upon my hands the worse for wearing; oh, damn'd Infidels! no, 'tis resolv'd, I'll live a Slave here, rather than enrich them.

1 *Turk.* Friend, you'll know your Destiny presently; for 'tis the custom of the Great *Turk* to view the Captives, and consider of their Ransoms and Liberties, according

to his pleasure. See, he is coming forth with the *Vizier Bassa*.

Enter Carlos *and* Guzman *as* Turks *with Followers*.

Most mighty Emperor, behold your Captive.

Fran. Is this the Great *Turk?*

1 *Turk.* Peace.

Fran. Bless me! as we at home describe him, I thought the Great *Turk* had been twice as big; but I shall find him Tyrant big enough, I'll warrant him.

Guz. Of what Nation art thou, Slave? speak to the Emperor, he understands thee, though he deign not to hold discourse with Christian Dogs.

Fran. Oh fearful!—*Spain*, so please you, Sir.

Guz. By *Mahomet*, he'll make a reverend Eunuch.

Fran. An Eunuch! oh, Lord!

1 *Turk.* Ay, Sir, to guard his Mistresses, 'tis an honour.

Fran. Oh! Mercy, Sir, that honour you may spare, Age has done my business already.

Guz. Fellow, what art?

Fran. An't please your Worship, I cannot tell.

Guz. How, not tell?

Fran. An't please your Lordship, my Fears have so transform'd me, I cannot tell whether I'm any thing or nothing.

Guz. Thy name, dull Mortal, know'st thou not that?

Fran. An't please your Grace, now I remember me, methinks I do.

Guz. Dog, how art thou call'd?

Fran. An't like your Excellence, Men call'd me Signior Don *Francisco*, but now they will call me Coxcomb.

Guz. Of what Trade?

Fran. An't please your Highness, a Gentleman.

Guz. How much dost thou get a day by that Trade? Hah!

Fran. An't like your Majesty, our Gentlemen never get but twice in all their lives; that is, when Fathers die,

they get good Estates; and when they marry, they get rich
Wives: but I know what your Mightiness wou'd get by
going into my Country and asking the Question.

Guz. What, Fool?

Fran. A good Cudgelling, an't please your Illustrious-
ness.

Guz. Slave! To my Face!—Take him away, and let
him have the Strapado.

Car. Baridama, Dermack.

Fran. Heavens, what says he?

1 *Turk.* He means to have you castrated.

Fran. Castrated! Oh, that's some dreadful thing, I'll
warrant,—Gracious Great *Turk*, for *Mahomet's* sake,
excuse me; alas, I've lost my wits.

Car. Galero Gardines?

Guz. The Emperor asks if thou art married, Fellow.

Fran. Hah—Married—I was, an't like your Mon-
sterousness, but, I doubt, your People have spoiled my
Property.

Guz. His Wife, with other Ladies, in a Pavillion in
the Garden, attend your Royal pleasure.

Car. Go, fetch her hither presently.   [*Ex.* Guz.

1 *Turk.* This is no common Honour, that the Great
Turk deigns to speak your Language; 'tis to sign you'll rise.

Fran. Yes, by the height of a pair of Horns.

Car. Is she handsom?

Fran. Oh, what an Ague shakes my Heart,—handsom!
alas, no, dread Sir; what shou'd such a deform'd Polecat
as I do with a handsom Wife?

Car. Is she young?

Fran. Young, what shou'd such an old doting Coxcomb
as I do with a young Wife? Pox on him for a Heathen
Whoremaster.

Car. Old is she then?

Fran. Ay, very old, an't please your Gloriousness.

Car. Is she not capable of Love?

Fran. Hum, so, so,—like Fire conceal'd in a Tinder-box,—I shall run mad.

Car. Is she witty?

Fran. I'm no competent Judge, an't like your Holiness,—This Catechism was certainly of the Devil's own making.   [*Aside.*

Enter Guzman, *bringing in* Julia, Clara, Isabella, Jacinta, Guiliom, Antonio, &c. *Women veil'd.*

Car. These, Sir, are all the Slaves of Note are taken.

Isa. Dost think, *Jacinta*, he'll chuse me?

Jac. I'll warrant you, Madam, if he looks with my Eyes.

Guz. Stand forth.   [*To the Men.*

Guil. Stand forth, Sir! why, so I can, Sir, I dare show my Face, Sir, before any Great *Turk* in Christendom.

Car. What are you, Sir?

Guil. What am I, Sir? Why, I'm a Lord, a Lord.

Fran. What, are you mad to own your Quality, he'll ask the Devil and all of a ransom.

Guil. No matter for that, I'll not lose an Inch of my Quality for a King's ransom; disgrace my self before my fair Mistress!

Isa. That's as the Great *Turk* and I shall agree.
                                                [*Scornfully.*

Car. What are you, Sir?

Ant. A Citizen of *Cadiz.*

Car. Set 'em by, we'll consider of their ransoms—now unveil the Ladies.   [*Guzman unveils Jacinta.*

Fran. Oh, dear Wife, now or never show thy Love, make a damnable face upon the filthy Ravisher,—glout thy Eyes thus—and thrust out thy upper lip, thus.—
                                        [*Guzman presents* Jacinta.

Guil. Oh, dear *Isabella*, do thee look like a Dog too.

Isa. No, Sir, I'm resolv'd I'll not lose an Inch of my Beauty, to save so trifling a thing as a Maiden head.

Car. Very agreeable, pretty and chearful—

[She is veil'd and set by : Then Clara is unveil'd.
A most divine bud of Beauty—all Nature's Excellence—
drawn to the life in little,—what are you, fair one?

Cla. Sir, I'm a Maid.

Fran. So, I hope he will pitch upon her.

Cla. Only, by promise, Sir, I've given my self away.

Car. What happy Man cou'd claim a title in thee,
And trust thee to such danger?

Isa. Heavens, shall I be defeated by this little Creature?
What pity 'twas he saw me not first?

Cla. I dare not name him, Sir, lest this small Beauty
which you say adorns me, shou'd gain him your displeasure ; he's in your presence, Sir, and is your Slave.

Car. Such Innocence this plain Confession shows, name
me the man, and I'll resign thee back to him.

Fran. A Pox of his Civility.

Ant. This Mercy makes me bold to claim my right.
                                             [Kneels.

Car. Take her, young Man, and with it both your
Ransoms.

Guil. Hum—hum—very noble, i'faith, we'll e'en confess
our loves too, *Isabella.*

Isa. S'life, he'll spoil all,—hold—pray let your Betters
be serv'd before you.

Guil. How! Is the Honour of my Love despised?—
wer't not i'th presence of the Great *Turk,* for whom I have
a reverence because he's a man of quality—by *Jove,* I'd
draw upon you.

Isa. Because you were my Lover once, when I'm
Queen I'll pardon you.

    *[*Guzman *unveils her, and leads her to* Carlos, *she
       making ridiculous actions of Civility.*

Car. What aukard, fond, conceited thing art thou?
Veil her, and take the taudry Creature hence.

Guil. Hum—your Majesty's humble Servant.
                              [Putting off his Hat ridiculously.

Fran. How! refuse my Daughter too! I see the Lot
of a Cuckold will fall to my share.

Guz. This is the Wife, Great Sir, of this old Slave.

                                  [*Unveils* Julia.

Car. Hah! what do I see, by *Mahomet*, she's fair.

Fran. So, so, she's condemn'd; oh, damn'd *Mahometan*
Cannibal! will nothing but raw flesh serve his turn.

Car. I'll see no more,—here I have fix'd my heart.

Fran. Oh, Monster of a *Grand Seignior!*

Guz. Have you a mind to be flead, Sir?

Car. Receive my Handkerchief.   [*Throws it to her.*

Fran. His Handkerchief! bless me, what does he mean?

Guz. To do her the honour to lie with her to night.

Fran. Oh, hold, most mighty *Turk.*   [*Kneeling.*

Guz. Slave, darest thou interrupt 'em,—die, Dog.

Fran. Hold, hold, I'm silent.

Car. I love you, fair one, and design to make you—

Fran. A most notorious Strumpet.   A Pox of his
Courtesy.

Car. What Eyes you have like Heaven blue and
charming, a pretty Mouth, Neck round and white as
polisht Alabaster, and a Complexion beauteous as an Angel,
a Hair fit to moke Bonds to insnare the God of Love,—
a sprightly Air,—a Hand like Lillies white, and Lips, no
Roses opening in a Morning are half so sweet and soft.

Fran. Oh, damn'd circumcised *Turk.*

Car. You shall be call'd the beautiful *Sultana,*
And rule in my Seraglio drest with Jewels.

Fran. Sure, I shall burst with Vengeance.

Jul. Sir, let your Virtue regulate your Passions;
For I can ne'er love any but my Husband.

Fran. Ah, dissembling Witch!

Jul. And wou'd not break my Marriage Vows to him,
For all the honour you can heap upon me.

Fran. Say, and hold; but *Sultana* and precious Stones
are damnable Temptations,—besides, the Rogue's young

and handsome,—What a scornful look she casts at me;
wou'd they were both handsomely at the Devil together.

Guz. Dog, do you mutter?

Fran. Oh! nothing, nothing, but the Palsy shook my
Lips a little.

Guz. Slave, go, and on your knees resign your Wife.

Fran. She's of years of discretion, and may dispose of her
self; but I can hold no longer: and is this your *Mahometan*
Conscience, to take other Mens Wives, as if there were not
single Harlots enough in the World?   [*In rage.*

Guz. Peace, thou diminutive Christian.

Fran. I say, Peace thou over-grown *Turk.*

Guz. Thou *Spanish* Cur.

Fran. Why, you're a *Mahometan* Bitch, and you go
to that.

Guz. Death, I'll dissect the bald-pated Slave.

Fran. I defy thee, thou foul filthy Cabbage-head, for
I am mad, and will be valiant.

               [*Guz. throws his Turbant at him.*

Car. What Insolence is this!—Mutes—strangle him.—

               [*They put a Bow-string about his neck.*

Jul. Mercy, dread Sir, I beg my Husband's life.

Car. No more,—this fair one bids you live,—henceforth, *Francisco*, I pronounce you a Widower, and shall
regard you, for the time to come, as the deceased Husband
of the Great *Sultana*, murmur not upon pain of being
made an Eunuch—take him away.

Jul. Go, and be satisfied, I'll die before I'll yield.

Fran. Is this my going to Sea?—the Plague of losing
Battels light on thee.

> *When ill success shall make thee idle lie,*
> *Mayst thou in bed be impotent as I.*

Car. Command our Slaves to give us some diversion;
Dismiss his Chains, and use him with respect, because he
was the Husband of our beloved *Sultana*.

Fran. I see your Cuckold might have a life good enough
if he cou'd be contented.   [*They pull off his Chains.*
                    [Carlos *and* Julia *sit under an Umbrella.*

The SONG.

How strangely does my Passion grow,
Divided equally twixt two?
Damon *had ne'er subdued my Heart,*
Had not Alexis *took his part :*
Nor cou'd Alexis *powerful prove,*
Without my Damon's *aid, to gain my Love.*

When my Alexis *present is,*
    Then I for Damon *sigh and mourn ;*
But when Alexis *I do miss,*
    Damon *gains nothing but my Scorn :*
And, if it chance they both are by,
For both, alas! I languish, sigh, and die.

Cure then, thou mighty winged God,
This raging Fever in my Blood.
One golden-pointed Dart take back ;
But which, O Cupid, *wilt thou take?*
If Damon's, *all my hopes are crost :*
Or, that of my Alexis, *I am lost.*

Enter Dancers, which dance an Antick.

Car. Come, my dear *Julia*, let's retire to shades.
                                [*Aside to her.*
Where only thou and I can find an entrance ;
These dull, these necessary delays of ours
Have drawn my Love to an impatient height.
—Attend these Captives, at a respectful distance.
                        [*Ex. all but* Isa. *who stays* Guil.
  Guil. What wou'd the Great *Sultana?*

Isa. Ah! do not pierce my Heart with this unkindness.

Guil. Ha, ha, ha,—Pages,—give order, I have Letters writ to *Sevil*, to my Merchant,—I will be ransomed instantly.

Isa. Ah, cruel Count!

Guil. Meaning me, Lady! ah, fy! no, I am a Scoundrel; I a Count, no, not I, a Dog, a very Chim—hum, —a Son of a Whore, I, not worthy your notice.

Isa. Oh, Heavens! must I lose you then? no, I'll die first.

Guil. Die, die, then; for your Betters must be served before you.

Isa. Oh! I shall rave; false and lovely as you are, did you not swear to marry me, and make me a Viscountess.

Guil. Ay, that was once when I was a Lover; but, now you are a Queen, you're too high i'th' mouth for me.

Isa. Ah! name it not; will you be still hard-hearted?

Guil. As a Flint, by *Jove*.

Isa. Have you forgot your Love?

Guil. I've a bad memory.

Isa. And will you let me die?

Guil. I know nothing of the matter.

Isa. Oh Heavens! and shall I be no Viscountess?

Guil. Not for me, fair Lady, by *Jupiter*,—no, no,— Queen's much better,—Death, affront a man of Honour, a Viscount that wou'd have took you to his Bed,—after half the Town had blown upon you,—without examining either Portion or Honesty, and wou'd have took you for better for worse—Death, I'll untile Houses, and demolish Chimneys, but I'll be revenged. [*Draws and is going out.*

Isa. Ah, hold! your Anger's just, I must confess: yet pardon the frailty of my Sex's vanity; behold my Tears that sue for pity to you. [*She weeps, he stands looking on her.*

Guil. My rage dissolves.

Isa. I ask but Death, or Pity.   [*He weeps.*

Guil. I cannot hold;—but if I shou'd forgive, and marry you, you wou'd be gadding after honour still, longing to be a she Great *Turk* again.

Isa. Break not my heart with such suspicions of me.

Guil. And is it pure and tender Love for my Person,
And not for my glorious Titles?

Isa. Name not your Titles, 'tis your self I love,
Your amiable, sweet and charming self,
And I cou'd almost wish you were not great,
To let you see my Love.

Guil. I am confirm'd—

'Tis no respect of Honour makes her weep ;
Her Love's the same shou'd I cry—Chimney Sweep. [*Ex.*

ACT V.

Scene I. *A Garden.*

Enter Francisco *alone.*

Fran. Now am I afraid to walk in this Garden, lest I
shou'd spy my own natural Wife lying with the Great
Turk in Fresco, upon some of these fine flowry Banks,
and learning how to make Cuckolds in *Turkey*.

Enter Guzman *and* Jacinta.

Guz. Nay, dear *Jacinta*, cast an eye of pity on me.
—What, deny the *Vizier Bassa?*

Jac. When you are honest *Guzman* again, I'll tell you
a piece of my mind.

Guz. But opportunity will not be kind to *Guzman*, as
to the Grand *Bassa ;* therefore, dear Rogue, let's retire
into these kind shades, or, if foolish Virtue be so squeamish,
and needless Reputation so nice, that Mr. *Vicar* must say
Amen to the bargain, there is an old lousy Frier, belonging
to this *Villa*, that will give us a cast of his Office ; for I
am a little impatient about this business, Greatness having
infus'd a certain itch in my Blood, which I felt not whilst
a common Man.

Fran. Um, why, what have we here, pert Mrs. *Jacinta*
and the *Bassa ?* I hope the Jade will be Turkefied with

a vengeance, and have Circumcision in abundance; and
the Devil shall ransom her for old *Francisco*.

Jac. Hah, the old Gentleman!

Fran. What, the Frolick is to go round, I see, you
Women have a happy time on't.

Guz. Men that have kind Wives may be as happy;
you'll have the honour of being made a Cuckold, Heaven
be prais'd.

Fran. Ay, Sir, I thank ye,—pray, under the Rose, how
does my Wife please his Grace the Great *Turk*?

Guz. Murmuring again, thou Slave.

Fran. Who, I? O Lord, Sir! not I, why, what hurt is
there in being a Cuckold?

Guz. Hurt, Sirrah, you shall be swinged into a belief,
that it is an honour for the Great *Turk* to borrow your Wife.

Fran. But for the Lender to pay Use-money, is some-
what severe;—but, see, he comes,—bless me, how grim
he looks!

Enter Carlos, *and* Mutes *attending*.

Car. Come hither, Slave,—why, was it that I gave you
Life? dismiss'd the Fetters from your aged Limbs?

Fran. For love of my Wife, and't please your Bar-
barousness.

Car. Gave you free leave to range the Palace round,
excepting my Apartment only?

Fran. Still for my Wife's sake, I say, and't like your
Hideousness.

Car. And yet this Wife, this most ungrateful Wife of
yours, again wou'd put your Chains on, expose your Life
to Dangers and new Torments, by a too stubborn Virtue,
she does refuse my Courtship, and foolishly is chaste.

Fran. Alas! what pity's that!

Car. I offer'd much, lov'd much, but all in vain;
Husband and Honour still was the reply.

Fran. Good lack! that she shou'd have no more Grace
before her Eyes.

Car. But, Slave, behold these Mutes; that fatal Instrument of Death behold too, and in 'em read thy doom, if this coy Wife of yours be not made flexible to my Addresses.

Fran. O Heavens! I make her.

Car. No more, thy Fate is fix'd—and, here attend, till he himself deliver his willing Wife into my Arms; *Bassa*, attend, and see it be perform'd—[*To his Mutes, then to* Guz.
[*Ex.* Car.

Guz. Go, one of you, and fetch the fair Slave hither.
[*Ex.* Turk.

Fran. I pimp for my own Wife! I hold the door to my own Flesh and Blood! *O monstrum horrendum!*

Guz. Nay, do't, and do't handsomly too, not with a snivelling Countenance, as if you were compell'd to't; but with the face of Authority, and the awful command of a Husband—or thou dyest.

Enter Turk *and* Julia.

Fran. My dear *Julia*, you are a Fool, my Love.

Jul. For what, dear Husband?

Fran. I say, a silly Fool, to refuse the Love of so great a *Turk*; why, what a Pox makes you so coy? [*Angrily.*

Jul. How! this from you, *Francisco*.

Fran. Now does my Heart begin to fail me; and yet I shall ne'er endure strangling neither; why, am not I your Lord and Master, hah?

Jul. Heavens! Husband, what wou'd you have me do?

Fran. Have you do;—why, I wou'd have ye—d'ye see—'twill not out; why, I wou'd have ye lie with the *Sultan*, Huswife; I wonder how the Devil you have the face to refuse him, so handsom, so young a Lover; come, come, let me hear no more of your Coyness, Mistress, for if I do, I shall be hang'd;   [*Aside.*
The Great *Turk's* a most worthy Gentleman, and therefore I advise you to do as he advises you; and the Devil take ye both.   [*Aside.*

Jul. This from my Husband, old *Francisco!* he advise me to part with my dear Honour.

Fran. Rather than part with his dear Life, I thank ye.
                                                    [*Aside.*

Jul. Have you considered the Virtue of a Wife?

Fran. No, but I have considered the Neck of a Husband.
                                                    [*Aside.*

Jul. Which Virtue, before I'll lose, I'll die a thousand Deaths.

Fran. So will not I one; a Pox of her Virtue,—these Women are always virtuous in a wrong place.   [*Aside.*
I say you shall be kind to the sweet *Sultan.*

Jul. And rob my Husband of his right!

Fran. Shaw, Exchange is no Robbery.

Jul. And forsake my Virtue, and make nown Dear a Cuckold.

Fran. Shaw, most of the Heroes of the World were so;—go, prithee, Hony, go, do me the favour to cuckold me a little, if not for Love, for Charity.

Jul. Are you in earnest?

Fran. I am.

Jul. And would it not displease you?

Fran. I say, no; had it been *Aquinius* his Case, to have sav'd the pinching of his Gullet he wou'd have been a Cuckold.   [*Aside.*

Jul. Fear has made you mad, or you're bewitcht; and I'll leave you to recover your Wits again.   [*Going out.*

Fran. O gracious Wife, leave me not in despair; [*Kneels to her and holds her.*] I'm not mad, no, nor no more bewitcht than I have been these forty years; 'tis you're bewitcht to refuse so handsom, so young, and so—a Pox on him, she'll ne'er relish me again after him.   [*Aside.*

Jul. Since you've lost your Honour with your wits, I'll try what mine will do.

Enter Carlos, Turks.

Fran. Oh, I am lost, I'm lost—dear Wife,—most

mighty Sir, I've brought her finely to't—do not make me
lose my credit with his *Mahometan* Grace,—my Wife has
a monstrous Affection for your Honour, but she's something bashful; but when alone your Magnanimousness
will find her a swinger.

Car. Fair Creature—

Jul. Do you believe my Husband, Sir? he's mad.

Car. Dog.   [*Offers to kill him.*

Fran. Hold, mighty Emperor; as I hope to be saved,
'tis but a copy of her Countenance—inhuman Wife—lead
her to your Apartment, Sir! barbarous honest Woman,—
to your Chamber, Sir,—wou'd I had married thee an errant
Strumpet; nay, to your Royal Bed, Sir, I'll warrant you she
gives you taunt for taunt: try her, Sir, try her. [*Puts 'em out.*

Jac. Hark you, Sir, are you possest, or is it real reformation in you? what mov'd this kind fit?

Fran. E'en Love to sweet Life; and I shall think my
self ever obliged to my dear Wife, for this kind Reprieve;
—had she been cruel, I had been strangled, or hung in the
Air like our Prophet's Tomb.

Enter First Turk.

1 *Turk.* Sir, boast the honour of the News I bring you.

Fran. Oh, my Head! how my Brows twinge.

1 *Turk.* The mighty *Sultan*, to do you honour, has set
your Daughter and her Lover free, ransomless;—and this
day gives 'em liberty to solemnize the Nuptials in the
Court;—but Christian Ceremonies must be private; but
you're to be admitted, and I'll conduct you to 'em.

Fran. Some Comfort, I shall be Father to a Viscount,
and for the rest—Patience—

> *All Nations Cuckolds breed, but I deny*
> *They had such need of Cuckolding as I.*

                          [*Goes out with the* Turk.

Enter Antonio, *and* Clara *to* Jacinta.

Jac. Madam, the rarest sport—Ha, ha, ha.

Ant. You need not tell us, we have been witness to all.
But to our own Affairs, my dearest *Clara*,
Let us not lose this blessed opportunity,
Which Art nor Industry can give again if this be idly lost.

Cla. Nay, hang me if it be my fault, *Antonio* : Charge it
to the number of your own Sins ; it shall not lie at my door.

Ant. 'Tis generously said, and take notice, my little dear
Virago, *Guzman* has a Priest ready to tie you to your word.

Cla. As fast as you please ; hang her that fears the con-
juring knot for me : But what will our Fathers say—mine
who expects me to be the Governor's Lady ; and yours,
who designs *Isabella* for a Daughter-in-Law ?

Ant. Mine will be glad of the Change ; and, for yours,
if he be not pleased, let him keep his Portion to himself
—that's the greatest mischief he can do us : and for my
Friend, the Governor, he's above their Anger.

Cla. Why do we lose precious time ? I long to be at
—I *Clara* take thee *Antonio*,—the very Ceremony will be
tedious, so much I wish thee mine ; and each delay gives
me a fear something will snatch me from thee.

Ant. No power of Man can do't, thou art so guarded ;
but now the Priest is employed in clapping up the honourable Marriage between the *False Count* and *Isabella*.

Jac. Lord, what a jest 'twill be to see 'em coupled, ha, ha.

Cla. Unmerciful *Antonio*, to drive the Jest so far ; 'tis
too unconscionable !

Ant. By Heaven, I'm so proud I cannot think my
Revenge sufficient for Affronts, nor does her Birth, her
Breeding and her Vanity—deserve a better Fortune ;
besides,—he has enough to set up for a modern Spark—
the Fool has just Wit and good Manners to pass for a Fop
of Fashion ; and, where he is not known, will gain the
Reputation of a fine accomplish'd Gentleman,—yet I'm
resolved she shall see him in his Geers, in his original Filthi-
ness, that my Revenge may be home upon the foolish Jilt.

Cla. Cruel *Antonio*, come, lets go give 'em Joy.

Ant. And finish our Affair with Mr. Vicar.

Enter Isabella, *her Train borne by the great* Page, Guiliom, *with the other great* Page, *and* Francisco *bare*.

—Joy to my noble Lord, and you, fair *Isabella!*

Isa. Thank thee, Fellow,—but, surely, I deserved my Titles from thee.

Cla. Your Honour I hope will pardon him.

Isa. How now, *Clara!*   [*Nodding to her.*

Jac. I give your Honour joy.

Isa. Thank thee, poor Creature.—

Fran. My Lord, this Honour you have done my Daughter is so signal, that whereas I designed her but five thousand Pound, I will this happy day settle on her ten.

Guil. Damn dirty trash, your Beauty is sufficient—hum —Signior Don *Antonio*, get the Writings ready. [*Aside.* Money—hang Money.

Fran. How generous these Lords are; nay, my Lord, you must not refuse a Father's Love, if I may presume to call you Son— I shall find enough besides for my Ransom, if the Tyrant be so unmerciful to ask more than my Wife pays him.

Guil. Nay, if you will force it upon me.

Isa. Ay, take it, the trifling sum will serve to buy our Honour Pins.

Ant. Well, Sir, since you will force it on him, my Cashier shall draw the Writings.

Guil. And have 'em signed by a publick Notary. [*Aside.*

Fran. With all my Soul, Sir, I'll go to give him order, and subscribe.   [*Ex.* Francisco.

Guil. Let him make 'em strong and sure—you shall go halves.   [*Aside.*

Ant. No, you will deserve it dearly, who have the plague of such a Wife with it;—but harkye, Count— these goods of Fortune are not to be afforded you, without Conditions.

Guil. Shaw, Conditions, any Conditions, noble *Antonio*.

Ant. You must disrobe anon, and do'n your native Habiliments—and in the Equipage give that fair Viscountess to understand the true quality of her Husband.

Guil. Hum—I'm afraid, 'tis a harder task to leap from a Lord to a Rogue, than 'tis from a Rogue to a Lord.

Ant. Not at all, we have examples of both daily.

Guil. Well, Sir, I'll show you my agility—but, Sir, I desire I may consummate, d'ye see,—consummate—a little like a Lord, to make the Marriage sure.

Ant. You have the Freedom to do so—the Writings I'll provide.

Guil. I'll about it then, the Priest waits within for you, and *Guzman* for you, *Jacinta*,—haste, for he is to arrive anon Ambassador from *Cadiz*.

Jac. I know not, this noise of Weddings has set me agog, and I'll e'en in, and try what 'tis.

[*Ex.* Antonio, Clara, *and* Jacinta.

Guil. Come, Madam, your Honour and I have something else to do, before I have fully dub'd you a Viscountess.

Isa. Ah, Heav'ns, what's that?

Guil. Why a certain Ceremony, which must be performed between a pair of Sheets,—but we'll let it alone till Night.

Isa. Till Night, no; whate'er it be, I wou'd not be without an Inch of that Ceremony, that may compleat my Honour for the World; no, for Heaven's sake, let's retire, and dub me presently.

Guil. Time enough, time enough.

Isa. You love me not, that can deny me this.

Guil. Love—no, we are married now, and People of our Quality never Love after Marriage; 'tis not great.

Isa. Nay, let's retire, and compleat my Quality, and you will find me a Wife of the Mode, I'll warrant you.

Guil. For once you have prevail'd.

Enter Francisco.

Fran. Whither away?

Isa. Only to consummate a little, pray keep your distance.　　　　　　　　　　　　　[*She pulls off his hat.*

Fran. Consummate!

Isa. Ay, Sir, that is to make me an absolute Viscountess —we cannot stay—farewel.　　　[*Guiliom leads her out.*

Fran. Hum—this *Turkey* Air has a notable faculty, where the Women are all plaguy kind.

Enter Carlos *and* Julia.

Car. By Heav'n, each Moment makes me more your Slave.

Fran. The Business is done.

Jul. My Husband!　　　　　　　　　　　　[*Aside.*

Car. And all this constant love to old *Francisco* has but engaged me more.

Fran. Ha, Love to me?　　　　　　　　　　[*Aside.*

Jul. Sir, if this Virtue be but real in you, how happy I shou'd be; but you'll relapse again, and tempt my virtue, which if you do—

Fran. I'll warrant she wou'd kill herself.　　[*Aside.*

Jul. I should be sure to yield.　[*In a soft tone to him.*

Car. No, thou hast made an absolute Conquest o'er me—and if that Beauty tempt me every hour, I shall still be the same I was the last.

Fran. Pray Heaven he be *John.*

Enter First Turk.

1 *Turk.* Most mighty Emperor, a Messenger from *Cadiz* has Letters for your Highness.

Car. Conduct him in; in this retreat of ours we use no State.

Enter Guzman, *as himself, gives* Carlos *Letters.*

Guz. Don *Carlos*, Governor of *Cadiz*, greets your Highness.

Carlos *reads.*

High and Mighty,
FOR *seven* Christian *Slaves, taken lately by a Galley of yours,*

we offer you twice the number of Mahometans *taken from you by us.—If this suffice not,—propose your Ransoms, and they shall be paid by*

> Don Carlos, *Governor of* Cadiz.

—Know you this *Carlos* offers so fair for you?

Fran. Most potent Lord, I do, and wonder at the Compliment,—and yet I am not jealous—I have so over-acted the complaisant Husband, that I shall never fall into the other Extreme again.

Car. Go, let the Christian Governor understand his Request is granted.

Guz. The Slaves are ready, Sir, and a Galley to carry off the Christians.

Jul. How shall we make this Governor amends?

Fran. I do even weep for joy; alas, I must leave it to thee, Love.

Jul. To me, Sir? do you mock me?

Fran. Mock thee! no; I know thy Virtue, and will no more be jealous, believe me, Chicken, I was an old Fool.

Car. Your Wife is chaste—she overcame my unruly Passion with her Prayers and Tears.

Enter Isabella *at one door;* Clara, Antonio, Jacinta, *at another;* Isabella's *Train carried up.*

Fran. Rare News,—we are all free and ransom'd! All's well, and the Man has his Mare again.

Isa. You still forget your Duty and your Distance.

Fran. A pox of your troublesom Honour; a man can't be overjoy'd in quiet for't.

Enter Baltazer *and* Sebastian.

Seb. Sure, I am not mistaken, this is the House of my Son *Antonio.*

Bal. Let it be whose house 'twill, I think the Devil's broke loose in't.

Seb. —Or the *Turks;* for I have yet met with ne'er a Christian thing in't.

Fran. Hah,—do I dream, or is that my Father-in-law, and Signior *Sebastian?*

Ant. My Father here?

Car. Baltazer!   [*Aside.*

Bal. Son *Francisco*, why do you gaze on me so?

Fran. Bless me, Sir, are you taken by the Great *Turk* too?

Bal. Taken,—Great *Turk*,—what do mean?

Fran. Mean, Sir! why, how the Devil came you into *Turkey?*

Bal. Sure, Jealousy has crack'd his brains.

Fran. Crack me no Cracks, good Father mine;—am not I a Slave in *Turkey?* and is not this the *Grand Seignior's* Palace?

Car. So,—all will come out, there's no prevention.[*Aside.*

Seb. Some that are wiser answer us: You, Son,—are you infected too?—was not yesterday to have been your Wedding-day?

Ant. To day has done as well, Sir, I have only chang'd *Isabella* for *Clara.*

Seb. How, *Francisco*, have you juggled with me?

Fran. My Daughter's a Lady, Sir.

Bal. And you, Mistress, you have married *Antonio*, and left the Governor.

Cla. I thought him the fitter Match, Sir, and hope your Pardon.

Jul. We cannot scape.

Fran. But how came you hither, Gentlemen, how durst you venture?

Seb. Whither, Sir, to my own Son's house; is there such danger in coming a mile or two out of *Cadiz?*

Fran. Is the Devil in you, or me, or both? Am not I in the Possession of *Turks* and Infidels?

Bal. No, Sir; safe in *Antonio Villa*, within a League of *Cadiz.*

Fran. Why, what a Pox, is not this the Great *Turk* himself?

Bal. This, Sir,—cry mercy, my Lord,—'tis Don *Carlos*, Sir, the Governor.

Fran. The Governor! the worst Great *Turk* of all; so, I am cozened,—most rarely cheated; why, what a horrid Plot's here carried on, to bring in heretical Cuckoldom?

Car. Well, Sir, since you have found it out, I'll own my Passion.

Jul. Well, if I have been kind you forced me to't, nay, begged on your knees, to give my self away.

Fran. Guilty, guilty, I confess,—but 'twas to the Great *Turk*, Mistress, not Don *Carlos*.

Jul. And was the Sin the greater?

Fran. No, but the Honour was less.

Bal. Oh horrid! What, intreat his Wife to be a Whore?

Car. Sir, you're mistaken, she was my Wife in sight of Heaven before; and I but seiz'd my own.

Fran. Oh,—Sir, she's at your Service still.

Car. I thank you, Sir, and take her as my own.

Bal. Hold, my Honour's concerned.

Fran. Not at all, Father mine, she's my Wife, my Lumber now, and, I hope, I may dispose of my Goods and Chattels—if he takes her we are upon equal terms, for he makes himself my Cuckold, as he has already made me his;—for, if my memory fail me not, we did once upon a time consummate, as my Daughter has it.

Enter Guiliom *in his own dress; crying Chimney-Sweep.*

Guil. Chimney-sweep,—by your leave, Gentlemen.

Ant. Whither away, Sirrah?

Guil. What's that to you, Sir?—

Ant. Not to me, Sirrah;—who wou'd you speak with?

Guil. What's that to you, Sir? why, what a Pox, may not a man speak with his own Lady and Wife?

Cla. Heavens! his Wife! to look for his Wife amongst Persons of Quality!

Car. Kick out the Rascal.

Guil. As soon as you please, my Lord; but let me take my Wife along with me.   [*Takes* Isa. *by the hand.*

Isa. Faugh! what means the Devil?

Guil. Devil; 'twas not long since you found me a human creature within there.

Isa. Villain, Dog; help me to tear his Eyes out.

Guil. What, those Eyes, those lovely Eyes, that wounded you so deeply?

Fran. What's the meaning of all this? why, what, am I cozen'd? and is my Daughter cozen'd?

Guil. Cozen'd! why, I am a Man, Sir.

Fran. The Devil you are, Sir, how shall I know that?

Guil. Your Daughter does, Sir; and that's all one.

Isa. Oh! I'm undone; am I no Viscountess then.

Guil. Hang Titles; 'twas my self you lov'd, my amiable sweet and charming self: In fine, sweet-heart, I am your Husband; no Viscount, but honest *Guiliom*, the Chimney-sweeper.—I heard your Father design'd to marry you to a Tradesman, and you were for a Don; and to please you both, you see how well I have managed matters.

Fran. I'll not give her a farthing.

Guil. No matter, her Love's worth a million; and, that's so great, that I'm sure she'll be content to carry my Soot basket after me.

Isa. Ah! I die, I die.

Guil. What, and I so kind?   [*Goes and kisses her, and*
Isa. Help! murder, murder!   *blacks her face.*

Guil. Well, Gentlemen, I am something a better fortune than you believe me, by some thousands.

[*Shows* Car. *his Writings.*

Car. Substantial and good! faith, Sir, I know not where you'll find a better fortune for your Daughter, as cases stand.   [*To* Francisco.

Guil. And, for the Viscount, Sir, gay Clothes, Money and Confidence will set me up for one, in any ground in Christendom.

Car. Faith, Sir, he's i'th' right ; take him home to *Sevil*, your Neighbours know him not, and he may pass for what you please to make him ; the Fellow's honest, witty and handsom.

Fran. Well, I have considered the matter : I was but a Leather-seller my self, and am grown up to a Gentleman ; and, who knows but he, being a Chimney-sweeper, may, in time, grow up to a Lord ? Faith, I'll trust to Fortune, for once—here—take her and rid me of one Plague, as you, I thank you, Sir, have done of another. [*To* Carlos.

Guil. Prithee be pacified, thou shalt see me within this hour as pretty a fluttering Spark as any's in Town.—My noble Lord, I give you thanks and joy ; for, you are happy too.

Car. As Love and Beauty can make me.

Fran. And I, as no damn'd Wife, proud Daughter, or tormenting Chamber-maid can make me.

Ant. And I, as Heaven and *Clara* can.

—*You base-born Beauties, whose ill-manner'd Pride,*
Th' industrious noble Citizens deride,
May you all meet with Isabella's *doom.*

Guil. —*And all such Husbands as the Count* Guiliome.

EPILOGUE.

Spoken by Mrs. *Barry*, made by a Person of Quality.

> *I Come not a Petitioner to sue,*
> *This Play the Author has writ down to you ;*
> *'Tis a slight Farce, five Days brought forth with ease,*
> *So very foolish that it needs must please ;*
> *For though each day good Judges take offence,*
> *And Satir arms in Comedy's defence,*
> *You are still true to your* Jack-Pudding *Sense.*
> *No Buffoonry can miss your Approbation,*
> *You love it as you do a new* French *Fashion :*
> *Thus in true hate of Sense, and Wit's despite,*
> *Bantring and Shamming is your dear delight.*

Thus among all the Folly's here abounding,
None took like the new Ape-trick of Dumfounding.
If to make People laugh the business be,
You Sparks better Comedians are than we ;
You every day out-fool ev'n Nokes *and* Lee.
They're forc'd to stop, and their own Farces quit,
T'admire the Merry-Andrews of the Pit ;
But if your Mirth so grate the Critick's ear,
Your Love will yet more Harlequin appear.
—You everlasting Grievance of the Boxes,
You wither'd Ruins of stum'd Wine and Poxes ;
What strange Green-sickness do you hope in Women
Shou'd make 'em love old Fools in new Point Linen ?
The Race of Life you run off-hand too fast,
Your fiery Metal is too hot to last ;
Your Fevers come so thick, your Claps so plenty,
Most of you are threescore at five and twenty.
Our Town-bred Ladys know you well enough,
Your courting Women's like your taking Snuff ;
Out of mere Idleness you keep a pother,
You've no more need of one than of the other.
   Ladies—
Wou'd you be quit of their insipid noise,
And vain pretending take a Fool's advice ;
Of the faux Braves I've had some little trial,
There's nothing gives 'em credit but Denial :
As when a Coward will pretend to Huffing,
Offer to fight, away sneaks Bully-Ruffian,
So when these Sparks, whose business is addressing,
In Love pursuits grow troublesom and pressing ;
When they affect to keep still in your eye,
When they send Grisons *every where to spy,*
And full of Coxcomb dress and ogle high ;
Seem to receive their Charge, and face about,
I'll pawn my life they never stand it out.

ABDELAZER; OR,
THE MOOR'S REVENGE.

ABDELAZER;

or, The Moor's Revenge.

PROLOGUE.

GALLANTS, you have so long been absent hence,
That you have almost cool'd your Diligence;
For while we study or revive a Play,
You, like good Husbands, in the Country stay,
There frugally wear out your Summer Suit,
And in Frize Jerkin after Beagles toot;
Or, in Montero-Caps, at Feldfares shoot.
Nay, some are so obdurate in their Sin,
That they swear never to come up again,
But all their Charge of Clothes and Treat retrench,
To Gloves and Stockings for some Country Wench:
Even they, who in the Summer had Mishaps,
Send up to Town for Physick for their Claps.
The Ladies too are as resolved as they,
And having Debts unknown to them, they stay,
And with the Gain of Cheese and Poultry pay.
Even in their Visits, they from Banquets fall,
To entertain with Nuts and Bottle-Ale;
And in Discourse with Secresy report
State-News, that past a Twelve-month since at Court.
Those of them who are most refin'd, and gay,
Now learn the Songs of the last Summer's Play:
While the young Daughter does in private mourn,
Her Love's in Town, and hopes not to return.
These Country Grievances too great appear:
But cruel Ladies, we have greater here;

You come not sharp, as you are wont, to Plays;
But only on the first and second Days:
This made our Poet, in her Visits, look
What new strange Courses, for your time you took,
And to her great Regret she found too soon,
Damn'd Beasts and Ombre spent the Afternoon;
So that we cannot hope to see you here
Before the little Net-work Purse be clear.
Suppose you should have Luck—
Yet sitting up so late, as I am told,
You'll lose in Beauty what you win in Gold:
And what each Lady of another says,
Will make you new Lampoons, and us new Plays.

DRAMATIS PERSONÆ.

MEN.

Ferdinand, a young King of *Spain*, in love with *Florella*,	Mr. *Harris*.
Philip, his Brother,	Mr. *Smith*.
Abdelazer, the Moor,	Mr. *Betterton*.
Mendozo, Prince Cardinal, in love with the Queen,	Mr. *Medburne*.
Alonzo, a young Nobleman of *Spain*, contracted to *Leonora*,	Mr. *Crosbie*.
Roderigo, a Creature to the Moor,	Mr. *Norris*.
Antonio, *Sebastian*, } Two Officers of *Phillip's*,	Mr. *John Lee*.
Osmin, *Zarrack*, } Moors and Officers to *Abdelazer*,	Mr. *Percivall*. Mr. *Richards*.
Ordonio, a Courtier.	
A Swain, and Shepherds.	

Courtiers, Officers, Guards, Soldiers, Moors, Pages, and Attendants.

WOMEN.

Isabella, Queen of *Spain*, Mother to *Ferdinand* and *Philip*, in love with *Abdelazer*,	Mrs. *Lee*.
Leonora, her Daughter, Sister to *Ferdinand* and *Philip*,	Mrs. *Barrey*.
Florella, Wife to *Abdelazer*, and Sister to *Alonzo*,	Mrs. *Betterton*.
Elvira, Woman to the Queen,	Mrs. *Osborne*.
A Nymph, and Shepherdesses.	

Other Women Attendants.

SCENE *Spain*, and in the Camp.

ACT I.

Scene I. *A rich Chamber.*

A Table with Lights, Abdelazer *sullenly leaning his Head on his Hands: after a little while, still Musick plays.*

SONG.

LOVE in fantastick Triumph sat,
  Whilst bleeding Hearts around him flow'd,
For whom fresh Pains he did create,
  And strange Tyrannick Pow'r he shew'd ;
From thy bright Eyes he took his Fires,
  Which round about in sport he hurl'd ;
But 'twas from mine he took Desires,
  Enough t'undo the amorous World.

From me he took his Sighs and Tears,
  From thee his Pride and Cruelty ;
From me his Languishments and Fears,
  And ev'ry killing Dart from thee :
Thus thou, and I, the God have arm'd,
  And set him up a Deity ;
But my poor Heart alone is harm'd,
  Whilst thine the Victor is, and free.

       [After which he rouzes, and gazes.

Abd. On me this Musick lost?—this Sound on me
That hates all Softness?—What, ho, my Slaves!

     Enter Osmin, Zarrack.

Osm. My gracious Lord— *[Enter* Queen, Elvira.
Qu. My dearest *Abdelazer*—
Abd. Oh, are you there?—Ye Dogs, how came she in?
Did I not charge you on your Lives to watch,
That none disturb my Privacy?

Qu. My gentle *Abdelazer*, 'tis thy Queen,
Who 'as laid aside the Business of her State,
To wanton in the kinder Joys of Love—
Play all your sweetest Notes, such as inspire
The active Soul with new and soft Desire,

      [*To the Musick, they play softly.*
Whilst we from Eyes—thus dying, fan the Fire.

        [*She sits down by him.*

 Abd. Cease that ungrateful Noise. [*Musick ceases.*

 Qu. Can ought that I command displease my Moor?

 Abd. Away, fond Woman.

 Qu. Nay, prithee be more kind.

 Abd. Nay, prithee, good Queen, leave me—I am dull,
Unfit for Dalliance now.

 Qu. Why dost thou frown?—to whom was that Curse
  sent?

 Abd. To thee—

 Qu. To me?—it cannot be—to me, sweet Moor?—
No, no, it cannot—prithee smile upon me—
Smile, whilst a thousand *Cupids* shall descend
And call thee *Jove*, and wait upon thy Smiles,
Deck thy smooth Brow with Flowers;
Whilst in my Eyes, needing no other Glass,
Thou shalt behold and wonder at thy Beauty.

 Abd. Away, away, be gone—

 Qu. Where hast thou learnt this Language, that can say
But those rude Words—Away, away, be gone?
Am I grown ugly now?

 Abd. Ugly as Hell—

 Qu. Didst thou not love me once, and swore that Heav'n
Dwelt in my Face and Eyes?

 Abd. Thy Face and Eyes!—Baud, fetch me here a
  Glass,   [*To* Elvira.
And thou shalt see the Balls of both those Eyes
Burning with Fire of Lust:
That Blood that dances in thy Cheeks so hot,

That have not I to cool it
Made an Extraction even of my Soul,
Decay'd my Youth, only to feed thy Lust?
And wou'dst thou still pursue me to my Grave?

Qu. All this to me, my *Abdelazer?*

Abd. I cannot ride through the *Castilian* Streets,
But thousand Eyes throw killing Looks at me,
And cry—That's he that does abuse our King—
There goes the Minion of the *Spanish* Queen,
Who, on the lazy Pleasures of his Love,
Spends the Revenues of the King of *Spain*—
This many-headed Beast your Lust has arm'd.

Qu. How dare you, Sir, upbraid me with my Love?

Abd. I will not answer thee, nor hear thee speak.

Qu. Not hear me speak!—Yes, and in Thunder too;
Since all my Passion, all my soft Intreaties
Can do no good upon thee,
I'll see (since thou hast banish'd all thy Love,
That Love, to which I've sacrific'd my Honour)
If thou hast any Sense of Gratitude,
For all the mighty Graces I have done thee.

Abd. Do;—and in thy Story too, do not leave out
How dear those mighty Graces I have purchas'd;
My blooming Youth, my healthful vigorous Youth,
Which Nature gave me for more noble Actions
Than to lie fawning at a Woman's Feet,
And pass my Hours in Idleness and Love—
If I cou'd blush, I shou'd thro all this Cloud
Send forth my Sense of Shame into my Cheeks.

Qu. Ingrate!
Have I for this abus'd the best of Men,
My noble Husband?
Depriving him of all the Joys of Love,
To bring them all intirely to thy Bed;
Neglected all my Vows, and sworn 'em here a-new,
Here, on thy Lips—

Exhausted Treasures that wou'd purchase Crowns,
To buy thy Smiles—to buy a gentle Look ;
And when thou didst repay me—blest the Giver?
Oh, *Abdelazer*, more than this I've done—
This very Hour, the last the King can live,
Urg'd by thy Witch-craft, I his Life betray'd ;
And is it thus my Bounties are repaid?
Whate'er a Crime so great deserves from Heav'n,
By *Abdelazer* might have been forgiven: [*Weeps.*
But I will be reveng'd by penitence,
And e'er the King dies, own my black Offence—
And yet that's not enough—*Elvira*—   [*Pauses.*
Cry murder, murder, help, help.

> [*She and her Women cry aloud, he is surpriz'd, the*
> Queen *falls, he draws a Dagger at* Elvira.

Elv. Help, murder, murder !—

Abd. Hell, what's this?—peace, Baud—'sdeath,
They'll raise the Court upon me, and then I'm lost—
My Queen—my Goddess—Oh raise your lovely Eyes,
I have dissembled Coldness all this while ;
And that Deceit was but to try thy Faith.

> [*Takes her up, sets her in a Chair, then kneels.*

Look up—by Heav'n, 'twas Jealousy—
Pardon your Slave—pardon your poor Adorer.

Qu. Thou didst upbraid me with my shameful Passion.

Abd. I'll tear my Tongue out for its Profanation.

Qu. And when I woo'd thee but to smile upon me,
Thou cry'st—Away, I'm dull, unfit for Dalliance.

Abd. Call back the frighted Blood into thy Cheeks,
And I'll obey the Dictates of my Love,
And smile, and kiss, and dwell for ever here—

> *Enter* Osmin *hastily.*

How now—why star'st thou so ?

Osm. My Lord—the King is dead.

Abd. The King dead !—'Twas time then to dissemble.
          [*Aside.*

What means this Rudeness?—   [*One knocks.*

Enter Zarrack.

Zar. My Lord—the Cardinal inquiring for the Queen,
The Court is in an uproar, none can find her.

Abd. Not find the Queen! and wou'd they search her
here?

Qu. What shall I do? I must not here be found.

Abd. Oh, do not fear—no Cardinal enters here;
No King—no God, that means to be secure—
Slaves guard the Doors, and suffer none to enter,
Whilst I, my charming Queen, provide for your Security—
You know there is a Vault deep under Ground,
Into the which the busy Sun ne'er enter'd,
But all is dark, as are the Shades of Hell,
Thro which in dead of Night I oft have pass'd,
Guided by Love, to your Apartment, Madam—
They knock agen—thither, my lovely Mistress, [*Knock.*
Suffer your self to be conducted—
Osmin, attend the Queen—descend in haste,

        [*Queen, Osm. and Elv. descend the Vault.*
My Lodgings are beset.

Zar. I cannot guard the Lodgings longer—
Don *Ordonio,* Sir, to seek the Queen—

Abd. How dare they seek her here?

Zar. My Lord, the King has swounded twice,
And being recover'd, calls for her Majesty.

Abd. The King not dead!—go, *Zarrack,* and aloud
Tell Don *Ordonio* and the Cardinal,
He that dares enter here to seek the Queen,

        [*Puts his Hand to his Sword.*
Had better snatch the She from the fierce side
Of a young amorous Lion, and 'twere safer.—
Again, more knocking!—   [*Knocking.*

Zar. My gracious Lord, it is your Brother, Don *Alonzo.*

Abd. I will not have him enter—I am disorder'd.

Zar. My Lord, 'tis now too late.

Enter Alonzo.

Alon. Saw you not the Queen, my Lord?

Abd. My Lord!

Alon. Was not the Queen here with you?

Abd. The Queen with me!
Because, Sir, I am married to your Sister,
You, like your Sister, must be jealous too:
The Queen with me! with me! a Moor! a Devil!
A Slave of *Barbary!* for so
Your gay young Courtiers christen me—But, Don,
Altho my Skin be black, within my Veins
Runs Blood as red, and royal as the best.—
My Father, Great *Abdela*, with his Life
Lost too his Crown; both most unjustly ravish'd
By Tyrant *Philip*, your old King I mean.
How many Wounds his valiant Breast receiv'd
E'er he would yield to part with Life and Empire:
Methinks I see him cover'd o'er with Blood,
Fainting amidst those numbers he had conquer'd.
I was but young, yet old enough to grieve,
Tho not revenge, or to defy my Fetters:
For then began my Slavery; and e'er since
Have seen that Diadem by this Tyrant worn,
Which crown'd the sacred Temples of my Father,
And shou'd adorn mine now—shou'd! nay, and must—
Go tell him what I say—'twill be but Death—
Go, Sir,—the Queen's not here.

Alon. Do not mistake me, Sir,—or if I wou'd,
I've no old King to tell—the King is dead—
And I am answer'd, Sir, to what I came for,
And so good night.   [*Exit.*

Abd. Now all that's brave and villain seize my Soul,
Reform each Faculty that is not ill,
And make it fit for Vengeance, noble Vengeance.

Oh glorious Word! fit only for the Gods,
For which they form'd their Thunder,
Till Man usurp'd their Power, and by Revenge
Sway'd Destiny as well as they, and took their trade of
    killing.
And thou, almighty Love,
Dance in a thousand forms about my Person,
That this same Queen, this easy *Spanish* Dame,
May be bewitch'd, and dote upon me still;
Whilst I make use of the insatiate Flame
To set all *Spain* on fire.—
Mischief, erect thy Throne,
And sit on high; here, here upon my Head.
Let Fools fear Fate, thus I my Stars defy:
The influence of this—must raise my Glory high.
            [*Pointing to his Sword.*   [*Exit.*

Scene II. *A Room in the Palace.*

Enter Ferdinand *weeping,* Ordonio *bearing the Crown,*
followed by Alonzo, *leading* Leonora *weeping;* Florella,
Roderigo, Mendozo, *met by the* Queen *weeping;*
Elvira *and* Women.

  Qu. What doleful Cry was that, which like the Voice
Of angry Heav'n struck thro my trembling Soul?
Nothing but horrid Shrieks, nothing but Death;
Whilst I, bowing my Knees to the cold Earth,
Drowning my Cheeks in Rivulets of Tears,
Sending up Prayers in Sighs, t' implore from Heaven
Health for the Royal Majesty of *Spain*—
All cry'd, the Majesty of *Spain* is dead.
Whilst the sad Sound flew through the ecchoing Air,
And reach'd my frighted Soul—Inform my Fears,
Oh my *Fernando,* oh my gentle Son—   [*Weeps.*
  King. Madam, read here the truth, if looks can shew
That which I cannot speak, and you wou'd know:

The common Fare in ev'ry face appears;
A King's great loss the publick Grief declares,
But 'tis a Father's Death that claims my Tears.

                [*Card. leads in the* Queen *attended.*

    Leon. Ah, Sir !
If you thus grieve, who ascend by what y'ave lost,
To all the Greatness that a King can boast;
What Tributes from my Eyes and Heart are due,
Who've lost at once a King and Father too?

    King. My *Leonora* cannot think my Grief
Can from those empty Glories find relief;
Nature within my Soul has equal share,
And that and Love surmount my Glory there.
Had Heav'n continu'd Royal *Philip's* Life,
And giv'n me bright *Florella* for a Wife, [*Bows to* Florella.
To Crown and Scepters I had made no claim,
But ow'd my Blessings only to my Flame.
But Heav'n well knew in giving thee away,   [*To* Flor.
I had no bus'ness for another Joy.   [*Weeps.*
The King, *Alonzo*, with his dying Breath,

            [*Turns to* Alon. *and* Leon.

To you my beauteous Sister did bequeath;
And I his Generosity approve,
And think you worthy *Leonora's* Love.

      Enter Card. *and* Queen *weeping.*

    Alon. Too gloriously my Services are paid,
In the possession of this Royal Maid,
To whom my guilty Heart durst ne'er aspire,
But rather chose to languish in its Fire.

     Enter Philip *in a Rage,* Antonio *and* Sebastian.

    Phil. I know he is not dead; what envious Powers
Durst snatch him hence? he was all great and good,
As fit to be ador'd as they above.
Where is the Body of my Royal Father?
That Body which inspir'd by's sacred Soul,

Aw'd all the Universe with ev'ry Frown,
And taught 'em all Obedience with his Smiles.
Why stand you thus distracted—Mother—Brother—
My Lords—Prince Cardinal—
Has Sorrow struck you dumb?
Is this my Welcome from the Toils of War?
When in his Bosom I shou'd find repose,
To meet it cold and pale!—Oh, guide me to him,
And with my Sighs I'll breathe new Life into't.

    King. There's all that's left of Royal *Philip* now,
                              [Phil. *goes out.*
Pay all thy Sorrow there—whilst mine alone
Are swoln too high t' admit of Lookers on.
                            [*Ex.* King *weeping.*
               Philip *returns weeping.*
    Phil. His Soul is fled to all Eternity;
And yet methought it did inform his Body,
That I, his darling *Philip*, was arriv'd
With Conquest on my Sword; and even in Death
Sent me his Joy in Smiles.
    Qu. If Souls can after Death have any Sense
Of human things, his will be proud to know
That *Philip* is a Conqueror.
               Enter Abdelazer.
But do not drown thy Laurels thus in Tears,
Such Tributes leave to us, thou art a Soldier.
    Phil. Gods! this shou'd be my Mother—
    Men. It is, great Sir, the Queen.
    Phil. Oh, she's too foul for one or t'other Title.
    Qu. How, Sir, do you not know me?
    Phil. When you were just, I did,
And with a Reverence, such as we pay Heav'n,
I paid my awful Duty;—
But as you have abus'd my Royal Father,
For such a Sin the basest of your Slaves
Wou'd blush to call you Mother.

Qu. What means my Son?

Phil. Son! by Heav'n, I scorn the Title.

Qu. Oh Insolence!—out of my sight, rude Boy.

Phil. We must not part so, Madam;
I first must let you know your Sin and Shame;—
Nay, hear me calmly—for, by Heav'n, you shall—
My Father whilst he liv'd, tir'd his strong Arm
With numerous Battles 'gainst the Enemy,
Wasting his Brains in warlike Stratagems;
To bring Confusion on the faithless Moors,
Whilst you, lull'd in soft Peace at home, betray'd
His Name to everlasting Infamy;
Suffer'd his Bed to be defil'd with Lust,
Gave up your self, your Honour, and your Vows,
To wanton in yon sooty Lecher's Arms. [*Points to* Abd.

Abd. Me, dost thou mean?

Phil. Yes, Villain, thee, thou Hell-begotten Fiend,
'Tis thee I mean.

Qu. Oh most unnatural, to dishonour me!

Phil. That Dog you mean, that has dishonour'd you,
Dishonour'd me, these Lords, nay, and all *Spain;*
This Devil's he, that—

Abd. That—what—Oh pardon me if I throw off
All Ties of Duty:—wert thou ten King's Sons,
And I as many Souls as I have Sins,
Thus I would hazard all. [*Draws, they all run between.*

Phil. Stand off—or I'll make way upon thy Bosom.

Abd. How got you, Sir, this daring?

Phil. From injur'd *Philip's* Death,
Who, whilst he liv'd, unjustly cherish'd thee,
And set thee up beyond the reach of Fate;
Blind with thy brutal Valor, deaf with thy Flatteries,
Discover'd not the Treason thou didst act,
Nor none durst let him know 'em—but did he live,
I wou'd aloud proclaim them in his Ears.

Abd. You durst as well been damn'd.

Phil. Hell seize me if I want Revenge for this—
Not dare!
Arise, thou injur'd Ghost of my dead King,
And thro thy dreadful Paleness dart a Horror,
May fright this pair of Vipers from their Sins.

Abd. Oh insupportable! dost hear me, Boy?

Qu. Are ye all mute, and hear me thus upbraided?
　　　　　　　　　　　　　　　　[To the Lords.

Phil. Dare ye detain me whilst the Traitor braves me?

Men. Forbear, my Prince, keep in that noble Heat
That shou'd be better us'd than on a Slave.

Abd. You politick Cheat—

Men. Abdelazer—
By the Authority of my Government,
Which yet I hold over the King of *Spain*,
By Warrant of a Council from the Peers,
And (as an Unbeliever) from the Church,
I utterly deprive thee of that Greatness,
Those Offices and Trusts you hold in *Spain*.

Abd. Cardinal—who lent thee this Commission?
Grandees of *Spain*, do you consent to this?

All. We do.

Alon. What Reason for it? let his Faith be try'd.

Men. It needs no tryal, the Proofs are evident,
And his Religion was his Veil for Treason.

Alon. Why should you question his Religion, Sir?
He does profess Christianity.

Men. Yes, witness his Habit which he still retains
In scorn to ours—
His Principles are too as unalterable.

Abd. Is that the only Argument you bring?
I tell thee, Cardinal, not thy Holy Gown
Covers a Soul more sanctify'd than this
Moorish Robe.

Phil. Damn his Religion—he has a thousand Crimes
That will yet better justify your Sentence.

Men. Come not within the Court ; for if you do,
Worse mischief shall ensue—you have your Sentence.
                                    [*Ex.* Phil. *and* Men.

Alon. My Brother banish'd ! 'tis very sudden ;
For thy sake, Sister, this must be recall'd.   [*To* Flor.

Qu. Alonzo, join with me, I'll to the King,
And check the Pride of this insulting Cardinal.
                        [*Exeunt all, except* Abdelazer, Florella.

Abd. Banish'd ! if I digest this Gall,
May Cowards pluck the Wreath from off my Brow,
Which I have purchas'd with so many Wounds,
And all for *Spain ;* for *Spain !* ingrateful *Spain !*—
Oh, my *Florella*, all my Glory's vanish'd,
The Cardinal (Oh damn him) wou'd have me banish'd.

Flor. But, Sir, I hope you will not tamely go.

Abd. Tamely !—ha, ha, ha,—yes, by all means—
A very honest and religious Cardinal !

Flor. I wou'd not for the World you should be banish'd.

Abd. Not *Spain*, you mean—for then she leaves the
        King.   [*Aside.*
What if I be?—Fools ! not to know—All parts o'th' World
Allow enough for Villany ; for I'll be brave no more.
It is a Crime—and then I can live any where—
But say I go from hence—I leave behind me
A Cardinal that will laugh—I leave behind me
A *Philip* that will clap his Hands in sport—
But the worst Wound is this, I leave my Wrongs,
Dishonours, and my Discontents, all unreveng'd—
Leave me, *Florella*—prithee do not weep ;
I love thee, love thee wondrously—go leave me—
I am not now at leisure to be fond—
Go to your Chamber—go.

Flor. No, to the King I'll fly,
And beg him to revenge thy Infamy.   [*Ex.* Flor.
                        To him Alonzo.

Alon. The Cardinal's mad to have thee banish'd *Spain*.

I've left the Queen in angry Contradiction,
But yet I fear the Cardinal's Reasoning.

Abd. This Prince's Hate proceeds from Love,
He's jealous of the Queen, and fears my Power. [*Aside.*

Alon. Come, rouse thy wonted Spirits, awake thy Soul,
And arm thy Justice with a brave Revenge.

Abd. I'll arm no Justice with a brave Revenge.
　　　　　　　　　　　　　　　　[*Sullenly.*

Alon. Shall they then triumph o'er thee, who were once
Proud to attend thy conqu'ring Chariot-Wheels?

Abd. I care not—I am a Dog, and can bear wrongs.

Alon. But, Sir, my Honour is concern'd with yours,
Since my lov'd Sister did become your Wife;
And if yours suffer, mine too is unsafe.

Abd. I cannot help it—

Alon. What Ice has chill'd thy Blood?
This Patience was not wont to dwell with thee.

Abd. 'Tis true; but now the World is chang'd you see.
Thou art too brave to know what I resolve— [*Aside.*
No more—here comes the King with my *Florella.*
He loves her, and she swears to me she's chaste;
'Tis well, if true—well too, if it be false: [*Aside.*
I care not, 'tis Revenge
That I must sacrifice my Love and Pleasure to.
　　　　　　　　　　　[*Alon. and* Abd. *stand aside.*

Enter King, *Lords,* Guards *passing over the Stage,*
　　Florella *in a suppliant posture weeping.*

King. Thou woo'st me to reverse thy Husband's Doom,
And I woo thee for Mercy on my self,
Why shoud'st thou sue to him for Life and Liberty,
For any other, who himself lies dying,
Imploring from thy Eyes a little Pity?

Flor. Oh mighty King! in whose sole Power, like Heav'n,
The Lives and Safeties of your Slaves remain,
Hear and redress my *Abdelazer's* Wrongs.

King. All Lives and Safeties in my Power remain!
Mistaken charming Creature, if my Power
Be such, who kneel and bow to thee,
What must thine be,
Who hast the Sovereign Command o'er me and it?
Wou'dst thou give Life? turn but thy lovely Eyes
Upon the wretched thing that wants it,
And he will surely live, and live for ever.
Canst thou do this, and com'st to beg of me?

Flor. Alas, Sir, what I beg's what you alone can give,
My *Abdelazer's* Pardon.

King. Pardon! can any thing ally'd to thee offend?
Thou art so sacred and so innocent,
That but to know thee, and to look on thee,
Must change even Vice to Virtue.
Oh my *Florella!*
So perfectly thou dost possess my Soul,
That ev'ry Wish of thine shall be obey'd:
Say, wou'dst thou have thy Husband share my Crown?
Do but submit to love me, and I yield it.

Flor. Such Love as humble Subjects owe their King.
                              [*Kneels, he takes her up.*
And such as I dare pay, I offer here.

King. I must confess it is a Price too glorious:
But, my *Florella*—

Abd. I'll interrupt your amorous Discourse.   [*Aside.*
                              [Abel. *comes up to them.*

Flor. Sir, *Abdelazer's* here.

King. His Presence never was less welcome to me;—
                                        [*Aside.*
But, Madam, durst the Cardinal use this Insolence?
Where is your noble Husband?

Abd. He sees me, yet inquires for me.   [*Aside.*

Flor. Sir, my Lord is here.

King. Abdelazer, I have heard with much surprize,
O'th' Injuries you've receiv'd, and mean to right you:

My Father lov'd you well, made you his General,
I think you worthy of that Honour still.

   Abd. True—for my Wife's sake.   *[Aside.*

   King. When my Coronation is solemnized,
Be present there, and re-assume your wonted State and
     Place;
And see how I will check the insolent Cardinal.

   Abd. I humbly thank my Sovereign—

               [Kneels, and kisses the King's Hand.
That he loves my Wife so well.   *[Aside.*
                                [Exeunt.

Manent Abdelazer, Florella.

   Flor. Wilt thou not pay my Service with one Smile?
Have I not acted well the Suppliant's part?

   Abd. Oh wonderfully! y'ave learnt the Art to move.
Go, leave me.

   Flor. Still out of humour, thoughtful and displeas'd?
And why at me, my *Abdelazer?* what have I done?

   Abd. Rarely! you cannot do amiss you are so beautiful.
So very fair—Go, get you in, I say—

                         [Turns her in roughly.
She has the art of dallying with my Soul,
Teaching it lazy softness from her Looks.
But now a nobler Passion's enter'd there,
And blows it thus—to Air—Idol Ambition,
Florella must to thee a Victim fall:
Revenge,—to thee—a Cardinal and Prince:
And to my Love and Jealousy, a King—
More yet, my mighty Deities, I'll do,
None that you e'er inspir'd like me shall act;
That fawning servile Crew shall follow next,
Who with the Cardinal cry'd, banish *Abdelazer.*

    Like Eastern Monarchs I'll adorn thy Fate,
    And to the Shades thou shalt descend in State.   *[Exit.*

ACT II.

Scene I. *A Chamber of State.*

Enter the King *crown'd,* Philip, Mendozo, Queen, Leonora,
Florella, Elvira, Alonzo, Roderigo, Ordonio, Sebastian,
Antonio, *Officers and Guards; met by* Abdelazer *follow'd
by* Osmin, Zarrack, *and Moors attending. He comes in
with Pride, staring on* Philip *and* Mendozo,
and takes his stand next the King.

Phil. Why stares the Devil thus, as if he meant
From his infectious Eyes to scatter Plagues,
And poison all the World? Was he not banish'd?
How dares the Traitor venture into th' Presence?—
Guards, spurn the Villain forth.

Abd. Who spurns the *Moor*
Were better set his foot upon the Devil—
Do, spurn me, and this Hand thus justly arm'd,
Shall like a Thunder-bolt, breaking the Clouds,
Divide his Body from his Soul—stand back—

[To the Guards.

Spurn *Abdelazer!*—

Phil. Death, shall we bear this Insolence?

Alon. Great Sir, I think his Sentence was unjust.

[To the King.

Men. Sir, you're too partial to be judge in this,
And shall not give your Voice.

Abd. Proud Cardinal—but he shall—and give it loud.
And shall not!—who shall hinder him?

Phil. This—and cut his Wind-pipe too. [*Offers to draw.*
To spoil his whisp'ring. [Abd. *offers to draw, his Attendants do the same.*

King. What means this Violence?
Forbear to draw your Swords—'tis we command.

Abd. Sir, do me Justice, I demand no more.

[Kneels, and offers his Sword.

And at your Feet we lay our Weapons down.

Men. Sir, *Abdelazer* has had Justice done,
And stands by me banish'd the Court of *Spain*.

King. How, Prince Cardinal!
From whence do you derive Authority
To banish him the Court without our leave?

Men. Sir, from my Care unto your royal Person,
As I'm your Governor—then for the Kingdom's Safety.

King. Because I was a Boy, must I be still so?
Time, Sir, has given me in that formal Ceremony,
And I am of an age to rule alone;
And from henceforth discharge you of your Care.
We know your near relation to this Crown,
And wanting Heirs, that you must fill the Throne;
Till when, Sir, I am absolute Monarch here,
And you must learn Obedience.

Men. Pardon my zealous Duty, which I hope
You will approve, and not recal his Banishment.

King. Sir, but I will; and who dares contradict
It, is a Traitor.

Phil. I dare the first, yet do defy the last.

King. My hot-brain'd Sir, I'll talk to you anon.

Men. Sir, I am wrong'd, and will appeal to *Rome*.

Phil. By Heav'n, I'll to the Camp—Brother, farewel,
When next I meet thee, it shall be in Arms,
If thou can'st get loose from thy Mistress' Chains,
Where thou ly'st drown'd in idle wanton Love.

Abd. Hah—his Mistress—who is't Prince *Philip* means?

Phil. Thy Wife, thy Wife, proud Moor, whom thou'rt
    content
To sell for Honour to eternal Infamy—
Does't make thee snarl?—Bite on, whilst thou shalt see,
I go for Vengeance, and 'twill come with me.
                          [*Going out, turns and draws.*

Abd. Stay! for 'tis here already—turn, proud Boy.
                          [Abd. *draws.*

King. What mean you, *Philip*?— [*Talks to him aside.*

Qu. Cease, cease your most impolitick Rage. [*To* Abd.
Is this a time to shew't?—Dear Son, you are a King,
And may allay this Tempest.

King. How dare you disobey my Will and Pleasure?
[*To* Abd.

Abd. Shall I be calm, and hear my Wife call'd Whore?
Were he great *Jove*, and arm'd with all his Lightning,
By Heav'n, I could not hold my just Resentment.

Qu. 'Twas in his Passion, noble *Abdelazer*—
[King *talking to* Phil. *aside.*

Imprudently thou dost disarm thy Rage,
And giv'st the Foe a warning, e'er thou strik'st;
When with thy Smiles thou might'st securely kill.
You know the Passion that the Cardinal bears me;
His Pow'r too o'er *Philip*, which well manag'd
Will serve to ruin both : put up your Sword—
When next you draw it, teach it how to act.

Abd. You shame me, and command me.

Qu. Why all this Rage?—does it become you, Sir?
[*To* Men. *aside.*

What is't you mean to do?

Men. You need not care, whilst *Abdelazer's* safe.

Qu. Jealousy, upon my Life—how gay it looks!

Men. Madam, you want that pitying Regard
To value what I do, or what I am;
I'll therefore lay my Cardinal's Hat aside,
And in bright Arms demand my Honour back.

Qu. Is't thus, my Lord, you give me Proofs of Love?
Have then my Eyes lost all their wonted Power?
And can you quit the hope of gaining me,
To follow your Revenge?—go—go to fight,
Bear Arms against your Country, and your King,
All for a little worthless Honour lost.

Men. What is it, Madam, you would have me do?

Qu. Not side with *Philip*, as you hope my Grace—
Now, Sir, you know my Pleasure, think on't well.

Men. Madam, you know your Power o'er your Slave,
And use it too tyrannically—but dispose
The Fate of him, whose Honour, and whose Life,
Lies at your Mercy—
I'll stay and die, since 'tis your gracious Pleasure.

King. Philip, upon your Life,
Upon your strict Allegiance, I conjure you
To remain at Court, till I have reconcil'd you.

Phil. Never, Sir;
Nor can you bend my Temper to that Tameness.

King. 'Tis in my Power to charge you as a Prisoner;
But you're my Brother—yet remember too
I am your King—No more.

Phil. I will obey.

King. Abdelazer,
I beg you will forget your Cause of Hate
Against my Brother *Philip,* and the Cardinal;
He's young, and rash, but will be better temper'd.

Abd. Sir, I have done, and beg your royal Pardon.

King. Come, *Philip,* give him your Hand.

Phil. I can forgive without a Ceremony.

King. And to confirm ye Friends,
I invite you all to Night to banquet with me;
Pray see you give Attendance—Come, Brother,
You must along with us.

                    [*Exeunt all but* Abd. Queen *and Women.*

Qu. Leave me—   [*To the Women, who go out.*
Now my dear Moor.

Abd. Madam.

Qu. Why dost thou answer with that cold Reserve—
Is that a Look—an Action for a Lover?

Abd. Ah, Madam—

Qu. Have I not taken off thy Banishment?
Restor'd thee to thy former State and Honours?
Nay, and heap'd new ones too, too mighty for thy
     Hopes;

And still to raise thee equal to this Heart,
Where thou must ever reign.

 Abd. 'Tis true, my bounteous Mistress, all this you've
  done—
But—

 Qu. But what, my *Abdelazer?*

 Abd. I will not call it to your Memory.

 Qu. What canst thou mean?

 Abd. Why was the King remov'd?

 Qu. To make thy way more easy to my Arms.

 Abd. Was that all?

 Qu. All!

 Abd. Not but it is a Blessing Gods would languish for—
But as you've made it free, so make it just.

 Qu. Thou mean'st, marry thee.

 Abd. No, by the Gods—   [*Aside.*
Not marry thee, unless I were a King.

 Qu. What signifies the Name to him that rules one?

 Abd. What use has he of Life, that cannot live
Without a Ruler?

 Qu. Thou wouldst not have me kill him.

 Abd. Oh, by no means, not for my wretched Life!
What, kill a King!—forbid it, Heaven :
Angels stand like his Guards about his Person.
The King!
Not so many Worlds as there be Stars
Twinkling upon the embroider'd Firmament!
The King!
He loves my Wife *Florella*, shou'd he die—
I know none else durst love her.

 Qu. And that's the Reason you wou'd send him hence.

 Abd. I must confess, I wou'd not bear a wrong :
But do not take me for a Villain, Madam ;
He is my King, and may do what he pleases.

 Qu. 'Tis well, Sir.

 Abd. Again that Frown, it renders thee more charming

Than any other Dress thou could'st put on.

Qu. Away, you do not love me.

Abd. Now mayst thou hate me, if this be not pretty.

Qu. Oh, you can flatter finely—

Abd. Not I, by Heaven:

Oh, that this Head were circled in a Crown,
And I were King, by Fortune, as by Birth!
And that I was, till by thy Husband's Power
I was divested in my Infancy—
Then you shou'd see, I do not flatter ye.
But I, instead of that, must see my Crown
Bandy'd from Head to Head, and tamely see it:
And in this wretched state I live, 'tis true;
But with what Joy, you, if you lov'd, might guess.

Qu. We need no Crowns; Love best contented is
In shady Groves, and humble Cottages,
Where when 'twould sport, it safely may retreat,
Free from the Noise and Danger of the Great;
Where Victors are ambitious of no Bays,
But what their Nymphs bestow on Holy-days;
Nor Envy can the amorous Shepherd move,
Unless against a Rival in his Love.

Abd. Love and Ambition are the same to me,
In either I'll no Rivals brook.

Qu. Nor I:
And when the King you urge me to remove,
It may be from Ambition, not from Love.

Abd. Those Scruples did not in your Bosom dwell,
When you a King did in a Husband kill.

Qu. How, Sir, dare you upbraid me with that Sin,
To which your Perjuries first drew me in?

Abd. You interrupt my Sense; I only meant
A Sacrifice to Love so well begun
Shou'd not Devotion want to finish it;
And if that stop to all our Joys were gone,
The envying World wou'd to our Power submit:

But Kings are sacred, and the Gods alone
Their Crimes must judge, and punish too, or none—
Yet he alone destroys his Happiness.

  Qu. There's yet one more—

  Abd. One more! give me his Name,
And I will turn it to a Magick Spell,
To bind him ever fast.

  Qu. Florella.

  Abd. Florella! Oh, I cou'd gnaw my Chains ⎫
That humble me so low as to adore her :   ⎬ [*Aside.*
But the fond Blaze must out—while I erect ⎭
A nobler Fire more fit for my Ambition.

—*Florella* dies—a Victim to your Will.
I will not let you lose one single Wish,
For a poor Life, or two ;
Tho I must see my Glories made a Prey,
And not demand 'em from the Ravisher ;
Nor yet complain—because he is my King :
But *Philip's* Brow no sacred Ointment deifies,
If he do wrong, stands fair for the Revenger.

  Qu. Philip! instruct me how t' undo that Boy I hate ;
The publick Infamy I have receiv'd,
I will revenge with nothing less than Death.

  Abd. 'Tis well we can agree in our Resentments,
For I have vow'd he shall not live a day ;
He has an Art to pry into our Secrets :
To all besides our Love is either hid,
Or else they dare not see—But this Prince
Has a most dangerous Spirit must be calm'd.

  Qu. I have resolv'd his Death,
And now have waiting in my Cabinet,
Engines to carry on this mighty Work of my Revenge,

  Abd. Leave that to me, who equally am injur'd ;
You, like the Gods, need only but command,
And I will execute your sacred Will—
That done, there's none dare whisper what we do.

Qu. Nature, be gone, I chase thee from my Soul,
Who Love's almighty Empire does controul :
And she that will to thy dull Laws submit,
In spite of thee, betrays the Hypocrite.
No rigid Virtue shall my Soul possess,
Let Gown-men preach against the Wickedness ;
Pleasures were made by Gods, and meant for us,
And not t'enjoy 'em, were ridiculous.

Abd. Oh perfect, great and glorious of thy Sex !
Like thy great self 'twas spoke, resolv'd and brave—
I must attend the King—where I will watch
All *Philip's* Motions.

Qu. And—after that—if you will beg Admittance,
I'll give you leave to visit me to Night.

Abd. Madam, that Blessing now must be defer'd.

[*Leads her to the Door.*

My Wrongs and I will be retir'd to Night,
And bring forth Vengeance with the Morning's Light.

Enter Osmin, Zarrack.

Osm. My gracious Lord.

Abd. Come near—and take a Secret from my Lips ;
And he who keeps not silent hears his Death.—
This Night the Prince and Cardinal—do you mark me—
Are murder'd.

Osm. Where, Sir ?

Abd. Here in the Court.

Osm. By whom, great Sir ?

Abd. By thee—I know thou darst.

Osm. Whatever you command.

Abd. Good !—then see it be perform'd.
Osmin, how goes the Night ?

Osm. About the hour of Eight,
And you're expected at the Banquet, Sir :
Prince *Philip* storms, and swears you're with the Queen.

Abd. Let him storm on ; the Tempest will be laid—
Where's my Wife ?

Osm. In the Presence, Sir, with the Princess and
Other Ladies.

Abd. She's wondrous forward !—what the King—
(I am not jealous tho)—but he makes court to her.
—Hah, *Osmin* !
He throws out Love from Eyes all languishing ;—
Come tell me,—he does sigh to her,—no matter if he do—
And fawns upon her Hand,—and kneels ;—tell me, Slave !

Osm. Sir, I saw nothing like to Love ; he only treats her
Equal to her Quality.

Abd. Oh, damn her Quality.

Zar. I came just now
From waiting on his Person to the Banquet,
And heard him ask, if he might visit her to Night,
Having something to impart to her, that concern'd his Life.

Abd. And so it shall, by Heav'n !   [*Aside.*

Zar. But she deny'd, and he the more intreated—
But all in vain, Sir.

Abd. Go, *Osmin*, (you the Captain of my Guard of
     Moors)
Chuse out the best affected Officers,
To keep the Watch to Night—
Let every Guard be doubled—you may be liberal too—
And when I gave the Word, be ready all.

Osm. What shall the Word be?   [*Ex.* Zarrack.

Abd. Why—Treason—mean time make it your Business,
To watch the Prince's coming from the Banquet ;
Heated with Wine, and fearless of his Person,
You'll find him easily to be attack'd.

Osm. Sir, do not doubt my Management nor Success.
                              [*Ex.* Osmin.

Abd. So, I thank thee, Nature, that in making me,
Thou didst design me Villain ;
Hitting each Faculty for active Mischief :
Thou skilful Artist, thank thee for my Face,
It will discover nought that's hid within.

Thus arm'd for Ills,
Darkness, and Horrour, I invoke your aid;
And thou dread Night, shade all your busy Stars
In blackest Clouds,
And let my Dagger's Brightness only serve
To guide me to the Mark—and guide it so,
It may undo a Kingdom at one Blow.   [*Exit.*

SCENE II. *A Banqueting Hall.*

A Banquet, under a Canopy the King, Leonora, Florella,
Ladies waiting; Philip, Mendozo, Alonzo, Ordonio,
  Antonio, Sebastian, *Lords and Attendants: As soon as
  the Scene draws off, they all rise, and come forward.*

  King. My Lords, you're sad to Night; give us loud
      Musick—
I have a double Cause to mourn;
And Grief has taken up his dwelling here—
Beyond the Art of Love, or Wine to conquer—
'Tis true, my Father's dead—and possibly
'Tis not so decent to appear thus gay;
But Life, and Death, are equal to the wretched,
And whilst *Florella* frowns—'tis in that Number [*To* Flor.
I must account her Slave—*Alonzo,*
How came thy Father so bewitch'd to Valour,
(For *Abdelazer* has no other Virtue)
To recompense it with so fair a Creature?
Was this—a Treasure t' inrich the Devil with?

  Alon. Sir, he has many Virtues, more than Courage,
Royally born, serv'd well his King, and Country;
My Father brought him up to martial Toils,
And taught him to be brave; I hope, and good;—
Beside, he was your Royal Father's Favourite.

  King. No, *Alonzo,* 'twas not his Love to Virtue,
But nice Obedience to his King, and Master,
Who seeing my increase of Passion for her,
To kill my Hopes, he gave her to this *Moor.*

Alon. She's now a virtuous Woman, Sir.

King. Politick Sir, who would have made her other?
Against her Will, he forc'd her to his Arms,
Whilst all the World was wondring at his Madness.

Alon. He did it with her Approbation, Sir.

King. With thine, *Florella!* cou'dst thou be so criminal?

Flor. Sir, I was ever taught Obedience;
My humble Thoughts durst ne'er aspire to you,
And next to that—Death, or the Moor, or any thing.

King. Oh God! had I then told my Tale
So feebly, it could not gain Belief.
Oh my *Florella!* this little Faith of thine
Has quite undone thy King—*Alonzo,*
Why didst not thou forbid this fatal Marriage,
She being thy only Sister?

Alon. Great Sir, I did oppose it with what Violence
My Duty would permit; and wou'd have dy'd
In a just Quarrel of her dear Defence;
And, Sir, though I submitted to my Father,
The Moor and I stand on unequal Terms.

Phil. Come, who dares drink Confusion to this Moor?

Ant. That, Sir, will I.

Sebast. And I.

Phil. Page, fill my Glass, I will begin the Round,
Ye all shall pledge it—*Alonzo,* first to thee.   [*Drinks.*

Alon. To me, Sir!

Phil. Why, yes, thou lovest him—therefore—
Nay, you shall drink it, tho 'twere o'th' *Stygian* Lake.
Take it—by Heaven, thoud'st pimp for him to my
        Mother—
Nay, and after that, give him another Sister.

Alon. 'Tis well you are my Prince.

Phil. I'd rather be a Prince of Curs—come pledge me—

Alon. Well, Sir, I'll give you way.   [*Drinks.*

Phil. So wou'dst thou any—though they trod on thee.
So—nay, Prince Cardinal, tho it be not decent

For one so sanctify'd to drink a Health;
Yet 'tis your Office both to damn and bless—
Come, drink and damn the Moor.

   Men. Sir, I'm for no carousing.

   Phil. I'm in an Humour now to be obey'd,
And must not be deny'd—But see, the Moor

           Enter Abdelazer, *gazes on them.*

Just come to pledge at last—Page, fill again—

   Abd. I'll do you Reason, Prince, what'er it be.

                        [*Gives him the Glass.*

   Phil. 'Twas kindly said—Confusion to the Moor.

   Abd. Confusion to the Moor—if this vain Boy,
See the next rising Sun.   [*Aside.*

   Phil. Well done, my Lad.

   King. Abdelazer, you have been missing long,
The publick Good takes up your whole Concern,
But we shall shortly ease you of that Load—
Come, let's have some Musick;
Ordonio, did I not call for Musick?

   Ord. You did, Sir.

   Abd. Roderigo!

   Rod. My gracious Lord— [*Roderigo whispers to* Abd.

   Abd. No more—the Prince observes us.

   Phil. There's no good towards when you are whisp'ring.

   Ord. The Musick you commanded, Sir, is ready.

SONG.

Nymph.   *MAKE haste,* Amintas, *come away,*
        The Sun is up and will not stay;
     And oh how very short's a Lover's Day!
        Make haste, Amintas, *to this Grove,*
        Beneath whose Shade so oft I've sat,
        And heard my dear lov'd Swain repeat,
        How much he Galatea *lov'd;*
      Whilst all the list'ning Birds around,
   Sung to the Musick of the blessed Sound.

> *Make haste*, Amintas, *come away,*
> *The Sun is up and will not stay ;*
> *And oh how very short's a Lover's Day !*

Swain enters, with Shepherds and Shepherdesses, and
Pipes.

> *I hear thy charming Voice, my Fair,*
> *And see, bright Nymph, thy Swain is here ;*
> *Who his Devotions had much earlier paid,*
> *But that a Lamb of thine was stray'd ;*
> *And I the little Wanderer have brought,*
> *That with one angry Look from thy fair Eyes,*
> *Thou may'st the little Fugitive chastise,*
> *Too great a Punishment for any Fault.*
>   *Come,* Galatea, *haste away,*
>   *The Sun is up and will not stay,*
> *And oh how very short's a Lover's Day !*   [*Dance.*

King. How likes *Florella* this?

Flor. Sir, all Delight's so banish'd from my Soul,
I've lost the Taste of every single Joy.

Abd. God's ! this is fine ! Give me your Art of Flattery,
Or something more of this, will ruin me—
Tho I've resolv'd her Death, yet whilst she's mine,
I would not have her blown by Summer Flies.

Phil. Mark how he snarls upon the King !
The Cur will bite anon.

Abd. Come, my *Florella*, is't not Bed-time, Love ?

Flor. I'll wait upon you, Sir.   [*Going out.*

Phil. The Moor has ta'en away, we may depart.

Abd. What has he ta'en away ?   [*Turns about.*

Phil. The fine gay play-thing, that made us all so merry.

Abd. Was this your Sport ?   [*To his Wife.*

King. *Abdelazer*, keep your way—Good night, fair
     Creature !

Abd. I will obey for once.   [*Ex.* Abd. *and* Flor.

King. Why this Resentment, Brother, and in publick ?

Phil. Because he gives me Cause, and that in Publick.
And, Sir, I was not born to bear with Insolence;
I saw him dart Revenge from both his Eyes,
And bite his angry Lip between his Teeth,
To keep his Jealousy from breaking forth,
Which, when it does—stand fast, my King.

King. But, *Philip*, we will find a way to check him;
Till when we must dissemble—take my Counsel—Good
    night.

Phil. I cannot, nor I will not—yet good Night.
               [*Exit* King, *and all but* Philip's *Party.*
Well, Friends, I see the King will sleep away his Anger,
And tamely see us murder'd by this Moor;
But I'll be active, Boys—
Therefore, *Antonio*, you command the Horse;
Get what more Numbers to our Cause you can:
'Tis a good Cause, and will advance our Credit.
We will awake this King out of his Lethargy of Love,
And make him absolute—Go to your Charge,
And early in the Morning I'll be with you—
                  [*Ex. all but* Phil.
If all fail, *Portugal* shall be my Refuge,
Those whom so late I conquer'd, shall protect me—
But this *Alonzo* I shou'd make an Interest in;
Cou'd I but flatter—'tis a Youth that's brave.

Enter Cardinal *in haste.*

Men. Fly, fly, my Prince, we are betray'd and lost else.

Phil. Betray'd and lost! Dreams, idle Coward Dreams.

Men. Sir, by my Holy Order, I'm in earnest,
And you must either quickly fly, or die;
'Tis so ordain'd—nor have I time to tell
By what strange Miracle I learn'd our Fate.

Phil. Nor care I, I will stay, and brave it.

Men. That, Sir, you shall not, there's no safety here,
And 'tis the Army only can secure us.

Phil. Where had you this Intelligence?

Men. I'll tell you as we go to my Apartment;
Where we must put ourselves in Holy Dress;
For so the Guards are set in every Place,
(And those all Moors, the Slaves of *Abdelazer*)
That 'tis impossible in any other Habit to escape.
Come, haste with me, and let us put 'em on.

Phil. I had rather stay and kill till I am weary—
Let's to the Queen's Apartment and seize this Moor;
I'm sure there the Mongrel's kennel'd.

Men. Sir, we lose time in talking—Come with me.

Phil. Where be these lousy Gaberdines?

Men. I will conduct you to 'em.

Phil. Mother—and Moor, farewel,
I'll visit you again; and if I do,
My black Infernal, I will conjure you.   [*Exeunt.*

ACT III.
SCENE I. *A Gallery in the Palace.*
Enter Abdelazer *and* Zarrack.

Zar. Osmin (my Lord) by this has done his Task,
And *Philip* is no more among the living:
Will you not rest to night?

Abd. Is this a time for Sleep and Idleness—dull Slaves?

Zar. The Bus'ness we have Order, Sir, to do,
We can without your Aid.

Enter Osmin.

Abd. Osmin!
Thy ominous Looks presage an ill Success;
Thy Eyes no joyful News of Murders tell:
I thought I shou'd have seen thee drest in Blood—
Speak! Speak thy News—
Say that he lives, and let it be thy last.

Osm. Yes, Sir, he lives.

Abd. Lives! thou ly'st, base Coward—lives!—renounce
thy Gods!

It were a Sin less dangerous—speak again.

   Osm. Sir, *Philip* lives.

   Abd. Oh treacherous Slave !

   Osm. Not by my Fault, by Heav'n !

   Abd. By what curst Chance,
If not from thee, could he evade his Fate?

   Osm. By some Intelligence from his good Angel.

   Abd. From his good Devil !
Gods ! must the Earth another Day at once
Bear him and me alive?

   Osm. Another Day !—an Age for ought I know ;
For, Sir, the Prince is fled, the Cardinal too.

   Abd. Fled ! fled—say'st thou?
Oh, I cou'd curse the Stars, that rule this Night :
'Tis to the Camp they're fled ; the only Refuge
That Gods, or Men cou'd give 'em—
Where got you this Intelligence?

   Osm. My Lord, inquiring for the Prince
At the Apartment of the Cardinal, (whither he went)
His Pages answer'd me, he was at his Devotions :
A lucky time (I thought) to do the Deed ;
And breaking in, found only their empty Habits,
And a poor sleepy Groom, who with much threatning,
Confess'd that they were fled, in holy Robes.

   Abd. That Case of Sanctity was first ordain'd,
To cheat the honest World :
'Twas an unlucky Chance—but we are idle—
Let's see, how from this Ill, we may advance a good—
                                      [*Pauses.*
'Tis now dead time of Night, when Rapes, and Murders
Are hid beneath the horrid Veil of Darkness—
I'll ring thro all the Court, with doleful Sound
The sad Alarms of Murder—Murder—*Zarrack*,
Take up thy standing yonder—*Osmin*, thou
At the Queen's Apartment—cry out, Murder :
Whilst I, like his ill Genius, do awake the King ;

Perhaps in this Disorder I may kill him.   [*Aside.*
—Treason—Murder—Murder—Treason.

Enter Alonzo, *and Courtiers.*

Alon. What dismal Crys are these?—
Abd. Where is the King?—Treason—Murder!
Where is the sleeping Queen?—Arise, arise.
Osm. The Devil taught him all his Arts of Falshood.
                                              [*Aside.*

Enter King *in a Night-Gown, with Lights.*

King. Who frights our quiet Slumbers with this Noise?

Enter Queen *and Women, with Lights.*

Qu. Was it a Dream, or did I hear the Sound
Of Treason, call me from my silent Griefs?
King. Who rais'd this Rumour, *Abdelazer,* you?
Abd. I did, Great Sir.
King. Your Reasons.
Abd. Oh Sir, your Brother *Philip,* and the Cardinal,
Both animated by a Sense of Wrongs,
(And envying, Sir, the Fortune of your Slave)
Had laid a Plot this Night, to murder you:
And 'cause they knew it was my waiting Night,
They wou'd have laid the Treason, Sir, on me.
King. The Cardinal, and my Brother! bring them forth,
Their Lives shall answer it.
Abd. Sir, 'tis impossible:
For when they found their Villany discover'd,
They in two Friers Habits made escape.
King. That Cardinal is subtle, and ambitious,
And from him *Philip* learnt his dangerous Principles.
Qu. The Ambition of the one infects the other,
And they are both too dangerous to live—
But might a Mother's Counsel be obey'd,
I wou'd advise you, send the valiant Moor
To fetch 'em back, e'er they can reach the Camp:

For thither they are fled—where they will find
A Welcome fatal to us all.

    King. Madam, you counsel well; and, *Abdelazer,*
Make it your Care to fetch these Traitors back,
Not only for my Safety, and the Kingdom's,
But as they are your Enemies; and th' envious World
Will say, you made this story to undo 'em.

    Abd. Sir, I'll obey; nor will I know reposc,
Till I have justify'd this fatal Truth.

                [Abd. *goes to the* Queen, *and talks to her.*

    King. Mean time I will to my *Florella's* Lodging,
Silence, and Night, are the best Advocates   [*Aside.*
To plead a Lover's Cause—*Abdelazer*—haste.
Madam, I'll wait on you to your Chamber.

    Abd. Sir, that's my Duty.

    King. Madam, good Night—*Alonzo,* to your rest.

                [*Ex. all but* Qu. *and* Abd.

    Qu. Philip escap'd!
Oh, that I were upon some Desart Shoar,
Where I might only to the Waves and Winds
Breathe out my Sense of Rage for this Defeat.

    Abd. Oh, 'tis no time for Rage, but Action, Madam.

    Qu. Give me but any Hopes of blest Revenge,
And I will be as calm as happy Lovers.

    Abd. There is a way, and is but that alone;
But such a way, as never must be nam'd.

    Qu. How! not be nam'd! Oh, swear thou hat'st me rather,
It were a Torment equal to thy Silence.

    Abd. I'll shew my Passion rather in that Silence.

    Qu. Kind Torturer, what mean'st thou?

    Abd. To shew you, Madam, I had rather live
Wrong'd and contemn'd by *Philip,*
Than have your dearer Name made infamous.

    Qu. Heavens! dost thou mock my Rage? can any Sin
I could commit, undo my Honour more

Than his late Insolence?
Oh, name me something may revenge that Shame:
I wou'd encounter killing Plagues, or Fire,
To meet it—Come, oh quickly give me ease.

 Abd. I dare no more reveal the guilty Secret,
Than you dare execute it when 'tis told.

 Qu. How little I am understood by thee—
Come, tell me instantly, for I grow impatient;
You shall obey me—nay, I do command you.

 Abd. Durst you proclaim—*Philip* a Bastard, Madam?

 Qu. Hah! proclaim my self—what he wou'd have me
  thought!
What mean'st thou?—

 Abd. Instruct you in the way to your Revenge.

 Qu. Upon my self thou meanest—

 Abd. No—
He's now fled to th' Camp, where he'll be fortify'd
Beyond our Power to hurt, but by this means;
Which takes away his Hopes of being a King,
(For he'd no other Aim in taking Arms)
And leaves him open to the People's Scorn;
Whom own'd as King, Numbers wou'd assist him,
And then our Lives he may dispose,
As he has done our Honours.

 Qu. There's Reason in thy Words: but oh my Fame!

 Abd. Which I, by Heaven, am much more tender of,
Than my own Life or Honour; and I've a way
To save that too, which I'll at leisure tell you.
In the mean time send for your Confessor,
And with a borrow'd Penitence confess,
Their Idol *Philip* is a Bastard;
And zealously pretend you're urg'd by Conscience,
A cheap Pretence to cozen Fools withal.

 Qu. Revenge, although I court you with my fatal Ruin,
I must enjoy thee: there's no other way,
And I'm resolv'd upon the mighty Pleasure;

He has profan'd my purer Flame for thee,
And merits to partake the Infamy.   [*He leads her out.*

 Abd. Now have at my young King—
I know he means to cuckold me to Night,
Whilst he believes I'll tamely step aside—
No, let *Philip* and the Cardinal gain the Camp,
I will not hinder 'em—
I have a nobler Sacrifice to make
To my declining Honour, shall redeem it,
And pay it back with Interest—well, then in order to't,
I'll watch about the Lodgings of *Florella*,
And if I see this hot young Lover enter,
I'll save my Wife the trouble of allaying
The amorous Heat—this—will more nimbly do't,
       [*Snatches out his Dagger.*
And do it once for all—

   Enter Florella *in her Night-Clothes.*

 Flor. My *Abdelazer*—why in that fierce posture,
As if thy Thoughts were always bent on Death?
Why is that Dagger out?—against whom drawn?
 Abd. Or stay,—suppose I let him see *Florella*,
And when he's high with the expected Bliss,
Then take him thus—Oh, 'twere a fine surprize!
 Flor. My Lord—dear *Abdelazer*.
 Abd. Or say—I made her kill him—that were yet
An Action much more worthy of my Vengeance.
 Flor. Will you not speak to me? what have I done?
 Abd. By Heaven, it shall be so.
 Flor. What shall be so?
 Abd. Hah—
 Flor. Why dost thou dress thy Eyes in such unusual
  wonder?
There's nothing here that is a stranger to thee,
Or what is not intirely thine own.
 Abd. Mine!

Flor. Thou canst not doubt it.

Abd. No,—and for a proof that thou art so,—take this
Dagger.

Flor. Alas, Sir !—what to do?

Abd. To stab a Heart, *Florella*, a Heart that loves thee.

Flor. Heaven forbid !

Abd. No matter what Heaven will, I say it must—

Flor. What must?

Abd. That Dagger must enter the Heart of him
That loves thee best, *Florella* ;—guess the Man.

Abd. What means my Moor?
Wouldst thou have me kill thy self?

Abd. Yes—when I love thee better than the King.

Flor. Ah, Sir ! what mean you?

Abd. To have you kill this King,
When next he does pursue thee with his Love—
What, do you weep?—
By Heaven, they shall be bloody Tears then.

Flor. I shall deserve them—when I suffer Love
That is not fit to hear ;—but for the King,
That which he pays me, is so innocent—

Abd. So innocent ! damn thy dissembling Tongue ;
Did I not see, with what fierce wishing Eyes
He gazed upon thy Face, whilst yours as wantonly
Returned, and understood the amorous Language?

Flor. Admit it true, that such his Passions were,
As (Heaven's my witness) I've no cause to fear ;
Have not I Virtue to resist his Flame,
Without a pointed Steel?

Abd. Your Virtue !—Curse on the weak Defence ;
Your Virtue's equal to his Innocence.
Here, take this Dagger, and if this Night he visit thee,
When he least thinks on't—send it to his Heart.

Flor. If you suspect me, do not leave me, Sir.

Abd. Oh—I'm dispatch'd away—to leave you free—
About a wonderful Affair—mean time,

I know you will be visited—but as you wish to live,
At my return let me behold him dead.—
Be sure you do't—'tis for thy Honour's safety—
I love thee so, that I can take no rest,
Till thou hast kill'd thy Image in his Breast.
—Adieu, my dear *Florella*. [*Exit.*

Flor. Murder my King! the Man that loves me too—
What Fiend, what Fury such an act wou'd do?
My trembling Hand wou'd not the Weapon bear,
And I should sooner strike it here—than there.

[*Pointing to her Breast.*

No! though of all I am, this Hand alone
Is what thou canst command, as being thy own;
Yet this has plighted no such cruel Vow;
No Duty binds me to obey thee now.
To save my King's, my Life I will expose,
No Martyr dies in a more glorious Cause. [*Exit.*

SCENE II. *The* Queen's *Apartments.*

Enter the Queen *in an undress alone, with a Light.*

Qu. Thou grateful Night, to whom all happy Lovers
Make their devout and humble Invocations;
Thou Court of Silence, where the God of Love,
Lays by the awful Terror of a Deity,
And every harmful Dart, and deals around
His kind Desires; whilst thou, blest Friend to Joys,
Draw'st all thy Curtains, made of gloomy Shades,
To veil the Blushes of soft yielding Maids;
Beneath thy Covert grant the Love-sick King,
May find admittance to *Florella's* Arms;
And being there, keep back the busy Day;
Maintain thy Empire till my Moor returns;
Where in her Lodgings he shall find his Wife,
Amidst her amorous Dalliance with my Son.—
My watchful Spies are waiting for the Knowledge;

Which when to me imparted, I'll improve,
Till my Revenge be equal to my Love.

Enter Elvira.

—*Elvira*, in thy Looks I read Success ;
What hast thou learnt ?

  Elv. Madam, the King is gone as you imagin'd,
To fair *Florella's* Lodging.

  Qu. But art thou sure he gain'd Admittance ?

  Elv. Yes, Madam ;
But what Welcome he has found, to me's unknown ;
But I believe it must be great, and kind.

  Qu. I am of thy Opinion.—
But now, *Elvira*, for a well-laid Plot,
To ruin this *Florella* ; —though she be innocent,
Yet she must die ; so hard a Destiny
My Passion for her Husband does decree :
But 'tis the way I stop at.—
His Jealousy already I have rais'd ;
That's not enough, his Honour must be touch'd.
This Meeting twixt the King and fair *Florella*,
Must then be render'd publick ;
'Tis the Disgrace, not Action, must incense him—
Go you to Don *Alonzo's* Lodging strait,
Whilst I prepare my Story for his Ear.—   [*Exit* Elvira.
Assist me all that's ill in Woman-kind,
And furnish me with Sighs, and feigned Tears,
That may express a Grief for this Discovery.—
My Son, be like thy Mother, hot and bold ;
And like the noble Ravisher of *Rome*,
Court her with Daggers, when thy Tongue grows faint,
Till thou hast made a Conquest o'er her Virtue.

Enter Alonzo, Elvira.

—Oh, *Alonzo*, I have strange News to tell thee !

  Alon. It must be strange indeed, that makes my Queen
Dress her fair Eyes in Sorrow.

Qu. It is a Dress that thou wilt be in love with,
When thou shalt hear my Story.—
You had a Sister once.

Alon. Had !

Qu. Yes, had,—whilst she was like thy self, all Virtue ;
Till her bewitching Eyes kindled such Flames,
As will undo us all.

Alon. My Sister, Madam ! sure it cannot be :—
What Eyes ? what Flames ?—inform me strait.

Qu. Alonzo, thou art honest, just and brave :
And should I tell thee more,—
(Knowing thy Loyalty's above all Nature)
It would oblige thee to commit an Outrage,
Which baser Spirits will call Cruelty.

Alon. Gods, Madam ! do not praise my Virtue thus,
Which is so poor, it scarce affords me patience
To attend the end of what you wou'd deliver—
Come, Madam, say my Sister—is a Whore.
I know 'tis so you mean ; and being so,
Where shall I kneel for Justice ?
Since he that shou'd afford it me,
Has made her Criminal.—
Pardon me, Madam, 'tis the King I mean.

Qu. I grieve to own, all thy prophetick Fears
Are true, *Alonzo*, 'tis indeed the King.

Alon. Then I'm disarm'd,
For Heaven can only punish him.

Qu. But, *Alonzo*,
Whilst that religious Patience dwells about thee,
All *Spain* must suffer, nay, Ages that shall ensue
Shall curse thy Name, and Family ;
From whom a Race of Bastards shall proceed,
To wear that Crown.

Alon. No, Madam, not for mine,
My Sister's in my power, her Honour's mine ;
I can command her Life, though not my King's.

Her Mother is a Saint, and shou'd she now
Look down from Heaven upon a Deed so foul,
I think even there she wou'd invent a Curse,
To thunder on her Head.——
But, Madam, whence was this Intelligence?

    Qu. *Elvira* saw the King enter her Lodgings,
With Lover's haste, and Joy.

    Alon. Her Lodgings!——when?

    Qu. Now, not an Hour ago,
Now, since the Moor departed.

    Alon. Damnation on her! can she be thus false?
Come, lead me to the Lodgings of this Strumpet,
And make me see this truth,   [*To* Elvira.
Or I will leave thee dead, for thus abusing me.

    Qu. Nay, dear *Alonzo*, do not go inrag'd,
Stay till your Temper wears a calmer look;
That if, by chance, you shou'd behold the Wantons,
In little harmless Dalliance, such as Lovers
(Aided with Silence, and the shades of Night)
May possibly commit,
You may not do that which you may repent of.

    Alon. Gods! should I play the Pander!
And with my Patience, aid the amorous Sin——
No, I shall scarce have so much Tameness left,
To mind me of my Duty to my King.
Ye Gods! behold the Sacrifice I make
To my lost Honour: behold, and aid my Justice.

                             [*Ex.* Alon.

    Qu. It will concern me too to see this Wonder,
For yet I scarce can credit it.   [*Exeunt.*

SCENE III.   *Florella's Lodgings.*

Enter the King, *leading in* Florella *all in fear.*

    Flor. Ah, Sir, the Gods and you would be more merciful,
If by a Death less cruel than my Fears,

You would preserve my Honour; begin it quickly,
And after that I will retain my Duty,
And at your Feet breathe Thanks in dying Sighs.

   King. Where learnt you, Fairest, so much Cruelty
To charge me with the Power of injuring thee?
Not from my Eyes, where Love and Languishment
Too sensibly inform thee of my Heart.

   Flor. Call it not Injury, Sir, to free my Soul
From fears which such a Visit must create,
In dead of Night, when nought but frightful Ghosts
Of restless Souls departed walk the Round.

   King. That fleeting thing am I, whom all Repose,
All Joys, and every good of Life abandon'd,
That fatal Hour thou gavest thy self away;
And I was doom'd to endless Desperation:
Yet whilst I liv'd, all glorious with my hopes,
Some sacred Treasures in thy Breast I hid,
And near thee still my greedy Soul will hover.

   Flor. Ah, rather like a Ravisher you come,
With Love and Fierceness in your dangerous Eyes;
And both will equally be fatal to me.

   King. Oh, do not fear me, as the fair *Lucretia*
Did the fierce *Roman* Youth; I mean no Rapes,
Thou canst not think that I wou'd force those Joys,
Which cease to be so, when compell'd, *Florella*—
No, I would sooner pierce this faithful Heart,
Whose Flame appears too criminal for your Mercy.

   Flor. Why do you fright me, Sir? methinks your Looks
All pale, your Eyes thus fixt, and trembling Hands,
The awful Horror of the dark and silent Night,
Strike a cold Terror round my fainting Heart,
That does presage some fatal Accident.

   King. 'Tis in your cruel Eyes the Danger lies—
Wou'd you receive me with that usual Tenderness,
Which did express it self in every Smile,
I should dismiss this Horror from my Face,

And place again its native Calmness there;
And all my Veins shall re-assume their Heat,
And with a new and grateful Ardour beat.

 Flor. Sir, all my Soul is taken up with fear,
And you advance your Fate, by staying here—
Fly, fly, this place of Death—if *Abdelazer*
Shou'd find you here—all the Divinity
About your sacred Person could not guard you.

 Flor. Ah, my *Florella*, cease thy needless Fear,
And in thy Soul let nothing reign but Love;
Love, that with soft Desires may fill thy Eyes,
And save thy Tongue the pain t' instruct my Heart,
In the most grateful Knowledge Heaven can give me.

 Flor. That Knowledge, Sir, wou'd make us both more
   wretched,
Since you, I know, wou'd still be wishing on,
And I shou'd grant, till we were both undone.
And, Sir, how little she were worth your care,
Cou'd part with all her honourable Fame,
For an inglorious Life—short and despis'd—

 King. Canst thou believe a Flame thy Eyes have kindled,
Can urge me to an infamous pursuit?—
No, my *Florella*, I adore thy Virtue,
And none profane those Shrines, to whom they offer;
—Say but thou lov'st—and I thus low will bow— [*Kneels.*
And sue to thee, to be my Sovereign Queen?
I'll circle thy bright Forehead with the Crowns
Of *Castile*, *Portugal*, and *Arragon;*
And all those petty Kingdoms, which do bow
Their Tributary Knees to thy Adorer.

 Flor. Ah, Sir! have you forgot my sacred Vow?
All that I am, is *Abdelazer's* now.

 King. By Heav'n, it was a sacrilegious Theft;
But I the Treasure from his Breast will tear,
And reach his Heart, though thou art seated there.

 Flor. A Deed like that my Virtue wou'd undo,

And leave a Stain upon your Glories too;
A Sin, that wou'd my Hate, not Passion move;
I owe a Duty, where I cannot love.

King. Thou think'st it then no Sin to kill thy King;
For I must die, without thy Love, *Florella.*

Flor. How tamely, Sir, you with the Serpent play,
Whose fatal Poison must your Life betray;
And though a King, cannot divine your Fate;
Kings only differ from the Gods in that.—
See, Sir, with this—I am your Murderer made;

　　　　　　　　　　　　　　[*Holds up a Dagger.*

By those we love, we soonest are betray'd.

King. How! can that fair Hand acquaint it self with
　　Death?
—What wilt thou do, *Florella?*

Flor. Your Destiny divert,
And give my Heart those Wounds design'd for yours.
—If you advance, I'll give the deadly Blow.

King. Hold!—I command thee hold thy impious Hand,
My Heart dwells there, and if you strike—I die.

Enter Queen, Alonzo, *and* Elvira.

Qu. Florella! arm'd against the King?

　　　　　[*Snatches the Dagger and stabs her: the* King *rises.*
Oh Traitress!

King. Hold, hold, inhuman Murdress;
What hast thou done, most barbarous of thy Sex!

　　　　　　　　　　　　　[*Takes Flor. in his Arms.*

Qu. Destroy'd thy Murdress,—and my too fair Rival.

　　　　　　　　　　　　　　　　　　[*Aside.*

King. My Murdress!—what Devil did inspire thee
With Thoughts so black and sinful? cou'd this fair Saint
Be guilty of a Murder?—No, no, too cruel Mother,
With her Eyes, her charming lovely Eyes,
She might have kill'd, and her too virtuous Cruelty.
—Oh my *Florella!* Sacred lovely Creature!

Flor. My Death was kind, since it prevented yours,
And by that Hand, which sav'd mine from a Guilt.

[*Points to the* Queen.

—That Dagger I receiv'd of *Abdelazer*,
To stab that Heart,—he said, that lov'd me best;
But I design'd to overcome your Passion,
And then to have vanquish'd *Abdelazer's* Jealousy:
But finding you too faithful to be happy,
I did resolve to die—and have my wish.
—Farewel—my King—my Soul begins its flight,
—And now—is hovering—in eternal—Night.   [*Dies.*

King. She's gone—she's gone—her sacred Soul is fled
To that Divinity, of which it is a part;
Too excellent to inhabit Earthly Bodies.

Alon. Oh, Sir, you grieve too much, for one so foul.

King. What profane Breath was that pronounc'd her
    foul?
Thy Mother's Soul, though turn'd into a Cherubim,
Was black to hers—Oh, she was all divine.
—*Alonzo*, was it thou?—her Brother!

Alon. When she was good, I own'd that Title, Sir.

King. Good!—by all the Gods, she was as chaste as
    Vestals,
As Saints translated to Divine Abodes.
I offer'd her to be my Queen, *Alonzo*,
To share the growing Glories of my Youth;
But uncorrupted she my Crown contemn'd,
And on her Virtue's Guard stood thus defended.

[*Alon. weeps.*

—Oh my *Florella!* let me here lie fix'd,   [*Kneels.*
And never rise, till I am cold and pale
As thou, fair Saint, art now—But sure
She cou'd not die;—that noble generous Heart,
That arm'd with Love and Honour, did rebate
All the fierce Sieges of my amorous Flame,
Might sure defend it self against those Wounds

Given by a Woman's Hand,—or rather 'twas a Devil's.

                                   [Rises.

—What dost thou merit for this Treachery?
Thou vilest of thy Sex—
But thou'rt a thing I have miscall'd a Mother,
And therefore will not touch thee—live to suffer
By a more shameful way;—but here she lies,
Whom I, though dead, must still adore as living.

    Alon. Sir, pray retire, there's danger in your stay;
When I reflect upon this Night's Disorder,
And the Queen's Art to raise my Jealousy;
And after that my Sister's being murder'd,
I must believe there is some deeper Plot,
Something design'd against your sacred Person.

    King. Alonzo, raise the Court, I'll find it, *[Ex.* Alonzo.
Tho 'twere hid within my Mother's Soul.

    Qu. My gentle Son, pardon my kind mistake,
I did believe her arm'd against thy Life.

    King. Peace, Fury! Not ill boding Raven Shrieks,
Nor midnight Cries of murder'd Ghosts, are more
Ungrateful, than thy faint and dull Excuses.
—Be gone! and trouble not the silent Griefs,
Which will insensibly decay my Life,
Till like a Marble Statue I am fixt,
Dropping continual Tears upon her Tomb.

                  [Kneels and weeps at Florella's *Feet.*

    Abd. [*Within.*] Guard all the Chamber-Doors—Fire
    and Confusion
Consume the *Spanish* Dogs—was I for this
Sent to fetch back a *Philip,* and a Cardinal,
To have my Wife abus'd?

                Enter Abdelazer.

    Qu. Patience, dear *Abdelazer.*

    Abd. Patience and I am Foes : where's my *Florella?*
The King! and in *Florella's* Bed-Chamber!
Florella dead too!—

Rise, thou eternal Author of my Shame;
Gay thing—to you I speak,   [*King rises.*
And thus throw off Allegiance.

 Qu. Oh, stay your Fury, generous *Abdelazer*,
 Abd. Away, fond Woman. [*Throws her from him.*
 King. Villain, to me this Language?
 Abd. To thee, young amorous King.
How at this dead and silent time of Night,
Durst you approach the Lodgings of my Wife?
 King. I scorn to answer thee.
 Abd. I'll search it in thy Heart then.
  [*They fight*, Queen *and* Elv. *run out crying Treason.*
 King. The Devil's not yet ready for his Soul,
And will not claim his due.—Oh, I am wounded. [*Falls.*
 Abd. No doubt on't, Sir, these are no Wounds of Love.
 King. Whate'er they be, you might have spar'd 'em now,
Since those *Florella* give me were sufficient:
—And yet a little longer, fixing thus
Thou'dst seen me turn to Earth, without thy aid.
Florella!—*Florella!*—is thy Soul fled so far
It cannot answer me, and call me on?
And yet like dying Ecchoes in my Ears,
I hear thee cry, my Love—I come—I come, fair Soul.
—Thus at thy Feet—my Heart shall bleeding—lie.
Who since it liv'd for thee—for thee—will die. [*Dies.*
 Abd. So—thou art gone—there was a King but now,
And now a senseless, dull, and breathless nothing.
    [*A noise of fighting without.*
    Enter Queen *running.*
 Qu. Oh Heavens! my Son—the King, the King is
  kill'd!—
Yet I must save his Murderer:—Fly, my Moor;
Alonzo, Sir, assisted by some Friends,
Has set upon your Guards,
And with resistless Fury is making hither.
 Abd. Let him come on.

Enter Alonzo *and others, led in by* Osmin, Zarrack,
and Moors.

Oh, are you fast?   [*Takes away their Swords.*

  Alon. What mean'st thou, Villain?

  Abd. To put your Swords to better uses, Sir,
Than to defend the cause of Ravishers.

  Alon. Oh Heavens, the King is murder'd!

  Abd. Look on that Object,
Thy Sister and my Wife, who's doubly murder'd,
First in her spotless Honour, then her Life.

  Alon. Heaven is more guilty than the King in this.

  Qu. My Lords, be calm; and since your King is murder'd.
Think of your own dear Safeties; chuse a new King,
That may defend you from the Tyrant's Rage.

  Alon. Who should we chuse? Prince *Philip* is our King.

  Abd. By Heaven, but *Philip* shall not be my King;
Philip's a Bastard, and Traytor to his Country:
He braves us with an Army at our Walls,
Threatning the Kingdom with a fatal Ruin.
And who shall lead you forth to Conquest now,
But *Abdelazer*, whose Sword reap'd Victory,
As oft as 'twas unsheath'd?—and all for *Spain*
—How many Laurels has this Head adorn'd?
Witness the many Battles I have won;
In which I've emptied all my youthful Veins!—
And all for *Spain!*—ungrateful of my Favours!
—I do not boast my Birth,
Nor will not urge to you my Kingdom's Ruin;
But loss of Blood, and numerous Wounds receiv'd—
And still for *Spain!*—
And can you think, that after all my Toils,
I wou'd be still a Slave?—to Bastard *Philip* too?
That dangerous Foe, who with the Cardinal,
Threatens with Fire and Sword.—I'll quench those Flames,
Such an esteem I still preserve for *Spain*.

  Alon. What means this long Harangue? what does it
    aim at?

Abd. To be Protector of the Crown of *Spain*,
Till we agree about a lawful Successor.

Alon. Oh Devil!

Qu. We are betray'd, and round beset with Horrors;
If we deny him this—the Power being his,
We're all undone, and Slaves unto his Mercy.—
Besides—Oh, give me leave to blush when I declare,
That *Philip* is—as he has rendred him.—
But I in love to you, love to my *Spain*,
Chose rather to proclaim my Infamy,
Than an ambitious Bastard should be crown'd.

Alon. Here's a fine Plot,
What Devil reigns in Woman, when she doats?   [*Aside.*

Rod. My Lords, I see no remedy but he must be Pro-
    tector.

Alon. Oh, Treachery—have you so soon forgot
The noble *Philip*, and his glorious Heir,
The murder'd *Ferdinand?*—
And, Madam, you so soon forgot a Mother's Name,
That you wou'd give him Power that kill'd your Son?

Abd. The Modesty wherewith I'll use that Power,
Shall let you see, I have no other Interest
But what's intirely *Spain's.*—Restore their Swords,
And he amongst you all who is dissatisfy'd,
I set him free this minute.

Alon. I take thee at thy word—
And instantly to *Philip's* Camp will fly.   [*Exit.*

Abd. By all the Gods my Ancestors ador'd,
But that I scorn the envying World shou'd think
I took delight in Blood—I wou'd not part so with you.
—But you, my Lords, who value *Spain's* Repose,
Must for it instantly with me take Arms.
Prince *Philip*, and the Cardinal, now ride
Like *Jove* in Thunder; we in Storms must meet them.
To Arms! to Arms! and then to Victory,
Resolv'd to conquer, or resolv'd to die.   [*Exeunt.*

ACT IV.

Scene I. Abdelazer's *Tent*.

Enter Abdelazer, Osmin *bearing his Helmet of Feathers*, Zarrack *with his Sword and Truncheon*.

Abd. Come, *Osmin*, arm me quickly; for the Day
Comes on apace, and the fierce Enemy
Will take advantages by our delay.

Enter Queen *and* Elvira.

Qu. Oh, my dear Moor!
The rude, exclaiming, ill-affected Multitude
(Tempestuous as the Sea) run up and down,
Some crying, kill the Bastard—some the Moor;
These for King *Philip*,—those for *Abdelazer*.

Abd. Your Fears are idle,—blow 'em into Air.
I rush'd amongst the thickest of their Crouds,
And with the awful Splendor of my Eyes,
Like the imperious Sun, dispers'd the Clouds.
But I must combat now a fiercer Foe,
The hot-brain'd *Philip*, and a jealous Cardinal.

Qu. And must you go, before I make you mine?

Abd. That's my Misfortune—when I return with Victory,
And lay my Wreaths of Laurel at your Feet,
You shall exchange them for your glorious Fetters.

Qu. How canst thou hope for Victory, when their Numbers
So far exceed thy Powers?

Abd. What's wanting there, we must supply with Conduct.
I know you will not stop at any thing
That may advance our Interest, and Enjoyment.

Qu. Look back on what I have already done;
And after that look forward with Assurance.

Abd. You then (with only Women in your Train)
Must to the Camp, and to the Cardinal's Tent;—

Tell him, your Love to him hath drawn you thither:
Then undermine his Soul—you know the way on't.
And sooth him into a Belief, that the best way
To gain your Heart, is to leave *Philip's* Interest;
Urge 'tis the Kingdom's safety, and your own;
And use your fiercest Threats, to draw him to a Peace
    with me;
Not that you love me, but for the Kingdom's good:
Then in a Tent which I will pitch on purpose,
Get him to meet me: He being drawn off,
Thousands of Bigots (who think to cheat the World
Into an Opinion, that fighting for the Cardinal is
A pious Work) will (when he leaves the Camp)
Desert it too.

    Qu. I understand you, and more than I have time to be
Instructed in, I will perform; and possibly
Before you can begin, I'll end my Conquests.

    Abd. 'Twill be a Victory worthy of your Beauty.
—I must to Horse, farewel, my generous Mistress.

    Qu. Farewel! and may thy Arms as happy prove,
As shall my Art, when it dissembles Love.   [*Exeunt.*

Scene II. Philip's *Tent.*

Enter Philip, Alonzo, *and Guards.*

    Phil. 'Tis a sad Story thou hast told, *Alonzo;*
Yet 'twill not make me shed one single Tear:
They must be all of Blood that I will offer
To my dear Brother's Ghost—
But, gallant Friend, this Good his Ills have done,
To turn thee over to our juster Interest,
For thou didst love him once.

    Alon. Whilst I believ'd him honest, and for my Sister's
    sake;
But since, his Crimes have made a Convert of me.

    Phil. Gods! is it possible the Queen should countenance
His horrid Villanies?

Alon. Nay, worse than so, 'tis thought she'll marry him.

Phil. Marry him! then here upon my Knees I vow,
[*Kneels.*

To shake all Duty from my Soul;
And all that Reverence Children owe a Parent,
Shall henceforth be converted into Hate.   [*Rises.*
—Damnation! marry him! Oh, I cou'd curse my Birth!
This will confirm the World in their Opinion,
That she's the worst of Women;
That I am basely born too, (as she gives it out)
That Thought alone does a just Rage inspire,
And kindles round my Heart an active Fire.

Alon. A Disobedience, Sir, to such a Parent,
Heaven must forgive the Sin, if this be one:
—Yet do not, Sir, in Words abate that Fire,
Which will assist you a more effectual way.

Phil. Death! I could talk of it an Age;
And, like a Woman, fret my Anger high:
Till like my Rage, I have advanc'd my Courage,
Able to fight the World against my Mother.

Alon. Our Wrongs without a Rage, will make us fight,
Wrongs that wou'd make a Coward resolute.

Phil. Come, noble Youth,
Let us join both our several Wrongs in one,
And from them make a solemn Resolution,
Never to part our Interest, till this Moor,
This worse than Devil Moor be sent to Hell.

Alon. I do.

Phil. Hark—hark—the Charge is sounded, let's to
Horse,

St. *Jaques* for the Right of *Spain* and me.   [*Exeunt.*

SCENE III. *A Grove.*

*Drums and Trumpets afar off, with noise of fighting at a
distance: After a little while, enter* Philip *in a Rage.*

Phil. Oh unjust Powers! why d'ye protect this Monster?—

And this damn'd Cardinal, that comes not up
With the *Castilian* Troops? curse on his formal Politicks—

Enter Alonzo.

—*Alonzo*, where's the Moor?
Alon. The Moor—a Devil—never did Fiend of Hell,
Compell'd by some Magician's Charms,
Break thro the Prison of the folded Earth
With more swift Horrour, than this Prince of Fate
Breaks thro our Troops in spite of Opposition.
Phil. Death! 'tis not his single Arm that works the
Wonders,
But our Cowardice—Oh, this Dog Cardinal!

Enter Antonio.

Ant. Sound a Retreat, or else the Day is lost.
Phil. I'll beat that Cur to Death that sounds Retreat.

Enter Sebastian.

Sebast. Sound a Retreat.
Phil. Who is't that tempts my Sword?—continue the
Alarm,
Fight on Pell-mell—fight—kill—be damn'd—do any
thing
But sound Retreat—Oh, this damn'd Coward Cardinal!
[*Exeunt.*

The noise of fighting near; after a little while enter
Philip *again.*

Phil. Not yet, ye Gods! Oh, this eternal Coward!

Enter Alonzo.

Alon. Sir, bring up your Reserves, or all is lost;
Ambition plumes the Moor, that makes him act
Deeds of such Wonder, that even you wou'd envy them.
Phil. 'Tis well—I'll raise my Glories to that dazling
height,
Shall darken his, or set in endless Night.   [*Exeunt.*

SCENE IV. *A Grove.*

Enter Card. *and* Queen; *the noise of a Battel continuing afar off all the Scene.*

Qu. By all thy Love, by all thy Languishments,
By all those Sighs and Tears paid to my Cruelty,
By all thy Vows, thy passionate Letters sent,
I do conjure thee, go not forth to fight:
Command your Troops not to engage with *Philip*,
Who aims at nothing but the Kingdom's ruin.
—*Fernando's* kill'd—the Moor has gain'd the Power,
A Power that you nor *Philip* can withstand;
And is't not better he were lost than *Spain*,
Since one must be a Sacrifice?
Besides—if I durst tell it,
There's something I cou'd whisper to thy Soul,
Wou'd make thee blush at ev'ry single Good
Thou'ast done that insolent Boy;—But 'tis not now
A time for Stories of so strange a Nature,—
Which when you know, you will conclude with me,
That every Man that arms for *Philip's* Cause,
Merits the name of Traitor.—
Be wise in time, and leave his shameful Interest,
An Interest thou wilt curse thy self for taking;
Be wise, and make Alliance with the Moor.

Card. And, Madam, should I lay aside my Wrongs,
Those publick Injuries I have receiv'd,
And make a mean and humble Peace with him?
—No, let *Spain* be ruin'd by our Civil Swords,
E'er for its safety I forego mine Honour.—

Enter an Officer.

Offi. Advance, Sir, with your Troops, or we are lost.

Card. Give order—

Qu. That they stir not on their Lives;
Is this the Duty that you owe your Country?
Is this your Sanctity—and Love to me?

Is't thus you treat the Glory I have offer'd
To raise you to my Bed?
To rule a Kingdom, be a Nation's Safety,
To advance in hostile manner to their Walls;
Walls that confine your Countrymen, and Friends,
And Queen, to whom you've vow'd eternal Peace,
Eternal Love? And will you court in Arms?
Such rude Addresses wou'd but ill become you.
No, from this hour renounce all Claims to me,
Or *Philip's* Interest; for let me tell you, Cardinal,
This Love, and that Revenge, are inconsistent.

   Card. But, Madam—
   Qu. No more—disband your Rebel Troops,
And strait with me to *Abdelazer's* Tent,
Where all his Claims he shall resign to you,
Both in my self, the Kingdom, and the Crown:
You being departed, thousands more will leave him,
And you're alone the Prop to his Rebellion.

Enter Sebastian.

   Sebast. Advance, advance, my Lord, with all your Force,
Or else the Prince and Victory is lost,
Which now depends upon his single Valour;
Who, like some ancient Hero, or some God,
Thunders amongst the thickest of his Enemies,
Destroying all before him in such numbers,
That Piles of Dead obstruct his passage to the living—
Relieve him strait, my Lord, with our last Cavalry and
      Hopes.

   Card. I'll follow instantly.—   [*Ex.* Sebast.
   Qu. Sir, but you shall not, unless it be to Death—
Shall you preserve the only Man I hate,
And hate with so much reason?—let him fall
A Victim to an injur'd Mother's Honour.
—Come, I will be obey'd—indeed I must— [*Fawns on him.*
   Card. When you're thus soft, can I retain my Anger?

Oh, look but ever thus—in spite of Injuries—
I shall become as tame and peaceable,
As are your charming Eyes, when dress'd in Love,
Which melting down my Rage, leave me defenceless.
—Ah, Madam, have a generous care of me,
For I have now resign'd my Power to you.   [*Shouts within.*

Qu. What Shouts are these?

Enter Sebastian.

Sebast. My Lord, the Enemy is giving ground,
And *Philip*'s Arm alone sustains the day :
Advance, Sir, and compleat the Victory.   [*Exit.*

Qu. Give order strait, that a Retreat be sounded ;
And whilst they do so, by me conducted,
We'll instantly to *Abdelazer*'s Tent—
Haste—haste, my Lord, whilst I attend you here.

[*Ex. severally.*

Cardinal *going out, is met by* Philip.

Phil. Oh, damn your lazy Order, where have you been,
   Sir ?
—But 'tis no time for Questions,
Move forward with your Reserves.

Card. I will not, Sir.

Phil. How, will not !

Card. Now to advance would be impolitick ;
Already by your desperate Attempts,
You've lost the best part of our Hopes.

Phil. Death ! you lye.

Card. Lye, Sir !

Phil. Yes, lye, Sir,—therefore come on,
Follow the desperate Reer-Guard, which is mine,
And where I'll die, or conquer—follow my Sword
The bloody way it leads, or else, by Heaven,
I'll give the Moor the Victory in spite,
And turn my Force on thee—
Plague of your Cowardice—Come, follow me. [*Ex. Card.*

SCENE V. *The Grove.*

As Philip *is going off, he is overtook by* Alonzo, Antonio,
Sebastian, *and other Officers : At the other side some Moors,
and other of* Abdelazer's *Party, enter and fall on* Philip *and
the rest—the Moors are beaten off—one left
dead on the Stage.—*

Enter Abdelazer, *with* Roderigo *and some others.*

Abd. Oh, for more Work—more Souls to send to Hell !
—Ha, ha, ha, here's one going thither,—Sirrah—Slave
Moor—who kill'd thee ?—how he grins—this Breast,
Had it been temper'd and made proof like mine,
It never wou'd have been a Mark for Fools.

Abd. *going out : Enter* Philip, Alonzo, Sebastian, Antonio,
and Officers, as passing over the Stage.

Phil. I'll wear my Sword to th' Hilt, but I will find
The Subject of my Vengeance.—
Moor, 'tis for thee I seek, where art thou, Slave ?—
Abd. Here, *Philip.*   [Abd. *turns.*
Phil. Fate and Revenge, I thank thee.—
Abd. Why—thou art brave, whoe'er begot thee.
Phil. Villain, a King begot me.
Abd. I know not that,
But I'll be sworn thy Mother was a Queen,
And I will kill thee handsomly for her sake.
                    [*Offers to fight, their Parties hinder them.*
Alon. Hold—hold, my Prince.
Osm. Great Sir, what mean you ?   [*To* Abd.
The Victory being yours, to give your Life away
On one so mad and desperate.   [*Their Parties draw.*
Phil. Alonzo, hold,
We two will be the Fate of this great Day.
Abd. And I'll forego all I've already won,
And claim no Conquest ; the whole heaps of Bodies,
Which this Right-hand has slain, declare me Victor.

Phil. No matter who's the Victor; I have thee in my
    view,
And will not leave thee,
Till thou hast crown'd those Heaps, and made 'em all
The glorious Trophies of my Victory—Come on, Sir.

Alon. You shall not fight thus single;
If you begin, by Heaven, we'll all fall on.

Phil. Dost thou suspect my Power?
Oh, I am arm'd with more than compleat Steel,
The Justice of my Quarrel; when I look
Upon my Father's Wrongs, my Brother's Wounds,
My Mother's Infamy, *Spain's* Misery,
I am all Fire; and yet I am too cold
To let out Blood enough for my Revenge:
—Therefore stir not a Sword on my side.

Abd. Nor on mine.

> *They fight; both their Parties engage on either side; the*
> *Scene draws off, and discovers both the Armies, which*
> *all fall on and make the main Battel: Philip prevails,*
> *the Moors give ground: Then the Scene closes to the*
> *the Grove. Enter some Moors flying in disorder.*

SCENE VI.   *Changes to a Tent.*

Enter Abdelazer, Roderigo, Osmin, Zarrack, *and some*
others of his Party.

Rod. Oh, fly, my Lord, fly, for the Day is lost.

Abd. There are three hundred and odd Days i'th Year,
And cannot we lose one? dismiss thy Fears,
They'll make a Coward of thee.

Osm. Sir, all the noble *Spaniards* have forsook you;
Your Soldiers faint, are round beset with Enemies,
Nor can you shun your Fate, but by your Flight.

Abd. I can—and must—in spite of Fate:
The Wheel of War shall turn about again,
And dash the Current of his Victories.—

This is the Tent I've pitched, at distance from the Armies,
To meet the Queen and Cardinal ;
Charm'd with the Magick of Dissimulation,
I know by this h'as furl'd his Ensigns up,
And is become a tame and coward Ass.

> [*A Retreat is sounded.*

—Hark—hark, 'tis done : oh, my inchanting Engine !
—Dost thou not hear Retreat sounded ?

   Rod. Sure 'tis impossible.

   Abd. She has prevail'd—a Woman's Tongue and Eyes
Are Forces stronger than Artilleries.

Enter Queen, Cardinal, *Women, and Soldiers.*

—We are betray'd—

   Qu. What means this Jealousy ? lay by your Weapons.
And embrace—the sight of these beget Suspicion :
—*Abdelazer*, by my Birth he comes in peace ;
Lord Cardinal, on my Honour so comes he.

   Abd. Let him withdraw his Troops then.

   Qu. They're Guards for all our Safeties :
Give me your Hand, Prince Cardinal—thine, *Abdelazer*—

> [*She brings them together, they embrace.*

This blest Accord I do behold with Joy.

   Card. Abdelazer,
I at the Queen's Command have met you here,
To know what 'tis you will propose to us.

   Abd. Peace and eternal Friendship 'twixt us two.
How much against my Will I took up Arms,
Be witness, Heav'n : nor was it in revenge to you,
But to let out th' infected Blood of *Philip,*
Whose sole aim
Is to be King—which *Spain* will never suffer ;
Spain gave me Education, though not Birth,
Which has intitled it my native Home,
To which such Reverence and Esteem I bear,
I will preserve it from the Tyrant's Rage.

The People who once lov'd him, now abhor him,
And 'tis your Power alone that buoys him up :
And when you've lifted him into a Throne,
'Tis time to shake you off.

Card. Whilst I behold him as my native Prince,
My Honour and Religion bids me serve him ;
Yet not when I'm convinc'd that whilst I do so,
I injure *Spain*.

Abd. If he were so, the Powers above forbid
We should not serve, adore, and fight for him ;
But *Philip* is a Bastard :—nay, 'twill surprize ye,
But that 'tis Truth, the Queen will satisfy you.

Qu. With one bold Word he has undone my Honour.
                                                    [*Weeps.*

Too bluntly, *Abdelazer*, you repeat
That which by slow Degrees you shou'd have utter'd.

Abd. Pardon my Roughness, Madam, I meant well.

Card. *Philip* a Bastard !
If by such Arts you wou'd divide me from him,
I shall suspect you wou'd betray us both.

Qu. Sir, he informs you Truth ; and I blush less
To own him so, than that he is a Traitor.

Card. *Philip* a Bastard ! oh, it cannot be—
Madam, take heed you do not for Revenge,
Barter your dearer Honour, and lose both.

Qu. I know what's due to Honour, and Revenge,
But better what I owe to *Spain*, and you—
You are a Prince o'th' Blood, and may put off
The Cardinal when you please, and be a Monarch.

Card. Though my Ambition's equal to my Passion,
Neither shall make me act against those Principles
My Honour ever taught me to obey.
—And, Madam—
'Tis less a Sin, not to believe you her,
Than 'tis to doubt your Virtue.

Qu. I wish it were untold, if it must forfeit

The least of your Esteem—but that 'tis Truth,
Be witness, Heav'n, my Shame, my Sighs, and Tears.

                                [Weeps.

    Card. Why, Madam, was't so long conceal'd from me?

    Qu. The Circumstances I shall at leisure tell you:
And for the present,
Let it suffice, he cannot rule in *Spain*,
Nor can you side with him, without being made
As much incapable to reign as he.

    Card. Though Love and Honour I have always made
The Business of my Life;
My Soul retains too so much of Ambition,
As puts me still in mind of what I am,
A Prince, and Heir to *Spain:*
Nor shall my blinded Zeal to Loyalty,
Make me that glorious Interest resign,
Since *Philip's* Claims are not so great as mine.
—Madam, tho I'm convinc'd I've done amiss
In taking Arms for *Philip*,
Yet 'twill be difficult to disengage my self.

    Abd. Most easily—
Proclaim it in the head of all your Troops,
The Justice of your Cause for leaving him;
And tell 'em, 'tis a Work of Piety
To follow your Example.
The giddy Rout are guided by Religion,
More than by Justice, Reason, or Allegiance.
—The Crown which I as a good Husband keep,
I will lay down upon the empty Throne;
Marry you the Queen, and fill it—and for me,
I'll ever pay you Duty as a Subject.   *[Bows low.*

    Card. On these Conditions all I am is yours;
Philip we cannot fear, all he can do
Is to retire for refuge into *Portugal.*

    Abd. That wou'd be dangerous—
Is there no Arts to get him in our Power?

Card. Perhaps by Policy, and seeming Friendship,
For we have reason yet to fear his Force ;
And since I'm satisfy'd he's not my lawful Prince,
I cannot think it an Impiety
To sacrifice him to the Peace of *Spain*,
And every Spirit that loves Liberty :
First we'll our Forces join, and make 'em yours,
Then give me your Authority to arrest him ;
If so we can surprize him, we'll spare the hazard
Of a second Battel.

Abd. My Lord, retire into my inner Tent,
And all things shall be instantly perform'd. [*Exeunt all.*

Scene VII.   *The Grove.*

Enter some of Philip's *Party running over the Stage,
pursu'd by* Philip, Alonzo, Sebastian, Antonio,
and some few Officers more.

Alon. Do not pursue 'em, Sir, such coward Slaves
Deserve not Death from that illustrate Hand.

Phil. Eternal Plagues consume 'em in their flight ;
Oh, this damn'd coward Cardinal has betray'd us !
When all our Swords were nobly dy'd in Blood,
When with red Sweat that trickled from our Wounds
We'ad dearly earn'd the long disputed Victory,
Then to lose all, then to sound base Retreat,
It swells my Anger up to perfect Madness.

Alon. Indeed 'twas wondrous strange.

Sebast. I'm glad, Sir——

Phil. Art glad of it ? art glad we are abandon'd ?
That I, and thou have lost the hopeful'st Day——

Sebast. Great Sir, I'm glad that you came off alive.

Phil. Thou hast a lean Face—and a carrion Heart——
A plague upon the Moor, and thee——Oh, *Alonzo,*
To run away—follow'd by all the Army !
Oh, I cou'd tear my Hair, and curse my Soul to Air !

—Cardinal—thou Traitor, *Judas*, that would'st sell
Thy God again, as thou hast done thy Prince.
—But come—we're yet a few,
And we will fight till there be left but one—
If I prove him, I'll die a glorious death.

Ant. Yes, but the Cardinal has took pious Care
It shall be in our Beds.

Sebast. We are as bad as one already, Sir ; for all our
Fellows are crawl'd home, some with ne'er a Leg, others
with ne'er a Arm, some with their Brains beat out, and
glad they escaped so.

Phil. But, my dear Countrymen, you'll stick to me.

1 *Sold.* Ay, wou'd I were well off—   [*Aside.*

Phil. Speak, stout *Sceva*, wilt thou not ?

1 *Sold. Sceva*, Sir, who's that ?

Phil. A gallant *Roman*, that fought by *Cæsar's* side,
Till all his Body cover'd o'er with Arrows,
Shew'd like a monstrous Porcupine.

1 *Sold.* And did he die, Sir ?

Phil. He wou'd not but have dy'd for *Cæsar's* Empire.

1 *Sold.* Hah—why, Sir, I'm none of *Sceva*, but honest
Diego, yet would as willingly die as he, but that I have
a Wife and Children ; and if I die they beg.

Phil. For every drop of Blood which thou shalt lose,
I'll give thy Wife—a Diadem.

Sold. Stark mad, as I am valiant !

Enter Card. *Officers and Soldiers :* Philip *offers to run on
him, is held by* Alonzo.

Phil. Oh Heav'n ! is not that the Cardinal ?
Traitor, how dar'st thou tempt my Rage, and Justice ?

Card. Your Pardon, Sir, I come in humble Love
To offer happy Peace.

Phil. Was that thy aim when base Retreat was sounded ?
Oh, thou false Cardinal—let me go, *Alonzo*—
Death ! offer happy Peace ! no, offer War,

Bring Fire and Sword—Hell and Damnation—Peace !
Oh, damn your musty Peace—No, will you fight and cry,
Down with the Moor ! and then I'll die in peace.
I have a Heart, two Arms, a Soul, a Head,
I'll hazard these—I can but hazard all—
Come—I will kneel to thee—and be thy Slave—[*Kneels.*
I'll let thee tread on me, do any thing,
So this damn'd Moor may fall.

　　Card. Yes, Sir, he shall—

　　Phil. Gods ! shall he—thy noble Hand upon't,
And for this Promise, take my grateful Heart.

[*Embraces him.*

—Shall *Abdelazer* fall ?

　　Card. Yes, upon thee—
Like the tall Ruins of a falling Tower,
To crush thee into Dust—

[*As they embrace, the Guards seize him and the rest.*

Traitor and Bastard, I arrest thee of High-Treason.

　　Phil. Hah !—Traitor !—and Bastard—and from thee !

[*They hold* Philip's *Hands.*

　　Card. Guards, to your Hands the Prisoner is committed.
There's your Warrant—*Alonzo*, you are free. [*Ex.* Card.

　　Phil. Prithee lend me one Hand—to wipe my Eyes,
And see who 'tis dares authorize this Warrant :
—The Devil and his Dam !—the Moor and Queen !
Their Warrant !—Gods ! *Alonzo*, must we obey it ?
Villains, you cannot be my Jailors ; there's no Prison,
No Dungeon deep enough ; no Gate so strong,
To keep a Man confin'd—so mad with Wrong.
—Oh, dost thou weep, *Alonzo* ?

　　Alon. I wou'd fain shed a Tear,
But from my Tears so many Show'rs are gone,
They are too poor to pay your Sorrow's Tribute ;
There is no Remedy, we must to Prison.

　　Phil. Yes, and from thence to Death—
I thought I should have had a Tomb hung round

With tatter'd Ensigns, broken Spears and Javelins;
And that my Body, with a thousand Wounds,
Shou'd have been borne on some triumphant Chariot,
With solemn Mourning, Drums, and Trumpets sounding;
Whilst all the wondring World with Grief and Envy,
Had wish'd my glorious Destiny their own:
But now, *Alonzo*—like a Beast I fall,
And hardly Pity waits my Funeral.   [*Exeunt.*

ACT V.

SCENE I.   *A Presence-Chamber, with a Throne and Canopy.*

Enter Abdelazer, Cardinal, Alonzo, Ordonio, Roderigo,
*and other Lords, one bearing the Crown, which is laid on
the Table on a Cushion; the* Queen, Leonora, *and Ladies.*
*They all seat themselves, leaving the Throne and Chair
of State empty.* Abdelazer *rises and bows,* Roderigo
kneeling, presents him with the Crown.

Abd. Grandees of *Spain*, if in this royal Presence
There breathes a Man, who having laid his hold
So fast on such a Jewel, and dares wear it,
In the Contempt of Envy, as I dare;
Yet uncompell'd (as freely as the Gods
Bestow their Blessings) wou'd give such Wealth away;
Let such a Man stand forth—are ye all fix'd?
No wonder, since a King's a Deity.
And who'd not be a God?
This glorious Prospect, when I first saw the Light,
Met with my Infant Hopes; nor have those Fetters
(Which e'er they grew towards Men, *Spain* taught me
        how to wear)
Made me forget what's due to that illustrious Birth;
—Yet thus—I cast aside the Rays of Majesty—
                [*Kneels, and lays the Crown on the Table.*
And on my Knee do humbly offer up
This splendid powerful thing, and ease your Fears
Of Usurpation and of Tyranny.

Alon. What new Device is this ?   [*Aside.*

Card. This is an Action generous and just—
Let us proceed to new Election.

Abd. Stay, Peers of *Spain*,
If young Prince *Philip* be King *Philip*'s Son,
Then is he Heir to *Philip*, and his Crown ;
But if a Bastard, then he is a Rebel,
And as a Traitor to the Crown shou'd bleed :
That dangerous popular Spirit must be laid,
Or *Spain* must languish under civil Swords ;
And *Portugal* taking advantage of those Disorders,
(Assisted by the Male-contents within,
If *Philip* live) will bring Confusion home.
—Our Remedy for this is first to prove,
And then proclaim him Bastard.

Alon. That Project wou'd be worth your Politicks
                                          [*Aside.*
—How shou'd we prove him Bastard ?

Abd. Her Majesty being lately urg'd by Conscience,
And much above her Honour prizing *Spain*,
Declar'd this Secret, but has not nam'd the Man ;
If he be noble and a *Spaniard* born,
He shall repair her Fame by marrying her.

Card. No ; *Spaniard*, or Moor, the daring Slave shall die.

Qu. Would I were cover'd with a Veil of Night,
                                          [*Weeps.*
That I might hide the Blushes on my Cheeks !
But when your Safety comes into Dispute,
My Honour, nor my Life must come in competition.
—I'll therefore hide my Eyes, and blushing own,
That *Philip*'s Father is i'th' Presence now.

Alon. I'th' Presence ! name him.

Qu. The Cardinal—   [*All rise in Amazement.*

Card. How's this, Madam !

Abd. How ! the Cardinal !

Card. I *Philip*'s Father, Madam !

Qu. Dull Lover—is not all this done for thee !
Dost thou not see a Kingdom and my self,
By this Confession, thrown into thy Arms ?

Card. On Terms so infamous I must despise it.

Qu. Have I thrown by all Sense of Modesty,
To render you the Master of my Bed,
To be refus'd—was there any other way ?—

Card. I cannot yield ; this Cruelty transcends
All you have ever done me—Heavens ! what a Contest
Of Love and Honour swells my rising Heart !

Qu. By all my Love, if you refuse me now,
Now when I have remov'd all Difficulties,
I'll be reveng'd a thousand killing ways.

Card. Madam, I cannot own so false a thing,
My Conscience and Religion will not suffer me.

Qu. Away with all this Canting ; Conscience, and
      Religion !
No, take advice from nothing but from Love.

Card. 'Tis certain I'm bewitch'd—she has a Spell
Hid in those charming Lips.

Alon. Prince Cardinal, what say you to this ?

Card. I cannot bring it forth—

Qu. Do't, or thou'rt lost for ever.

Card. Death ! What's a Woman's Power !
And yet I can resist it.

Qu. And dare you disobey me ?

Card. Is't not enough I've given you up my Power,
Nay, and resign'd my Life into your Hands,
But you wou'd damn me too—I will not yield—
Oh, now I find a very Hell within me ;
How am I misguided by my Passion !

Alon. Sir, we attend your Answer.

Qu. 'Tis now near twenty Years, when newly married,
(And 'tis the Custom here to marry young,)
King *Philip* made a War in *Barbary*,
Won *Tunis*, conquer'd *Fez*, and hand to hand

Slew great *Abdela*, King of *Fez*, and Father
To this *Barbarian* Prince.

   Abd. I was but young, and yet I well remember
My Father's Wound—poor *Barbary*—but no more.

   Qu. In absence of my King I liv'd retir'd,
Shut up in my Apartment with my Women,
Suffering no Visits, but the Cardinal's,
To whom the King had left me as his Charge ;
But he, unworthy of that Trust repos'd,
Soon turned his Business into Love.

   Card. Heavens ! how will this Story end ?   [*Aside.*

   Qu. A Tale, alas ! unpleasant to my Ear,
And for the which I banish'd him my Presence,
But oh, the power of Gold ! he bribes my Women,
That they should tell me (as a Secret too)
The King (whose Wars were finish'd) would return
Without acquainting any with the time ;
He being as jealous, as I was fair and young,
Meant to surprize me in the dead of Night :
This pass'd upon my Youth, which ne'er knew Art.

   Card. Gods ! is there any Hell but Woman's Falshood !
                                 [*Aside.*

   Qu. The following Night I hasted to my Bed,
To wait my expected Bliss—nor was it long
Before his gentle Steps approach'd my Ears.
Undress'd he came, and with a vigorous haste
Flew to my yielding Arms : I call'd him King,
My dear lov'd Lord ; and in return he breath'd
Into my Bosom, in soft gentle Whispers,
My Queen ! my Angel ! my lov'd *Isabella* !
And at that word—I need not tell the rest.

   Alon. What's all this, Madam, to the Cardinal ?

   Qu. Ah, Sir, the Night too short for his Caresses,
Made room for Day, Day that betray'd my Shame ;
For in my guilty Arms I found the Cardinal.

   Alon. Madam, why did not you complain of this ?

Qu. Alas, I was but young, and full of Fears;
Bashful, and doubtful of a just Belief,
Knowing King *Philip's* rash and jealous Temper;
But from your Justice I expect Revenge.

Rod. His Crime, my Lords, is Death, by all our Laws.

Card. Have you betray'd me by my too much Faith?
Oh shameless Creature, am I disarm'd for this?
Had I but so much Ease to be inrag'd,
Sure I shou'd kill thee for this Treachery:
But I'm all Shame, and Grief—By all that's holy,
My Lords, I never did commit this Crime.

Abd. 'Tis but in vain, Prince Cardinal, to deny it.

Qu. Do not believe him, Lords;—
Revenge—let Sentence pass upon the Traitor.

Card. I own that Name with Horror, which you drew
    me to,
When I betray'd the best of Men, and Princes;
And 'tis but just you fit me for Despairs,
That may instruct me how to follow him in Death:
Yet as I'm Prince o'th Blood, and Cardinal too,
You cannot be my Judges.

Abd. You shall be try'd, Sir, as becomes your Quality.
Osmin, we commit the Cardinal to your Charge.

Card. Heaven! should I live to that! No,
I have within me a private Shame,
That shall secure me from the publick one.

Alon. A pretty turn of State!—we shall all follow, Sir.

Card. The Powers above are just:
Thus I my Prince a Sacrifice first made,
And now my self am on the Altar laid.

                              [*Ex.* Card. *guarded.*

Abd. Madam, retire, you've acted so divinely,
You've fill'd my Soul with new admiring Passion:
I'll wait on you in your Apartment instantly,
And at your Feet pay all my Thanks, and Love.

Qu. Make haste, my dearest Moor, whilst I retire,

And fit my Soul to meet thy kind Desire.

> [*Ex.* Queen *and her Train ;* Leon. *advancing to follow, is staid by* Abd.

Abd. Stay, beauteous Maid, stay, and receive that Crown,

> [*Leads her back.*

Which as your due, Heav'n and all *Spain* present you with.

Alon. But granting *Philip* is—that thing you call him,
If we must grant him so, who then shall reign?
Not that we do not know who ought to reign,
But ask who 'tis you will permit to do so.   [*To* Abd.

Abd. Who but bright *Leonora !* the Royal Off-spring
Of noble *Philip,* whose Innocence and Beauty,
Without th' advantage of her glorious Birth,
Merits all Adoration.

All. With Joy we do salute her Queen.

Abd. Live *Leonora !* beauteous Queen of *Spain !* [*Shout.*

Alon. From *Abdelazer* this ! it cannot be,
At least not real.   [*Aside.*

Abd. My Lords,
Be it now your Care magnificently to provide
Both for the Coronation, and the Marriage
Of the fair Queen ;
Let nothing be omitted that may shew,
How we can pay, where we so vastly owe.   [*Bows.*

Alon. I am much bound to *Spain,* and you, my Lords,
For this great Condescenion.

Leo. My Lords, I thank ye all,
And most the gallant Moor—I am not well—

> [*Turns to* Alon.

Something surrounds my Heart so full of Death,
I must retire to give my Sorrow Breath.

> [*Ex.* Leo. *follow'd by all but* Abd. *and* Rod. *who looks on* Abd.

Rod. Sir,—what have you done?

Abd. What every Man that loves like me shou'd do;
Undone my self for ever, to beget

One Moment's thought in her, that I adore her ;
That she may know, none ever lov'd like me,
I've thrown away the Diadem of *Spain*—
—'Tis gone ! and there's no more to set but this—
(My Heart) at all, and at this one last Cast,
Sweep up my former Losses, or be undone.

    Rod. You court at a vast Rate, Sir.

    Abd. Oh, she's a Goddess ! a Creature made by Heaven
To make my prosperous Toils all sweet and charming !
She must be Queen, I and the Gods decree it.

    Rod. Sir, is she not designed *Alonzo's* Bride ?

    Abd. Yes, so her self and he have ill agreed ;
But Heav'n and I am of another Mind,
And must be first obey'd.

    Rod. *Alonzo* will not yield his Interest easily.

    Abd. Wou'd that were all my stop to Happiness ;
But, *Roderigo*, this fond amorous Queen
Sits heavy on my Heart.

    Rod. She's but a Woman, nor has more Lives than one.

    Abd. True, *Roderigo*, and thou hast dealt in Murders,
And knowest the safest way to—

    Rod. How, Sir !—

    Abd. Thou dar'st not sure pretend to any Virtue ;
Had Hell inspir'd thee with less Excellency
Than Arts of killing Kings, thou'dst ne'er been rais'd
To that exalted Height, t' have known my Secrets.

    Rod. But, Sir—

    Abd. Slave, look back upon the Wretchedness I took
      thee from ;
What Merits had thou to deserve my Bounty,
But Vice, brave prosperous Vice ?
Thou'rt neither wise, nor valiant.

    Rod. I own my self that Creature rais'd by you,
And live but to repay you, name the way.

    Abd. My business is—to have the Queen remov'd ;
She does expect my coming this very Hour ;

And when she does so, 'tis her Custom to be retir'd,
Dismissing all attendance, but *Elvira*.

   Rod. The rest I need not be instructed in. [*Ex.* Rod.

Enter Osmin.

   Osm. The Cardinal, Sir, is close confin'd with *Philip.*

   Abd. 'Tis well.

   Osm. And do you think it fit, Sir, they shou'd live?

   Abd. No, this day they both must die, some sort of Death,
That may be thought was given them by themselves:
I'm sure I give them cause—*Osmin*, view well this Ring;
Whoever brings this Token to your Hands,
Without considering Sex, or Quality,
Let 'em be kill'd.

   Osm. Your Will shall be obey'd in every thing.

[*Exeunt severally.*

SCENE II.   *A fine Chamber.   A Table and Chair.*

Enter Queen *and* Elvira.

   Qu. Elvira, hast thou drest my Lodgings up,
Fit to receive my Moor?
Are they all gay, as Altars, when some Monarch
Is there to offer up rich Sacrifices?
Hast thou strew'd all the Floor his Feet must press,
With the soft new-born Beauties of the Spring?

   Elv. Madam, I've done as you commanded me.

   Qu. Let all the Chambers too be fill'd with Lights;
There's a Solemnity methinks in Night,
That does insinuate Love into the Soul,
And make the bashful Lover more assur'd.

   Elv. Madam,
You speak as if this were your first Enjoyment.

   Qu. My first! Oh *Elvira*, his Power, like his Charms,
His Wit, or Bravery, every hour renews;
Love gathers Sweets like Flow'rs, which grow more fragrant,
The nearer they approach Maturity.   [*Knock.*

—Hark! 'tis my Moor,—give him admittance strait,
The Thought comes o'er me like a gentle Gale,
Raising my Blood into a thousand Curls.

Elv. Madam, it is a Priest—

Qu. A Priest! Oh, send him quickly hence;
I wou'd not have so cold and dull an Object,
Meet with my nobler Sense, 'tis mortifying.

Elv. Perhaps 'tis some Petition from the Cardinal.

Qu. Why, what have I to do with Priest or Cardinal?
Let him not enter—   [*Elv. goes out, and returns with*
                              Roderigo *drest like a Fryar.*

Elv. From *Abdelazer*, Madam.

Qu. H'as named a Word will make all Places free.

Rod. Madam, be pleas'd to send your Woman hence,
I've something to deliver from the Moor,
Which you alone must be acquainted with.

Qu. Well, your Formality shall be allowed—retire—
                              [*To* Elv.   *Exit* Elv.
What have you to deliver to me now?

Rod. This—   [*Shews a Dagger, and takes her roughly*
Qu. Hah!—   *by the Hands.*
Rod. You must not call for help, unless to Heaven.
Qu. What daring thing art thou?
Rod. One that has now no time to answer thee.
                    [*Stabs her, she struggles, her Arm bleeds.*
Qu. Oh, hold thy killing Hand! I am thy Queen.
Rod. Thou may'st be Devil too, for ought I know;
I'll try thy Substance thus—   [*Stabs again.*
Qu. Oh, *Abdelazer!*—

Thou hast well reveng'd me—on my Sins of Love;—
                              [*He seats her in the Chair.*
But shall I die thus tamely unreveng'd?—
—Help—murder—help—   [*He offers to stab again.*
              Enter Elvira, *and other Women.*

Elv. Oh Heavens! the Queen is murder'd—help the
    Queen!   [Rod. *offers to stab* Elv.

Enter Abdelazer.

Abd. Hah ! the Queen ! what sacrilegious Hand,
Or Heart so brutal—
Durst thus profane the Shrine ador'd by me ?
Guard well the Passages.—

Qu. Thou art that sacrilegious—brutal thing !—
And false as are the Deities thou worship'st.

Abd. Gods ! let me not understand that killing Language ?
—Inform me quickly, how you came thus wounded,
Lest looking on that sacred Stream of Blood,
I die e'er I've reveng'd you on your Murderer.

Qu. Haste then, and kill thy self; thou art my Murderer.
Nor had his Hand, if not by thee instructed,
Aim'd at a Sin so dangerous—

Abd. Surely she'll live—[*Aside.*]—This !—
Can Mischief dwell beneath this reverend Shape ?
Confess who taught thee so much Cruelty.
Confess, or I will kill thee.

Rod. The Cardinal.

Qu. The Cardinal !

Abd. Oh impious Traitor !
How came I mention'd then ?

Rod. To get Admittance.

Abd. But why do I delay thy Punishment ?
Die,—and be damn'd together. [*Aside.*]   [*Stabs him.*
But oh, my Queen !—*Elvira*, call for help.
Have I remov'd all that oppos'd our Flame,   [*Kneels.*
To have it thus blown out, thus in a Minute ?
When I, all full of youthful Fire, all Love,
Had rais'd my Soul with Hopes of near Delights,
To meet thee cold, and pale ; to find those Eyes,
Those charming Eyes thus dying—Oh ye Powers !
Take all the Prospect of my future Joys,
And turn it to Despair, since thou art gone.

Qu. Cease,—cease—your kind Complaints—my struggling Soul,

'Twixt Death—and Love—holds an uneasy Contest;
This will not let it stay—nor that depart;—
And whilst I hear thy Voice—thus breathing Love,
It hovers still—about—the grateful—Sound.
My Eyes—have took—an everlasting Leave—
Of all that blest their Sight; and now a gloomy Darkness
Benights the wishing Sense,—that vainly strives—
To take another View;—but 'tis too late,—
And Life—and Love—must yield—to Death—and—
    Fate.   [*Dies.*

   Abd. Farewell, my greatest Plague, [*He rises with Joy.*
Thou wert a most impolitick loving thing;
And having done my Bus'ness which thou wert born for,
'Twas time thou shouldst retire,
And leave me free to love, and reign alone.

   Enter Leonora, Alonzo, Ordonio, *and other Men
and Women.*

Come all the World, and pay your Sorrows here,
Since all the World has Interest in this Loss.
   Alon. The Moor in Tears! nay, then the Sin was his.
   Leon. The Queen my Mother dead!
How many Sorrows will my Heart let in,
E'er it will break in pieces.   [*Weeps over her.*
   Alon. I know the Source of all this Villany,
And need not ask you how the Queen came murder'd.
   Elv. My Lord, that Fryer, from the Cardinal, did it.
   Alon. The Cardinal!
'Tis possible,—for the Injuries she did him
Cou'd be repaid with nothing less than Death.   [*Aside.*
My Fair, your Griefs have been so just of late,
I dare not beg that you would weep no more;
Though every Tear those lovely Eyes let fall,
Give me a killing Wound—Remove the Body.
   [*Guards remove the Body. Ex. all but* Alon. *and* Leon.
Such Objects suit not Souls so soft as thine.

Leon. With Horrors I am grown of late familiar;
I saw my Father die, and liv'd the while;
I saw my beauteous Friend, and thy lov'd Sister,
Florella, whilst her Breast was bleeding fresh;
Nay, and my Brother's too, all full of Wounds,
The best and kindest Brother that ever Maid was blest with;
Poor *Philip* bound, and led like Victims for a Sacrifice;
All this I saw and liv'd—
And canst thou hope for Pity from that Heart,
Whose harden'd Sense is Proof 'gainst all these Miseries?
This Moor, *Alonzo*, is a subtle Villain,
Yet of such Power we scarce dare think him such.

Alon. 'Tis true, my charming Fair, he is that Villain,
As ill and powerful too; yet he has a Heart
That may be reach'd with this—but 'tis not time,

[*Points to his Sword.*

We must dissemble yet, which is an Art
Too foul for Souls so innocent as thine.

Enter Abdelazer.

The *Moor!*
Hell! will he not allow us sorrowing time?

Abd. Madam, I come to pay my humblest Duty,
And know what Service you command your Slave.

Leon. Alas, I've no Commands; or if I had,
I am too wretched now to be obey'd.

Abd. Can one so fair, and great, ask any thing
Of Men, or Heaven, they wou'd not grant with Joy?

Leon. Hea'vns Will I'm not permitted to dispute,
And may implore in vain; but 'tis in you
To grant me what may yet preserve my Life.

Abd. In me! in me! the humblest of your Creatures!
By yon bright Sun, or your more splendid Eyes,
I wou'd divest my self of every Hope,
To gratify one single Wish of yours.
—Name but the way.

Leon. I am so unhappy, that the only thing
I have to ask, is what you must deny;
—The Liberty of *Philip*—

Abd. How! *Philip*'s Liberty—and must I grant it?
I (in whose Hands Fortune had put the Crown)
Had I not lov'd the Good and Peace of *Spain*,
Might have dispos'd it to my own Advantage;
And shall that Peace,
Which I've preferr'd above my proper Glories,
Be lost again in him, in him a Bastard?

Alon. That he's a Bastard, is not, Sir, believ'd;
And she that cou'd love you, might after that
Do any other Sin, and 'twas the least
Of all the Number to declare him Bastard.

Abd. How, Sir! that cou'd love me! what is there here,
Or in my Soul, or Person, may not be belov'd?

Alon. I spoke without Reflection on your Person,
But of dishonest Love, which was too plain,
From whence came all the Ills we have endur'd;
And now being warm in Mischiefs,
Thou dost pursue the Game, till all be thine.

Abd. Mine!

Alon. Yes, thine—
The little humble Mask which you put on
Upon the Face of Falshood, and Ambition,
Is easily seen thro; you gave a Crown,
But you'll command the Kingly Power still,
Arm and disband, destroy or save at Pleasure.

Abd. Vain Boy, (whose highest Fame,
Is that thou art the great *Alvaro*'s Son)
Where learnt you so much daring, to upbraid
My generous Power thus falsly—do you know me?

Alon. Yes, Prince, and 'tis that Knowledge makes me
   dare;
I know thy Fame in Arms; I know in Battels
Thou hast perform'd Deeds much above thy Years:

My Infant Courage too

(By the same Master taught) grew up to thine,

When thou in Rage out-didst me, not in Bravery.

—I know thou'st greater Power too—thank thy Treachery!

Abd. Dost thou not fear that Power?

Alon. By Heaven, not I,

Whilst I can this—command.

[*Lays his Hand on his Sword.*

Abd. I too command a Sword.

[Abd. *lays his Hand on his, and comes close up to him.*

But not to draw on thee, *Alonzo;*

Since I can prove thy Accusation false

By ways more grateful—take this Ring, *Alonzo;*

The sight of it will break down Prison-Gates,

And set all free, as was the first-born Man.

Alon. What means this turn?

Abd. To enlarge *Philip;* but on such Conditions,

As you think fit to make for my Security:

And as thou'rt brave, deal with me as I merit.

Alon. Art thou in earnest?

Abd. I am, by all that's sacred.

Leon. Oh, let me fall before you, and ne'er rise,

Till I have made you know what Gratitude

Is fit for such a Bounty!—

Haste, my *Alonzo*—haste—and treat with *Philip;*

Nor do I wish his Freedom, but on such Terms

As may be advantageous to the Moor.

Alon. Nor I, by Heaven! I know the Prince's Soul,

Though it be fierce, has Gratitude and Honour;

And for a Deed like this, will make returns,

Such as are worthy of the brave Obliger.   [*Exit Alon.*

Abd. Yes, if he be not gone to Heaven before you

    come.   [*Aside.*

—What will become of *Abdelazer* now,

Who with his Power has thrown away his Liberty?

Leon. Your Liberty! Oh, Heaven forbid that you,

Who can so generously give Liberty,
Should be depriv'd of it!
It must not be whilst *Leonora* lives.

   Abd. 'Tis she that takes it from me.

   Leon. I! Alas, I wou'd not for the World
Give you one minute's Pain.

   Abd. You cannot help it, 'tis against your Will;
Your Eyes insensibly do wound and kill.

   Leon. What can you mean? and yet I fear to know.

   Abd. Most charming of your Sex! had Nature made
This clouded Face, like to my Heart, all Love,
It might have spar'd that Language which you dread;
Whose rough harsh sound, unfit for tender Ears,
Will ill express the Business of my Life.

   Leon. Forbear it, if that Business, Sir, be Love.

   Abd. Gods!
Because I want the art to tell my Story
In that soft way, which those can do whose Business
Is to be still so idly employ'd,
I must be silent and endure my Pain,
Which Heaven ne'er gave me so much tameness for.
Love in my Soul is not that gentle thing
It is in other Breasts; instead of Calms,
It ruffles mine into uneasy Storms.
—I wou'd not love, if I cou'd help it, Madam;
But since 'tis not to be resisted here—
You must permit it to approach your Ear.

   Leon. Not when I cannot hear it, Sir, with Honour.

   Abd. With Honour!
Nay, I can talk in the Defence of that:
By all that's sacred, 'tis a Flame as virtuous,
As every Thought inhabits your fair Soul,
And it shall learn to be as gentle too;
—For I must merit you—

   Leon. I will not hear this Language; merit me!

   Abd. Yes—why not?

You're but the Daughter of the King of *Spain*,
And I am Heir to great *Abdela*, Madam;
I can command this Kingdom you possess,
(Of which my Passion only made you Queen)
And re-assume that which your Father took
From mine—a Crown as bright as that of *Spain*.

　Leon. You said you wou'd be gentle—

　Abd. I will; this sullen Heart shall learn to bow,
And keep it self within the Bounds of Love;
Its Language I'll deliver out in Sighs,
Soft as the Whispers of a yielding Virgin.
I cou'd transform my Soul to any Shape;
Nay, I could even teach my Eyes the Art
To change their natural Fierceness into Smiles;
—What is't I wou'd not do to gain that Heart!

　Leon. Which never can be yours! that and my Vows,
Are to *Alonzo* given; which he lays claim to
By the most sacred Ties, Love and Obedience;
All *Spain* esteems him worthy of that Love.

　Abd. More worthy it than I! it was a Woman,
A nice, vain, peevish Creature that pronounc'd it;
Had it been Man, 't had been his last Transgression.
—His Birth! his glorious Actions! are they like mine?

　Leon. Perhaps his Birth wants those Advantages,
Which Nature has laid out in Beauty on his Person.

　Abd. Ay! there's your Cause of Hate! Curst be my
　　Birth,
And curst be Nature that has dy'd my Skin
With this ungrateful Colour! cou'd not the Gods
Have given me equal Beauty with *Alonzo*!
—Yet as I am, I've been in vain ador'd,
And Beauties great as thine have languish'd for me.
The Lights put out, thou in thy naked Arms
Will find me soft and smooth as polish'd Ebony;
And all my Kisses on thy balmy Lips as sweet,
As are the Breezes, breath'd amidst the Groves

Of ripening Spices in the height of Day:
As vigorous too,
As if each Night were the first happy Moment
I laid thy panting Body to my Bosom.
Oh, that transporting Thought—
See— I can bend as low, and sigh as often,   [*Kneels.*
And sue for Blessings only you can grant;
As any fair and soft *Alonzo* can—
If you could pity me as well—
But you are deaf, and in your Eyes I read
                              [*Rises with Anger.*
A Scorn which animates my Love and Anger;
Nor know I which I should dismiss or cherish.

    Leon. The last is much more welcome than the first;
Your Anger can but kill; but, Sir, your Love—
Will make me ever wretched, since 'tis impossible
I ever can return it.

    Abd. Why, kill me then! you must do one or t'other.
                              [*Kneels.*
For thus—I cannot live—why dost thou weep?
Thy every Tear's enough to drown my Soul!
How tame Love renders every feeble Sense!   [*Rises.*
—Gods! I shall turn Woman, and my Eyes inform me
The Transformation's near—Death! I'll not endure it,
I'll fly before sh'as quite undone my Soul—   [*Offers to go.*
But 'tis not in my Power—she holds it fast—
And I can now command no single part—   [*Returns.*
Tell me, bright Maid, if I were amiable,
And you were uningag'd, could you then love me?

    Leon. No! I could die first.

    Abd. Hah!—awake, my Soul, from out this drousy Fit,
And with thy wonted Bravery scorn thy Fetters.
By Heaven, 'tis gone! and I am now my self.
Be gone, my dull Submission! my lazy Flame
Grows sensible, and knows for what 'twas kindled.
Coy Mistress, you must yield, and quickly too:

Were you devout as Vestals, pure as their Fire,
Yet I wou'd wanton in the rifled Spoils
Of all that sacred Innocence and Beauty.
—Oh, my Desire's grown high !
Raging as midnight Flames let loose in Cities,
And, like that too, will ruin where it lights.
Come, this Apartment was design'd for Pleasure,
And made thus silent, and thus gay for me ;
There I'll convince that Error, that vainly made thee think
I was not meant for Love.

Leon. Am I betray'd ? are all my Women gone ?
And have I nought but Heaven for my Defence ?

Abd. None else, and that's too distant to befriend you.

Leon. Oh, take my Life, and spare my dearer Honour !
—Help, help, ye Powers that favour Innocence.

[*Enter Women.*

Just as the Moor *is going to force in* Leonora, *enters to him* Osmin *in haste.*

Osm. My Lord, *Alonzo*—

Abd. What of him, you Slave—is he not secur'd ?
Speak, dull Intruder, that know'st not times and seasons,
Or get thee hence.

Osm. Not till I've done the Business which I came for.

Abd. Slave !—that thou cam'st for.

[*Stabs him in the Arm.*

Osm. No, 'twas to tell you, that *Alonzo*,
Finding himself betray'd, made brave resistance ;
Some of your Slaves h'as killed, and some h'as wounded.

Abd. 'Tis time he were secured ;
I must assist my Guards, or all is lost.   [*Exit.*

Leon. Sure, *Osmin*, from the Gods thou cam'st,
To hinder my undoing ; and if thou dy'st,
Heaven will almost forgive thy other Sins
For this one pious Deed.—
But yet I hope thy Wound's not mortal.

Osm. 'Tis only in my Arm—and, Madam, for this pity,
I'll live to do you Service.

Leon. What Service can the Favourite of the Moor,
Train'd up in Blood and Mischiefs, render me?

Osm. Why, Madam, I command the Guard of Moors,
Who will all die, when e'er I give the Word.
Madam, 'twas I caus'd *Philip* and the Cardinal
To fly to th' Camp,
And gave 'em warning of approaching Death.

Leon. Heaven bless thee for thy Goodness.

Osm. I am weary now of being a Tyrant's Slave,
And bearing Blows too; the rest I could have suffer'd.
Madam, I'll free the Prince.
But see, the Moor returns.

Leon. That Monster's Presence I must fly, as from a
        killing Plague.   [*Ex. with her Women.*

Enter Abdelazer *with* Zarrack, *and a Train of* Moors.

Abd. It is prodigious, that a single Man
Should with such Bravery defend his Life
Amongst so many Swords;—but he is safe.
Osmin, I am not us'd to sue for Pardon,
And when I do, you ought to grant it me.

Osm. I did not merit, Sir, so harsh a Usage.

Abd. No more; I'm asham'd to be upbraided,
And will repair the Injury I did thee.

Osm. Acknowledgment from you is pay sufficient.

Abd. Yet, *Osmin*, I shou'd chide your Negligence,
Since by it *Philip* lives still, and the Cardinal.

Osm. I had design'd it, Sir, this Evening's Sacrifice.

Abd. *Zarrack* shall now perform it—and instantly:
Alonzo too must bear 'em company.

Zar. I'll shew my Duty in my haste, my Lord.
                                        [*Ex. Zar.*

Osm. Death! I'm undone; I'll after him, and kill him.
                                        [*Offers to go.*

Abd. Osmin, I've business with you.—

[*Osm. comes back bowing.*

As they are going off, enter Leonora, Ordonio, *other
Lords, and Women.*

Leon. Oh Prince! for Pity hear and grant my Suit. [*Kneels.*

Abd. When so much Beauty's prostrate at my Feet,
What is't I can deny?—rise, thou brightest Virgin
That ever Nature made;
Rise, and command my Life, my Soul, my Honour.

Leon. No, let me hang for ever on your Knees,
Unless you'll grant *Alonzo* Liberty.

Abd. Rise, I will grant it; though *Alonzo*, Madam,
Betray'd that Trust I had repos'd in him.

Leon. I know there's some Mistake; let me negotiate
Between my Brother and the Gallant Moor.
I cannot force your Guards,
There is no Danger in a Woman's Arm.

Abd. In your bright Eyes there is, that may corrupt
'em more
Than all the Treasures of the Eastern Kings.
Yet, Madam, here I do resign my Power;
Act as you please, dismiss *Alonzo's* Chains.
And since you are so generous, to despise
This Crown, which I have given you,
Philip shall owe his Greatness to your Bounty,
And whilst he makes me safe, shall rule in *Spain.*
—Osmin—   [*Whispers.*

Ord. And will you trust him, Madam?

Leon. If he deceive me, 'tis more happy far
To die with them, than live where he inhabits.

Osm. It shall be done.

Abd. Go, *Osmin*, wait upon the Queen;
And when she is confin'd, I'll visit her,
Where if she yield, she reigns; if not, she dies. [*Aside.*

[*Ex. Abd. one way,* Leon. Osm. *and the rest another.*

SCENE III.   *A Prison.*

Discovers Philip *chain'd to a Post, and over against him
the* Cardinal *and* Alonzo *in Chains.*

Phil. Oh, all ye cruel Powers! is't not enough
I am depriv'd of Empire, and of Honour?
Have my bright Name stol'n from me, with my Crown!
Divested of all Power! all Liberty!
And here am chain'd like the sad *Andromede*,
To wait Destruction from the dreadful Monster!
Is not all this enough, without being damn'd,
To have thee, Cardinal, in my full view?
If I cou'd reach my Eyes, I'd be reveng'd
On the officious and accursed Lights,
For guiding so much torment to my Soul.
   Card. My much wrong'd Prince! you need not wish
      to kill
By ways more certain, than by upbraiding me
With my too credulous, shameful past misdeeds.
   Phil. If that wou'd kill, I'd weary out my Tongue
With an eternal repetition of thy Treachery;—
Nay, and it shou'd forget all other Language,
But Traitor! Cardinal! which I wou'd repeat,
Till I had made my self as raging mad,
As the wild Sea, when all the Winds are up;
And in that Storm, I might forget my Grief.
   Card. Wou'd I cou'd take the killing Object from your
      Eyes.
   Phil. Oh *Alonzo*, to add to my Distraction,
Must I find thee a sharer in my Fate?
   Alon. It is my Duty, Sir, to die with you.—
But, Sir, my Princess
Has here—a more than equal claim to Grief;
And Fear for her dear Safety will deprive me
Of this poor Life, that shou'd have been your Sacrifice.

Enter Zarrack *with a Dagger ; gazes on* Philip.

Phil. Kind Murderer, welcome ! quickly free my Soul,
And I will kiss the sooty Hand that wounds me.

Zar. Oh, I see you can be humble.

Phil. Humble ! I'll be as gentle as a Love-sick Youth,
When his dear Conqu'ress sighs a Hope into him,
If thou wilt kill me !—Pity me and kill me.

Zar. I hope to see your own Hand do that Office.

Phil. Oh, thou wert brave indeed,
If thou wou'dst lend me but the use of one.

Zar. You'll want a Dagger then.

Phil. By Heaven, no, I'd run it down my Throat,
Or strike my pointed Fingers through my Breast.

Zar. Ha, ha, ha, what pity 'tis you want a Hand.

Enter Osmin.

Phil. Osmin, sure thou wilt be so kind to kill me !
Thou hadst a Soul was humane.

Osm. Indeed I will not, Sir, you are my King.

[*Unbinds him.*

Phil. What mean'st thou?

Osm. To set you free, my Prince.

Phil. Thou art some Angel sure, in that dark Cloud.

Zar. What mean'st thou, Traitor?

Osm. Wait till your Eyes inform you.

Card. Good Gods ! what mean'st thou?

Osm. Sir, arm your Hand with this.

[*Gives* Phil. *a Sword, goes to undo* Alonzo.

Zar. Thou art half-damn'd for this !
I'll to my Prince—

Phil. I'll stop you on your way—lie there—your
    Tongue   [*Kills him.*
Shall tell no Tales to day—Now, Cardinal—but hold,
I scorn to strike thee whilst thou art unarm'd,
Yet so thou didst to me ;
For which I have not leisure now to kill thee.

—Here, take thy Liberty;—nay, do not thank me;
By Heaven, I do not mean it as a Grace.

   Osm. My Lord, take this—   [*To* Alon. *and the* Card.
And this—to arm your Highness.

   Alon. Thou dost amaze me!

   Osm. Keep in your Wonder with your Doubts, my Lord.

   Phil. We cannot doubt, whilst we're thus fortify'd—
                              [*Looks on his Sword.*
Come, *Osmin*, let us fall upon the Guards.

   Osm. There are no Guards, great Sir, but what are
     yours;
And see—your Friends I've brought to serve ye too.
                            [*Opens a back Door.*

    Enter Leonora *and Women*, Ordonio, Sebastian,
               Antonio, *&c.*

   Phil. My dearest Sister safe!

   Leon. Whilst in your Presence, Sir, and you thus arm'd.

   Osm. The Moor approaches,—now be ready all.

   Phil. That Name I never heard with Joy till now;
Let him come on, and arm'd with all his Powers,
Thus singly I defy him.   [*Draws.*
            Enter Abdelazer.
                 [Osmin *secures the Doors.*

   Abd. Hah! betray'd! and by my Slaves! by *Osmin* too!

   Phil. Now, thou damn'd Villain! true-born Soul of Hell!
Not one of thy infernal Kin shall save thee.

   Abd. Base Coward Prince!
Whom the admiring World mistakes for Brave;
When all thy boasted Valour, fierce and hot
As was thy Mother in her height of Lust,
Can with the aid of all these—treacherous Swords,
Take but a single Life; but such a Life,
As amongst all their Store the envying Gods
Have not another such to breathe in Man.

   Phil. Vaunt on, thou monstrous Instrument of Hell!
For I'm so pleas'd to have thee in my Power,

That I can hear thee number up thy Sins,
And yet be calm, whilst thou art near Damnation.

Abd. Thou ly'st, thou canst not keep thy Temper in;
For hadst thou so much Bravery of Mind,
Thou'dst fight me singly; which thou dar'st not do.

Phil. Not dare!
By Heaven, if thou wert twenty Villains more,
And I had all thy Weight of Sins about me,
I durst thus venture on;—forbear, *Alonzo.*

Alon. I will not, Sir.

Phil. I was indeed too rash; 'tis such a Villain,
As shou'd receive his Death from nought but Slaves.

Abd. Thou'st Reason, Prince! nor can they wound
       my Body
More than I've done thy Fame; for my first step
To my Revenge, I whor'd the Queen thy Mother.

Phil. Death! though this I knew before, yet the hard
       Word
Runs harshly thro my Heart;—
If thou hadst murder'd fifty Royal *Ferdinands,*
And with inglorious Chains as many Years
Had loaded all my Limbs, 't had been more pardonable
Than this eternal Stain upon my Name:
—Oh, thou hast breath'd thy worst of Venom now.

Abd. My next advance was poisoning of thy Father.

Phil. My Father poison'd! and by thee, thou Dog!
Oh, that thou hadst a thousand Lives to lose,
Or that the World depended on thy single one,
That I might make a Victim
Worthy to offer up to his wrong'd Ghost.—
But stay, there's something of thy Count of Sins untold,
That I must know; not that I doubt, by Heaven,
That I am *Philip's* Son—

Abd. Not for thy Ease, but to declare my Malice,
Know, Prince, I made thy amorous Mother
Proclaim thee Bastard, when I miss'd of killing thee.

Phil. Gods! let me contain my Rage!

Abd. I made her too betray the credulous Cardinal,
And having then no farther use of her,
Satiated with her Lust,
I set *Roderigo* on to murder her.
Thy Death had next succeeded; and thy Crown
I wou'd have laid at *Leonora's* Feet.

Alon. How! durst you love the Princess?

Abd. Fool, durst! had I been born a Slave,
I durst with this same Soul do any thing;
Yes, and the last Sense that will remain about me,
Will be my Passion for that charming Maid,
Whom I'd enjoy'd e'er now, but for thy Treachery.

[*To* Osmin.

Phil. Deflour'd my Sister! Heaven punish me eternally,
If thou out-liv'st the Minute thou'st declar'd it.

Abd. I will, in spite of all that thou canst do.
—Stand off, fool-hardy Youth, if thou'dst be safe,
And do not draw thy certain Ruin on,
Or think that e'er this Hand was arm'd in vain.

Phil. Poor angry Slave, how I contemn thee now!

Abd. As humble Huntsmen do the generous Lion;
Now thou darst see me lash my Sides, and roar,
And bite my Snare in vain; who with one Look
(Had I been free) hadst shrunk into the Earth,
For shelter from my Rage:
And like that noble Beast, though thus betray'd,
I've yet an awful Fierceness in my Looks,
Which makes thee fear t'approach; and 'tis at distance
That thou dar'st kill me; for come but in my reach,
And with one Grasp I wou'd confound thy Hopes.

Phil. I'll let thee see how vain thy Boastings are,
And unassisted, by one single Rage,
Thus—make an easy Passage to thy Heart.

[*Runs on him, all the rest do the like in the same Minute.* Abd.
aims at the Prince, *and kills* Osmin, *and falls dead himself.*

—Die with thy Sins unpardon'd, and forgotten—

[*Shout within.*

Alon. Great Sir, your Throne and Kingdom want you
now ;
Your People rude with Joy, do fill each Street,
And long to see their King—whom Heaven preserve.

All. Long live *Philip*, King of *Spain*—

Phil. I thank ye all ;—and now, my dear *Alonzo*,
Receive the Recompence of all thy Sufferings,
Whilst I create thee Duke of *Salamancha*.

Alon. Thus low I take the Bounty from your Hands.

[*Kneels.*

Leon. Rise, Sir, my Brother now has made us equal.

Card. And shall this joyful Day, that has restor'd you
To all the Glories of your Birth and Merits,
That has restor'd all *Spain* the greatest Treasure
That ever happy Monarchy possess'd,
Leave only me unhappy, when, Sir, my Crime
Was only too much Faith?—Thus low I fall,   [*Kneels.*
And from that Store of Mercy Heaven has given you,
Implore you wou'd dispense a little here.

Phil. Rise, (though with much ado) I will forgive you.

Leon. Come, my dear Brother, to that glorious business,
Our Birth and Fortunes call us, let us haste,
For here methinks we are in danger still.

Phil. So after Storms, the joyful Mariner
Beholds the distant wish'd-for Shore afar,
And longs to bring the rich-fraight Vessel in,
Fearing to trust the faithless Seas again.

EPILOGUE.

Spoken by little Mrs. *Ariell*.

WITH late Success being blest, I'm come agen ;
You see what Kindness can do, Gentlemen,
Which when once shewn, our Sex cannot refrain.
Yet spite of such a Censure I'll proceed,
And for our Poetess will intercede :
Before, a Poet's wheedling Words prevail'd,
Whose melting Speech my tender Heart assail'd,
And I the flatt'ring Scribler's Cause maintain'd ;
So by my means the Fop Applauses gain'd.
'Twas wisely done to chuse m' his Advocate,
Since I have prov'd to be his better Fate ;
For what I lik'd, I thought you could not hate.
Respect for you, Gallants, made me comply,
Though I confess he did my Passion try,
And I am too good-natur'd to deny.
But now not Pity, but my Sex's Cause,
Whose Beauty does, like Monarchs, give you Laws,
Should now command, being join'd with Wit, Applause.
Yet since our Beauty's Power's not absolute,
She'll not the Privilege of your Sex dispute,
But does by me submit.—Yet since you've been
For my sake kind, repeat it once agen.
Your Kindness, Gallants, I shall soon repay,
If you'll but favour my Design to Day :
Your last Applauses, like refreshing Showers,
Made me spring up and bud like early Flow'rs ;
Since then I'm grown at least an Inch in height,
And shall e'er long be full-blown for Delight.

Written by a Friend.